PAPER TRAIL

Writings from the Front-Line of Peace Action
Quaker House/Fort Bragg North Carolina
2001-2012

Chuck Fager

Kimo Press
2013

ISBN: 978-0-945177-59-3

The photos on the front and back cover are of homemade banners
hung along the road to Camp Lejeune, a major Marine base in
North Carolina, where they will be seen by troops returning
from combat tours. Photos © by Chuck Fager.

Kimo Press
P.O. Box 3811
Durham NC 27701

CONTENTS

Introduction

I'm a writer, who has had a writer's career. That is, I've held various jobs to stay relatively solvent while doing the writing I needed to do, much of which didn't pay.

That's how it is for most published writers, so this is not a complaint. Besides, my own work-to-write path was reinforced by a couple of anti-commercial peculiarities, which I couldn't shake: first, as a writer I've been more interested in Quakers than just about anything else. But there aren't enough Quakers to make a living writing about them – unless, perhaps, your name is Jessamyn West, or one wanted to build an academic career around Richard Nixon or Herbert Hoover. The presidents, while interesting, were not of central concern to me; and Jessamyn West, alas, was not only already taken, but had produced many excellent books. (I still aspire to live up to her example, though.)

The other problem was that my life, as both an American and a writer, has been pretty well defined and marked out by wars: one after another (including some, the worst of all, that fortunately haven't quite happened; yet). There were writers who made it big from these wars, especially World War Two, which I was born into, down to Iraq and Afghanistan. That's a path I might also have taken, except that I stumbled first on the work of Dr. Martin Luther King, Jr., and then the Quakers, at just about the time I would have been sent off to Vietnam, the war of (and on) my generation.

These two in tandem persuaded me that war-making – and war-celebrating, which most popular war writing amounted to – was not for me. If America's recurring wars could not be avoided as topics, my question was how to limit, mitigate, resist, and if at all possible prevent them.

There was plenty to be written along this line, to be sure; but with a few honorable exceptions (such as David Halberstam's Vietnam-era classic, *The Best and the Brightest*), it had little hope of gaining a wide audience. By and large, the American public prefers either to glorify its wars, or if that is too difficult, ignore them. Discussions of how to do without them are usually relegated to the margins, and subsist in obscurity.

And so it was for me, beginning with my first published piece in 1966, titled "Dilemma for Dr. King," which urged the civil rights leader to speak out against the Vietnam War. Through the following three-plus decades, I kept writing about Quakers, and about (mostly against) war; meanwhile, to pay bills I delivered mail, toiled on a congressional staff, drove cabs, taught college classes, wrote for newspapers, and the like. A hodge-podge of occupations in support of a writer's vocation; and I have few regrets.

This book is an outgrowth of the last decade of this active work life, when by chance or providence the threads of career and occupation unexpectedly came together: in late 2001, I became Director of Quaker House, a peace project near Fort Bragg in Fayetteville, North Carolina, a post I held til November 2012. Here it was all in a package: steady work; not just one but two wars (plus some secret ones) to try to end; Quakers of all stripes; and the chance to write about all of it.

Yes, there was lots of practical work to do at Quaker House: counseling soldiers struggling with their conscience about war; visiting resisters in jail; organizing too many peace vigils and rallies to count; planning conferences on the war, torture, and related issues; and more. But alongside this there was writing practically all the time: fund appeal letters to meet our budget; newsletters to spread the word; plus presentations, articles, pamphlets, even books. And on the side, a short story at least once a year. In sum, I worked and wrote full-time and full-tilt.

Moreover, in the writing I was often able to look beyond the daily flux and chaos of these war years, toward broader issues that I saw reflected through them: the meaning of torture for free government; the cumulative impact of the Military industrial Complex; the toll of wars on families and the larger society. Then there was the whole Quaker side: what did the forty years of witness at Quaker House mean in the longer history of what Friends call their "Peace Testimony"? What was the place of religion beyond our sect in all that was happening? Overall, had we learned anything there near Fort Bragg that could be of use in the future and in other places? I thought so, and worked to suggest what that might be.

When I retired from Quaker House in November 2012, one transitional task was reflecting on the writing that had been produced in those years. From this the sense emerged that here was a unique body of work emerging from a unique venture, not to mention one representing a major chunk of my writing career.

And so I set out to compile the major pieces, and many shorter ones as well into the present collection. The result makes no pretense of being comprehensive; nor does it present a single "story" of those eleven years; meant for browsing and reference, it is more of a mosaic of telling vignettes and "snapshots." Nor is it autobiography, although much is ineluctably personal. (I'm at work separately on a memoir of the period.)

Instead, my hope is that for some readers it will provide vivid glimpses of work on the "front-line" of peace action in this decade; for others, "think pieces" of review and substantive analysis to engage and mull over. For still others, a casebook of applied peace witness, one with a definite Quaker character. And don't forget the stories; fiction opens another set of windows through which to seek understanding and illumination of this crowded, troubled era.

In the biblical book of Ecclesiastes, the last chapter laments that, "of the making of books there is no end." That's more true today than the Biblical writer ever imagined. This volume adds one more to the stack; and is of uncertain significance in the grand scheme of things. But for those who want to see a different side of warmaking and peace work in the era of the "War On Terror," I think they will find that this book is not a waste of their time.

II

About the "Chapters": organizing this material was neither easy nor tidy. The first two "chapters" proceed chronologically, and offer informal, anecdotal glimpses from the runup to the Iraq and Afghanistan wars, and some of our support work with soldiers who refused to be part of it. (Full disclosure: among them are segments from fund appeal letters, minus the pleas for donations; such missives depend on vivid reportage for their success, and we had much that was vivid to report.)

The next two sections take different slants: beginning in 2005, I submitted OpEd columns to the Fayetteville *Observer* every few months. Most of these were published, almost twenty in all. While staunchly pro-military, the *Observer* was a better paper than I expected, and its openness to running my anti-war messages was evidence. It's fair to say that this military community had never seen such a series of antiwar messages presented in its main public medium, and it seemed right to bring them together.

The same goes for the book reviews in the fourth section. There were many books in these years that taught me a great deal.; it's not simply an intellectual exercise. I've also been reviewing books for many years; this is a form of intellectual engagement and debate which, with the rise of the internet, has become much more wide open.

Something similar dictated bringing together many of my longer essays in the Fifth "Chapter." Here there are extended reflections on many aspects of the experience of staffing a pacifist outpost on the edge of one of the largest cogs in the far-flung American war machine.

Here too are attempts to make sense of it in religious and

7

theological terms; Quaker House is, after all, a church project, not a political or secular one. Moreover, it soon became clear to me that what I call "American War Christianity" was a central pillar and font of American militarism, but one that has almost never been addressed by peace movements, Quaker or otherwise. Naming and tackling this death cult became a continuing part of the work as I saw it.

So did the tide of domestic destruction and self-destruction that washed over the city and the military generally almost from the first month I was in Fayetteville. Few headlines from those years are more true and abiding than "The War At Home."

The same goes for the issue of torture in "Chapter" Seven, though here the headlines were slower coming, because few among either readers or writers really wanted to deal with it. Nor did I; but by mid-2005 it was becoming clear that Fort Bragg and our region of North Carolina were, perhaps not the epicenter of the Torture Industrial complex, but still in the thick of it.

Further, I soon realized one of the bitterest truths about it: beyond the pain inflicted on victims, the legitimation of torture as government practice strikes at the very heart of what we have been taught to think of as government based on laws, with protection of our liberties and human rights. Thus even as the public flees from even the memory of what has been done – and what is now legal to do whenever our rulers so choose – I have been unable to keep silent about it.

Many of these themes are woven into the oral presentations that are the basis for "Chapter" Eight. In length they range from over an hour ("A Quaker Declaration of War"), to about seven minutes for "American War Christianity." The latter was obliged to be concise, because it was delivered as part of a "cattle-call" session at the 2010 North Carolina Yearly Meeting (FUM).

This latter talk deserves a bit of context. For some reason the yearly meeting chose to designate 2010 as its "Year of Peace," even though the sections in its book of Faith and Practice containing the traditional statements of Quaker pacifism are ignored by most of the membership, displaced by identification with standard southern white hyper-patriotic and pro-war attitudes. In line with this outlook, "outside Quaker organizations" were marginalized on their program: customarily all their representatives were called to the platform, seated in a row of chairs, then given five minutes each to make their pitch (usually for donations). The yearly meeting gave no support to Quaker House, but each year I dutifully trekked across the state and took a place in the lineup, if only to "show the flag."

In 2010, with the "year of peace" designation as a starting point, I was moved to compress all my concern about "American War Christianity" into as close to five minutes as I could get, and preached it as plainly as I could.

The next year, the yearly meeting procedures were "revised," and Quaker House was no longer invited.

This banishment was not exactly "paying dues," but there were such times, as "Chapter" Nine shows. The call to appear on the Fox News "Bill O'Reilly Show" was definitely a challenge, as described here. More serious were the weeks spent in suspense, as 2005 turned to 2006, while my friend Tom Fox was held captive in Iraq, and then murdered. Although I was thousands of miles away, the impact was deep. The piece here was for a booklet of memorial reflections that I compiled.

Yet the most grueling of these experiences came about wholly by happenstance, when the mayor of Fayetteville decided it was time to give Vietnam veterans the "Heroes' Homecoming" they had never received, along with a week-long series of events looking back at that war as it was lived in Fayetteville.

Okay, but what was that to us? It seems that someone suggested to him that Quaker House should have a part in this look back.

The idea certainly made historical sense: the project was started, in response to continuing protests generated and led by soldiers opposed to the Vietnam War, and the military draft that was sending them into it. This GI uprising was very real, very noisy and very disruptive, at Fort Bragg and across the army generally. Also, in Fayetteville only Quaker House had preserved an archive of documents, posters and other memorabilia from these events.

The mayor agreed, and I was summoned to a private lunch with him in late 2010, to hear the plan and give him feedback. I told him we would do what we could, but cautioned that this part of the story, which included such notables as Jane Fonda, would likely be controversial. He said that would be no problem and not to worry.

But the mayor was wrong. The rest, which you can read below, became the toughest time during my tenure at Quaker House.

As the big Iraqistan war wound down, the war machine kept turning, and the current administration shifted from overt and large-scale combat to hidden wars, using drones and secret units. Fort Bragg again played a major role in all this. "Chapter" Ten includes several pieces that record our glimpses of this changing military landscape. It continues to evolve, but that course is for others to chart.

And last but not least, there are some stories. A bit of background on these: one summer about 1990, while visiting Friends Music Camp, at the Olney Friends School in Barnesville, Ohio, I was asked to fill a gap in the evening program, by reading some short stories I had written, originally for my own children. The stories were a hit, and I've been returning to the camp to read every year since.

Most years I have brought a new story as well. But in

Fayetteville, the Latin adage came true: *inter arma silent musae,* "Amid the noise of war, the muses fall silent." Story ideas came more rarely; and in several – four of those here – the wars seeped in. I didn't much like this; the campers were an alert lot, and probably carried enough of the generalized post-9/11 anxiety without my reminding them of it.

But like it or not, here they came, artifacts of their world. So here they are too, along with an early vignette, which might have been dismissed as paranoid fantasy when penned in early 2003– if, alas, there weren't enough subsequent real-life versions of it to fill many books.

– Chuck Fager
Durham NC

ONE: Digging Potholes In the Road to War

Chuck Fager
Bellefonte Pennsylvania

November 30, 2001

Dear Friend,

Did opening this letter take a bit of courage? Did you hesitate before tearing the envelope, watchful for unidentified substances, wondering, "What if?"

Welcome to our new war, where we're all potential targets, and even your mailbox can be a weapon.

It hasn't been easy to deal with what's happened since September 11. So much has changed for so many. This letter is about one of these changes. Mine:

I'm joining up.

Not enlisting in the military; I'm too old for that, and out of shape.

But I'm not exaggerating, either. I'm about to become the Director of Quaker House, a Friends peace project in Fayetteville, North Carolina. Fayetteville is the home of Ft. Bragg, one of America's largest military bases. I'm already starting to pack, and will be moving there in a few weeks. I'd like your support in this new mission, and want to keep in touch with you about it.

Ft. Bragg and Fayetteville have been in the news lately – many U.S. troops in action in and around Afghanistan are based there. Ft. Bragg has been a key incubator for American military campaigns for more than half a century. Fayetteville, deep in Jesse Helms country, also has a reputation as a tough town: "Fayettenam," and "Fatalville" are two of its more printable nicknames.

There's nothing like Quaker House anywhere near there. Opened in 1969 to be a symbol of and a home for the Quaker Peace Testimony in a time of war, Quaker House has counseled GIs since its inception in the Vietnam War, and persisted as a forward outpost of peace witness ever since. Now Quaker House is being reinvented to meet the daunting challenges of a new and very different war. I've been asked to lead this effort, and plan to give it my best shot.

This revamping will be a major challenge. Vietnam, after all, was an unpopular war, fought halfway around the world. Our dying was done largely by draftees whose families couldn't pull strings to get safe

National Guard slots or other deferments. Protests for peace were frequent, noisy and often massive.

Those were the days.

But this time war has come to us. After the September attacks, increased security efforts, even retaliatory strikes, were predictable and predictably popular. But support for the expanding holy war against "evildoers" is not quite unanimous, and I'm among the dissenters. For me, the reaction has gone much too far– now the cure threatens to become worse than the disease. It alarms me to see:

– Liberal civil libertarians nod and shrug as more than a thousand people are swept into indefinite detention without warrant, charge, bail, or any idea when, how, or even if they might be tried, deported or released.

– Secret military tribunals being set up in place of our court system.

– Civil liberties being mugged in the name of "fighting terrorism."

– Dissenters mocked and pilloried, on campus and off.

– Racial profiling and dragnets aimed at thousands of American Muslims.

– Hordes of new refugees fleeing our bombs into poorly equipped, overcrowded camps as a bitter winter closes in.

– And, as this is written, broad hints from the White House about expanding the fighting into one or several other countries.

This list could be longer. Yes, there are real threats to "freedom and democracy" out there. Yet increasingly it looks like our civil liberties are being eroded in the name of national security. I don't know about you, but these tendencies certainly don't make me feel any safer.

Some may call this criticism un-American. I disagree completely. To me, speaking up for freedom imperilled is more patriotic than covering my car or lawn with flags. For me as a Quaker, it's also a religious duty.

So, what is Quaker House going to do about all this? The short answer is: whatever we can. Even without a draft, Quaker House still counsels dissident GIs. But we hope to do more. We want to contribute to:

Helping shorten this war, and make it less destructive.

Supporting just and peaceful steps toward national security.

Lifting, whenever we can, the thickening veil of official secrecy.

Promoting interreligious understanding and reconciliation.

Helping build a supportive network among other like-minded folk.

In short, upholding a Quaker peace witness in every way possible.

In this work, the board knows what I bring to the table, and has told me, in effect, to do my best to develop programs and strategies to

13

counter the increasing violence in American society. I've been an investigative reporter, and written or edited several books on Quaker peace work in various wars. More recently, I've built websites on peace issues, for Quakers and others. And I've organized several national Quaker peace conferences, as well as numerous smaller gatherings. As way opens, I'll likely be doing all of these from Fayetteville, on a full-time basis.

The board hopes to see the Quaker House ministry become regional or even national in its outreach. In the age of the World Wide Web, all this is now within our reach if we find the financial support.

It's a tall order, for what the government tells us will be a long war. That's a tragedy, but Quaker House has been going for 32 years; we know about the long haul. With your support, we'll keep at it for the duration of this war too.

So, will you help us get started? First, we need to share ideas you've heard some of ours; now we want to hear yours; there's a brief questionnaire here to get that going. We also need contacts for our network: meetings, churches, email addresses of others who question the militarist and repressive responses to the present dangers. Just as New Yorkers came together after the attacks, we can come together to find and support alternative ways to make the world safer.

And, of course, Quaker House needs financial help. . . .

Is it an emergency?

What do you think?

Let me close on a personal note. Frankly, Quaker House is a name which would not have occurred to me even late last summer. I've been here in central Pennsylvania for four years, busy and safe in what the locals call "Happy Valley," and indeed I have been happy here. All this is now to be turned upside down.

A real war does that. When this proposal came, with the images of the flaming, falling towers still vivid, I couldn't say no. It felt like being "called up" from the peace reserves, back to "active duty."

I don't know if anyone will ever ask me, "What did you do for peace in the terror war?" But I've been asking it of myself, and this is a step toward finding an answer.

Will you join me?

Peace,

Chuck Fager

PS. There's a new book, *Homefront*, by Catherine Lutz (Beacon Press), with an in-depth study of Fayetteville/Ft. Bragg. It makes revealing and unsettling reading: besides the connection to international warmaking, the

14

area has a long history of more local violence and terror, aimed at natives, then blacks, for the Confederacy, the Klan, and against others deemed different or insufficiently patriotic. Of Quaker House, in the Vietnam years Lutz says it "was under close surveillance by Army Intelligence and the FBI." In May, 1970, the first Quaker House was mysteriously burned to the ground. Things had been quieter since Vietnam ended; but now there's a new war, and who knows what I'm heading into? Will you help keep the Quaker House peace witness alive in wartime? Let us hear from you!

Pineland Journal
Quaker House, Fayetteville North Carolina
Monday, March 18, 2002

Dear Friend,

("Pineland" is the army's name for Fayetteville, NC and nearby areas, which are often used as playing fields for their big war games. The name fits the Carolina Sandhills region, or at least its landscape. As for the games, they all seem to center around a fictional country [Pineland], which is "occupied" by a bunch of oppressive evildoers, and which the Green Berets repeatedly wrench free from their iniquitous clutches. How well that scenario fits here is another, more complicated matter.)

< I >

This could be a day off, since I worked through most of the weekend. But there's a grant application on my desk that's close to being finished, for a deadline that's approaching, if not quite imminent. And anyway, a small nonprofit director's work is never done.

Even so, I was hoping to sleep in; but the phone rings early, waking me; then rings again.

The third time, I pick it up, and it's a GI from Ft. Bragg, wanting advice.

Most such calls go to our 800 number, and are taken by Steve or Lenore, the couple who most of our GI counseling, from their Catholic Worker farm. They keep an orderly schedule, however, which doesn't start at this hour.

But – this is why we're here, right? If somebody really wants to talk about conscientious objection or getting a discharge right this minute, okay.

Except that conscience is not on this GI's mind, and a discharge is the least of his problems. It seems he's facing county charges of assault with a deadly weapon. His civilian attorney tells him she can knock it down and maybe make it go away. But now he's heard that the army wants to go after him with an attempted murder rap, under military law.

I see. This is not in our usual line, and I have to coax him to focus on what he wants to know from me, which turns out to be: Are the JAGs, the army prosecutors, really allowed to talk to his ex-wife?

There's a metallic squealing noise in the background that sounds

16

like toilet stall doors in need of attention; and he soon adds that he's not supposed to make phone calls without an MP present. So I get that he's probably in the john, using a buddy's cell.

But what, I ask, does your ex-wife have to do with it?

Well, it seems she's the victim.

As they say in the service, this is way above my pay grade. I repeat several times that I am not a lawyer, and the best advice I can offer is that he needs one, preferably a civilian who knows army law. But, I add, in my strictly nonprofessional opinion it's not so outlandish to think the prosecutors might want to talk to the alleged victim.

Why, I wonder after he hangs up, would the army want to go after him for attempted murder, if the county can't make the lesser charge stick?

Only later does an explanation come to me: it's well-known around here that the military has a bad numbers problem with spouse abuse: rates are measurably higher in uniform.

Nor is this simply an academic squabble: just a few weeks ago a GI, who had been jailed by the county for beating his ex-wife, was somehow let out on bail. Following her to a local restaurant, he grabbed her as she came out from lunch, stabbed her and slashed her throat, and left her crumpled and dying in the doorway, in broad daylight.

But the kicker, from this angle, is that just a few days before, the army had pushed through a quick discharge, so the guy was, by just a few AMs and PMs, officially not their problem anymore.

The cops soon tracked the guy down, found him cowering in a nearby motel. But the shudders from that killing are still reverberating quietly through the city; and now this anonymous GI who woke me up is probably caught in the backwash: the army can't afford to let another armed wife-stalker walk, even an alleged one. Not just yet anyway. And as our GI rights handbook remarks drily, "Rates of conviction at court-martial are very high."

Rumbles and thuds from outside break up these musings. It's artillery, the big guns are booming out in the pines somewhere. Hardly unusual, but the games at Fort Bragg must be hot and heavy this week; maybe it's the army's version of March Madness: the windows rattle, the floor vibrates. Wonder who's winning the war in Pineland today?

< II >

Pretty soon it's time for my daily constitutional, heading downtown toward the big post office.

We're on a nice street here, in what the signs say is the Haymount Historic District, very respectable and, for Fayetteville, even venerable. Quaker House itself, according to a small plaque on the mantle, was once owned by a former governor-senator-Duke University president. (Which title, in North Carolina, is the more prestigious?) A respected former congressman grew up down the block.

What's a subversive operation like ours doing here? That's a story for another time. In the front yard, creamy buds are starting to unfurl on the moss-hung dogwoods, while chickadees hop along their branches. Down the block, pink and lavender azaleas are out.

Before leaving I read the Fayetteville *Observer*, the surprisingly good local daily. Most of the front-page is taken up with a lengthy, furrowed-brow treatise, the second of a series, on the long-running, seemingly insoluble problem of how to revive Fayetteville's downtown, make it attractive to locals and tourists.

The city bigwigs have certainly tried. A decade ago they cleared out the notorious and violence-plagued GI bars and strip joints which were the hallmark of Hay Street, the main drag. Then they built a new city hall, put a big war museum across from it, got Radisson to gentrify the seedy Prince Charles hotel, put in a few blocks of brick pavement and fancy street lamps. Soon came the requisite coffee bars with cutesy names, an "art cinema" and a few upscale shops, including a Birkenstock boutique.

All this cost lots of tax money. And it hasn't yet worked. Downtown is nearly deserted this Monday morning, as it is almost every time I walk through it. The newspaper disclosed that the army is keeping the hotel afloat by stashing called-up reservists there. The Birkenstock store just closed, to reopen in one of the larger malls on the Ft. Bragg side of town. I wonder how long the "art cinema" can last. Many other storefronts stand empty.

Everybody's a critic, of course. There are half a dozen overlapping and competing urban improvement groups thrashing around the area, and everybody's got a Big Plan for downtown, which they paid some consultant or architect Big Bucks to design.

So why be shy? Based on three months here, my theory of the case is simpler, and they can have it for free. The executive summary is:

Give it up, folks. Downtown Fayetteville is haunted. There's enough unresolved karma here to fill all the long freight trains that roll through it in a week. The steepled Market House which is its centerpiece and symbol is mainly known for selling slaves, with all the baggage that represents. And there's an unseen yet unyielding residue of the seven decades of GI hellraising on Hay Street, what was a forced and frenzied revelry aimed at coping with the weight of dozens of wars, large and small.

Even harder to untangle is the fact that this is a weight laid on Fayetteville, by a nation which never tires of celebrating its wars as media spectacles but prefers, thank you very much, not to see them or their

18

human victims at close range. Especially the recent ones.

"Fayetteville's story is America's story," says the city's latest chronicler, a UNC anthropologist named Catherine Lutz. Her fine new book *Homefront: A Military City and the American twentieth Century*, shows this in vivid and convincing detail, and is of course, widely despised here for that. But the downtown part of this mutual story is something neither Fayetteville nor America much wants to remember or hear about.

So downtown has been "cleaned up," and that's good; but it isn't enough. After all, the Hay Street sleaze didn't disappear; it just moved, and continues to take its toll. To make real progress, the city needs something more like redemption, and probably an exorcism. But with the winds of war blowing stronger all the time, such a project of spiritual urban renewal, always unlikely, seems even more remote now.

See? Consulting advice worth every penny.

A group of us will try a kind of exorcism soon. An annual Pilgrimage for Justice and Peace, planned largely by some activists from Raleigh, will start a Holy week trek across the state here after church this coming Sunday. In a ragtag procession, we'll tour downtown, stopping for a kind of stations of the cross at various sites freighted with this unremarked but unforgotten side of its history. I doubt we'll attract much notice; downtown on a Sunday afternoon will likely be even more empty than usual.

I've agreed to prepare the text for two of the stops: The first is right by where the Amtrak station is now, where a black GI named Ned Turman was murdered by a white MP in 1942. Then, a few blocks away on Ray Street, is the site of the original Quaker House. It was opened there in 1969 and firebombed in 1970. A few blocks in the other direction, a black couple was killed at random by neonazi GIs in 1995, in a particularly notorious case. Karma indeed.

I listen to the artillery booming all the way back up the slope to Haymount.

< III >

Once at home, the mail sorted, what else is there to do but sit down at the computer? The grant application is still waiting. But first I yield to the urge to do some surfing about a short news piece I saw somewhere a couple days ago.

Google-the-All-Knowing soon spits it out: a report that the army is preparing to shut down its Peacekeeping Institute at the Army war College in Pennsylvania, the one such project in all the American military.

In Washington, a few dozen liberal House members have fired off

19

a letter to the Pentagon trying to save it, and the Institute's director told the Associated Press he wonders what message its closure will send to the world.

It's a rhetorical question. And more than that, a sign of desperation. The real operators handle these things behind the scenes, with the press noticing, if at all, only after the deals are done and the bodies are buried.

Same goes for the letter from the congressional liberals. Prominent among the signers is Barbara Lee. Sure, she's a hero to me for voting against the war; but how much ice will her name cut with the Joint Chiefs? Get real.

Looking this stuff up is not entirely an excuse to procrastinate. Army peacekeeping has been in my purview for awhile now; this could be something to spread the word about. In years past, I visited the place a couple times, and even worked with its staff on peace gatherings. An army institute talking openly with Quakers? No wonder it's in the cross-hairs.

To find out more, though, it's necessary to make some calls, to congress and the Pentagon. But nobody seems to be home. All I'm able to talk to on the Hill are junior aides and interns. Then I remember from my own time there that it's Monday, after all, and Congress doesn't get seriously back to work til Tuesday. (In their defense, many of them work weekends too.) Nor is there any answer at the Pentagon numbers I turn up; but then, the AP article says nobody called them back about it either.

Finally I track down a former Peacekeeping Institute staffer. He says yeah, it's probably going down. But he has hopes that something like it might pop up elsewhere in the defense establishment; he always did have an optimistic streak. In any case, nowadays he's actually more concerned about the planning for the US attack on Iraq, which he expects by summer. "Chuck," he says, "I'm afraid it will be a disaster."

That's encouraging.

Then a key congressional press aide unexpectedly calls me back. Yes, she was taking the day off. Can she get back to me tomorrow, and she'll have the background I need?

Of course; I'm easy when I'm not on deadline.

Okay, time to get down to it and finish the grant application. Quaker House needs more money to keep up with an expanding war, and an escalating workload. Gotta keep rattling the cup.

The artillery booms on, almost a steady rumble now.

< IV >

Dinnertime. I've made a big salad, for a potluck. There's a dozen or so of us who have been struggling to create a Fayetteville peace group,

20

and it's time for our monthly meeting, at a nearby church. The highlight tonight is a visit by Catherine Lutz, author of "Homefront." I've heard her speak before, as a UNC Professor at the Cumberland Country Library downtown, before a large and ambivalent crowd; but tonight she's Cathy, and here she's one of us.

In the church social room, twenty or so people sit at tables pulled into a square. This is a large crowd of dissenters for Fayetteville, even subtracting the three grad students who followed Lutz down from Chapel Hill. As we eat, she talks, and then takes questions.

Lutz is full of optimism about a revival of the peace movement, both nationally and in North Carolina. She passes out copies of two new antiwar papers, one national, the other for the state. There are also cheap bus tickets to be had, she tells us, for rides to the Washington peace march set for April 20.

I feel of two minds about all this. On the one hand, as a newcomer to the Tar Heel state, I've been surprised to find a small but stubbornly vigorous peace constituency here. On Martin Luther King day, 500 people braved a pouring rain for a peace march at the capitol in Raleigh. An antiwar coalition is meeting monthly in Greensboro. And look at us, here.

But on the other hand, I'm not sanguine about the prospects for any large-scale upsurge of activism anytime soon.

Why not? To sort that out, I've been looking for an analogy: what earlier year most resembles 2002 as far as public sentiment goes?

In Greensboro not long ago some diehard socialists tried to convince us that this year was like 1969: a mass antiwar movement was ready to burst out any minute, they prophesied, with resistance to the Bush regime's war propaganda spreading like wildfire, even in the military.

Not a chance, I thought, and told them so. Sure, Bush is a full-time propagandist; but he didn't foist this war on an unwilling or distracted public; September 11 did that job, and the impact of that day can't be erased. The polls showing 80 percent backing for the war are not faked, and I don't expect them to change soon.

More recently, an activist Quaker scholar agreed this scenario was fanciful. Instead, he argued that this year was actually more like 1964, when the Vietnam peace movement was still small, scattered and easy to ignore, but gathering momentum for the mass movement to come in a couple of years.

My head likes this image better, but my gut doesn't really buy it. The September attacks have been often compared to Pearl Harbor, persuasively to me. And that would make our time more like 1942 or 1943, when a large majority of the public was solidly behind the war effort, regardless of the cost and for the duration, and peace advocates were effectively silenced or subjected to internal exile. COs were sent off to rural camps, kept out of sight and out the public mind.

And in these years COs were not, of course, the only ones in camps. Two of those at our tables tonight are of Japanese-American descent, and they speak up, to make plain that the possibility of being forcibly silenced and kept invisible is not hyperbole to them, but intimate family history.

Cathy Lutz sticks to her optimism. But she qualifies it now, agreeing that if there are more terror attacks, we could see very substantial losses of what remains of our democratic and civil rights. Which makes me wonder if the right year for comparison might not be 1933 in Germany, when the Reichstag fire was used to usher in totalitarian rule.

One of the Japanese-Americans is thinking along similar lines. She leans forward and asks Lutz point-blank: If something like that happens, "Do you have a Plan B?"

Here Lutz's optimism falters. From her stumbling answer, it sounds to me like she doesn't have a plan B.

But then, who among us does? We look around the table, more or less mutually inarticulate.

Are we paranoid? Sure. But do *you* have a Plan B?

< V >

The talk starts up again, and someone asks Lutz how we can become more visible in our dissent here, without being typecast and dismissed as anti-GI and anti-Fayetteville, common charges hurled at local critics of all stripes.

To my surprise, Lutz brushes off this concern, saying essentially that it can't be helped, and isn't worth the energy drain. She insists that no one who has read her book thinks she is anti-GI or anti-Fayetteville.

This latter item I agree with; she spent six years working on it, interviewed dozens of people, on the post and off, military and civilian, ransacked piles of forgotten historical records, and her writing shows great empathy as well as scholarship. I've read "Homefront" twice, with profit each time.

Even so, she and her book have both been trashed repeatedly in the Fayetteville Observer, with the anti-GI and anti-Fayetteville accusations being flung at her right and left. Such stereotyping may not bother her in Chapel Hill; but what about those of us who live here?

It concerns me, certainly. Last Friday, when an Observer reporter approached me while I was protesting George Bush's visit to Ft. Bragg, my first sentence was an avowal of respect for the men and women in uniform, distinguishing them from the war and the policies that generate

22

it. The hope was to position myself outside this stereotypical box, if only rhetorically. The reporter got it, and the small report about our protest in the next day's paper repeated the statement.

That distinction is meaningful to me, and I'll work to sustain it as long as possible, even knowing it could easily be buried in an avalanche of anti-pacifist propaganda.

It's getting close to ten, and the meeting breaks up. I take my gloomy thoughts back to Quaker House, where I figure to start on another grant proposal before packing it in. The artillery is still rumbling out there in the night, but more intermittently now.

Damn – missed my favorite TV show, "Once and Again." But it should be on tape, if I have managed to program the VCR correctly at long last.

That's enough with the proposal. I wrap it up, then turn to email to write to Lynne, back home in Pennsylvania. it's not easy living apart. We work at being in touch by email most every weekday, then burn up free cellphone minutes on the weekends. But war is hell.

Then it's time to chill with my book of the moment: *A Stone Bridge North,* by Kate Maloy. It's a journal/memoir by a woman Quaker who got her life together after a divorce. She met her true soulmate online, quit the urban ratrace, moved with him and her son to a fixer-upper in the Vermont woods, and found God again in a small Friends meeting nearby. The book recounts the first full year of this Friendly Green Mountain idyll.

Now that's an escape for you. Nothing to worry about but snow, black flies, dozing off during meeting, and whether this is the year Canada gets fed up and decides to invade. I'm enjoying the book.

Finally to bed, but first a pause to check for overlooked voicemails: There's one, electronically designated as "urgent," from a traveling Friend, seeking hospitality this Friday night.

I won't be here then; committee meetings in Virginia. I'm on the road a lot. Maybe a local Friend can help; but I'm not optimistic; the Fayetteville meeting is tiny.

Crawling into bed, I wonder if Pineland has been "liberated" yet again. In any case, the artillery is finally quiet.

Except for the echoes in my dreams.

An Urgent Letter from Quaker House

November 2002

Dear Friends,

Do you believe the countdown to war has begun? I do.

Why? First there are the signs we've all seen and heard:

– the congressional war resolution;

– the steady buildup of weapons and equipment in the Gulf area;

– the brushing aside of dissenters, whether they be generals, former secretaries of state, even a Nobel peace laureate ex-president, not to mention a full-throat chorus in the United Nations.

– And of course, the midterm elections are now out of the way.

Yes, we've all seen and heard these.

But second, this past month in Fayetteville there were a couple signs others didn't see. They're things we get to see from Quaker House, as a forward outpost of Friends peace witness.

One sign came out of the blue, when the doorbell rang on a quiet Fall afternoon. On the porch stood a tall Airborne paratrooper in full combat uniform: shiny black boots, green camouflage uniform, red beret. "I want to find out how to file a conscientious objector claim," he said.

"Come in," I shook his hand. "That's what we do here. No charge."

Let's call him Adam. "I was in Afghanistan, last summer," he added when we sat down. What he saw there sickened him. War solves nothing, he decided then, and he wanted nothing more to do with it.

Even so, Adam will probably face war again soon: he's in line to be shipped out at a moment's notice, this next time to Iraq. He said that almost all the equipment and weaponry for a pre-emptive attack is already in place, much of it in Afghanistan.

Adam expects the invasion to start before year's end. He'd be sent in as an infantryman, one of those likely to end up fighting block-by-block in Baghdad. Could Quaker House be of any help, he asked?

Well, at least we can offer GIs like him accurate information, and encouragement to follow their conscience. I showed him the detailed Army regulations about conscientious objector claims, and reviewed the Pentagon's elaborate procedures for handling them. I made him copies of old Quaker House newsletters describing the experiences of previous

24

Army COs.

As we talked, Adam became increasingly curious about Quaker House, and Quakers. Who, he wondered aloud, would set up and sustain a place like this, talking peace, conscience and resistance in a flag-waving Army town like Fayetteville?

Good question! The answer, of course, is: You. Friends and meetings.

Switching to Outreach mode, I handed him some brochures on Quakerism, talked about the Peace Testimony, and invited him to meeting. When Adam left, I wished him well, but with a sinking feeling.

I had tried to tell him the truth, which is that his way forward won't be easy: At its best the Army takes months to process a CO claim, and as war gets closer, the brass shows ever less sympathy for them.

So Adam could well face orders to board a flight to Iraq before any decision on a CO claim could be made. Then what? If he gets on the plane, he may well find himself in a war that not only threatens his life but also violates his conscience. If he refuses, he'll likely end up behind bars.

Quaker House can't save him from this cruel dilemma. What we can offer, besides the good information (which the Army won't), is some relief from his spiritual and emotional isolation, and help finding a civilian attorney if it comes to that. Plus we can follow up to see what happens.

This is what we do; it's our form of "front-line" Friends peace witness. That's how Quaker House started in 1969, as a response to a GI named Dean Holland, who also wanted to be a CO. But then he had to hitch-hike 75 miles from Fayetteville to the Friends Meeting in Chapel Hill to find someone ready to listen to his plea.

Dean Holland got the Friendly help he needed, his CO claim succeeded, and he became the first Director of Quaker House. At one time there were dozens of GI projects like it near bases around the country; but they're all gone now, victims of repression, emptied bank accounts and burnout.

Quaker House has had its own trials: a firebombing, military and FBI spying, staff turnover, budget troubles. But Friends don't give up easily. And 32 years later Adam found us on the web, still here, right across town from his barracks.

If there's no way to know what Adam will face in the coming months, we can be sure of one thing: Unlike Dean Holland, he won't be alone–as of last June, GI calls to our counseling line were up 20 per cent over 2001. (We had 3200 calls last year; we're on a pace to take 4000+ in 2002.)

That's where the other sign comes in: it was a call from Washington DC and the Center On Conscience and War, one of our sister groups. They were convening an emergency meeting of GI counselors, to talk about how to cope with a war-induced influx of new CO claims and cases. If the army is mobilizing, we better be too.

We're already feeling the impact. Besides making more work for me and our two counselors, Steve Woolford and Lenore Yarger, it's increasing many of our costs: telephone, transportation, printing, postage, training.

After all, GI counseling is not all we do here. Quaker House had its start amid an active local antiwar struggle. In fact, last spring we rediscovered and displayed the suppressed history of the Vietnam-era GI peace movement here at Ft. Bragg. (You can see much of the resulting exhibit at our website: www.quakerhouse.org)

The heady days of the Sixties may not be returning soon, but the peace movement is alive and growing. All of us here are involved: vigils at the gates of Ft. Bragg; local programs; peace workshops for meetings and churches; talking with young Friends and parents about draft/CO issues. More of all of these is coming.

Wars are like that around here: too much work, not enough money. Our board recently adopted a budget for 2003 which anticipates a $16,000 increase in expenses (with, for the record, no staff pay raises). Given what's coming, this expense figure looks realistic to me. I also hope it's realistic to think we can raise this much; we'll see.

Thanks and Peace,

Chuck Fager,
Director

PS. While writing this, the phone rang again. It was another GI, one we've been working with for almost a year. He applied for CO status last spring, just before his first child was born. Now he's expecting orders to Afghanistan anytime, and isn't sure whether to go or refuse. Whatever he decides, we're going to walk with him, his wife and young son as long as it takes.

Pineland Journal, February 7, 2003:

Smith, Jones, and War on Iraq –
A Debate With a Special Forces Officer

By Chuck Fager

Fayetteville, NC– It's February 7, 2003, and out on Fort Bragg the big guns are booming again, part of some new round of war games. And what seemed to echo distantly in their muffled roars this time last year now sounds like the leading edge of a terrible storm, the real thing about to burst over Iraq, and us, with the torrents and thunderbolts of war.

An even more vivid and unsettling harbinger of this war came yesterday, when I sat on a panel about the war with one of its defense intellectual advocates.

It was my second such foray. The first, at Duke almost three months ago now, had me seated next to an academic, pleasant, articulate and dogged; let's call him Smith. He quietly insisted that the invasion of Iraq was necessary, and would be ultimately beneficial for the Iraqis and the rest of the world.

I challenged the value of the war to the Iraqis, and based this objection above all on the prospect of high civilian casualties. Smith calmly replied that this was no problem, because the US military was the most careful such force in history when it came to minimizing them.

Perhaps so in theory and even intention, I retorted, but two big doubts about that notion linger for me. First, even if US generals get "collateral damage" down to a seemingly tiny percentage of, say, bombs dropped or missiles fired, the overwhelming volleys likely to be loosed by our forces argue for many civilian deaths just by the law of averages; and the record of the first Gulf War shows that many of the 'smart": bombs were really rather destructively dumb.

Moreover, I argued, in such a calculus, the counting does not end once the jets or the drones fly away. When US bombs destroy electricity and water purification plants–as they did many in Iraq the last time--the names of the children who die months or even years later from lack of safe water also belong on the casualty list, even if the bombing itself was done "cleanly," without hitting civilians at the moment of the attack.

By such reckoning the toll of the first Gulf War and the years of sanctions that ensued must be, has to be huge, and has been reckoned by credible estimates in the hundreds of thousands. Smith still scoffed at this

27

number, but had little concrete to offer in rebuttal beyond repeating that US wars were run in a primly fastidious manner. When I pointed to the million-plus Vietnamese civilian fatalities in our adventure there, a figure widely acknowledged, Smith shrugged, insisting he was talking about current–and impending–wars, not troubled missions bungled by a previous generation, mine.

So much for my first cavil. The second went simply unanswered, and to me is even more damning. It is that the Pentagon has resolutely refused even to discuss the question of civilian casualties in Iraq, either in the first or now the second Gulf war. No estimates, no explanations, no comment. The subject is off the table, and this policy of zipped lips has been decried even by staunchly pro-military analysts. Thus the basis for Smith's insistence that US war planners take pains to avoid them is strictly secondhand and unofficial. This by definition makes his contention unverifiable at best, and at worst no more than propaganda repeated.

Whatever goes on behind the scenes, this official refusal to engage diverges sharply from the public stance of hyper-morality that suffuses the current pentagon regime. It is no wonder that their reaction is to pass over it in silence whenever possible. And this was the response of my second panel colleague, at yesterday's face-off: let's call him Jones.

Jones is a fast-track Special Forces major who took time out from his schedule of intensive war preparation to join the panel at a local college. Trim and articulate, he had been president of his class at West Point; quoted Clausewitz at every opportunity, and stayed on message, offering no comment at all when I again presented my civilian casualty calculus as an objection to a new war. Instead, Jones preferred to talk about the coming war itself, which he was positively eager to see begin.

For him, Smith's modulated claim of a favorable outcome for the Iraqis was far too modest: this war, Jones enthused, would be a tremendous boon to all mankind, the golden door to peace, democracy and prosperity, not only in the currently turbulent Middle East region, but for as far as the eye could see. It would even, he believed, push the Israelis and Palestinians to the brink of a rapprochement.

My initial challenge to this scenario was to brandish a sheaf of articles and statements by generals, intelligence analysts, diplomats, political conservatives and even Republican donors, all decrying the plan as foolhardy and dangerous to American interests. The "Peace Hawks and Un-Usual Suspects" I called this unlikely band. The kicker was the January 13 full-page ad in the Wall Street Journal placed by a group of corporate CEOs who had backed G.W. Bush in 2000 but oppose the Iraq war and were now demanding, "We want our money back. We want our country back."

The willingness of all these people to go public, I contended, showed there is a real debate over the wisdom of this plan underway that crosses party and political lines, even though it has been largely ignored and marginalized by the administration.

Jones's response was patronizing and dismissive; the debate was great, he said; it showed America at its best. But it was also over, because we were going in, and soon, and a good thing too.

When a questioning student saw the specter of a new American imperialism in his pronouncements, Jones was trigger-quick with denial: No way – the US did not intend to "plant the flag" in Iraq or anywhere else. Of course, this rejoinder was quickly challenged; yet cries from me and others that imperialism could take other forms than formal colonization did not faze him.

We would soon bomb our way into Iraq, Jones agreed, but would then march in as liberators, not "overlords." He confidently predicted that the Iraqis (those who survived, I griped) would be greeting the 82d Airborne with cheers and flags, and it was evident Jones didn't intend to miss out on the party. While he did acknowledge that we'd need to be involved there for awhile, to ensure its proper transition to an acceptable version of democracy, the terms "occupation" or "colonialism" could in no way be attached to these outcomes.

Very well, then; I said; what's in a name? Though "imperialism" is now being used openly and without apology in such establishment journals as the New York Times Magazine. But if it must be a blood-red rose (or cruise missile) by some other name, what then to call the enterprise our rulers are about to launch?

Where to look for an answer was suggested by a religion professor. He named the association of the present leadership with politicized fundamentalism, which sees in the current struggle the latest and possibly most ominous locale for its end-times biblical preoccupation. This was, the professor opined, a very hazardous combination.

But Jones was having none of it. He hadn't, we were informed, seen Jerry Falwell or Pat Robertson at any of the policy conferences or seminars he'd recently attended with various policy wonks and high-mucky-mucks. Those in charge–he was now slightly indignant--were not religious fanatics, but very smart, rational people, making thoughtful, clear-sighted decisions. End of story.

Such political and cultural naivete was touching, even if it was not to be taken seriously in a person who undoubtedly knows how to spell the word "Ashcroft." here are, major, more policy conferences in Washington than those you were invited to. In any event, the light dawned and an alternative to the dreaded "imperialism" was rolling off my tongue:

"Messianic Hegemonism." That is, the US is not out to conquer Iraq (and the world), but to bring it salvation, in the form of our "values," especially democracy (as long as they learn to vote for the right sort of democrats, who among other things won't mess with our control of their oil.) That's the messianic part.

And we're bringing them this salvation even if they didn't ask for it, and not counting how many of them we'll have to kill to deliver it. Which is the "hegemonic" part.

I argued that this program was a recipe for permanent wars, loss of civil liberties and ever-deepening militarization of our society, which would (among other things) likely force the return of the draft, even though Rumsfeld and the White House don't want it: the world is simply too big to manage with the army we have or are likely to get without it. (Cf. North Korea, et al.)

Jones sneered at this, saying the army "could not afford" the draft. This was a curious response from one who has argued in print for doubling the military budget, and seems confident that we can afford an endless convoy of new high-tech, astronomically-priced weapons.

Okay, so "messianic hegemonism" doesn't have the sound-bite ring of "Axis of Evil." But the religion professor chuckled and agreed, as did some of the other panelists. Jones shrugged it off, as I expected. But I knew I was onto something when he went on to set the Iraq crusade in the context of the National Security Strategy document issued by the White House last September. Unlike earlier such documents, Jones said, this one was a very "big picture" manifesto, worldwide in scope and combining the advancement of our values with the determination to thwart any challengers to our preeminence."

Advancing our "values" while protecting our preeminence? Aha! I had him cold.

That document is the very scripture of Messianic hegemonism, pure and simple. Jones's response was paradoxical, or contradictory: dismissing imperialism or messianic hegemonism, he simultaneously gushed with awe at the new strategy's worldwide sweep. He found its vision thrilling. I frankly found it chilling.

Part of the difference in our reactions, I am convinced, was generational as much as political or even– though I doubt he would admit to this-- theological: his combat experience came in Panama in 1989, and stints in the little wars of the 90s. To me, the grizzled antiwar veteran shaped and scarred by Vietnam, Jones seemed impossibly young (he's 38) and idealistic. He hadn't seen or lived through the experience of watching national hubris shatter not only much of Vietnam but also large sectors of the US Army. I'm sure he's studied all that at West Point, and is confident he knows how to avoid repeating the mistakes of that generation of generals. Oh yes, I recognize such ardor, though mine came in a different costume and with flowers in its hair; but now it does not fool me. Does that qualify as older and wiser? Older, at least.

When he couldn't make headway with us by praising the new imperial vision, Jones fell back to the hard-nosed soldier's mantra that war was necessary because (pointing at me): "There are some very dangerous people out there who hate you and are determined to kill YOU." And he was ready to lead the charge to kill them first; which was, he knew, the only possible and moral response.

At which point the student moderator asked the standard, and entirely reasonable question, "But why do they hate us so much?"

When one of the faculty members started to talk about the US propping up dictators, hogging the oil, and abetting Israeli oppression of Palestinians, Jones quickly pulled the pin on the line that's supposed to explode all such talk like a concussion grenade: This is Hate-America stuff, he charged, which excuses and even supports terrorism.

But I fired right back, citing my work with Dr. King in Selma, Alabama as evidence that figuring out why people hate each other, and how to address this nonviolently can and does work, and benefits rather than threatens America. As evidence, I contrasted the success of the 1965 nonviolent campaign there in bringing "democracy" to the Black Belt with the failure of the Union Army to achieve any comparable result in an 1865 assault, despite its military "victory" in Selma and the South.

This response seemed to catch him off guard, I suppose because it wasn't a familiar sound bite. Further, I was speaking from first-hand experience, as real as his parachuting into Panama with guns blazing. On reflection it seems clear that the "hate-America" canard can be effectively countered by assertive statements of alternative approaches, especially with something to back them up.

(I would now add an analogy to disease research: we don't accuse cancer researchers of "siding with the disease" when they seek to understand why and how carcinomas start and grow; such understanding is crucial to overcoming it. For that matter, Jones's charge doesn't pass the hypocrisy test, because the military has battalions of intelligence staff analyzing every bit of available data about Iraqi and other terrorists, trying to "understand" them for military purposes.)

These were only debating sallies, though, and however well I and others may have blunted them in the discussion, Jones still had the trump cards, which he gladly showed when a young woman asked when he thought the attack would start. Disclaiming any "inside information," Jones nonetheless opined that he expected the bombing to begin late in February, shortly after the Hajj in Mecca concluded, with a ground invasion to follow in short order. And he thought it would all be over quickly.

I couldn't argue with most of this scenario; all the evidence points to it. And I want to acknowledge the integrity of Jones's advocacy: unlike the chickenhawks and draft-dodgers at the top, he will put himself in harm's way for this adopted vision. But I'm still doubtful about the last part: will it all be over quickly, the way 1991's Desert Storm (but not the dying of Iraqi civilians) ended after a few days?

As this debate proceeded, an eerie sense of role reversal crept over me: gone was my radical persona of the Sixties. That night, on that panel, Jones was the radical – nay an outright, unashamed revolutionary–while I was the querulous conservative: warning against unintended consequences and the hazards of social engineering, lamenting the erosion of constitutional traditions, arguing for limits and incremental rather than drastic change in Iraq. How did it happen, I wondered, that it was me waving a page from the Wall Street Journal, quoting Republican CEOs, generals, and Jesus?

So it goes. And after the debate, the countdown to war continued unabated.

Heading home, two quotes came to me, as supplements to the Clausewitz Jones cited so regularly. The first is from Robert E. Lee at the battle of Fredericksburg in 1862: "It is well that war is so terrible," he told James Longstreet, "or we should grow too fond of it."

Is Jones too fond of it? As far as the fire to be visited upon Iraq, I fear the answer is yes.

The other is from the sociologist Peter Berger, in a 1970 book called *Movement and Revolution:* "When it comes to revolutionaries," he wrote, "only trust the sad ones. The enthusiastic ones are the oppressors of tomorrow–or else they are only kidding."

That night Jones was surely not kidding; but perhaps I was melancholy enough for both of us.

Postscript from the *New Yorker,* February 10, 2003: "The other day, Secretary of State Colin Powell was reminded that his boss is in bed by ten and sleeps like a baby. Powell reportedly replied, "I sleep like a baby too–every two hours I wake up screaming."

[NOTE: In early 2003, First lady Laura Bush announced plans for a "literary salon" to be held at the White House on February 12. The theme was to be "Poetry and the American Voice," and numerous prominent poets were invited.

However, this was also the time when plans were made known for the "Shock and Awe" bomb and missile attack on Iraq – which began the following month– and antiwar protests against the impending invasion were widespread and breaking records for turnout. When several of the invited poets let it be known that they wold be reading antiwar verse to the event, it was abruptly "postponed," indefinitely.

In response, poets all over the nation held public readings of poetry on February 12, under the umbrella of "Poets Against the War. They were invited to submit their verse to a web archive, and within a few months the site had collected well over 12,000 poems, without question the most massive outburst of public poetry in American history.

One such reading was held at the historic Market House in downtown Fayetteville. And below is my original poem recited at the event.]

Overheard at the Department of Homeland Metonymy, Where They're Doing
A strategic Threat Assessment of Poets Against the War

A tribute to Poets Against the War <www.poetsagainstthewar.org>

by Chuck Fager

Red Alert, Boss!

Look out the window–
What's that? A fusillade of cruise missives?
And right behind them–
My god, right over there–
It's a hail of incoming SCUDs
          (Stanzas Calculated to Undo Destruction)
And behind us, all the mailboxes are stuffed with
unmarked envelopes full of powdered sonnets.

Christ! Call in the 82nd Airborne Revision,
or it will be too late
To stop these rogue scriveners from launching their own TIA

(Total Imagination Awareness) Program.
And then where will we be–?

It's the nightmare scenario!
I think I'm gonna onomatopoeia my pants.
The Petrarchan Act won't help us now, with
Unmanned iambic pentameters droning everywhere.
And trucks smuggling cargoes of chemical limericks
        and biologically active alliteration,
            all over the country, speeding off at a moment's notice,
Always ten feet and a spondee ahead of the doggerel inspectors.

And when we run out of duct tape and plastic sheeting
        to protect against the effects of
            aerosol-dispersed terza rima,
Then, Boss, we can just kiss our assonance goodby!

Even the sealed rooms won't keep out the
Laser-guided quatrains, and heat-seeking couplets
And if we somehow manage to get out, there's still the minefields of
        dual-use haiku to pick our way through.
In fact, if they're not stopped soon,
        one of these loose canons is sure to go nuclear,
figuring out how to rhyme
        "irrelevant," "Condoleeza," or even "Poindexter."

Add it up, we confront the unmistakable and growing proliferation
        of weapons of mass construction.

Let's face it, guys:
We're surrounded, and
This war just doesn't scan.

Just finished a book that I'd call a "must-read" for Friends, with special interest for women: "Driving By Moonlight," by Kristin Henderson, just out from Seal Press.

WARNING: Do NOT start this book when you have a lot of work to do. It was very hard to put down, and I stayed up way too late (even for me) over the past few nights to finish it.

While it can be called a memoir, and is, as she says, "a true story -- both true and a story," it's also a "road book", built around an 8000-mile trip she made across the country and back in a Corvette right after 9-11. But of course, the journey is also an archetypal Quest, and a Spiritual Pilgrimage. And interwoven with that are three other major themes, each richly and achingly detailed:

Her marriage, which is a good one, but with very serious strains – among them:

Her consuming lust to have a child, which only intensifies through 8 years of excruciating struggles with infertility.

Her Quakerism, which encompasses devotion to and questions about it. The questions swirl around both the peace testimony after the Twin Towers, as well as the "whole Christian thing." She's "worn orthodoxy as long as she canst," but belief in it is slipping away from her, no matter how hard she tries to hold on, and even as she becomes more firmly settled as a Quaker.

All this circles back to her marriage, because her husband is a devoutly believing Lutheran minister, who counts on their always having a love of Jesus Christ as divine savior in common.

And he's not just a minister, but one who has lusted to be a chaplain in the Marines, and finally achieves his goal. He heads for Afghanistan on a troopship as she heads west in the Corvette, leaving her to agonize both about his personal fate and about how his acting on his faith connects with her efforts to act on hers.

This is soap opera material, but there's not a hint of bathos here: Henderson can write.

While most Friends will have issues that differ from hers, there will be parallels and overlaps for most of us too, and I expect many a box of Kleenex will be get soggy while readers miss appointments and neglect chores to see how it turns out.

"Driving By Moonlight" really ought to be an Oprah bestseller; but I suspect it won't make the cut: it's too real and painful in too many places. That's not a criticism in my book, but a truth of marketing. Famine relief groups know they can't raise money using pictures of children who are actually starving; American readers recoil from such realistic images, turn away in denial.

Henderson is frequently funny, and regularly insightful--aphoristic gems sparkle from her quickly-turning pages. Yet she doesn't soften anything, doesn't turn away, and my hat is off to her for that.

"Driving By Moonlight" is real Quaker truth-speaking, something all-too rare among Friends (as everywhere else), and would deserve to be cherished for that witness alone. Fortunately there is more here to make it memorable reading. Much more.

Don't miss it.

When the War Begins, Peace Witness Does NOT End

March 17, 2003

Friends–

What does the beginning of the Iraq war mean for Quakers?

Consider an analogy: most fire departments work hard at fire prevention, and each actual fire means a setback for this goal.

Yet a blaze does not put the firefighters out of action. To the contrary-- they then redouble their efforts, take risks, and absorb casualties, in a struggle to contain the fire, roll it back and ultimately put it out. Once this is done, they catch their breath and return to their prevention campaign.

Friends are, I believe, in a parallel situation. The outbreak of war surely marks a setback for our months of marching, vigiling, writing and FAXing to head it off. But it does not spell defeat, and much less a reason for withdrawal into depression, indifference or escape.

There is still much To Do. And even more, there is still much To Be.

Here I'll pass by what To Do; there are many possibilities and opportunities for action, and they are widely advertised.

Rather, let me focus briefly on what, for Quakers, there is To Be.

At bottom it is straightforward and simple, so much so that it can be easily overlooked: It is, in George Fox's phrase, to "keep to our meetings," that is, to maintain and deepen our life as a worshiping community.

This cultivation of a deep center will not only help sustain us as individuals in a dark time (which it will). It also, and perhaps more importantly, has a public aspect: it can maintain our meetinghouses as places of refuge from the spirit of war.

The importance of this "witness of worship," the "action" of "being," came home to me on the morning the First Gulf War's ground invasion began in Second Month 1991. It was First Day, but a work day for me, at the post office. All that morning, it felt as if the winds of war were howling around me like a hurricane: screaming from the radio and TV, echoing in the voices of my co-workers, both anxious and excited, all reinforcing a crescendo of mass violence.

In those years they let me punch out for a couple of hours to attend meeting. And when I arrived at our modest building and stepped inside (a bit late, as so often happened), the door that closed behind me marked a transit into a qualitatively different space: a place of quiet, in which the noise of war was muffled, kept at bay, even if only briefly. In that small, fragile building, a different spirit was being evoked and maintained.

It is hard to overstate the contrast of this worshipful atmosphere with what was outside and all around it. At one level the meeting was typical and unremarkable: Friends sat in somber silence; the few messages, not especially eloquent, voiced grief and anguish in the face of what was happening without; one or two Friends wept quietly.

Yet for me it was a lifesaver, a miracle, a resource that made it possible to maintain some sense of balance and hope in that maelstrom. It enabled me to finish my shift at the post office with some composure, and then to turn to my other "job" of planning and taking part in outward witness.

This was my personal experience; yet it was not mine alone. In those bloody weeks, our meetinghouse filled up with pilgrims. They were seeking a similar respite from the war-spirit, and somehow figured that among Friends they would find it; and they were not mistaken. By "simply" being who we were, the meeting sustained a public witness, ministering to many who did not know where else to turn.

From a worldly perspective, the meeting did not "accomplish" much. Our feeble public protests (like the others) were ignored or ridiculed, and the ugly war ground on to its foolishly triumphalist conclusion, planting the seeds of the wars to come.

Yet we did achieve something, which I am convinced is more lasting than many a noisy protest: the meeting's presence and character helped sustain the hope of many. It certainly sustained me. By the time the tide of that war receded, I was convinced this was one of our most important tasks during wartime: the task of being, rather than, or better yet, undergirding all our doing.

It also seemed likely to me that this task would come to us again. And so, regrettably, it has. As we continue to rush about doing all that we can to stem the tide of war, let us not forget that much of our most potent peace witness will grow out of our being, as a worshiping community, rather than our doing.

Chuck Fager
Quaker House
Fayetteville NC

TWO: Resistance – In Uniform & Out

Quaker House - October 2002

Dear Friend,

Do you believe the countdown to war has begun? I do.
Why? First there are the signs we've all seen and heard:

– the congressional war resolution;
– the steady buildup of weapons and equipment in the Gulf area;
– the brushing aside of dissenters, whether they be generals, former secretaries of state, even a Nobel peace laureate ex-president, not to mention a full-throat chorus in the United Nations.

Yes, we've all seen and heard these.
But second, this past week in Fayetteville there were a couple signs others didn't see. And they're a big part of why I'm asking for your renewed support of Quaker House, as a forward outpost of Friends peace witness.
One sign came out of the blue, when the doorbell rang on a quiet Fall afternoon. At the door stood a tall Airborne paratrooper in full combat uniform: shiny black boots, green camouflage uniform, red beret. "I want to find out how to file a conscientious objector claim," he said.
"Come in," I shook his hand. "That's what we do here. No charge."
Let's call him Adam. "I was in Afghanistan, last summer," he added when we sat down. What he saw there sickened him. War solves nothing, he decided then, and he wanted nothing more to do with it.
Even so, Adam will probably face war again soon: he's in line to be shipped out at a moment's notice, this next time to Iraq. He said that almost all the equipment and weaponry for a pre-emptive attack is already in place, much of it in Afghanistan.
Adam expects the invasion to start before year's end. He'd be sent in as an infantryman, one of those likely to end up fighting block-by-block in Baghdad. Could Quaker House be of any help, he asked?
Well, at least we can offer GIs like him accurate information, and encouragement to follow their conscience. I showed him the detailed Army regulations about conscientious objector claims, and reviewed the

40

Pentagon's elaborate procedures for handling them. I made him copies of old Quaker House newsletters describing the experiences of previous Army COs.

As we talked, Adam became increasingly curious about Quaker House, and Quakers. Who, he wondered aloud, would set up and sustain a place like this, talking peace, conscience and resistance in a flag-waving Army town like Fayetteville?

Good question! The answer, of course, is: You.

Switching to Outreach mode, I handed him some brochures about Friends, talked about the Peace Testimony, and invited him to meeting. When Adam left, I wished him well, but with a sinking feeling.

I had tried to tell him the truth, which is that his way forward won't be easy: At its best the Army takes months to process a CO claim, and as war gets closer, the brass shows ever less sympathy for them.

So Adam will likely face orders to board a flight to Iraq before any decision on a CO claim could be made. Then what? If he gets on the plane, he may well find himself in a war that not only threatens his life but also violates his conscience. If he refuses, he'll likely end up behind bars.

Quaker House can't save him from this cruel dilemma. What we can offer, besides the good information (which the Army won't), is some relief from his spiritual and emotional isolation, and help finding a civilian attorney if it comes to that. Plus we can follow up to see what happens.

This is what we do; it's our form of "front-line" Friends peace witness. That's how Quaker House started in 1969, as a response to a GI named Dean Holland, who also wanted to be a CO. But then he had to hitch-hike 75 miles from Fayetteville to the Friends Meeting in Chapel Hill to find someone ready to listen to his plea.

Dean Holland got the Friendly help he needed, his CO claim succeeded, and he became the first Director of Quaker House. At one time there were dozens of GI projects like it at bases around the country; but they're all gone now, victims of repression, emptied bank accounts and burnout.

Quaker House had its own trials: a firebombing, military and FBI spying, staff turnover, budget troubles. But Friends don't give up easily. And 32 years later Adam found us on the web, still here, right across town from his barracks.

If there's no way to know what Adam will face in the coming months, we can be sure of one thing: Unlike Dean Holland, he won't be alone as of last June, GI calls to our counseling line were up 20 per cent over 2001. (We had 3200 calls last year; we're on a pace to take 4000+ in 2002.)

That's where the other sign comes in: it was a call from Washington

DC and the Center On Conscience and War, one of our sister groups. They're convening an emergency meeting of GI counselors, to talk about how to cope with a war-induced influx of new CO claims and cases. If the army is mobilizing; we better be too.

We're already feeling the impact. Besides making more work for me and our two counselors, Steve Woolford and Lenore Yarger, it's increasing many of our costs: telephone, transportation, printing, postage, training.

After all, GI counseling is not all we do here. Quaker House had its start amid an active local antiwar movement. In fact, last spring we rediscovered and displayed the suppressed history of the Vietnam-era GI peace movement here at Ft. Bragg. (You can see much of the resulting exhibit at our website: www.quakerhouse.org)

The heady days of the Sixties may not be returning soon, but the peace movement is alive and growing. All of us here are involved: vigils at the gates of Ft. Bragg; local programs; peace workshops for meetings and churches; talking with young Friends and parents about draft/CO issues. More of all of these is coming.

Wars are like that around here: too much work, not enough money. Our board recently adopted a budget for 2003 which anticipates a $16,000 increase in expenses (with, for the record, no staff pay raises).

Thanks, and

Peace,

Chuck Fager,
Director

PS. While writing this, the phone rang again. It was another GI, one we've been working with for almost a year. He applied for CO status last spring, just before his first child was born. Now he's expecting orders to Afghanistan anytime, and isn't sure whether to go or refuse. Whatever he decides, we're going to walk with him, his wife and young son as long as it takes.

Toronto, February 7—The *Globe & Mail*, a major Canadian newspaper, reported today that Jeremy Hinzman, an army private from Ft. Bragg, has arrived there and applied for retugee status. Jeremy's attorney is
asserting that the invasion of Iraq violated international law, and that Jeremy will be persecuted for his beliefs in nonviolence it he returns to lie US.

Jeremy and his family were regular attenders at Fayettevite Friends Meeting, and Quaker House assisted him in preparing a CO claim, which he filed in 2002.

Despite his claim, be was sent to Afghanistan later in 2002, and his unit was deployed to Iraq in January 2004, a few days after he left for Canada.

Canadian legal experts say Jeremy's chances of being granted retugee status are slim. What will happen then is impossible to predict. In the US, Jeremy would face charges of desertion, a serious telony.

March 20, 2004 Fayetteville Peace Rally: A New GI Peace Movement Finds Its Voices

As the Iraq War gets bloodier and ever more pointless, a distinctive GI Resistance is now emerging. On March 20, 2004, in Fayetteville, this resistance found its voices. Beth Pratt and Norma Castillo were two of them.

The March 20 peace march and rally was the largest local antiwar protest since May of 1970; Quaker House was among the key organizers of both events.

On the platform of the March 20 rally, the largest group of speakers was made up of veterans and family members of active duty soldiers. Their words were varied, but the message was consistent and summed up in the large banner hung above the stage: a call to show "real support" for the troops by bringing them home now.

This new GI resistance is quite different from the movement flourishing here at the time of the 1970 rally, held in the same park at the height of the Vietnam War. (For an eyewitness account, see the letter on page 2.) At Quaker House we maintain an extensive exhibit of documents and images from this earlier wave of GI protest, drawn from our archives. (Much of it is online at our website, www.quakerhouse.org)

That earlier GI movement was a large – at moments even a mass – phenomenon: it produced underground newspapers, noisy protest groups, vivid, irreverent graphics, public statements by dissident officers, and large antiwar rallies.

As reporters and others have viewed our exhibit, some have asked, "Do you really expect to see something like this again?" The query echoes with another question, unspoken and sardonic: "You're still hoping to revive the Sixties, right?"

The answer to this last has always been NO: we document and celebrate this hidden past, but we don't live in it, and are not interested in reviving the Sixties. But we are interested in seeing what the GI resistance to this Iraq war will look and sound like; and now we're finding out.

It's not a "movement" exactly, at least not yet. But there are now enough voices and persons stepping forward to make it more than an isolated phenomenon. And as it grows, I believe it will make a big impact.

The army is different today than it was in 1970: all "volunteer," and with a much higher percentage of married GIs. Most servicepeople joined up because of the "carrots" (college money, job training) rather than the "sticks" (the draft). Thus, many feel they have more to lose from speaking up than did the restive single men of 35 years ago. And the "sticks"are not gone either–the military has moved forcefully against many who have spoken out.

Our last newsletter featured two early voices in this resistance – Jeremy Hinzman, who sought refuge in Canada in January – and Stephen Funk, who went AWOL last year to publicize his antiwar stand, and served six months in a Marine brig for his witness.

But the public military dissenters today are as likely to be military spouses or family members as GIs themselves.

Beth Pratt, for instance; she is a nurse in Fayetteville. Her husband was deployed in Iraq when she stepped up to the microphone at the March 20, 2004 rally. He drove trucks in Iraq, one of the most dangerous duties there.

"If we're lucky he'll be back home next month, and then maybe I can relax," Beth said. "But not for long, probably – he's been told that his unit will be sent back to Afghanistan soon, for a year. And then I'll get to go through this again, just like thousands of other army and reservists' wives and family members.

"He's due to get out of the army on October 23, 2006 – that's a date I've had memorized ever since he signed up. But maybe he won't be done then – now I know that they could put on a stop-loss order and keep him in indefinitely.

"What kind of a life is that? It's my life, unless we can get this war stopped....

"If I believed in this war, maybe it would be easier to deal with this separation. But I don't. . . .

"I want to thank all of you who have come out here today," she said, "because it takes courage to speak up about these issues. It's taken all the courage I have to stand up here myself and speak for these few minutes. If you're of a different mindset around here, you can feel very isolated and alone. So a peace rally like this one where people can speak up has been a great source of support for me, and will hopefully be to others."

Norma Castillo is the aunt of Sgt. Camilo Mejia, a soldier who refused orders to return for a second tour in Iraq, went AWOL, and then filed a CO claim when he turned himself in last month. He was invited to speak at the Fayetteville peace rally, but his commander refused to let him leave Fort Stewart, Georgia, where he has been charged with desertion.

Castillo came in his place, and read a statement from Mejia. It said, in part:

"I would like to thank everyone for coming here today. I cannot get tired of saying that what I have done and what you people are doing today is something that goes far beyond one man, or even one nation. We are asking for an end to a war that represents a crime against all mankind. We are doing this for the soldiers and their families who are victims of this war. We are doing this for the people of Iraq, who are being oppressed for the oil. We are doing this for humanity, which has already paid a high price for this in every war. Thank you for uniting with me with this cause, which is the cause of peace. Pray with me to put an end to this and every war."

Regrettably there is not space here to summarize more of the statements made at the rally. Numerous pictures and more descriptions were posted on our website, along with excerpts from various press reports. The most important fact is that it happened, it was peaceful and festive, and it gained an international audience for the voices of respectful pro-troop and anti-war dissent, right in the heart of one of America's key military communities.

An E-mail to Quaker House, May 4, 2004:

Dear Friends,

My draft-age son and I (and many of his friends) are horrified at the violence and war in Iraq. My son is not sleeping worrying over what he will do if a draft returns, which is likely. Please advise us about any links in Canada and any refuge provided there by the Quaker church (we are not Quaker but do wholeheartedly subscribe to nonviolence). In the Quaker view, is leaving one's country because of an unjust "war" alright in the eyes of God?

SJ

Dear SJ,

Thanks for your note. It is a tragedy that your son has to worry about the return of the draft; but there it is.

As for refuge in Canada if the draft returns, there were many groups and individuals in Canada who helped young men find refuge there during the Vietnam war draft.

However, laws in Canada today are different and much more restrictive regarding immigration, and your son needs to inform himself carefully about current legal matters there. . . . .

For information about the experience of current military resisters who are seeking refuge in Canada, let me also suggest that you google the name "Jeremy Hinzman." Jeremy is a US soldier who went to Canada after his army unit received orders to go to Iraq. He is applying for refugee status there. At the website you will find an extensive collection of articles and other information about his case.

One other point: At the website for Quaker House, www.quakerhouse.org, you can find an article on the possible return of the draft, which suggests that next year, 2005, is when the chances of reviving the draft will likely be the greatest. If this turns out to be the case, that will be the time to pay close attention to the actions in Washington, and make plans accordingly.

I wish you and your son the best!

Peace,
Chuck Fager

PS. to Friends: "In the Quaker view, is leaving one's country because of an unjust war alright in the eyes of God?"
Good question. What's the answer?

Quaker House

Dear Friend,

It's autumn – time for a fund appeal letter. But it hasn't been easy to get it done. There are too many distractions – including a stack of unopened mail. There are bills in many of the envelopes, so that's a big incentive to get started.

We have plenty to write a letter about. The war goes on, and GI Hotline calls are up. 2004 seems sure to be another record year – there were almost 29,000 calls in 2003; at the current rate, this year's total will be near 35,000; our share will top 6000. – Or I could mention our 35th anniversary as the only Quaker peace project next to a major military post, and the Interfaith Peace Seminar we held in June to mark it.

Then there was the arrival of a new baby, Geneva Magdalena Yarger Woolford, to Steve & Lenore, our main GI Hotline counselors.

That's about all the good news. On the other side, the house needs a lot of expensive repair work. Plus, we have an $83,000 operating budget to raise. And over the past few months, my phone at the house has also been ringing more and more frequently with urgent counseling calls. As the war continues, our workload keeps growing.

So it's hard to stay focused when the phone keeps ringing and people need our help.

There it goes, ringing now.

This call also turns out to be good news, about an army paratrooper whose CO claim was rejected. He's been in the brig for almost two weeks, after a punitive court-martial.

But now the word is he's on the way home. The army has finally seen the light and agreed to discharge him. While behind bars, he and his wife were showered with supportive letters from Friends – you came through again! His struggle has gone on for almost two years, and we've been walking with him all the way. That's what your support makes possible – the kind of call we like. But I don't get to savor it long before the phone rings again.

This time it's a Marine just out of boot camp, at Camp Lejeune. Horrified by the reality of training to kill with a bayonet, he's been struggling with depression and an urge to go AWOL. I've already been talking with both his parents about the details of preparing a CO claim.

The family is Catholic, and the father is a career Navy officer. None of them ever heard of conscientious objection until they found our website a few days ago. I've been explaining that there is actually a strong Catholic antiwar witness, led by a guy they've probably heard of, named John Paul II. This is evidently news to them. But the son wants to have a CO claim ready within the next few days, before the next phase of his combat training starts. The parents are hoping that if they make their case clearly and follow the rules, it will all turn out okay. They're optimists. I think about the paratrooper getting out of the brig, his two years of struggle, and figure they'll be calling back before long.

I hang up, and head for the desk to get to the stack of mail, with those bills.

Then – there's another call, again from Camp Lejeune. This time it's a Marine who's been in for 14 months, and hates it. A recent suicide attempt put him in a naval hospital, where they said he was faking and returned him to his unit. He says the stress is such that he can't bear it.

I can believe it. I've been to Lejeune – making visits to Stephen Funk, another Marine CO and resister. He did six months in the brig there last winter. Friends like you sent him over a thousand cards and letters to keep his morale up – and it worked! Now Stephen is out, and back in school, getting on with it. Marines from Lejeune are doing a lot of the heavy lifting in Iraq, taking many of the casualties. Our is a unique ministry, to Stephen Funk, and this new caller.

With this new Marine I go over the procedures for seeking a discharge based on mental distress. Turns out he has a therapist back home who may be able to help who will believe him when the military docs won't. He seems calmer when we're finished. Maybe he's found a bit of relief from the stress, some ground for hope. That's often the most important thing we can give: hope. We offer it free of charge.

Besides calls, there are emails waiting, asking whether the draft will return, and what to do about it. These questions come in almost daily now. The threat looks real and growing from here, and the recent "No" vote in Congress meant nothing. Our latest Quaker House newsletter included a fact sheet about how to get ready if/when the draft returns. I copy it and send it off.

Okay, back to the snailmail. *But there's the phone again.* This time, the caller has a thick British accent – he's a reporter, from Liverpool. Foreign reporters are nothing new these days. But this Brit writes for a large Spanish daily in Barcelona. He's coming to watch a presidential debate in Fayetteville, plans to talk about the campaign with some military families, and wants to learn about Quaker House.

So why not? A Liverpudlian scribe is covering the U.S. election from

Fayetteville, for a paper in Spain. Go figure. I explain carefully that I don't talk politics (on the record, anyway), but am happy to tell about our work. We make an appointment.

Barcelona – another city to add to the list: this past year Quaker House and our local peace work has been on TV in Australia, Japan, France, England, and Canada. Once we even made it onto a station in Raleigh, 70 miles up the road.

Calls from reporters have been an almost everyday thing since our peace rally last March 20, the anniversary of the Iraq invasion. At a thousand people or so, it was the largest in Fayetteville since Jane Fonda came during the Vietnam War. The queries and camera crews have come through steadily ever since March, even filming our sad peace vigil in September marking 1000 US casualties (and 10,000-20,000+ Iraqis).

Throughout, our message has been "YES to the Troops – NO to the War," and it looks to us like we're making headway. The old slurs on peace folks – that we hate soldiers and their families – don't seem to have much traction here these days.

Talking with reporters gives us a chance to get the word out, not only about Quaker House but about how our long-term, front-line peace witness works with and for GIs, not against them.

We're a standing challenge to the pervasive military view of the world here. The media exposure is gratifying, and the contacts will come in handy if Homeland Security ever comes after us. But they're a lot of work, and we don't get any donations from Tokyo or Paris. I talk to all the reporters who call, but Quaker House depends on you.

Later, another call confirms that the paratrooper has definitely made it home from the brig.

None of this letter is fiction, by the way; it was all part of a "normal" day here.

And somehow this fund appeal letter got finished. But that stack of mail is still mostly unopened.

Got to finish that. Right now.

Only there's the phone again. Better go grab it – I'll get back to you soon.

Thanks, and Peace,

Chuck Fager

PS. As this was written, a crucial national election was near. Remember, I don't talk politics (on the record, anyway), but this much can be said: no matter how the vote turns out, our workload will still grow, with no relief in sight.

Quaker House

May 2005

Dear Friend,

Visiting Camp Lejeune is always a sobering experience. The fences outside the gates are hung with many banners put up by family members to greet troops returning from Iraq. Marines from Lejeune have seen heavy and costly service there. I don't know what's done for those who don't return.

In early April, the Quaker House calendar included plans for another visit to Camp Lejeune, where a Marine Conscientious Objector, Joel Klimkewicz, was in the brig, serving seven months.

Joel's was a case that really stuck in the throat. His CO request was for non-combatant status; he didn't ask for a discharge; he said he was ready to serve in Iraq, even offered to take on dangerous duty like clearing mines provided only that he could do it unarmed.

Joel is a Seventh Day Adventist, and that was his understanding of the Gospel.

But instead, he was behind bars. That's because the Marines turned down his CO application, then ordered him to report for weapons training. He refused, and was court-martialed. We asked Friends to write to Joel, and to Marine higher-ups, to protest the unusually severe sentence. Many of you did, and I visited him several times, sharing the time with his wife and young daughter, Cameron.

Maybe the letters helped: the email excerpted below brought good news at last!

"I'm free in a literal sense but it appears the fight goes on! I want to thank you for all of your support and that of other Quakers. I was released by order of the [Marine Corps] Commandant . . . . It's a bit funny when I think about just two weeks earlier I was told my [court martial] Authority acted and all punishment was approved and forwarded to Navy Marine Court of Appeals, but a miracle took place when I heard April 5th I was going to be released.

There was a new line added to my [court martial] Authority action that states all confinement time after April 6th be suspended for a period of 12 months. How they changed something they had previously acted on

51

is in keeping with the highest standards of military tradition. God has truly blessed me through this entire thing and my freedom at least from the brig could not have come any sooner, I was starting to get a seriously negative attitude.

Let me tell you my fellow prisoners were just as happy to watch me go, everyone behind bars has a deep love for our first amendment. I have some books to send you so let me know if the address you sent me a letter from is a good one to send them. . . . Keep in touch and again I cannot thank you enough! Cameron's going to miss coloring with you.

Your Brother in Christ, Home
Joel David Klimkewicz"

Until late last year, Joel had been thinking of a (non-combatant) military career. Now he's planning to become a Seventh Day Adventist minister, maybe a prison chaplain. When I last saw Joel and his family, they were at a church service together. It was a surprise to see him dressed in something other than prisoner orange!

Thank you for the support that enables us to be Quaker companions to Joel, and the others.

Peace,

Chuck Fager

Quaker House

November 2005

Dear Friend,

For several weeks this past summer, I was afraid Quaker House might be seriously, even fatally, at risk.

The challenge came out of the blue, in June. Until then, the ongoing peace witness was keeping us extremely busy:

Among other work, our GI Rights Hotline, phone calls and emails were coming in at a pace well ahead of last year. In March, we'd helped organize Fayetteville's largest peace rally ever, and were still following up. Through the spring, there were visits to a Seventh Day Adventist marine CO in the brig at Camp Lejeune. And more.

The summer calendar was full too, with plans for workshops and presentations; and an intern was coming in August.

We were also helping plan two conferences – one in Indiana, for the three peace churches, Mennonite, Brethren & Quakers. The other, closer to home, was to be North Carolina's first ever statewide church peace conference. We partnered with the state Council of Churches for that project, set for November here in Fayetteville.

By that time, we figured, U.S. casualties in Iraq would have passed 2000. Yet along with that grim, looming landmark there came a sense – a hunch – that the logjam of public support for the Iraq war was cracking and about to break up.

So we were too busy to be paranoid. Or maybe just oblivious?

The challenge came in a letter from the county tax office.

I suppose we should have been expecting something. After all, while you are reading this, the FBI is using tens of thousands of "national security letters" – all issued with no court authorization or review – to snoop through citizen emails, snail mail, phone, library, credit and financial records.

Maybe yours. Maybe mine.

A new "National Clandestine Service," is now "coordinating" all federal intelligence and spy operations, domestic and foreign. Its director's name is itself a state secret. And it is now legal in America for citizens to be snatched off the street and held indefinitely without trial, charges, or counsel.

Nothing that dramatic happened here. Even so, the county's letter had my full attention, from the first line. The county wasn't sure, it said, that Quaker House really qualified for its exemption from local taxes, so our exempt status was up for "review."

Strictly routine, it said, nothing special.

Nonsense, snapped the local tax attorney we consulted.

In his decades of practice, such county "reviews" were almost unheard of. In his opinion, this one was neither random nor coincidental.

But don't panic, he went on. Sure, you're in jeopardy. But you're legitimate, doing what you say you do.

Right. It's what we've been doing for 36 years, and we can prove it.

The county tax issue could be fixed, the attorney said.

That was a relief.

Or it was, til we heard from the IRS.

It was early August. To that point, the summer had been going according to "plan." The hunch about a turn in public opinion was proving out. Our first real evidence came on June 28, when a presidential speech on Iraq was delivered at Ft. Bragg. The speech had been ballyhooed for days. It was to be the White House "magic bullet" to reverse the slide in public support for the war.

Calling together other area activists, we met the speech with an enlarged peace vigil downtown. Veterans of Iraq and other wars, children, senior citizens, black and white ignored a pouring rain to read the names of all the US casualties. A respectful international group of reporters and TV newspeople watched, listened, and broadcast. And whether or not our vigil helped, the "big" speech was a big bust.

Also, the heavy counseling load was yielding some remarkable cases. One was a soldier from Ft. Bragg we'll call "Ted." He sat in the living room on a warm afternoon and told me about the new kind of pornography his buddies were bringing back from Iraq: CDs full of gruesomely explicit digital photos of Iraqis killed in combat. His buddies were showing them off, Ted said, laughing and bragging about them.

Ted was clear he couldn't be a part of that. But, he wondered, what options did he have? (Ted has since filed for conscientious objector status.)

The Seventh Day Adventist CO, Joel Klimkewicz (his real name) got out of the brig at Camp Lejeune and headed to Tennessee with his family to enroll in college, planning to be a minister.

In early August, as we were preparing to greet a new intern, a woman who had given a brief, little-noted speech at our spring antiwar rally left the Veterans for Peace convention in Dallas headed for Crawford, Texas. That week, Cindy Sheehan stepped into history.

54

You could almost feel the logjam breaking up, the tide beginning to turn.

Was it a perfect time for some pushback, or what?

Whichever, that was the week we heard from the IRS – not directly, but even more disturbingly, via a potential donor. Their broker routinely checked the nonprofit tax status of intended beneficiaries – and found we didn't have any.

What? It seemed unbelievable at first – there's a 1973 IRS letter in our files confirming our nonprofit 501 (c) 3 status. I was on the phone to the IRS within the hour of hearing about this change. But their clerk in Cincinnati confirmed what the broker said: Quaker House's nonprofit tax status had been "suspended."

Now here was something to worry about.

It's a simple equation: – No nonprofit status = no donations = no Quaker House.

We didn't dawdle. A Quaker attorney from Baltimore offered to help us, and we accepted with alacrity.

If you've ever had to deal with the IRS, though, maybe you know how it can be like stumbling through the looking glass.

Despite all the attorney's phone calls, and mine, we could never find out when this suspension had been imposed. Or by whom. Never mind why.

Maybe, we were told, we had simply missed out on some routine paperwork. [Not likely; IRS mail is not neglected in this house.] But there were no specifics.

When this IRS issue came to light, we were just about to file the form with the county tax office. Was all this just coincidence? Who can say? In any event, the IRS said we could apply for reinstatement. We did; more fat packets of papers were gathered, mailed and faxed.

All the while, our ongoing work was, well, ongoing. The perennial work of GI counseling, peace action, networking, resource sharing. Plus a continuing search for new ideas.

One excellent new idea came from our intern, John Stephens from Alexandria Meeting in Virginia. John was interested in a Truth-in-Recruiting project: what, he suggested, about a cartoon character to guide potential recruits through the (many) pitfalls of the military enlistment agreement?

The idea was simple. Execution was challenging and time-consuming, but the result, "Sgt. Abe, The Honest Recruiter," was brilliant. "Sgt. Abe" is now being passed out to young people all over the country.

The Indiana peace church conference came and went. A Camp Casey caravan stopped in Fayetteville enroute from the president's texas ranch to Washington DC. Plans for the church peace conference, "Seek Peace and Pursue It," continued. Counseling calls kept coming in. We began to talk about organizing another large Fayetteville peace rally for the third anniversary of the Iraq occupation, next March. But over it all hung a nagging question mark.

Finally, on September 19, we caught a break: the IRS called, to say our nonprofit status was back on track. Retroactive, too – no donors would lose any deductions.

"Can I get that on paper?" was my first response. Within minutes, the fax was in my trembling hand.

A few days later I called the county tax office about our local exemption: no problem, they said nonchalantly; you're fine.

That's the happy ending to this story, for now.

And so, what was all this? A bad dream? A strange coincidence of lost or routine paperwork? Paranoia? A taste of things to come?

Whatever; it's behind us, for now, so we can stay focused on our other, positive work: the church peace conference, which just took place, successfully; GI counseling; peace action; networking and sharing resources with other groups – doing our bit to keep the turning tide, turning.

Focus. Please help us stay focused. And keep us in your prayers. Even if there's light at the end of the tunnel, the tunnel's end is still a long way off.

And even if we dodged the bullet this time, the IRS, the FBI, the "Patriot" Act, and the Clandestine Service are all still out there.

Have a good holiday season. Be good to those you love. Work for peace. And don't forget us.

In Friendship,

Chuck Fager

PS. A new item on our agenda is helping plan a Quaker conference on torture, slated for Guilford College next June. Watch for more details about it.

January 2006

To say it's been a busy autumn and early winter would be the understatement of the year, maybe the decade.

So much so, that an event which I would otherwise have regarded as possibly the biggest news of the season slipped past unnoticed here until weeks after it happened.

Welcome News From the North

I'm referring to a decision released in early November, with no fanfare and barely a mention even in the nation's press: A Canadian federal court granted Jeremy Hinzman's request to file an appeal of the government's rejection of his petition for refugee status.

Jeremy is our friend, formerly with the 82d Airborne at Ft. Bragg, whose application for CO status was turned aside by his superiors while he was deployed in Afghanistan. When his unit got orders for Iraq in December 2003, he went into exile with his wife and young son.

Since arriving in Toronto, Jeremy has become a spokesman for the growing number of other GI refugees who have surfaced in Canada.

He asked for official refugee status on the grounds that the war was illegal under international law, and that going there would make him complicit with war crimes. But the Canadian government has routinely denied refugee status to American citizens, arguing that the US is a respecter of human rights. At a hearing last December, Jeremy was denied the chance to argue the issue of the war's illegality.

Some conservative pundits like Bill O'Reilly of Fox News have demanded that Jeremy be returned to the US in handcuffs; and the initial rejection of his petition was announced last March, on the same day the Canadian prime minister was visiting the Texas White House in Crawford.

A hearing on the case in a Canadian federal court is slated for February. Jeremy's attorney, Jeffry House, has said the process will enable him to raise the issue of the war's legality, which has been a part of successful appeals involving refugees from other wars.

Predictions are risky, but it seems quite possible that Jeremy's appeal could become a landmark case.

In a message dated 9/8/2006 3:35:58 PM Eastern Standard Time, sxxxx@earlham.edu writes:

Dear Chuck,

I am a 22-year-old (former) non-registrant who was mistakenly registered in the filling out of my Federal Application For Student Aid this spring. I've filed the corrective paperwork with FAFSA, but the Selective Service says there's no mechanism for un-registering short of a letter to the President of the United States. Do you have any information or advice that could be helpful in getting me unregistered?

For peace in troubled times,
Jason
~~~~~~~~~~~~~~~~
Jason S------
Earlham College
Peace and Global Studies major ('07)
shenkja@earlham.edu
765.973.2984

Jason–

My advice to you is not to worry about the registration matter. If you were trying to avoid registration as a matter of laying groundwork for a potential future Conscientious Objector claim, being registered in no way limits your ability to make such a claim should the time come. There are numerous other things to do that will be more important in developing a "track record" for future use in a CO claim. (For more on this, go to: http://quakerhouse.org/Draft-FAQ.htm)

I'm not sure where you learned that a letter to the president would "un-register" you. I am unfamiliar with this concept, and can find no such provision anywhere on the Selective Service website. If you have some specific information about this procedutre, I'd like to see it. If this is secondhand or undocumented information, I would be very dubious about its reliability.

Further, if you were trying to avoid registering as a way of making some kind of public antiwar statement, my advice again is that this is not a very useful antiwar statement to make; there are many other more

58

visible ways to express such convictions.

About the only logical rationale I can conceptualize for refusing to register is a libertarian or anarchist belief that the government should not have the power to coerce such information from a free citizen. I can respect such a philosophical position, but must note that anyone attending a US college in 2006 is in a very poor position to enforce it: both public and private agencies at all levels in our society today have many ways of gathering information about all such persons, and they DO gather it, all the time. Certainly anyone who uses email or a credit card is exposed to many such information-gathering technologies; there's really no such thing as "privacy" on the net.

If I wanted to become practically speaking "invisible" to this pervasive information-gathering regime, I would explore one of three main options:

1. Join the Amish, who stay outside the Social Security system and thus escape one of the keystone databases, and dress alike to make individuals hard to identify. (Do YOU have a Social security Number? If so, you're busted.)

2. Join one of the more cloistered Catholic religious orders which will take in lay brothers; some of these communities, I am told, will take people in without asking too many questions; the members adopt new names, wear the same clothes, and the authorities are slow to question them as well.

3. Leave the country.

Failing any of the above, my prediction is that even if you were to manage to get "un-registered" in your current situation, you will have difficulty avoiding being registered again involuntarily. For instance, if you have or acquire a driver's license, in 35 states that means you are already registered by that route -- and even in the other 15 states, that information is at the command of the feds and Selective Service when they want to come and get it.

I wish this were not so. But you asked my advice, and I'm committed to giving you the best I have. And this is it: don't sweat the registration. Ignore it and get to work stopping the war, fundamentalist terror and militarism. (For my thoughts on how to begin doing that, see this page: http://quakerhouse.org/declaration-01.htm) There's plenty of resources for serious preparation for this work at Earlham. Worrying about registration is a distraction and a waste of your precious time.

Peace,

Chuck Fager
Quaker House
Fayetteville / Ft. Bragg NC
www.quakerhouse.org

Sgt. Ricky Clousing: Another Iraq Veteran Says no

When Sgt. Ricky Clousing took the stand at his court martial on October 12 at Ft. Bragg, the military judge looked irritated. As Ricky described the pattern of routine abuse he saw on the streets of occupied Iraq, the judge's irritation seemed to deepen.

There was no way to stop this riveting story. Even though Ricky had pled guilty to going AWOL, he was entitled to testify in his own behalf. It was his chance to present "mitigating" points, in hopes of gaining a lighter sentence from the judge.

There was little chance of that, and all of us in the courtroom knew it: a plea agreement had been made with Ricky's commander, limiting jail time to a maximum of three months. The judge knew there was a deal, but not the specifics. Only if his sentence turned out to be less than the agreed upon term – not likely – would it stand; anything longer would automatically be reduced to the three months.

All this arcane military math aside, there were other audiences for Ricky's testimony: one was half a dozen other soldiers who had also been AWOL and are now awaiting their fate. They sat in the courtroom, listening closely and rooting quietly for Ricky.

The other audience was a row of reporters, who were being closely monitored by a major and a sergeant from Ft. Bragg's Public Affairs Office. Through the media, Ricky hoped to have his story heard across the country.

To some extent, Ricky succeeded in this last goal: the *New York Times* sent a reporter, who wrote a fine report, as did the Fayetteville *Observer*. And his GI buddies went out of their way to wish him well when the trial was over, as he prepared to head off to confinement.

This success was no thanks to the judge, who interrupted Ricky frequently, and refused to let him read excerpts from his journal detailing his early struggles of conscience in Iraq. Even so, the main elements of a compelling story were told:

How Clousing was a born-again Christian who joined the army after taking several mission trips with the evangelical group Youth With a Mission.

How he trained to be an interrogator for Army intelligence, was assigned to the 82d Airborne at Ft, Bragg, and performed well enough to be fast-tracked for promotion to sergeant in less than three years.

How he went on patrols in Baghdad and Mosul, inter-rogating scores of Iraqi civilians who were swept up in searches and raids, and reports about many more detainees.

How his own interrogations and the records he reviewed showed clearly that upwards of eighty-five percent of the Iraqis who were detained by occupation forces, often for months, with no legal rights and without their families knowing if they were dead or alive, were being held for no reason   they were, as he put it, "just in the wrong place at the wrong time."

And how he could see, and told his superiors, that this treatment of hundreds and thousands of innocent Iraqis, was self-defeating. Worse, it was turning them into supporters of the insurgency, creating much of the resistance that the occupation forces were fighting to eradicate.

How these pleas fell on deaf ears.

How he saw numerous abuses of Iraqis on the streets, including the killing of an unarmed Iraqi youth.

How after his return to Ft. Bragg, he sought help from the Army in resolving the questions of conscience that had been haunting him since his deployment   to no avail. A chaplain told him God approved war; a psychologist suggested he say he was gay or mentally ill, so he could get out of the army.

How Ricky considered filing a Conscientious Objector claim, but ultimately decided against it, because while he was sure the Iraq war was immoral, he wasn't sure all wars were.

How he finally decided that he had to separate himself from the Army and the war, by going AWOL for fourteen months.

And how many of the church groups of his youth didn't understand or sympathize with what he had been through, seeing the flag and the cross as essentially the same thing.

When Ricky was finished, the judge's sentence was eleven months, almost the maximum. But with the plea deal, Ricky should be out of jail in time for Christmas.

Once out of jail and out of the Army, what will Ricky do with this unique body of experience? He says he's eager to bear his testimony in full, uninterrupted, to anyone willing to hear it.

Quaker House

November 2006

Dear Friend,

Thanks to you, I'm going to jail. Again.

No, I haven't been arrested.

Nor am I planning any civil disobedience.

And I *hope* my name is not on a snatch-and-disappear list at Homeland Security.

But this fall, once again, I'm going to jail, and organizing other folks to do the same. This is an integral part of our work..

In a few weeks, it will be five years since I joined the Quaker House staff, and going to jail has been a recurring part of the job.

The jail is the Marine brig at Camp Lejeune, on the coast about 120 miles from Quaker House. The army sends prisoners there from Fort Bragg, since they don't have their own brig.

This fall I'm going to that jail to visit Ricky Clousing. Ricky used to be a sergeant in the U.S. Army. For several months last year he was a street interrogator in Iraq with the 82d Airborne Division. Ricky is bright and dedicated. He caught his superiors' eye, made sergeant more quickly than usual. He could have had a brilliant military career.

If only his conscience and faith hadn't gotten in the way.

But they did, and Ricky spent months in inner struggle and prayer over what he had seen and done in Iraq. He also talked to Quaker House; I remember the conversation well. Ricky considered filing a Conscientious Objector claim; but he wasn't sure war was *always* wrong.

On the other hand, he was sure the Iraq war *was* and *is* wrong.

Finally, rather than return to Iraq, or train others to do so, he went AWOL from Fort Bragg. He turned himself in last August. Now he's been court-martialed, stripped of his sergeant's stripes, fined several thousand dollars, and locked behind bars.

Despite all that, Ricky is lucky. Today he's in the brig, but soon enough he'll be out of there, and the army. His morale is good. And more important, his conscience is clear. He said NO to the Iraq war. NO to its massive and useless violence, its routinized abuses. And he made his refusal stick. For that, he's willing to pay the price of a jail term.

In the meantime, he has the support of Quaker House. Just as we've been doing since 1969, we've worked with Ricky from the time he returned to North Carolina. I was at his trial, and now during his confinement we're soliciting letter writing, organizing visits, talking with media, spreading the word.

This is the kind of work we plan to continue.

While Ricky Clousing is a remarkable individual, when I drive from Fayetteville to Camp Lejeune, I remember other GI resisters I've visited there for Quaker House in these past five years:

– **Stephen Funk** was the first: a Marine reservist who said no as the war was starting. Stephen's lawyer feared for his safety at Lejeune, because Funk had come out as gay. Fortunately, Stephen had no trouble in the brig. That was due mainly to his winning personality – but maybe our visits, and the thousand-plus letters that folks like you sent to him, didn't hurt either.

– **David Bunt,** whose deployment to Afghanistan turned him into a Conscientious Objector, even though the Army wouldn't believe him.

– **Luigi Pratt,** a gentle former surfer who drove a truck in Iraq, one of the most dangerous jobs there. He was appalled both by the pointless violence, and the widespread indifference to it among his younger, videogame-obsessed comrades. Back home, his wife Beth also bravely spoke out for him, and against the war.

– **Joel Klimkewicz,** another Marine, who joined the Seventh Dy Adventist church and then discovered that denomination's largely forgotten peace heritage. From there it was a small step to take Jesus' advice, "Blessed are the peacemakers," seriously enough to file for CO, put down his rifle, and refuse orders to pick it up again.

I went to jail for all of them.

Of course, Quaker House has dealt with many other dissenters in these five years, most of whom did not go to the brig. Thousands more have called our GI Rights Hotline. As the Iraq war grinds on, and servicepeople are being pushed past their limits, our GI Hotline calls are up 21 per cent over 2005. Call volume is on track to exceed 8000 in 2006.

Our highly experienced Hotline counselors, Steve Woolford & Lenore Yarger, are over-stretched trying to keep up with the calls. So we're about to hire a third part-time counselor, to give them some help.

More GI resisters will likely mean more trips to jail, plus other travel. And did I mention that we're still helping organize nonviolent peace actions in the region? I believe there will need to be more large peaceful protests before this ugly war is ended.

In addition, for months it's been my sense that GI war resistance, which has overall been sparse and subdued in the first three years of the Iraq occupation, is approaching a kind of boiling point. Certainly there's good reason for dissent in the ranks: US casualties are closing in on 3000, wounded are into the tens of thousands. Iraqi deaths are now credibly estimated as exceeding half a million. And for what?

It looks like some post-election changes are coming in Congress and the Pentagon. But around here the war machine grinds on, and we don't see much light at the end of this tunnel. Not yet. So we expect more GI dissent to surface. Already, there are several more soldier resisters besides Ricky who have garnered public attention, and they will be facing courts martial soon. Quaker House will be here for them, as we have been since 1969.

One impact of all this activity is on our costs: five years of expanding war and witness for peace have pushed our 2006-2007 Quaker House budget over $100,000, for the very first time in our history.

Frankly, I'm worried about our ability to meet this goal. But what else can we do? The demands of peace work in time of war keep growing, so to stay abreast we again turn to you. Will you send us a generous donation? We need it, to keep Quaker House going to jail.

And me too. After five years, I think I'm starting to get the hang of it.

Peace,

Chuck Fager

PS. Have you noticed the many shocking cases of military recruiter abuse making headlines this year? They've really been reaching new lows. We're countering with a brand-new flyer from our "Sgt. Abe, the Honest Recruiter." Of course, the Pentagon has us "outgunned" here by several hundred million dollars a year; but we're not intimidated.

Book Review

The Deserter's Tale, by Joshua Key, as told to Lawrence Hill. Anansi/HarperCollins Canada, 240 pages, paperback.

One passage in this compelling story stopped me cold.

Instead of returning to Iraq, Army Private First Class Joshua Key went AWOL in early 2004. During months underground, Key taught himself how to use a computer, and eventually figured out what "google" meant.

Then, he writes, "I started punching words such as 'AWOL' and 'soldier needs help' into various search engines. For the longest time I found nothing at all. I saw details about the G.I. Rights Hotline, but I couldn't imagine that any American organization would be of help to me now." (Emphasis added.)

In 2004, the GI Rights Hotline was ten years old, and received more than 30,000 calls. That's a lot, but even so, Key's dispirited comment shows how much more work we have to do to make it known and credible to similarly desperate GIs and their families.

Especially families like Key's. He grew up in a small Oklahoma town, endured much family violence, and left high school with few job prospects, a wife, and soon enough, two kids.

By 2002, after years of losing ground on fast-food wages, and with a third child on the way, he was easy pickings for an Army recruiter. When the recruiter assured Key that he would stay in the US, building bridges and learning the welding trade that had always fascinated him, the young father couldn't sign up fast enough.

The next chapter of the story is what you'd expect: Key didn't learn welding in the army; nor did he build bridges. Or anything else. Instead, he found himself in Iraq, on night missions, blowing open and looting houses full of terrified women and children. His unit did this night after night, searching for male "terrorists" and weapons that they never found. Along with these nerve-wracking night missions, he also saw more death and destruction than he'd ever imagined.

During nearly seven-months in Iraq, Key grew increasingly disillusioned about the war, and ashamed of his role in it. Toward the end of this time he asked his sergeant "about the point of the war.

"'There is no point, it's just your job,' he said.

"'But what's the justification for this war?'

"'The justification is that you signed a contract and you're told to be here.'

"'But when do I get to go home?' I said.

"'Private,' he said, 'we can keep you here just as long as we want, and we ain't never got to send you home.'"

Cold as it sounds, the sergeant's "explanation" contains practically all of the war's rationale as anyone else ever got.

In November 2003, Key's unit was given a two-week leave at their post, Ft. Carson, Colorado. Key brought back all the signs of serious PTSD:

"When I came home from Iraq I was a complete wreck. I had so many nightmares that I had to get a prescription for pills to stave off the bad dreams. I had blackouts. I would cry one moment and scream the next."

But his distress was intensified by a sense of guilt.

"I know right from wrong," he writes. "I had a conscience by the age of six. I had to suspend it for awhile in Iraq. . . .I am not a coward and I never flinched from danger. The easiest thing would have been to keep on doing what I was told to do. Ever so slowly, as the jets raced and the illumination rounds burned and the houses fell during the long Iraqi nights, my conscience returned. It could no longer be Army first, God second and family third. It had to be the tiny voice inside me that would not sleep any longer. I am not this man, I told myself. I cannot do these things any longer."

When his two week leave was up, Key hesitated, then in February 2004 he packed up his family and left Colorado. He headed east, without any clear destination except someplace where the Army couldn't find him. The family wound up near Philadelphia, living hand-to-mouth, doing odd jobs, moving from one cheap motel to another, five people often crammed into a single room.

Although Key couldn't believe what he read online about the GI Rights Hotline, another search he made late in 2004 caught his attention: an article about Jeremy Hinzman, the soldier from Ft. Bragg who had gone to Canada just weeks before Key went underground, and who was fighting to be allowed to stay there. In march of 2005, Key followed Hinzman's path across the border.

He's there today, struggling with both the outward uncertainty about his ability to stay in Canada, and with the inner demons that still lurk from his time in Iraq.

There are many, perhaps several hundred, other GI exiles now seeking refuge in Canada. Thousands more deserters are underground In the US. The Deserter's Tale is the first book to give voice to this anguished, scattered company.

It is an artlessly eloquent voice:

"I was made to be a criminal in Iraq," Key declares, "but I am a criminal no longer and I am never going back." And he adds that:

"Young people need to know that they don't have to live with the oral anguish of fighting an immoral war. It is not true that a soldier's first obligation is to the military. One's first obligation is to the moral truth buried deep inside our own souls. Every person knows what is right and wrong. And we have a duty to live up to it, regardless of what our leaders sometimes say."

This is a gripping book, an excellent way for both young and old to learn about the meaning of this duty.

QH Blog:

Friday, December 19, 2008

Thinking About Spring – Ready to March?

Friends,

It appears that an early spring national protest schedule is taking shape.

United for peace & Justice (UFPJ) is calling for a 3 month antiwar campaign, with LOCAL ACTIONS on Thursday March 19th, and a culminating national rally in New York City on April 4 2009. More information about the campaign outline is here.

Meanwhile, the rival ANSWER coalition is calling for A NATIONAL MARCH on the Pentagon on Saturday March 21.

A couple of comments: Lots of deja vu all over again here. The two big names of the national peace scene are not co-operating; so what else is new? There's no mention of April 4 in NYC on the ANSWER site, and UFPJ says zilch re: March 21 at the Pentagon.

But there's more involved here than the old leftie sectarian competition. On the one hand, UFPJ's Call for action notes that last fall it urged planning for a big DC rally next March. But given the economic crisis and Obama's election, they say they feel a need to "change gears."

They say that much of their constituency will likely not want to be protesting the new president only two months after he's inaugurated. (I think they're right.) They don't say, but there is reason to believe, that ANSWER has once again scooped up all the permits for DC sites on March 21, so they'd have to join them to do something in DC, and they don't want to do that.

One other internal item is also significant: UFPJ's longtime national coordinator Leslie Cagan is stepping down. A "help wanted" notice for her successor is on their site.

My view: both these groups are very weak. Neither has organized a successful large action since January 2007. And UFPJ is right that many activists will want to "wait and see" what the new president will do, and March will feel too soon to know.

Plus, the fact is that another BIG chunk of progressive folks worked their hearts out and their butts off for that same new president as the hope of change. And these and other folks already seem bound to put on what will be the biggest "rally" and "demonstration" maybe ever seen in DC on Jan. 20.

The notion that lots of those folks will then turn right around and go protest the object of all that adulation in mid-March – well, I wouldn't bet on it.

It will take some mental adjustment for some of us to not have the man in the White House as the object of rage the way so many of us have (with reason) gone after the current lame duck resident these past eight years. But it's an adjustment we need to start making, if only to avoid splintering our own base.

Here I'm recalling what I've read about when FDR came in. The New Deal sucked the air (and the mass base) out of the socialist groups, and the key struggles of those years went on in other, more specific contexts – such as union organizing. Not that FDR was beyond criticism (far from it). But the political situation had changed dramatically with his arrival. I wonder if we're entering into a similar period now.

Anyway, unless something big changes, my prediction is that the Pentagon march will be no big deal. NYC could be somewhat different, because the city is so large one can gather a hundred thousand without drawing from much beyond the suburbs. Yet what would be a huge crowd anywhere else will be merely respectable in NYC, and media attention will likely be tepid.

I would see the NYC rally as a kind of holding action, something to do that keeps UFPJ on the game board, but not much more, til maybe there's a turn against the new administration. It might be interesting, if the weather is good.

So, several options seem possible for local groups like those here in North Carolina (or wherever you are, Friend).

1. Ignore all these machinations entirely, do our own thing here, when we want, with whom we want, focused on the issues we want.

2. Or maybe pick Thursday March 19 for some local-regional event (s).

3. Or even do a local-regional action on Saturday March 21, ignoring the Pentagon march.

4. & 5. Buy train/bus/plane tickets for DC on March 21 and NYC on April 4.

What do folks think?

[NOTE: There were in fact no sizeable antiwar rallies in Washington in the spring of 2009.]

http://quakerhouse.blogspot.com/2008/12/thinking-about-spring-ready-to-march.html

QH Blog: Saturday, October 11, 2008

Dodging a Deportation Bullet – For Now

Private Jeremy Hinzman was one of the first soldiers I worked with after arriving at Quaker House at the end of 2001. He filed an application for conscientious objector status, which was turned aside, and he was deployed to Afghanistan. Several months after his return, in December 2003, he was ordered to head for Iraq.

Instead, he, his wife and infant son went to Canada, where they have been fighting ever since to stay. Last summer, a second child, a daughter, joined their family.

We've published numerous reports in our newsletters on this struggle. In sum, Jeremy has lost all his legal battles, and was issued a deportation order, to leave Canada on September 23, 2008.

But with one day to go, Jeremy won a round, as the newsclip below indicates. So this story is far from over.

Judge grants U.S. deserter's last-ditch effort to stave off deportation

Canadian Press – 4:10 PM Monday September 22, 2008

TORONTO – A high-profile American deserter has won a last-minute stay of deportation.

A [Canadian] Federal Court judge says Jeremy Hinzman can stay in Canada for now. Hinzman was due to get the boot to the U.S. Tuesday morning, where he would face prosecution for fleeing to Canada rather than deploying to Iraq. Ottawa has refused his family's application to remain in Canada on humanitarian and compassionate grounds.

The 29-year-old Hinzman, his wife and two young children asked for the stay while the courts decide if they will review that decision.

His lawyer argued today that deserters who have been publicly critical of the U.S.-led invasion of Iraq have received harsher punishment.

http://quakerhouse.blogspot.com/2008/10/dodging-bullet-for-now.html

[NOTE: Apropos of the Afghanistan escalation plans announced in early 2009, I re-read Rudyard Kipling's notorious 1899 poem "The White Man's Burden." Kipling was the bard of British imperialism, and many of his linesstill ring eerily true, evoking what's being pressed on Obama today. So I prepared this humble update, offered herewith.]

Chuck Fager

Take Up Obama's Burden, 2009
(with apologies to Kipling)

No more the White Man's Burden,
That phrase won't fly today.
It has to be re-packaged
If we're to make it play.

Let's speak of "the Imperative,"
And "nation-building" too,
A bow to Nine-Eleven
Should help to push it through.

Be sure to mention brand-new schools,
Young girls who shed the veil;
The sacred war for "hearts and minds' --
How could we let that fail?

The Afghans, theycan't helpthemselves,
Else they'd be done by now.
But Bagram and Guantanamo,
Will help to show them how.

Sotake up Obama's burden,
Send our best of every hue
To a fruitless war in a distant land --
Say they died for me and you.

The drone strikes here, the rockets there,
The Rangers' slashing blade;
Pile bodies in the village squares
To mark the progress made.

What if it takes a score of years,

A flood of casualties?
At tunnel's end a light will show
Our exit strategies.

We're sure to win this Afghan war,
Our generals know it well.
But what's the toll, the price-tag there?
On that, "Don't Ask, Don't Tell."

We'll hunt the poppy-growing warlord,
The scheming Taliban.
Where Britain stumbled, Russia failed–
We'll triumph: Yes, we can.

– Chuck Fager, Director

The White Man's Burden, 1899

Rudyard Kipling

Take up the White Man's burden–
Send forth the best ye breed–
Go bind your sons to exile
To serve your captives' need;
To wait in heavy harness,
On fluttered folk and wild–
Your new-caught, sullen peoples,
Half-devil and half-child.

Take up the White Man's burden–
The savage wars of peace–
Fill full the mouth of Famine
And bid the sickness cease;
And when your goal is nearest
The end for others sought,
Watch sloth and heathen Folly
Bring all your hopes to nought.

Take up the White Man's burden–
And reap his old reward:
The blame of those ye better,
The hate of those ye guard--
The cry of hosts ye humour
(Ah, slowly!) toward the light:–
"Why brought he us from bondage,
Our loved Egyptian night?"

Take up the White Man's burden–
Ye dare not stoop to less–
Nor call too loud on Freedom
To cloke your weariness;
By all ye cry or whisper,
By all ye leave or do,
The silent, sullen peoples
Shall weigh your gods and you.

QH Blog:

Thursday, March 19, 2009

Six Years Too Long - End the War

I'm feeling more than a little embarrassed as I write this post. Six years ago tonight, bombs and missiles began crashing down on Baghdad and other targets, in what was arrogantly billed as the "Shock & Awe" opening to the Iraq war.

Each year since, we've had some kind of protest or vigil. From 2004 through 2007, we helped organize sizeable peace rallies here in Fayetteville.

But this year, the anniversary crept up on me, and as I write we are scrambling to put on a small vigil downtown tomorrow. It's bound to be small; but as far as I can tell, it will be pretty much all the local action there is.

We're still pretty busy otherwise: our GI Rights Hotline is taking lots of calls; our "Sgt. Abe" character is still working to bring more Truth into Recruiting; and we're pressing for accountability for the torture that so disgraced the nation in recent years.

Yet there's no denying that the peace movement in March 2009 is in deep disarray. National groups are fading; uncertainty is widespread about how to project a strong peace message given the changes in Washington. And it seems that everything, even wars and rumors of war, is being swept from our field of vision by the noise and impact of the economic collapse.

No wonder it's been hard to stay focused lately. But here it is, the beginning of Year Seven of the Iraq war, and at Eugene O'Neill wrote in "Death of a Salesman," Attention must be paid.

So tomorrow I'll be carrying the poster I made in the summer of 2003, when the number of US casualties was about 250, a figure that was updated for each new vigil.

The sign is scuffed, smudged and battered now, held together with tape. But the message still appplies, the numbers are current, and the totals are depressingly familiar: 4200+ US troops killed; 500,000+ Iraqi civilians dead.

And there are more unhappy numbers that don't fit on the sign:

– Five million Iraqis turned into homeless refugees in their own homeland;

– More than 50,000 US troops seriously wounded;

– Hundreds more dead by suicide, in Iraq and afterward;

– Un-numbered military families torn apart by the stresses of repeated deployments;
– The financial costs of the war are well into multiple trillions of dollars (which
used to be a lot of money), with no end in sight.

And despite announced plans to pull out some troops from Iraq, there's another war in Afghanistan waiting to claim them.

Which reminds me – I was against the Afghanistan war first, all the way back in late 2001. And now, more than seven years later, this response has not dimmed: Afghanistan is a quagmire. Despite the skill and courage of US troops, I agree with military columnist and Vietnam veteran Joseph Galloway, who recently wrote:

"The Taliban insurgents now have a chokehold on as much as 70 percent of Afghanistan, and they're proving to be flexible and adaptive in their attacks on American, NATO and Afghan forces.

If the new American team has some new ideas about how to succeed in Afghanistan, now would be the time to lay them out. Nothing that Alexander the Great, Queen Victoria or Leonid Brezhnev tried in their attempts to subdue the quarrelsome Afghan tribes worked, and nothing we've tried in the last eight years has, either.

While we're waiting for a new strategy, perhaps we should break out some old Kipling:

"When wounded and left on Afghanistan's plain
"And the women come out to cut up your remains . . . ."
Etc., etc."

Current plans call for leaving at least 50,000 US troops in Iraq for the indefinite future. To me, that suggests that there may well be many more such anniversaries to mark, before the sentiment we saw on this Welcome Home banner at Camp Lejeune is fulfilled.

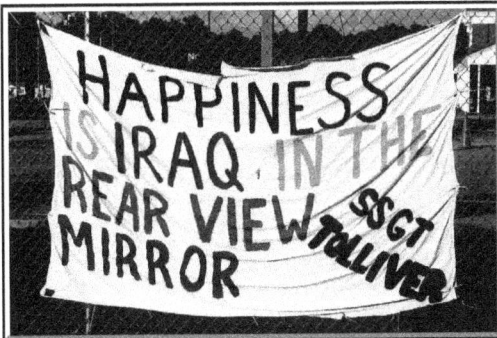

http://quakerhouse.blogspot.com/2009/03/six-years-too-long-end-war.html

Quaker House

2009-June

Dear Friend,

Sometimes the Iraq-Afghanistan wars break bodies. Just as often, they can break souls.

At Quaker House, we minister to both, as way opens.

This twofold task was brought home to me again – almost a year ago, while I was in the checkout line at one of Fayetteville's big box stores and the cash register froze up.

The clerk was doggedly cheerful, bantering with us as he coaxed the recalcitrant system to re-start. While waiting, I noticed a large button pinned next to his nametag. On it was a photo of a grinning youth, all teeth, sport shirt and crew cut.

Above the photo it said, "We Love You, Travis."Below, "Matthew 10:28."

By the time the register finally started up again, I had managed to surreptitiously google the Bible verse on my phone:

"And fear not them which kill the body, but are not able to kill the soul: but rather fear him which is able to destroy both soul and body in hell."

At my turn, I'd screwed up my courage. "What about Travis?" I asked, hoping it was – what?

The clerk deftly scanned my purchases. His expression didn't change. "Afghanistan," he said. "Travis stepped on a mine."

It sounds boorish, but I'd been hoping for something civilian – cancer maybe, or a drunken driver. Taking the receipt, I mumbled , "Um, I'm sorry for your loss," and he thanked me.

That was almost a year ago. It's been a busy twelve months for Quaker House – our 40th, in fact. And all along, we've been working on both body and soul.

Here's a small example: a soldier who sat in our living room a few weeks ago, red-eyed and at a loss. Call him Sgt Garcia.

He was no peacenik, no resister. For ten years he had served without question: record spotless, promotions rapid. He was well into a military career tracked for success and achievement, a full member of what is called "the Army family."

As such, Sgt. Garcia "went downrange" to Iraq without the doubts that have brought so many to us. He deployed and kept doing his duty, following his orders – even after the IED exploded near his vehicle.

Others were killed or had limbs blown off in the blast. Sgt. Garcia seemed okay, at first, and finished his tour. But back at Ft. Bragg, there came waves of headaches, progressive loss of focus, deepening anxiety. He was less and less able to function at work.

Doctors confirmed and re-confirmed the diagnosis: PTSD and TBI, or Traumatic Brain Injury, both with long-term impact. Sgt. Garcia needed help, lots of it. Instead he was given pills, but they only increased his confusion. As his condition became more clearly defined, it began to look as if a medical discharge might be the best possible outcome.

That's when the worst trouble started. After a decade of being assured he was a valued member of "the Army family," he was suddenly seen as a "problem," a burden. And the Army does not like "problem" soldiers.

The needed paperwork seemed endless, and increasingly difficult to get approved. Responses to his requests for information and action were slow and evasive.

It's a familiar story to us, but one new and alien to him. Sgt. Garcia's frustration and confusion grew, aggravated by the effects of TBI. When he complained about the side effects of the pills, he was given others that only made his confusion worse.

In fact, he got so – well, desperate, that one day he finally did the unthinkable:

He drove from Fort Bragg to Hillside Avenue, and rang the bell at Quaker House.

I didn't preach to him about pacifism. We focused on concrete ways he might be able to prod the wheels of a resistant military bureaucracy back into motion. There are several, all of them new to Sgt. Garcia. Our Hotline counselors followed up with more.

He was still getting used to the idea of being discarded after his years of loyalty, and having to deal with the Army as an adversary; but now that's the hard truth of the matter.

That abrupt change may have been the most devastating effect of Sgt. Garcia's injuries. If we helped him, the best measure of success will be that he regains some sense of dignity.

There are thousands of soldiers like him, too: loyal, brave – and cast aside. – There will be many more.

Last month I testified about another recent visitor, Private Dan Marble, at his court martial.

When he started Basic at Fort Benning in 2006, Dan Marble seemed to have the makings of a superior soldier. He was athletic, and enjoyed the physical rigors. His target shooting scores were tops in his unit. At paratrooper school he loved jumping out of airplanes.

After six months of intensive training, he graduated and got orders to report to the 82nd Airborne Division at Ft. Bragg, following two weeks leave.

The leave was what did it. "We never had time to think during training," he said. "But once I got home and actually thought about things, I knew I couldn't kill anyone. And that's what all the training was really about, killing. It just isn't me."

The two weeks passed, but Marble didn't report to Fort Bragg. Not until two and a half years later, not, that is, until he was arrested in February on an AWOL warrant. As he headed for town, his lawyer called, asking me to meet him at the bus station.

When I did, Dan was very agitated. He was worried about being forced onto a plane headed for Afghanistan or Iraq and the call to kill. Or being hauled off in handcuffs to the brig. In our living room he began to calm down, and we went over how he'd ended up AWOL, and then here.

Dan Marble had never heard of such a thing as a conscientious objector until I told him about it. But that's what he was. As he regained his composure he became clear that his refusal to kill was a conviction he could stick to with his head held high. He could face the consequences, even if they included jail time.

It soon looked like they were going to. The 82nd Airborne has been arresting and bringing in scores of AWOL GIs, some who had been gone for years.It was part of a frantic effort to "make numbers" for a big deployment to Afghanistan in April, part of the new "surge."

But "making numbers" wasn't easy. The 82nd's casualties, dead and wounded, have been in the thousands.Recruiters were (literally) killing themselves to bring in new enlistees. Reservists had already been called up. The National Guard too. But it wasn't enough.

Pressure was mounting. Orders had come from Washington.Make the numbers. Careers were at stake.A dragnet for AWOLs was one more tool. Those brought in were offered a deal: deploy "downrange" to combat and their cases would get resolved. Or else.

Dan Marble turned down the deal. His "or else" was a court martial for desertion. We supported him all the way, and I was summoned to testify about our mission at Quaker House – we don't often get a hearing on Ft. Bragg – and our work with him.

Dan was relatively lucky. His Army defense attorney was skilled: the prosecutor wanted him jailed for eight months, the general agreed to four; but the judge gave him a bad conduct discharge and no jail time. Dan left here with a record, but at least his soul is clear of killing.

As I write, we're supporting a second AWOL resister at Ft. Bragg, and another in the brig. Our GI Rights Hotline work continues.

One more recent set of visitors deserves mention here: a couple and their cat.

He had been a Special Forces medic, and they lived nearby.He was about to be medically retired – completely disabled by combat PTSD and TBI. His wife was now his caregiver.

They had come, she said, because of their cat. It was dead. Killed by a pack of dogs that have been roaming the area late at night. She said they hoped to warn other cat owners in the neighborhood; which would include us, to keep them inside after dark.

But once in the house, she also wanted to talk about how hard it had been to get the Army to do the right thing by her husband. Paperwork, hassles. And she noticed our wall exhibit about domestic homicides involving military wives and girlfriends.

Her husband mainly stood mute while she and I considered some of these melancholy matters. There was no sense of opposition to our antiwar ambiance from him; just a pained, almost catatonic withdrawal from all of that.

But he opened up once she showed the photos of their cat on her phone: a big gray striped Maine Coon, twenty pounds of unconditional love. "He was our therapy," she said. "I'd come in after dealing with the Army all day, and he'd just be there, purring all the time."

Her husband smiled at that, and at the small-screen snapshot of him snuggling with the pet. He began to talk. The dogs had attacked the cat right on their front porch, left him half ripped open. There was a photo of that too, to show that the threat was serious.

Cat therapy. It's not part of our regular GI counseling repertoire; but then our service is not all about paperwork and regulations either. So whatever works . . .

These are snapshots from what has been another big year for the wars, which despite the claims are not letting up. Also a year in which the post-9-11 peace movement has all but vanished from the national scene.

But Quaker House hasn't.

Peace,

Chuck Fager

PS. Two weeks ago, in line at the same big box store, I saw the clerk again. He was still resolutely cheerful. The button for Travis was still pinned beside his nametag. And I was able to remember the Bible verse.

Quaker House

November 2009

Dear Friend,

The same day the horrible massacre at Fort Hood** happened, Dustin Stevens left Fort Bragg, headed for home.

The Army won't thank him for it, but Dustin helped prevent a Fort Hood-type event here in Fayetteville.

At least for now.

He had to beat the Army to help it, and he did. Took him ten months.

We were there with him: we hooked him up with a fine, low-cost lawyer, tried to buck him up when he was down, kept in touch.

It's what we do, with your support. But Dustin also had two secret weapons.

At Bragg, he was put in Echo Platoon. Echo was where they put people who had been arrested after being AWOL, for months or longer.

Until late 2008, the Army usually dealt with long-term AWOLs quickly: an unfavorable "chapter" discharge, and good riddance. It made sense: cut the losses. There's a war on after all. Two.

Not anymore. Ft. Bragg's 82nd Airborne had been depleted by years of war and repeated long combat tours, with more coming. Echo Platoon was some Bragg commander's bright idea for filling a bunch of those empty slots.

No more Mr. Nice General: the 82nd would hunt down hundreds of AWOL GIs. Give them a choice: go "downrange" (i.e., deploy to combat) and get their records fixed. Or else face court martials and prison.

So new arrest warrants flew in all directions. By last January more than fifty AWOL soldiers had been picked up and crowded into Echo's old, dilapidated barracks.

A handful took the deployment deal. Others went to the brig. A lucky few still managed to eke out a "chapter" discharge, unfavorable but without jail time.

But the new plan soon ran into the old bureaucratic molasses. So for too many in Echo, their "sentence" included sitting in limbo, month after month after month, waiting for an apparently paralyzed or indifferent command to decide their fate.

Dustin's story, at first, was like most others, with a couple twists. After joining up in 2002, he soon decided war and killing were not for him. He became a committed pacifist, though he didn't learn the word til later. After he said, "I quit!" to his instructors enough times, a sergeant

80

told him to go home and await instructions.

He did; instructions never came. So Dustin went to work, got on with life; he didn't hide. Then last January, seven years later, he was arrested as a deserter.

Once at Fort Bragg, in Echo, Dustin firmly turned down the deployment deal. They told him he'd be court-martialed; so be it, he said. Just get it over with.

Instead the Army dithered. They kept him there, with scores of others, through the spring and summer. Not behind bars, exactly; yet not remotely free either.

Meanwhile, Echo's barracks was a dump, and the scene inside was increasingly like a madhouse, especially at night.

Much of what happened in Echo was predictable: many of the AWOL GIs there had serious "issues," mental health, drug use, PTSD, self-destructive behavior, mostly untreated, that were involved in their walking away in the first place.

Packing them in together only made things worse. So did the behavior of many unit staff: one sergeant was investigated for dealing drugs, others repeatedly sneered that everybody in Echo should just be taken out and shot.

One weekend a particularly disturbed soldier climbed out on the third floor roof and jumped. Somehow he was not seriously hurt.

Most GIs in Echo kept their heads down, grumbling or self-medicating, hoping to minimize their punishment. But the pressure kept building, and Dustin chose to resist.

He talked to reporters about the conditions; so did we. Few were interested; and the command laughed at these efforts. They weren't worried. Who would care about a bunch of AWOL "dirtbags"?

We did, for one. Sure, they'd broken regulations, and there would be consequences. But months of unofficial confinement at Echo was neither legal nor just. Nor was it smart, in a year when the Army was breaking records for suicides – with worse to come.

What a mess. By comparison, the military jail I visit frequently is quieter, cleaner, safer, and much more professionally run. Echo Platoon was a filthy powderkeg with a sputtering fuse, and a pointless one at that.

Still, summer turned to fall, with more dithering. Word came that Dustin's court martial wouldn't happen til spring.

What? Six months more of punitive waiting? That was too much: he became determined to bust things open. Not with violence, tho. Instead, he turned to the secret weapons.

The first was his cell phone. Which was also a camera. He took dozens of pictures of the moldy, decrepit barracks, and some of the troubled inmates.

The other was Facebook. Creating a page for Echo Platoon, with an upside-down U.S. flag (denoting an emergency) for its logo, he uploaded the pictures.

Then his supporters, including us, got busy, spreading the word.

And this time, finally, people began to notice. People in the Pentagon and above, reportedly at the highest levels, saw the pictures. And paid attention.

All at once, in late October, things began to happen. VIPs made unannounced visits to the Echo barracks. Calls came from Army headquarters. Fort Bragg commanders who had brusquely ignored complaints about Echo were suddenly all ears.

And then – bam – Echo Platoon was shut down: the barracks was cleared out, the inmates sent to regular units. Word is that a bunch of the GIs had their cases abruptly dealt with, after all the interminable delays. Cut the losses; there's a war on. Two.

Dustin was among them. Out of nowhere – or maybe cyberspace – on October 28, the threat of court martial and jail was dropped, and a chapter release approved.

Just like that. In the end, he'd won. Confronted by a "rogue" cell phone and a guerilla Facebook page – plus determined friends – the 82nd Airborne brass had met their match.

But the army didn't really lose. Like we said, as Dustin headed home his elation was shadowed by unfolding carnage at Fort Hood. Even 1300 miles away from Fayetteville, it felt close. For us too.

Still, his "secret weapons" and perseverance had done more than solve his personal problem. It also freed Fort Bragg from Echo Platoon, which was one more disaster waiting to happen.

There will be others. The combat forces and their families are still being put through hell, and from all reports, more is coming.

As with Dustin, we'll keep doing what we can to blunt the impact, and if possible, shorten the wars. It's a long haul; but in it, we have a secret weapon too.

It's you.

Peace,

Chuck Fager

** On November 5, 2009, an Army psychiatrist turned jihadist opened fire and killed 13 people at Fort Hood, Texas and injured more than 30 others. In August 2013 Major Nidal Malik Hasan, who acknowledged that he was the shooter, was convicted of murder and sentenced to death.

A Letter from the Brig at Camp Lejeune NC

Received December 8, 2009:

To Quaker House:

Hi. My name is Clifford Cornell. I'm currently serving 12 months at Camp Lejeune Brig. My time here is drawing short and I want to give special thanks to Chuck Fager for mentioning me in the Quaker House Newsletter and encouraging people to visit and to write. It really helped knowing there was a lot of support.

To Curt Torell for taking the time and to visit me whenever he could and making sure I had plenty of reading material.

To the hundreds who wrote to me, thanks. My favorite time of the day was mail call. I never knew who was writing or from where.

To all that managed to visit me, thanks. It was great seeing you all taking the time to visit. It helped break up the dull routine in here. And having someone to talk to, it really means a lot.

To Quaker House, for courage to resist, and to all, thanks. It hasn't been easy, but with your support, it's been manageable. It's great to see so many people ready to help.

Thanks,

Clifford Cornell

December 18, 2009

Dear Friend,

Clifford Cornell had a tough childhood, and was raised by adoptive grandparents in rural Arkansas. He joined the Army mainly to get job training.

As he learned more about the military and the Iraq war, he rejected both. Cliff went AWOL in 2005, and spent almost four years in Canada.

He found a home there, with steady work, and wanted to stay. But a hostile government there forced him out in early 2009.

Cliff was court-martialed as a deserter in April, and sent to the brig at Camp Lejeune, North Carolina.

This is where Quaker House came in. For years, my predecessors and I have visited resisters jailed at Camp Lejeune. It's one of the many ways

we say "Yes" to the troops, and "No" to the wars.
    We have been here for Cliff, because you have been here for us.

Thank you and have a blessed holiday season.

Peace,

Chuck Fager

QH Blog:

Saturday, January 16, 2010
GI Resister Cliff Cornell: Free At Last!

Sunrise at Camp Lejeune, NC. Quaker House board member Curt Torell and I (Chuck Fager, QH Director)are here to make a pickup.

It's cold, freezing. We're headed for the brig, to pick up Cliff Cornell, who is due to be released at 0730.

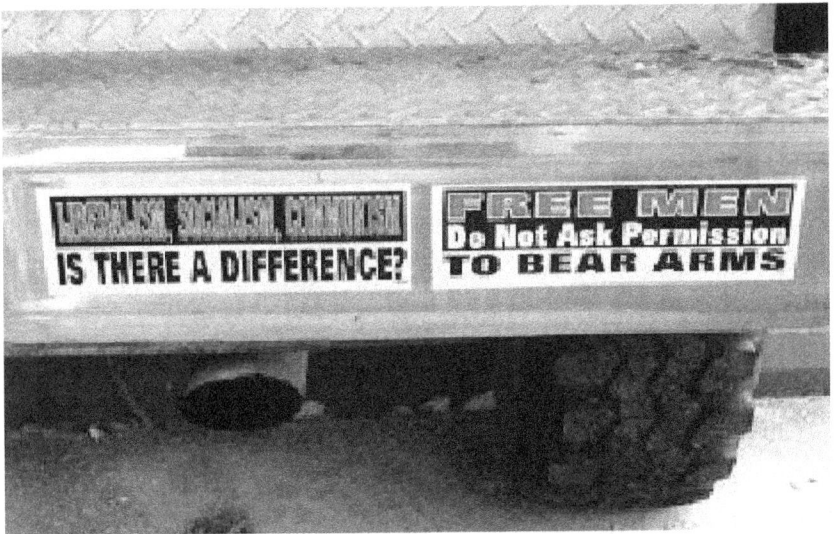

We arrive on time, at the side gate. Cliff isn't there yet, so we wait, huddling into ourselves against the cold.
Turning around I notice a pickup truck parked a few feet away.
What's this? A close look is in order . . . .

I see. And there's more . . . .
John Wayne? Oh, wait . . .
Intriguing. But enough of that, because there's action at the gate:

One more step . . .
And Cliff is Free! (That's him in shorts.)

Shorts? It's what he came in with. Fortunately, Curt brought him some long pants and a jacket.

Then it's on the first tastes of freedom: breakfast at Bojangles, a Pepsi, and a cigarette.(We didn't take a picture of the cancer stick.)

By lunchtime we're passing by Quaker House enroute to the next level of enjoyment . . .

. . .namely a look at the smash new film "Avatar." Cliff is a sci-fi/fantasy fan, and afterwards his review of the film, in full, is: "Awesome."

Around 4 PM Friends and friends gather for a welcoming reception at Quaker House.

A highlight was watching the YoutTube video just posted by folks from the War Resisters Support Committee in Toronto. It brought tears to Cliff's eyes, and you can watch it too, right now:

As things were winding down, Cliff made a brief YouTube appearance of his own, greeting all who have been supporting him through these long months (and years). It's here:

Cliff will head out for home in Arkansas in a day or so, and get on with his life. We wish him the best in this continuing journey, and want to add or thanks to all who have helped out with the support of his difficult stand of conscience.

http://quakerhouse.blogspot.com/2010/01/gi-resister-cliff-cornell-free-at-last.html

Quaker House

November 2011

Dear Friend,

I just got two early Christmas presents, and want to share them with you, right now.

What are they?

Hope.

The first gift of hope came at now-legendary Zuccotti Park, birthplace of the Occupy Wall Street movement, just a few days before it was cleared out. The youthful energy there, the seriousness, the creativity and resolve in insisting that economic justice be brought front and center into public and political discussion–they were a real, and very welcome, gift.

Also their openness. Twenty minutes in the park, and I had been invited to several working group sessions, joined a think tank discussion, and even took a turn on a stationary bike to power the press tent laptops (the city had banned other generators).

This "Occupy" movement has spread with amazing speed: it has even reached Fayetteville, where we've held two "Occupy" actions and are planning more. And what a relief from the past three years of frustration, disappointment and seeming paralysis on the social change front.

But.

Amid all the thrilling signs of change and action, from New York City to Fayetteville and beyond, one kind of sign has been all but absent from the Occupy upsurge: peace signs.

The focus so far has been mainly on banks and other financial marauders. Lord knows they deserve the scrutiny: their greed and wrongdoing had much to do with pushing our economy into the deep ditch where it's still stuck.

But you and I know a "secret" that's just as important: the drag of supporting a bloated war machine is–and has been–another major cause of our economic ills. And we also know there will be no real cure for them unless that bloat is tackled. Big-time.

Of course, the wars' calamitous waste of both fiscal and human resources is not really a secret. You and I have been repeating it, preaching it, shouting it for years. And we were not entirely alone.

Just mostly. In Washington, this year's spending on war will break all past records. And the war lobbies are determined to prevent any real cuts in the deficit-cutting talks.

Somehow this critical side of the equation hasn't yet made it into the

Occupiers' calculations. Or the broadened public debate it has sparked.

But sooner or later it will have to. If there's to be a new dawn of hope and opportunity for our children and grandchildren, that will require a sunset on our far-flung network of bases; major pruning of the gold-plated shopping list of (often useless) high-tech weaponry; a halt to the mushrooming of private armies of war contractors; and more. You know the list.

Who will raise this flag of peace in the Occupy movement?

At Quaker House, we're resolved to take up this challenge, and connect the dots. And besides working with the local Occupiers, we plan to charge into the brave new world of social media, to extend our reach and spread the message as widely as possible. We want to Occupy for Peace.

We're already at work on how best to present this message, and spread it across the movement spectrum.

And yes, we need your help.

You can help in several ways. We need your feedback on our message development. We also look to you to spread the word.

And of course, we need your financial support. In a year when war spending is at an all-time high, and a new social justice movement is rising, it's more important than ever.

And there's another reason. It's part of the second Christmas gift I spoke about.

Did I mention that this Christmas will be my last one at Quaker House? Yes, I'm in my final year as Director. So the other gift of hope is the strong likelihood that by the end of this holiday season, our board will select my successor as Director.

I want to hand Quaker House on to her/him in good shape. It's a tall order: repeatedly in its 42-plus years, such transitions have been tough for us. I had to train myself, on the job; that's the pits. Yet we're busy as ever now, so this time, we want to "break in" my successor over the coming months. There's no other "training school" for this job.

My hope is that this transition can be seamless: between the GI Rights Hotline and the rising Occupy movement, there's still too much work ahead for anything less. But it will cost us extra. And to make that happen, we'll need your support.

Here at the house, I've mainly followed the old plain Friends' tradition: no decorations, no tree; that day is holy, but not more than any other. And all of the ten Christmas seasons I have spent next door to Fort Bragg were haunted by war.

This year, we've been told, it should be different: Christmas 2011 will be marked by the "end" of the Iraq occupation and return of "all" US troops there.

More hope: that it really turns out that way. This terrible, massively expensive, needless war has weighed on our society and economy like a hundred-pound anvil dragging down a swimmer. And we're not finished paying for it; not by a long shot.

Besides, I keep recalling that the term "all" leaves out thousands of armed private contractors, plus cadres of shadowy Special Ops killing teams. They will all still be roaming Iraq after the official "end" of the war.

That's not to mention the bloody mess we'll be leaving behind: millions of refugees, warring factions, Iran stirring trouble.

Yes, as a grim quip put it, "I guess Iraq has been punished enough for having nothing to do with 9-11." (And no WMDs either.)

As the troops return, the TV screens will doubtless divert us from this backdrop of destruction, filling up with parades and ceremonies, booming salutes and flashing medals.

Will the pomp and glitter extend to the tens of thousands of troops not marching, because they came home disabled by wounds visible and invisible? Will the coverage highlight the veterans lining up at unemployment offices–at higher rates than non-vets–as the spectacle fades? Will it mention the several secret wars that are ongoing elsewhere, behind the double curtains of Special Ops secrecy and drone anonymity?

Still, even that much of a withdrawal could make this last Christmas different, and more hopeful, than many of the earlier ones These seasons have often been very intense times, for me personally and for Quaker House, marked by GI resistance, prison visits, work to end torture, and seemingly endless war. . . .

Write a note to the new Director-Designate: what does she or he need to hear about your concerns for peace witness in 2012 and beyond? Your hopes for Quaker House? Your ideas for ways to strengthen our work?

Thank you, and

Peace,

Chuck Fager

PS. Director of Quaker House is the best job I ever had, even though it's also been grueling, and I'm ready for a change. You made it all possible, so let me say thank you again. Will you stand with us now, as I prepare to hand it over?

THREE: Mano-a-Mano On the Op-Ed Page
– Columns in the Fayetteville *Observer*

From the Fayetteville NC *Observer*, April 25, 2005

Peace Rally An Asset To Fayetteville

Chuck Fager

It's been a month now since thousands of protesters gathered for Fayetteville's largest ever peace march and rally on March 19. Since then, there's been some grumbling about the rally being a burden to the city, especially for police services. Even though the rally was completely peaceful, one plausible figure put the cost to the city at $40,000.

Sure, providing security for several thousand protesters was expensive. But cost is only one side of the equation. For balance, let's also ask: what did the rally bring to the city?

A lot. In my view, a whole lot.

Let's start with money, since that's what the complaints mentioned.

Spending by the organizers on local products and services totaled well over $26,000, everything from catering to hotel rooms and portable toilets. Then there were uncounted hundreds of meals purchased at local establishments by visitors who stayed through the weekend, plus many tankfuls of gas to get them home.

So if $40,000 is the price tag, it's a fair estimate that the marchers spent at least that much, and probably more, while they were here. In sum, the city's economy was not drained. And we didn't leave a mess behind either; Park Department officials tell us that we were one of the tidiest groups to use Rowan Park.

But in my book, cash is not the best yardstick of the peace rally's impact. To get at the more important measure, consider a bit of background:

Since early 2002, when I moved here, the city has mounted several elaborate and expensive projects aimed at revamping the local image, trying to banish the gloomy specter of "Fayette-nam."

But these efforts have not succeeded very well. Perhaps the most spectacular fiasco was the big-ticket makeover program of spring 2002, which was just about to roll out whenwell, when the city was hit with a barrage of national publicity of a very different and painful sort. Other efforts have resulted in disappointing crowds, unpaid bills, and pleas for bailouts.

Now consider the peace rally in this light. Not only did it bring in as much, or more, spending than it might have cost, but more important, it brought scads of media to town as well, international as well as national and regional press. And these reporters and cameras dutifully spread the news of what they saw and heard here.

And what was that? Here's a clue: it was 99-plus percent positive. A peaceful, colorful march and rally, respectful of the troops in a military town, gathered in a lovely park, watched by police who were professional and courteous.

In the home of Ft. Bragg, the world saw freedom being exercised, and not only defended.

Checking Google a few days later, I found 290 news articles listed about the Fayetteville rally, reports in papers from the Washington Post to Japan.

What project or event in recent memory has brought Fayetteville 290 favorable reports in the world press? And how much is that kind of good press worth? My guess: a bundle.

Surea peace march and rally might not be quite what city boosters had in mind when planning and yearning for a municipal image makeover. But surprise! It was the peaceniks who got the job done.

There may be similar peace marches in Fayetteville's future. As they come, I hope fans ofthe city could regard them not as a burdensome intrusion, but as an asset, because that's what they really are.

Fayetteville: Where freedom is exercised, and not only defended.

It kind of has a ring to it, don't you think?

Chuck Fager is Director of Quaker House in Fayetteville.

Fayetteville *Observer* - Friday, July 29, 2005

Give recruits the truth

By Chuck Fager

Fayetteville- In the July 24 article, "He's in the Army now," Justin Willett reports blatantly illegal and abusive behavior by recruiters. Specifically, he wrote:

"The last stop at MEPS (Military Entrance Processing Station) is the swearing in. It's official, yet not official. All new recruits who go through MEPS must return a second time before shipping out to basic training or boot camp.

"The second swearing in is the one that really counts, MEPS officials said. Recruits are not prosecuted if they have a change of heart and fail to return for the second oath, the officials said."

This was said to Willett, accurately, because these recruits are formally in a delayed enlistment status.

But what the recruits were told was starkly different, and dishonest:

According to the article, a new recruit entered the "carpeted room with the military seals on the wall," and received a briefing on the Uniform Code of Criminal Justice, "in particular the sections titled absent without leave and desertion."

Recruits are told they could be court-martialed, which could result in the death penalty.

There are several levels of untruth and abuse here:

The first is flagrant exaggeration: The death penalty is on the books for desertion, but only two soldiers have been executed for it since 1864, and the last one was in World War II, 60 years ago. Typical sentences for desertion in recent years have been about a year, often less.

A second is that, as the recruiter admitted to Willett, these regulations do not yet apply to the recruits who were thus threatened.

A third is that this procedure clearly violates the Army's own rules -- specifically, an Army regulation (USAREC Reg 601-95), which states: "At no time will any (recruiter) tell a Delayed Enlistment Program enlistee he or she must "go in the Army or he or she will go to jail," or that " failure to enlist will result in a black mark on his or her credit record," or any other statement indicating adverse action will occur if the applicant fails to enlist."

In our military counseling at Quaker House, we often hear of such recruiter abuse. But seldom is it conducted so brazenly in the presence of a careful reporter.

I call on the Army to immediately cease this deceptive practice, and to discipline the recruiters involved.

Persons considering enlistment deserve truth in recruiting. The recruits in this case definitely did not get it.

For shame.

Chuck Fager is director of the Quaker House in Fayetteville.
http://zope.fayobserver.com/article_archive?year=2005&id=101488 0&q=chuck,Fager

Fayetteville NC *Observer* -March 16, 2006

Remembering The Peacemakers

Chuck Fager

Last Thursday, when we met at Quaker House to finalize the subjects and speakers for the annual peace march and rally in Rowan Park this Saturday, Tom Fox was not on the list.

Twenty-four hours later, he was.

Much of the peace rally program will recall the many who have fallen in the Iraq war–US troops, civilians, and innocent Iraqis. Tom is not the only civilian on that brutally long list. But he is the first fallen American who went to Baghdad as an unarmed peacemaker.

Tom's path to Iraq and an ignominious death was straightforward. We talked about it last August, when I saw him for the final time.

It was at our regional Quaker conferencein Virginia. Tom was between tours in Iraq, and we shared a meal and did some catching up.

We talked first about kids, as older dads will do. We both have a daughter and son the same age, and all grew up in the same Quaker meeting near Washington DC. They're in their twenties now, scattered across the continent, but still in touch. A few years back, our sons started a Quaker Hip Hop group called the Friendly Gangstaz Committee. The band caused quite a stir in our small Quaker world with startling, shouted renditions of well-worn hymns like "Simple Gifts." Tom and I chuckled ruefully about that.

We also talked about work. From that same faith community, Tom and I had traveled somewhat parallel paths, trying to be true to the meaning of texts like, "Blessed are the peacemakers,"(Matthew 5:9) and "seek peace and pursue it."(Proverbs 34:14)

How do you "pursue peace" in a violent world? My own seeking led, after a series of conventional jobs, to Fayetteville and Quaker House. Tom did twenty years in the Marine band, then was a baker at a growing health food supermarket. He was good at it, and his bosses wanted him to join management.

But Tom heard a "different drummer," especially after September 11, 2001. With a war on, he felt called to "pursue peace" in a concrete way. After much prayer and reflection, he joined the Christian Peacemaker Teams (CPT).

CPT sets out to bring the "weapons of the spirit" into the front lines of conflict, places where death and life are but a hair's breadth apart.

Tom's first assignment took him to the Occupied Territories of Palestine.

This was dangerous work, amid a conflict which seems hopelessly intractable. Tom stuck with it. Then, when the Iraq occupation shifted from the foolish illusion of "mission accomplished" to the grinding facts of guerilla and civil war, he headed there.

After Tom was kidnaped, Rush Limbaugh sneered that "part of me likes this," because, "I like any time a bunch of leftist feel-good hand-wringers are shown reality."

What's striking in this comment is not only the mean-spiritedness, but also the ignorance. Tom knew the reality of Baghdad's dangers firsthand. He talked frankly about them over that last August supper. Tom was calm but clear about it: kidnaping, torture, murder were on all sides there.

It was a CPT team, after all, that brought the first reports about the abuses at Abu Ghraib prison to reporter Seymour Hersh. They had seen other humanitarian workers kidnaped and some killed.

But there's more to it than that. The Christian Peacemaker Teams take their identity seriously. Their namesake, after all, was another unarmed troublemaker in an occupied country, who was tortured and then suffered an ignominious public execution. One other phrase that comes to mind is Matthew 10:24: "The disciple is not above his master, nor the servant above his lord."

So Tom has met his fate, and we mourn the loss. But at the peace rally this Saturday we will remember his witness. We will also remember that in the founding saga from which his team took its marching orders, death was a tragedy, but not the end of the story.

Chuck Fager is Director of Quaker House.

Fayetteville NC *Observer* - Sunday, July 16, 2006

Channeling the '60s

By Tim White, Editorial page editor

I know I'm setting myself up for a stern lecture from a peace protester or two, but someone has to tell them–the '60s are long gone. Dead and buried.

I was 20 years old . . . when the Chicago 7, Richard Daley (senior) and the Yippies had their summer of infamy. . . . The whole pop culture was roaring along to an anti-war, anti-establishment beat. . . . Some baby boomers still sit back and sigh   ah, those were the days. But nostalgia aside, those aren't the days anymore. . . .

Against this backdrop, we have a core of dedicated local peace activists who lately have been talking about more aggressive war protests. As Observer reporter Matt Leclercq wrote . . . the local anti-war folks (centering on Quaker House), are beginning to discuss more aggressive, albeit nonviolent, disruptions to make their point. They're talking about the kinds of actions where people get themselves arrested and then get themselves publicity that goes way farther afield than The Fayetteville Observer. . . .

We need more discussion, not more aggressive demonstrations. People are weary of the war. A large majority of Americans want it to end. They'll put more pressure on the politicians, but not if they are repulsed by old-timey demonstrations.

The – 60s are gone. So is the draft. They're not coming back in our lifetime.

Get over it.

Op-Ed response to Tim White, Fayetteville *Observer* - Published - 2006-07-19

Chuck Fager

It's always a pleasure to agree with Tim White; it confirms the suspicion that perhaps I am learning a thing or two in my near old age.

102

And today I get to do it twice.

First, let me join Tim in repeating the mantra:

"Yea, Verily, The Sixties Are Over."

Near as I can recall, they ended on January 1, 1970. Give or take a few.

With that stipulation, let me push on to what the discussion at Quaker House last week, which Tim lamented in his Sunday column, was actually aboutsomething only passingly mentioned in the *Observer*'s July 13 article about it.

Our focus was not nostalgia, or hope of turning back the clock. Rather, the agenda was much more immediate and concrete:

How, we wondered, could we bring more attention and consideration to the brave witness of several new American military heroes?

Specifically, we pondered the cases of First Lt. Ehren Watada, Spc. Suzanne Swift, and Sgt. Kevin Benderman.

Each of these three soldiers has recently said a loud NO to taking part in an Iraq war they regard as immoral, illegal, and destructive of the very integrity of the army.

We noted that two of them (Swift and Benderman) did so after serving in Iraq.

Lt. Watada took his stand after careful review of the rules and regulations that govern a military officer's conduct. He told ABC News that the "wholesale slaughter and mistreatment of the Iraqi people" is "a contradiction to the Army's own law of land warfare." We were told that rather than become a party to war crimes, Lt. Watada first tried to resign his commission; and only when that was denied did he refuse orders to deploy.

We heard that another burning issue was raised by Spc. Suzanne Swift. She has blown a loud whistle on the plague of sexual harassment to which so many female soldiers are subjected, and which left her afflicted with a double dose of PTSD.

Lt. Watada is the first army officer to refuse deployment. Sgt. Benderman is a ten-year veteran whose views changed drastically under the blows of hard experience.

All three of these soldiers are currently at Fort Lewis in Washington: Benderman is in the brig, serving eighteen months. Watada is awaiting a court-martial. Swift went AWOL rather than return to Iraq, and could face a desertion charge.

In our view these are not local matters. We felt strongly that the issues raised by these three cases – and there have been others – go to the heart of what the American military has been sent to do in Iraq from Day One.

It's a mission, we recalled, that more than seventy per cent of the US troops there surveyed for a *Stars and Stripes* poll last March, said should be ended within a year (and almost a quarter echoed our Rowan Park peace rally slogans, saying: "Bring Us Home Now.")

It seemed to us that these cases, especially the impending trial of Lt. Watada, ought to be of keen interest to the military-oriented public, here in Fayetteville and elsewhere.

But so far they've been barely noted. So we discussed a lot of ideas for helping raise their visibility. We'll be doing some more discussions.

And here is where I get to agree wholeheartedly with Tim again. He said "We need more discussion . . . " rather than nostalgic troublemaking.

Amen to that!

The issues raised by these three heroes deserve all the public discussion they can get.

We'll try do our part to promote that. I hope, Tim, that you and the *Observer* will do yours.

Chuck Fager is Director of Quaker House. He already knew the Sixties were over, in part because his sixties are not.

Fayetteville NC *Observer* - Thursday, July 10, 2008

Torturers may see justice

By Chuck Fager

Fayetteville- What are the chances that those responsible for torture in the U.S. "war on terror" will escape punishment?

According to Dick Marty, right now the chances are good.

Very good, in fact.

And Dick Marty should know. He's the Swiss equivalent of a U.S. senator — and the chief anti-torture investigator for the Council of Europe.

Marty produced two groundbreaking investigative reports that disclosed loads of hidden details about illegal U.S. torture flights to and across Europe. They also named Poland and Romania as the sites of similarly unlawful secret U.S. prisons.

The CIA shrugged off Marty's reports, and they got little notice in the U.S. But elsewhere they are recognized as landmarks, and haven't exactly burnished the U.S. image abroad.

I visited Europe this spring, giving talks to church groups, urging international action to stop torture. While there, I sought an appointment with Dick Marty. Having done investigative reporting myself, I wanted to give him props for a superb job, and chat about how he pulled it off.

More important, I hoped to get his candid view about the road ahead. I interviewed him in Lugano, his home town.

Knowing what he knows, I asked, is there any way to stop the perps from skating into the sunset on rollerblades of impunity?

Pardon the amateur crime-fighter argot, but it fits. Before Marty ran for the Swiss parliament, he was a tough prosecutor who bested mobsters and drug barons in his home canton of Ticino, which adjoins Italy.

Marty's English was limited, but his response was unmistakable: "That's exactly the right question to be asking," he said.

After that, he didn't have much immediate encouragement to offer. But then, he's not in the optimism business.

Sure, he agreed, torture is outlawed under both international and national laws. But, he added, at a secret NATO meeting in Athens in late 2001, the U.S. demanded and got assurances from all other member nations of impunity for its military and intelligence agencies, for any actions related to the "war on terror" on their territories. Several non-NATO nations, such as Ireland, later signed on as well.

Meanwhile, in U.S. courts, repeated assertions of the doctrine of "state secrets" have thus far stymied efforts, even by certifiably innocent torture victims like Khaled El Masri, to gain any redress.

So right now, it looks pretty well sewn up: tough luck, torture victims. And as for us lily-livered lovers of the Bill of Rights, better luck next time.

But that's the short-term view. Marty wasn't suggesting I go home and give up. "This will be a long work," Marty said. "It will require patience and determination."

Which means that, while the current forecast for torturers may be sunny, like Fayetteville weather, that can change.

How? In a lot of ways, mostly a bit at a time. Public pressure could continue to build, investigations begin, half-hearted at first, but picking up steam as the depth of the problem became clearer.

And eventually, prosecutions — most likely they'd start outside the United States. (Reliable reports are that cases are already being prepared in several countries, to surface in January.) And maybe a different U.S. president might just decide to keep out of their way.

Where would such a buildup of public pressure in the U.S. come from?

Believe it or not, the most likely place is American churches.

That's what happened, by the way, in the most famous anti-impunity case so far: the arrest of former Chilean dictator Augusto Pinochet in London in 1998. That bust took 10 years of persistent work, and the Catholic Church was a major factor.

There are already several inter-church, anti-torture coalitions at work in the U.S. And they include more than the usual liberal suspects. An evangelical conference against torture is planned for Atlanta in September.

I'll be there. I figure it's the least a follower of Jesus could do.

Any other Fayetteville Christians care to come along?

We can send Dick Marty a postcard.

How do you say "patience and determination" in Swiss-accented Italian?

Chuck Fager is director of Quaker House in Fayetteville, and is active with North Carolina Stop Torture Now.

http://www.fayobserver.com/print?id=1212674&type=archive

Intro from QH Blog:
Saturday, October 11, 2008

Keeping Up the Pressure on Torture

If I seem preoccupied with torture, that's due to two factors above all:
First, Fayetteville-Fort Bragg is surrounded by major components of what I call the "Torture Industrial Complex." So it's hard to ignore.

And second, in my study of this gruesome subject, it's become clear that legitimizing torture is a key step in the creation of a police state.
Anyway, here's another OpEd on the topic that I recently sent to the local paper.

Fayetteville NC *Observer*

Originally published on Sunday, September 28, 2008 in the Opinion category.

Don't forget "Torture Migration Day"

By Chuck Fager
Fayetteville

In this military town, much attention is given to important dates in military history: June 6, D-Day; Nov. 11, formerly Armistice, now Veterans Day; Dec. 7, Pearl Harbor Day.
Earlier this month, another major anniversary passed, with no notice but of huge importance, especially locally: Sept. 16. Migration Day. Torture Migration Day.
On Sept. 16, 2002, a conference began at the Special Warfare Center on Fort Bragg. At the session, the staff of the rapidly filling detention camp at Guantanamo were treated to detailed "demonstrations" of the Special Forces' SERE techniques.
SERE: Survival, Evasion, Resistance and Escape. It's the part of Special Forces training where aspiring operators are "captured" and then abused, under controlled conditions, to see how long they can resist breaking down and signing false confessions.
Reports are that the techniques, which grew out of the abuse of U.S. prisoners of war in the Korean War, can include waterboarding, religious

107

assaults, sensory and sleep deprivation, and extremes of heat and cold. Reports also say they are extremely effective at breaking down the trainees' will to resist, usually quickly.

The goal of the Bragg demonstration, according to Army investigators and the important new book, "The Dark Side," by New Yorker reporter Jane Mayer, was to show the Guantanamo officials how to get their prisoners to talk. Until then, the complaint was that the hundreds of detainees there were producing very little useful information.

From that fateful Sept. 16 meeting here, the SERE techniques, say investigators, "migrated" to Gitmo. And then to Afghanistan and Iraq, at Abu Ghraib and elsewhere. And then to the "black sites" operated by various OGAs, or Other Government Agencies – read CIA.

With this "migration," evidently many detainees started to talk, and didn't stop.

That's not surprising because these techniques really are not about interrogation. They're about torture. So yes, those subjected to them talked. They spewed reams of "confessions" and detailed "intelligence."

But over time, as numerous investigations have shown and Jane Mayer's book chillingly summarizes, little of this "intelligence" has proven authentic or useful.

And hundreds of the detainees, after such abuse, were released without charges – because they had no involvement with terrorism.

That is, they were not only innocent, they also were ignorant of the details of terror. Their confessions were mostly fabricated, to get the torture to stop.

Also in "The Dark Side," Mayer recounts that numerous administration officials – solid anti-terror conservatives and high military officers – came to see this "migration" as a tragic wrong turn and tried to stop it.

Without success.

There are many reasons to deplore the torture migration that was launched Sept. 16, 2002. Some, such as respect for the Geneva Conventions, the Constitution, U.S. federal anti-torture laws and God, can be dismissed as the cavils of bleeding hearts such as myself.

But others come from battle-seasoned military leaders.

One of these was former Joint Chiefs Chairman Gen. John Shalikashvili. He said that such practices "fostered greater animosity toward the United States, undermined our intelligence-gathering efforts, and added to the risks facing our troops serving around the world."

That's right: torture or "enhanced interrogation" by U.S. authorities endangers American troops.

This is "the Golden Rule" argument: if it's OK for the U.S. to torture and abuse detainees and prisoners – that makes it OK for our adversaries to do the same to our forces. "Do unto others ..."

Shalikashvili also states what can be called "the Bad Seed" argument:

Remember all those hundreds– more like thousands – of released detainees who weren't part of al-Qaida or other terror groups when they came in? Whose side do you suppose they're on now?

Right again: Torture helps recruit new terrorists and sympathizers. Which means, torture not only increases risks to our soldiers. It also endangers our national security.

While I hope the tide is beginning to turn against torture and so-called "enhanced interrogation," it's clear that this matter is far from over. The efforts to root it out will likely take years.

So while those efforts continue, I propose we add Sept. 16 to the calendar of unhappily memorable days on the military history calendar.

Torture Migration Day.

Let it not be forgotten.

And may it never happen again.

Chuck Fager is director of Quaker House in Fayetteville.

Fayetteville NC *Observer* – Wednesday, February 18, 2009 in the Opinion category.

Anti-torture stand deserves recognition

By Chuck Fager
Fayetteville

OK, so the *Observer* won a bunch of awards recently, from the North Carolina Press Association. Mostly seconds and thirds.

Congratulations, I guess.

But, if you ask me, the NCPA dropped the ball. They missed one at their rubber chicken confab. And it was a biggie.

A real biggie.

They forgot to hand the *Observer* the Special Citation for Editorial Courage and Excellence in the Fight to End Torture.

That's one award the editors earned, in spades. It should be hanging on the office wall right now, in a big shiny frame, in front of God and everybody.

Why? Do the math: Since 2005, this newspaper has published 10 – count 'em – editorials denouncing torture in the now obsolete "war on terror."

They have also printed a batch of anti-torture op-ed pieces, including two very powerful columns by Vietnam vet and military writer Joe Galloway, who knows what he's talking about.

That makes a dozen, and there were more. (Full disclosure: I wrote a couple of the other op-ed pieces, so we won't include them in the tally.)

How could the NCPA have missed out on recognizing this amazing record? Not only were the Observer's editorials consistent, they were eloquent as heck.

Recall just a few of these headlines:

"Our View: The only good policy regarding torture is zero tolerance" (Sept. 29, 2005).

"Our View: Americans can win wars without becoming what they despise" (Sept. 17, 2006).

"Our View: It's water torture, not an "enhanced technique" (Feb. 12, 2008).

"Our View: 'Abstinence only' is the sole honorable torture policy" (April 18, 2008).

There's lots more, but you get the idea.

This stunning achievement required more than mere eloquence and clear moral vision. In the America of working "the dark side, if you will," sneering at the Geneva Convention, and "All Hail Jack Bauer, Superstar," it took guts.

A lonely position

How lonely a stand was it? Well, for three years now, I've been making jaws drop on all my anti-torture activist buddies from the Triangle and other big cities, as I've shown them these clearly reasoned *cris de couer*, one after another, after another, after another.

You see, in those bigger, supposedly more sophisticated, cultured, and, well, "progressive" N.C. towns, the editorial voices against torture in their bigger, supposedly more sophisticated, etc., dailies have been mighty few and far between. One would think that for them, challenging torture was right up there with dissing NASCAR, basketball, barbecue and other timeless Tar Heel taboos.

So, maybe I can understand the NCPA's reluctance to honor the *Observer*'s principled consistency; to do so would show up too many of their colleagues around the state as the moral midgets they've been on this issue. For years.

And besides, that's all behind us now anyway, right? The New Order in Washington has declared torture off-limits, thank goodness. Let's move on, folks – nothing to see here. Especially not that pesky "accountability" aspect that Joe Galloway wrote about so forcefully in these pages just weeks back.

So no citation for the *Observer*. Oh, well. Yet, there is one consolation: If their fellow editors haven't been listening, maybe someone else has.

Come to think of it, those ringing declarations from the new White House resident about how America will no longer tolerate torture sounded like they were cribbed from the editorial columns of a small-city daily in the Sandhills. If they weren't, they sure could have been.

These echoes from the White House of what our paper has been saying for years ought to make local folks swell with pride.

And make a lot of other editors hang their heads in shame.

For that matter, maybe the NCPA isn't the *Observer*'s last chance to get its props.

Hello, Pulitzer Prize jury? Take note.

Chuck Fager is director of the Quaker House in Fayetteville.

111

Op-Ed -Fayetteville *Observer*- July 31, 2009

Canadian Health Care: A US Eyewitness In a Toronto ER

In the health-care melee, there's much alarmist talk and Canada-bashing, aimed at their single-payer health system.

A few days back, I had an unexpected chance to observe the Canadian system up close. What I saw was very instructive.

Here's what happened: on the last evening of a Toronto visit, I was invited to dinner by a young couple – let's call them Hank and Sue, for privacy.

Driving there, my cell buzzed. It was Hank, just home from work as a bicycle messenger: Sue was at the emergency room with Teddy, their seven year-old. He had broken his elbow in a playground fall. Hank was headed there; dinner was off.

Not so fast, said I. Let me pick you up and tag along. I could be moral support; and I had some bread, cheese and blueberries in a bag which might come in handy.

In fact, these snacks became our dinner. After relieving Sue, who took their fussy baby daughter home, Hank and I settled in with Teddy, to wait.

Waiting – that's one of the big knocks on Canadian health care. Teddy, arm in a makeshift sling, grimaced with pain but bore up bravely, watching a Harry Potter DVD. Hank and I grazed and caught up, and wondered what was taking so long.

Turned out there were two factors.

The first emerged when the chaplain dropped in. A Quebecer, we were just starting to chat about my favorite Canadian topic, Anglo-French issues, when her beeper chirped.

Glancing down at it, she frowned. "Sorry, got to go." Then, out of Teddy's earshot, "A child may be about to die." She hurried out.

So. Reason Number One was that ER basic: triage. Teddy was hurt and hurting, but in no real danger. Life-and-death cases properly came first.

And we weren't just left in limbo. A pediatric social worker came in several times, both to keep us posted and to distract Teddy when an IV was put in. She was, I noted, very good at both.

Reason Number Two became clear about nine o'clock, when finally it was show time: to reassemble Teddy's elbow involved a team of six, including an orthopedist, an anesthetist, a physician, X-ray tech, nurse and the social worker. In a big, busy hospital, getting this much expertise into the same room at the same time, ad hoc, was a challenge.

Once there, though, they made quick work of it, cast and all. Then it was only a matter of monitoring Teddy's recovery from the anesthetic. It was near four AM when I dropped them off; but it was done.

With four kids myself, I've had my share of ER visits. What did this unplanned field reconnaissance in the Canadian version reveal?

Two things above all:

First, I saw Teddy receive excellent, family-sensitive care.

And second, I observed how a personal injury did not become a family financial disaster.

Hank's messenger job is a no-frills, tough times gig: no sick days or bennies.In the US, that would mean no health insurance.

In Toronto, their out of pocket cost was zero. Here, his son's ordeal would have set cash registers jingling at every step: ambulance, ka-ching; ER visit, ka-ching; IV, X-rays, sedation, ka-ching, ka-ching, ka-ching. Not to mention the social worker and orthopedist: ka-double-ching!

In the US, when Hank got home, he would have carried not only his sleepy son, but a hospital bill of many thousands, likely five figures.

Hank and Sue are seriously thrifty folks: no mortgage, no car, no credit card balances. But down here, Teddy's accident would have crushed their discipline under a pile of medical debt.

Of course, there's no free lunch. Hank and Canadians pay for their care with higher taxes than here; I'm told that their wealthy even pay more.

That's what I witnessed.

So now, all you Canada-bashers, please line up to the right. And tell me again just how such a system is a godless socialist plot to destroy civilization.

Have at it. After all, who am I supposed to believe – you, or my lying eyes?

Chuck Fager is Director of Quaker House in Fayetteville. The views expressed here are his own.

Fayetteville NC *Observer*, Sept. 17, 2009

Domestic Acts of Terror Nothing New

When I saw the report that death threats against the president were up 400 per cent from those aimed at his predecessor, it gave me flashbacks.

The flashbacks were to several mornings in early 1965 in Selma, Alabama, where voting rights marches were led by Dr. Martin Luther King, Jr. Each time, several staff members marched close around Dr. King.

This was his unarmed, unofficial "secret service" delegation. Their task was simple: to block the aim of any snipers hiding on nearby rooftops.

I was one of those escorts. A green rookie, walking pretty well fit my skill set then – if it didn't include chewing gum at the same time.

Big James Orange was another. He was a movement veteran.

"But Jim," I said, when our orders came, "what if they pull the trigger and hit me instead?"

Orange laughed and slapped me on the back. "Don't worry, Chuck," he said. "If you get shot, I promise: Dr. King will preach at your funeral."

Which didn't make me feel much better. But I followed my orders. And nobody shot me – or Dr. King, then.

It wasn't for lack of trying, tho. Several years later, researching my book, "Selma 1965," I learned that the local police believed that during one of those marches there actually was a sniper lurking on a rooftop not far away.

So maybe I earned my $25 paycheck that week. Reading the report later still made the hair stand up on the back of my neck.

I learned some other lessons during those weeks. For one, death threats for Dr. King were an everyday thing; I saw several of the handwritten ones. Police in Los Angeles arrested one would-be assassin as Dr. King was arriving there for a speaking engagement: the guy had a garage full of armaments, and a heart full of murder.

Yes, there were plenty of plots to kill Dr. King. And of course as we know, in Memphis one finally succeeded.

But another thing I learned in Alabama was that Dr. King was not the only victim of the forces of rage and hate then loose in our land.

I could fill the rest of my time just listing some of their names: four young girls in a Birmingham church; Medgar Evers; Jimmie Lee Jackson; Lt. Col. Lemuel Penn; James Chaney.

Add to these two names which are almost unknown: Henry Hezekiah Dee and Charles Eddie Moore. They wereKlan victims whose bodies were found during a search for Chaney and two other murdered civil rights workers in Mississippi.

Whites were among the targets too: Michael Schwerner and Andrew Goodman, who were killed alongside James Chaney; Jonathan Daniels; Viola Liuzzo; James Reeb; and more.

This is not to mention the dozens of bombings, especially of churches.

Today, in 2009, this wave of domestic terrorism seems to have been all but forgotten. Many of us seem to cling to the idea that the kind of place where such organized violence against our own is unthinkable – or it happened so long ago that it's more the stuff of legend than a real danger.

But these aren't legends. This was home-grown terrorism that stalked much of America in my lifetime. And I speak of it now because some days lately, it feels as if we are edging very close to another outbreak. So I get flashbacks.

Looking back, it is easy to see how many of those who committed these crimes were incited, egged on, even mobilized by public voices of hate and racism. And looking around today, it is just as easy to hear similar voices again, many reaching much larger audiences than those of the 1960s.

What also rings in the memory is not only the old cries of hate, but the deafening, enabling silence that was the response of so many others with a voice –yes, especially in the predominantly white southern churches.

Are we hearing echoes of that complicit, abetting silence again? That's the kind of flashback that especially haunts me.

In the civil rights years, enough such public voices speaking against domestic hate and violence might have saved Dr. King, and many of the others.

Enough such voices today would make our president safer.

And many of the rest of us too. That would be real peace witness.

Do you hear the voices yet?

I don't.

Chuck Fager, the Director of Quaker House in Fayetteville, is the author of the books "Selma 1965: The March That Changed The South,"and "Eating Dr. King's Dinner: A Memoir."

http://zope.fayobserver.com/article_archive?year=2009&id=126098 6&q=chuck,fager

Fayetteville NC *Observer* -published January 31, 2010

Latest Gitmo Shocker Makes Waves

By Chuck Fager

Who would have guessed it?

The case of the three Guantanamo prisoners found dead in June, 2006, who were originally called suicides but maybe weren't, has many angles.

And one unexpected twist is that it might bring long-parted schoolmates together again.

In the early 1970s, "Billy" McRaven and Scott Horton were students at Theodore Roosevelt High School in San Antonio, Texas.

I talked with Horton in New York City earlier this week. He explained that he and "Billy' were both from military families. McRaven wound up in the Navy, while Horton went to law school. Each advanced in their profession.

Today, McRaven is an admiral. And he's commander of the Joint Special Operations Command.

JSOC, as it's called, may be the most secretive of the many secret groups based at Fort Bragg.

JSOC reputedly brings together such units as the Army's Delta Force, the Air Force's Combat Controllers, and other clandestine units for missions the rest of us are never supposed to hear about.

While details are few, indications are that in recent years JSOC has been particularly busy.

And how are they doing? Well, when the Washington Post's Bob Woodward asked the former president in his book, "The War Within," the reply was simply, "JSOC is awesome."

Whatever that means operationally, JSOC has also been extremely adroit in avoiding media or congressional scrutiny.

But could that start to change? This is where Admiral McRaven's old schoolmate enters the story.

Since high school in Texas, Scott Horton has successfully practiced international law, including human rights cases in many countries.

But he is no radical. When the "War On Terror" began after 9-11, he told me, he was not an antiwar skeptic or a pacifist. In fact, he had friends in both the military and intelligence agencies.

It was the off-the-record, uneasy reports from these contacts that got his attention. Alarmed talk of disappearances, torture, secret prison sites, a disregard for all the laws and rules of war. A cascade of deeds to make any honorable American soldier ashamed.

116

"This wasn't a question of occasional abuse," Horton told me.

"In any prison system you'll have some abuses. But this was a matter of torture as policy. Policy coming down from above."

And torture, as has been noted in this paper before, is a federal felony. It's also a war crime under international law.

These informal reports were followed by one public shock after another. There was Abu Ghraib, torture flights (most taking off from North Carolina), "black site" prisons, coverups (Pat Tillman, anyone?).

Following up these and other cases turned Scott Horton into one of the most determined and tenacious human rights attorneys and investigators working the ongoing "torture beat."

You ask me, we need more like him. The official probes of torture, such as they may be, are proceeding at a languid crawl behind tightly closed doors. Either that or they have yielded reports most notable for coverups, blackouts and whitewash.

Then earlier this month, Horton dropped a triple-barreled investigative bombshell into this set of polite croquet matches.

It came in a detailed report for *Harper's* Magazine, charging that the 2006 deaths at Guantanamo were not suicides at all.

Instead (Bombshell Number One), the three prisoners had been murdered, probably during torture.

Furthermore (Bombshell Number Two), the killings likely occurred at a previously undisclosed "black site," on the edge of Gitmo itself. It's been dubbed "Camp No," as in, "No, it does not exist." But it does.

And not least, as for where the culpability lies, Horton says all fingers of available information point at (Bombshell Number Three) JSOC.

Which brings us round to Admiral McRaven, Horton's old classmate.

Horton's report has been featured in hundreds of papers around the world (including this one). But so far it has been met with shifty "non-denial-denials" in Washington, and the SOP of stony silence from JSOC itself.

Horton's charges were backed up by the testimony of conscience-stricken soldiers, former Gitmo guards. They knew about Camp No, and they also knew that the original suicide story was false.

Horton told me he's since talked to more potential witnesses.

But despite this persistence, will Horton's new report get any real traction?

So far, the US torture impunity express has been chugging along without a bump, scarcely noting the change of Conductors a year ago this month.

Horton says he's hoping for public hearings in Congress. If his witnesses had the chance to tell their version of what happened, it might break through the coverup. And JSOC might even be obliged to answer some uncomfortable questions in public.

If it did, tho, and abuses were uncovered, Horton told me he would want them fixed. He's not out to get JSOC abolished. "There's a proper place for it in limited, very dangerous wartime situations," he insisted.

"But it looks as if JSOC's been shielded from scrutiny and accountability, so when mistakes have been made, they haven't been corrected."

Congress seems a weak reed to lean on these days, but Horton is not giving up.

I wish him luck. But maybe a more direct approach would also be worth a try.

Here's my scenario:

"Admiral McRaven, your old homey Scott Horton is on the line. Yes, THAT Scott Horton.

"Sure, he's got some issues. But like your former commander in chief, he too says that JSOC is awesome.

"It's just that the truth, especially about Camp No – that, sir, would be awesomer."

Chuck Fager is Director of Quaker House

Intro from QH Blog: Thursday, June 3, 2010

Ending "Don't Ask Don't Tell" - An Extended Exchange

As of 2010, I don't recall ever seeing an article in our local paper, the Fayetteville *Observer*, that was affirmative of GLBT issues, or in particular, supported the repeal of the military's "Don't Ask Don't Tell" policy.

This doesn't mean that the paper is a font of homophobic verbiage; but when anti-gay articles do appear, they usually go unanswered.

That silence is consistent with the general atmosphere of the community. Racial integration has been the policy of the military for sixty years, and federal law for almost fifty; racism surely still exists here, but it skulks in corners and speaks in code.

Homophobia is another matter. I am acquainted with a number of gays and lesbians here, some of whom are quite active in the community. But there is no visible gay presence in the city. No "Gay Pride Day," no vocal organizations, and the gay bars keep a very low profile.

Hence when an Op-Ed appeared in the *Observer* a couple of weeks ago, the chances were that it would go unanswered. The text of that commentary, by retired Chaplain Ronald Crews, is below, for reference.

But this communal closeting has long been a burden to me, and I decided to speak up for my own convictions, and perhaps those of some others who did not feel safe to speak.

My Op-Ed response was published in the Observer on Thursday June 3. It is posted here as well.

As advocacy goes, my piece is pretty mild. That reflects an effort to take the immediate audience into account. Several of the online comments for the paper's website are also pasted in here, to give an idea of the response.

So, here first is the original piece, by Ronald Crews, published May 26, 2010:

Fayetteville *Observer*, Wednesday, May 26, 2010

Let military decide gay issue

By Ronald A. Crews

President Barack Obama announced early in his administration his desire to repeal the law commonly known as the "Don't Ask, Don't Tell." Legislation has been introduced in the House and Senate to accomplish the president's desire and make a 180-degree change in military policy.

The Pentagon asked for a year to review the impact of repealing the policy that has been codified since the Clinton administration. Without waiting for this review, Congress has already begun hearings on the bill to fast-track this legislation.

As part of the Pentagon review, endorsing agents, those responsible for providing chaplains to our armed forces, were asked to submit information about the impact of this repeal on chaplains and their ministry. Grace Churches International currently endorses 14 chaplains on active duty with others in the pipeline to become chaplains.

As a retired Army chaplain, having served 29 years on active duty and in the reserve system, I am concerned about how the repeal of this policy will affect not only the ministry of chaplains, but also the morale and welfare of our soldiers, airmen, sailors and Marines.

We believe that military leaders, not politicians, should make this decision. This decision should be based on military needs and not a political agenda or payback to a special-interest group. Our military should not be used as a social experiment.

Further, this push is a distraction from providing the resources needed by our fighting forces as they continue one of the longest continual combat missions of our nation's history. This is not the time for such a radical change. We propose that Congress should be debating ways to support our men and women in uniform, not debating whether to make this radical change.

Grace Churches International chaplains, along with chaplains from other faith groups, serve the men and women of our armed forces regardless of their faith background or sexual practices. However, the repeal of Don't Ask, Don't Tell will impose a policy of how they serve a certain portion of the military population. This raises the following questions.

Preaching/teaching sound doctrine regarding sinful conduct: Like other Evangelical Christians, we believe that homosexual behavior is inconsistent with a Christian lifestyle. Our chaplains must be able to address sin as they see it, knowing that sinful behavior is harmful to individuals and to society at large. Chaplains must be able to speak against sin from the pulpit, as well as within a counseling session. Chaplains must also remain free to use the scripturally accurate depiction of the sinful nature of homosexual relations when necessary. Impact: Will chaplains be free to preach and counsel their convictions?

Counseling of soldiers who are affected by the conduct of homosexual personnel: Chaplains must feel free to validate a soldier's faith-based view of homosexuality as sin within the counseling environment. Chaplains must also be free to advise commanders in addressing the needs of soldiers who feel such conduct has violated their rights. Impact: Will chaplains be free to advise soldiers that they can maintain their convictions concerning homosexual behavior? Will chaplains be free to advise commanders of how soldiers have been adversely impacted by the homosexual behavior of peers and/or supervisors?

Strong Bonds: Strong Bonds marriage retreats are part of the commander's program for assisting married soldiers after deployments. Commanders will be required by law to protect the rights of homosexuals in their command to have equal access to the programs and services that a chaplain provides, leaving a chaplain's ministry vulnerable to Equal Opportunity violations. Impact: Will chaplains be required to include cohabiting homosexual couples in Strong Bonds events? If chaplains refuse to include homosexual couples, will they be guilty of Equal Opportunity violations?

Chaplains are often given chapel duties that require working with persons of different faith groups. One of the strengths of the Chaplain Corps has been the collegiality and respect for chaplains from other faiths. That said, chaplains often find themselves not able to share pulpit responsibilities with chaplains from faith groups they deem inconsistent with their belief system. Impact: Will chaplains be required to share pulpit duties with homosexual chaplains or lay-leaders?

Other considerations:

Adultery: Since most states and federal law still define marriage as the union of one man and one woman, will homosexuals living together open the door to the legitimization of adultery among all ranks in the military?

If homosexual soldiers can share rooms together in a barracks, will the same accommodation be afforded to heterosexual men and women?

If the Department of Defense maintains that same-sex relationships have the same value, dignity and honor as heterosexual relationships, will DoD seek to restrict or limit the recruitment of clergy from denominations that embrace the traditional teachings of Judaism and Christianity on this subject?

Will tolerance and promotion of same-sex relationships become a discriminator on officer and NCO efficiency reports?

Grace Churches International will not endorse chaplains who hold hatred toward any person, regardless of lifestyle. We believe in the commandment to love and serve all people. But muzzling chaplains and forcing them to preach a politically correct gospel would ultimately violate that commandment, and so we oppose replacing the military's current policy with special protections for homosexual behavior. May God grant His wisdom to our political leaders as they consider this radical change to military policy.

Ronald A. Crews, the executive director of Grace Churches International in Fayetteville, is a retired Army chaplain.

http://fayobserver.com/articles/2010/06/03/1003267?sac=Opin

My reply – which was in fact the only substantial rebuttal the paper published:

Fayetteville *Observer* - Thursday June 3, 2010

Op-Ed: Policy's death a boost for morale

By Chuck Fager

Fayetteville - Ronald Crews ("Let military decide gay issue," May 26) decries the likely end of "Don't Ask Don't Tell" and fears the impact of the change upon certain evangelical chaplains.

I'm all for ending DADT, for many reasons - and one of them is that Crews has much less to worry about than he thinks.

Crews insists that the military "should not be used for a social experiment." But isn't this much the same objection raised to desegregating the military 60 years ago? And didn't that "experiment" turn out rather well?

Crews also is worried about "the morale and welfare" of the troops, and calls DADT repeal a "distraction from providing the resources needed" for them.

Actually, repealing DADT will improve the morale and welfare of the troops. Especially that of the thousands of homosexual servicemen and women.

They're an important "resource," too. It will improve their welfare by removing an unnecessary risk from their lives - so they can better face the real ones, of which there are plenty.

For that matter, it will also improve the morale of many commanders. Enforcing DADT is a useless "distraction" they don't need. No question, the sooner DADT is gone, the better off all the services will be.

Chaplain conundrum

Yet, Crews wonders whether ending DADT will prevent some chaplains from preaching what they regard as "sound doctrine." Especially regarding the "scripturally accurate depiction of the sinful nature of homosexual relations when necessary."

But don't various churches already differ about many other issues?

Are chaplains "muzzled" when it comes to, say, the hotly disputed issue of abortion? Or evolution? This should be no different.

But maybe there's a point here that needs a closer look. The doctrinal statement of Crews' Grace Churches International asserts that the whole Bible is "free from error in the whole and in the part," and I'm sure that is part of their preaching.

I note, however, that in both the Old Testament (Leviticus 20:13) and the New (Romans 1:32) it teaches that homosexuals deserve to be put to death. And we know that in Uganda, for instance, there's currently an effort to enact those commandments into law.

On principle, I support the free speech of any military chaplain who feels obliged to uphold such "scripturally accurate" doctrines.

I swallow hard when saying that, but I do.

Even so, I hope the chaplain would add that acting on these "scripturally accurate" strictures is against U.S. military and civil law today, and could lead to a long prison sentence or even capital punishment. Full disclosure.

Crews asks whether post-DADT chaplains will "be free to advise commanders of how soldiers have been adversely affected by the homosexual behavior of peers and/or supervisors?"

The answer is that, post-DADT, sexual harassment and assaults, regardless of orientation, will still be crimes.

But if one of Crews' flock simply dislikes serving alongside open homosexuals, there's another adage which is applicable. It is not biblical, but I'm told it has something of scriptural weight in military circles.

It is: "Suck it up and drive on, soldier. Follow your orders."

Yet, as it also says in 1 Corinthians 12:31, there is a "more excellent way."

Crews himself pointed to it, when he stated that one of the "strengths of the Chaplains Corps has been the collegiality and respect for chaplains from other faiths."

This is good to hear, especially when we consider that several large U.S. Protestant denominations already accept homosexuals as members and clergy. Two of the three largest Jewish communities do, too. All are represented in the chaplaincy.

I suggest that the solution for the evangelical chaplains Crews is concerned about is straightforward: simply extend the "collegiality and respect" accorded to these other chaplains to all the troops, whether homosexual or not.

Or to put it another way: "Let him who is without sin cast the first stone" (John 8:7).

That should take care of it, really.

Chuck Fager is director of Quaker House in Fayetteville.

Online Reader Comments:

johnR - – Mr. Fager said, "Actually, repealing DADT will improve the morale and welfare of the troops. Especially that of the thousands of homosexual servicemen and women.

They're an important "resource," too. It will improve their welfare by removing an unnecessary risk from their lives - so they can better face the real ones, of which there are plenty".

Improve the morale and welfare of the troops?? The only group you gave any information about morale uplifting by repealing DADT are the gay folks. Nothing, and I mean nothing, you stated would improve the morale of the straight troops-it would only give THEM more to be concerned with.

Mr. Fager also said, "Crews insists that the military "should not be used for a social experiment." But isn't this much the same objection raised to desegregating the military 60 years ago? And didn't that "experiment" turn out rather well"?

Desegregating of the military was a fantastic idea and did turn out well. But, you are comparing apples to oranges. This is a completely different situation. One was to allow complete races to work side-by-side for a common good. The other is to allow what is considered to be by most in the military as a deviant lifestyle to force acceptance.

There are other countries that allow homosexuals in their military. I challenge anyone to compare our military with theirs....which one would you want defending your country?

Lumbee Against La Razists - Chuck, using the Bible, of all things to validate the queer lifestyle and trying to normalize this behaviour that was once medically considered an abnormality of the brain is deplorable and cheap.

Let's consider the following medical conditions that will have to be addressed in a deployment, as if there aren't enough serious injuries that need the attention of the physician in the field. Come, let us reason together. Isn't that in the Bible too?

Check this out. A doctor wrote it. I copied and pasted it for you. All facts. All medical conditions that accompany this lifestyle that heterosexuals do not encounter on a regular basis. I feel that an open policy will greatly destroy the cohesive nature of military duty, especially in the field. I feel that resources that would be better used on injury caused by enemy fire will be wasted on injury caused by the promiscuity that defines this "gay" sick lifestyle. Please read the following carefully. Again, these are medical facts:

The Health Risks of Gay Sex
JOHN R. DIGGS, JR., M.D.
(A long listing of awful diseases, all seen as consequences of gay sex; text deleted here for brevity)

johnR - Military medics don't have enough to worry about.......The field and outstations in OEF and OIF have inherent sanitation issues as it is, lets throw some more in there.

Lumbee Against La Razists - Chuck Fager is a NONNER, meaning, he never served his country a day in his entire life. He doesn't have a real voice in this matter because he is not active duty, nor is he a veteran, nor does he have a clue about military life other than what he has been told second-hand. In fact, it would be safe to say that he undermines the armed forces.

"In a 2008 military poll, 58% of active duty responders said they were against a repeal of "Don't Ask, Don't Tell." Based on the poll, National Review estimates that up to 10% of active duty forces would choose to quit the military if forced to cohabit with open homosexuals. The leading House Democrat on military policy himself unsuccessfully opposed the repeal. He said the law would create "disruption" while the military is in the middle of two major conflicts in Iraq and Afghanistan.

Merrill McPeak, Air Force chief in 1993 when the ban was passed, wrote an op-ed for the New York Times urging that it remain in place. He explains that under "Don't Ask, Don't Tell," service members are no longer asked whether they are homosexual; they no longer have to lie. They simply have to remain quiet about it. "Seventeen years ago, the chiefs – all four of us, plus the chairman and vice chairman – concluded that allowing open homosexuality in the ranks would probably damage the cohesiveness of our combat units."

Repeal advocates focus on the rights and job performance of individual homosexuals, says McPeak, but the military isn't about the individual. It is about group cohesion when facing deadly threats. The military has a right to exclude open homosexuals whose lifestyles weaken the warrior culture required for open combat.

McPeak also points out that the military has a special right to discriminate against candidates. Overweight candidates are routinely ejected from military training, and no one complains about the cost or damaged morale. "The services exclude, without challenge, many categories of prospective entrants. People cannot serve in uniform if they are too old or too young, too fat or too thin, too tall or too short, disabled, not sufficiently educated and so on. This, too, might be illegal in the civil sector. So why should exclusion of gay people rise to the status of a civil-rights issue, when denying entry to, say, unmarried individuals with sole custody of dependents under 18, does not?" If weight, height and education are substantive issue, then highly controversial and morally objectionable sexual behavior is even more so.

Although it is increasingly not recognized as anything but fringe "homophobia," many religious service members believe homosexuality is a very serious sin against God and man. Family Research Council says, "The courts have consistently upheld the military's 1993 homosexual ban and affirmed convincingly that the law is constitutional. Congress and the courts have long acknowledged that the military has the responsibility to focus on creating and preserving readiness. Military service is a privilege, not a right, and anything that detracts from the ability of our service personnel to fulfill their mission should be prohibited. The sexual tension that would be introduced by forced cohabition with homosexuals indispewtably fits into that category."

-Reverend Ted Pike, June 1, 2010, truthtellers.org

Rev. Jeffrey C. Long - Another bad idea. But coming from Mr. Fager and Quakerhouse, this is not at all surprising.

It is an especially cheap shot to try and equate "homosexual rights" with the Civil Rights movement and the opening of military service to Black Americans. As has been stated, this is of another category entirely. After all, being born dark skinned is what you are...being a homo is "what you DO," some of which as has been amply and disgustingly described above for us – lest we forget!

Furthermore, Mr. Fager, et al., most Black Americans take special umbrage at gays forever presuming to stow away on the Selma "freedom train." I will remind you that Seventy percent of them voted against prop 8 in California. Don't play the "race card" where it in no way remotely applies!

As a former Army officer I am appalled enough the way it is WITH DADT!

Open homosexuality is a threat to the morale, morals, and cohesion (not to mention the physical AND mental health) of any social unit and this is particularly true in a military unit. The corruption of the German Armed Forces by homosexual cadres is well documented and should serve as a warning to us in America today.

Unfortunately, Obama and most Democrats are hell bent to defy the lessons of history, believing they can escape their consequences, and this all as a matter of political payoff to extremist groups who have given them their support.

It is NOT being "Christian" to witness the pending destruction of men and women – which would be the inevitable entailment of such a ill-begotten policy without raising a voice against it.

Virginia - It's 2010 people, grow up! You're making an arguement about diseases and sexual practices which apply to BOTH homosexuals and heterosexuals. Besides, whether gay or straight these people are fighting for your freedom. How dare you criticize and judge someone who lays their life on the line so that you can live your life of ignorance.

johnR - With all due respect Virginia, though these things can and are done by both straight and gay folks-it is most prominent with homosexuals. The people that presently are fighting our wars do not need the extra self induced concerns that repealing DADT would cause. When the DOD's review comes out and they give the results of the polls of service members, you will see that the vast majority do not want to serve with homosexuals. That number will jump to near 100% if you ask direct combat troops e.g. Infantry, Rangers, SF, ect.....

Fayetteville NC *Observer* - Sunday, September 05, 2010

The price we paid for war

By Chuck Fager

On Tuesday [August 31, 2010], the president told us, "The bottom line is this: the war is ending. Like any sovereign, independent nation, Iraq is free to chart its own course."

I appreciated the muted rhetoric: no talk of "victory," or "mission accomplished" bluster.

It's also gratifying to see many troops actually coming home.

But when he added, "And by the end of next year, all of our troops will be home," I was not fully persuaded.

For one thing, *Army Times* has reported that "Special forces will continue to help Iraqis hunt for terrorists." In other words, secret warfare, this administration's preferred style, will go on. Further, besides uniformed special forces, whose numbers remain classified, there will be more "private" security contractors operating in Iraq, too.

Certainly the U.S. footprint has been reduced. And if in fact all the regular, non-clandestine forces are out by the end of 2011, that will indeed be change we can believe in.

Yet as far as a complete end to U.S. involvement in warfare there these are more than just loose ends.

Evaluating the costs

Meanwhile, if the president is muted in characterizing the Iraq invasion, others are not. Prominent war supporters such as Paul Wolfowitz and columnist David Brooks already have proclaimed it a big success.

But neither focused much on the war's costs. There are usually three kinds of costs mentioned: the more than 4,400 U.S. troops killed, 31,000 wounded, and a price tag of near $1 trillion.

But such figures are a substantial understatement.

Take casualties: Dr. Ronald Glasser, who researched it exhaustively for his book, "Wounded," said when he visited Fayetteville that the number of U.S. wounded was more like 70,000, and that the cost of their long-term care would be closer to $3 trillion. These figures are backed up by Nobel Prize-winning economist Joseph Stiglitz.

In short, the war's actual costs in blood and treasure will be a financial and a moral burden on our society for decades to come.

And that's only the beginning. Consider some others:

Based on lies, the war corroded public trust in government. From a phony connection to Sept. 11, to non-existent weapons of mass destruction, the Pat Tillman scandal and on and on, the lies kept piling up.

This cynicism has only deepened with exposure of some of the largest ripoffs and robberies in recorded history: billions of U.S. tax dollars were stolen from Iraq by crooks foreign and domestic, with little in the way of recovery or redress. Plus, about $5 billion more was wasted on unfinished or abandoned boondoggle construction projects.

The shocking legitimation of torture as U.S. policy, drastically undermining the rule of law. Sure, the president ordered it to stop. But he also has opposed any accountability for those responsible, which means he's only pressed the pause button; official torture can be restarted anytime, with no fear of consequences. And popular media have made U.S. torture almost a cultural norm, as long as we do the torturing.

The war made us less safe: Torture and the occupation were the best recruiting tools religious extremists in the region could ever have wanted, bringing in thousands of recruits burning for vengeance.

It has fed a growing and ugly strain of domestic anti-Islamic bigotry.

It damaged the U.S. military. After years of grueling deployments in a war without justification, record-high GI suicide rates are only one symptom of the internal havoc wrought on troops and families.

Iraq's burden

And then, what about the costs to Iraq? Yes, the tyrant Saddam Hussein was removed; elections were held, though a functioning government remains elusive at this writing. But what price did the Iraqi people pay for this uninvited mission of liberation? Here's my admittedly incomplete tally:

Between 500,000 and a million civilians killed.

Ongoing sectarian and political violence that kills hundreds more monthly.

Four million to 5 million Iraqis made refugees.

Hideously high rates of birth defects, childhood cancers and other horrors in battleground cities such as Fallujah.

The rights of women sharply curtailed by the new ruling groups.

The once numerous educated and professional population decimated or driven into exile.

Their ancient cultural heritage looted, destroyed or dispersed.

Public infrastructure such as electricity and water still barely functioning.

Unemployment rates in excess of 40 percent.

Venerable Christian and other religious minorities subjected to murderous persecution or driven from their homes.

I won't try to predict the future. But it would take a lot to make all this destruction even remotely worth the sacrifice of U.S. troops, and the greater sacrifices imposed on the Iraqi people.

Chuck Fager is director of Quaker House in Fayetteville.

http://zope.fayobserver.com/article_archive?year=2010&id=1303717&q=Chuck,Fager

Fayetteville NC *Observer* – Thursday November 4, 2010

Op-ed: An order of war news, hold the mayo

By Chuck Fager

Fayetteville – Tom Ricks was a heckuva war reporter in his Washington Post days. He's the furthest thing from a peacenik, but his book, "Fiasco," told the awful truth about the Iraq occupation's disastrous early years, and earned him mountains of respect.

Now he runs his own influential blog, "The Best Defense," where he's still telling it like he sees it.

And what Rick saw in the big Wikileaks document release was, in a word, "crap."

"Maybe I'm going soft," he wrote recently, "but the Wikileaks dump kind of makes me ill."

Why? "If the leaks brought great revelations, I might think differently, but so far I don't think I have been surprised by a single thing I've read."

But that's too mild. Tom's ultimate verdict is that "adding mayonnaise doesn't turn chicken (poop) into chicken salad. Here's my test: Tell me one thing we didn't know last week that we know now about the Iraq war."

Well, I hate to differ with one of my war reporter heroes, but here I have to stop and ask: Just who is included in this "we" you're talking about, Tom? Who knew all this already?

No doubt war-weary veteran reporters such as Ricks know tons more about what's happened "downrange" than I ever will.

But I have been paying attention these last eight years. And since the Wikileaks cascades, I've learned many things I didn't know before. To judge by the reaction of informed observers in many places, a lot of other people learned things, too, beyond what Ricks shrugged off as an "Iraqi version of a dog bites man story."

Here's a short list of some items this other "we" just learned, from the Wikileaks disclosures:

That U.S. forces were keeping detailed track of civilian casualties, even while loudly denying it. Which makes the denials a pack of lies, Tom. (OK, there were lots of such packs.)

That these civilian casualties were much higher than previously reported. So much higher that even the Iraq Body Count, always very conservative in its estimates, is adding more than 15,000 to its total. Is

131

that truly a so-what, Tom? Fifteen thousand extra dead civilians, and counting?

Then there's the documentation of massive torture and murder of civilians, not by insurgents but by U.S. "allies," including many women and children. And that U.S. commanders turned the victims over wholesale to Iraqi units notorious for such barbarous savagery.

More, we learned that this neglect of torture was a matter of policy, with top-down instructions for U.S. troops to ignore the carnage.

Torture

But wait a minute – could that mean it wasn't just a few low-rank "bad apples" such as the hapless Lynndie England and the sadistic Charles Graner, who were responsible for "abuses"? Really? Did Ricks know that, too?

Which brings us to the subject of power drills. No doubt Tom was aware of their deployment as instruments of torture and murder.

Actually, I knew about them too, since the months of 2005-06 when I monitored dozens of obscure news reports every night for news of my doomed hostage friend, Tom Fox. I recall those reports – particularly, because it was also when the Pentagon was consistently denying that there was a civil war raging around Baghdad.

But those were the bad guys, right? The ones our forces were there to stop? Only now I learn that the power drills were widely in use by U.S. "allies" against thousands of other Iraqis, mainly civilians.

OK, I admit it: homicide-by-power drill gives me the creeps. Maybe I'm going soft.

If so, that Wikileaks video of the laughing helicopter massacre had something to do with it. Sure, people get killed in war, and trigger judgments are split-second. But face it – the laughter is what pushed that video past horrible to shameful.

So maybe the U.N. torture investigator's call for a U.S. investigation of all this is just showboating. But then again, maybe not.

Ricks worries that "great newspapers are getting played" by all the Wikileaks fuss. And no doubt many documents do no more than confirm the adage, "War is hell."

But that chestnut can be a truth, or it can be an excuse.

For my part, dismissing the new hellish depths Wikileaks exposed sounds more like an excuse. No amount of mayonnaise will sweeten that verdict.

And by the way, what does mayonnaise do to a power drill?

Chuck Fager is director of Quaker House in Fayetteville.

http://fayobserver.com/articles/2010/11/04/1045210?sac=Opin

Fayetteville NC *Observer* May 19th, 2011

Cost of torture not worth benefits

By Chuck Fager

Let's suppose that the last administration's torture program actually did produce a tip that helped the SEALs hunt down Osama bin Laden. It seems unlikely, given all I've heard, but say it did.

Would that be the vindication the torture defenders want? Would it demolish the cavils of critics like me that even if torture "works," the U.S. government and military shouldn't use it?

I'll skip moral and legal angles here; let's talk practicalities.

The waterboarding (or other torture) that maybe squeezed out an al-Qaida courier's name in 2003 was not an isolated act. It was part of a larger program. And the killing of one man in a mansion in Abbottabad in 2011 was not its only outcome.

Against that benefit of torture, it's only fair, indeed imperative, to weigh the program's costs.

Former Joint Chiefs Chairman Gen. John Shalikashvili listed some of those costs to Congress in 2005. He said it "fostered greater animosity toward the United States, undermined our intelligence-gathering efforts, and added to the risks facing our troops serving around the world."

This warning was reinforced by interrogator Matthew Alexander, who conducted over a thousand interrogations in Iraq, including those of many "high-value" detainees, but without torture.

"When I was in Iraq," he said a few days ago, "I oversaw the interrogations of foreign fighters. And those foreign fighters, the majority of them, said, time and time again, the reason they had come to Iraq to fight was because of the torture and abuse of detainees at both Abu Ghraib and Guantanamo Bay.

"And this is not (only) my opinion. The Department of Defense tracked these statistics. And they were briefed, every interrogator who arrived there, that torture and abuse was al-Qaeda's number one recruiting tool.

"And remember," he added, "these foreign fighters that came to Iraq, they made up 90 percent of the suicide bombers. They killed hundreds, if not thousands, of American soldiers."

U.S. torture contributed directly to the deaths and wounding of

133

thousands of U.S. troops, and many more Iraqis and Afghans.

So, to sum up: on the one side, a big prize – Osama bin Laden.

Yet on the other side, the torture program's cost in lives and national security is undeniably vast and far from played out. Yet were these costs necessary?

Chuck Fager is director of Quaker House in Fayetteville.

Fayetteville NC *Observer* – August 4, 2011

Agent Orange's Painful Legacy

One of the many terms associated with the Vietnam War that evoke strong and often angry reactions.

Why mention it now, and risk stirring those responses again?

Partly, it's the calendar: August 10 will mark fifty years since the first load of powerful defoliant was sprayed by US forces on the Vietnam landscape in 1961. It was the beginning of what was initially called Operation Hades, then was soon renamed and expanded into Operation Ranch Hand.

The name came from the color of the label on the barrels; other defoliant "Agents" used were coded Blue, White, Purple, Pink, and Green. But Agent Orange made up sixty per cent of the sprays.

The idea was that by withering the jungle, Agent Orange would depriveHo Chi Minh's guerillas of cover. And by withering crops, it would help move rural farmers into towns under the control of the SouthVietnamese government.

Over the ten years of Operation Ranch Hand, planes and trucks sprayed some 20 million gallons of such defoliants across parts of Vietnam that added up to an area as large as Massachusetts.

Yet Agent Orange is not only about the painful past. It remains a present specter hanging over many of those who served in the Vietnam War -- and the generations since.

Hundreds of thousands of US troops camped, marched and fought their way through areas heavily sprayed with it. Airmen and sailors handled thousands of barrels of it. And soon after their return home, many veterans began experiencing illnesses, often fatal, that they believed were related to that exposure.

They had good reason for their fears. Most of the defoliant chemicals were contaminated with dioxin, one of the most potent toxic chemicals around. Dioxin has been linked to diabetes, spina bifida and other birth defects, along with various cancers and nerve disorders.

In the US, dioxin made national news in 1978. The Love Canal area of Niagara Falls, New York was found to have been built on a toxic waste dump laced with dioxin.

Surveys showed that as many as half the children born in the neighborhood suffered birth defects or serious childhood illnesses and cancer. After years of local denial, President Jimmy Carter declared a federal emergency there. More than 800 houses were demolished and the families relocated. Love Canal resulted in creation of the federal Superfund program, aimed at cleaning up such toxic sites.

As Love Canal showed, the effects of Agent Orange use in Vietnam were not limited to those who had served there. Among their children, and now grandchildren, there have been higher rates of birth defects and other congenital conditions.

The struggle of these veterans and their families for recognition, treatment, and compensation for Agent Orange-related conditions has been a lengthy and often bitter one. Nor is it over.

But what about the people of Vietnam, who have had to live with the legacy of Agent Orange at close quarters?

Dioxin is a long-lasting toxin. After the rain washes it off the plants, it settles in the soil and the sediment of rivers. There it enters the food chain via fish and ducks, frequent items in the Vietnamese diet.

Their government estimates that up to five million of its people were exposed to long-lived toxic elements of Agent Orange, with up to three million suffering physical symptoms. Many are children and grandchildren of the war generation.

The Vietnam War ended thirty-six years ago. The U.S. Established diplomatic relations with Vietnam sixteen years ago. In 2010, trade between the two nations totaled nearly $19 billion dollars.

In this state of relative amity, Vietnamese support groups have visited the U.S., seeking help from private groups and Congress, and filing lawsuits against the manufacturers.

The lawsuits did not succeed. But their lobbying efforts may have begun to show results. In June, a joint U.S. And Vietnamese government cleanup project was launched at the site of the Da Nang airfield, where large quantities of Agent Orange were stored. Da Nang is one of dozens of "hot spots" in Vietnam where wartime toxic contamination lingers at high levels.

Such cleanup efforts have a long way to go – as does the work of coping with the impact of Agent Orange on US veterans and families.

It has been fifty years since Operation Hades began. For both its American and Vietnamese victims, there has recently been some positive steps taken. But the story of Agent Orange is far from over.

Fayetteville NC *Observer* – Sunday February 26, 2012

Iraq War Over? Officials silent on torture

By Chuck Fager

The Iraq war is over, right? And Afghanistan is winding down.

Well, mostly. But a big unfinished piece of their business recently crossed the North Carolina media horizon. It was like a gray cloud marring the sunny vista of homecoming.

The unfinished business was North Carolina's legacy of torture.

The cloud centered about 40 miles north of here, over a company called Aero Contractors, in Johnston County. But its shadow reached to Cumberland County, too.

On Jan. 19, a faculty-student team from the UNC law school released a damning 75-page report on Aero's years-long involvement in the sordid saga of "extraordinary rendition."

That's doublespeak for torture flights.

Aero's torture connections were not exactly unknown; the New York Times had disclosed the basics in 2005. But the new report pulled together stacks of new evidence from national and international sources.

The report showed that planes from Aero regularly took off from Johnston County's airport. Then they picked up CIA snatch teams, who filled them with blindfolded, chained and drugged detainees. These captives were then carried to torture sites in Europe, Africa and Asia.

After torture and imprisonment, often for years, almost all of Aero's unwilling passengers were ultimately released. Their lives and families were shattered, for nothing.

The report included signed affidavits from two men who were taken to torture in Aero's planes. The statements are dry but harrowing. After years of torture and imprisonment, neither was ever charged with terrorism. There are many more like them.

The UNC team delivered the report first to top staff members of Gov. Bev Perdue and state Attorney General Roy Cooper, calling on them to investigate these amply supported charges.

Then they took it to a press conference at the Johnston County Airport. Aero Contractors is still operating there.

Business must be good: their facilities have expanded, with new, higher fences. Behind them the hundred-plus employees repeat a single mantra: "No comment."

At both places the report's backers emphasized that an investigation is urgently needed above all because torture is a crime.

Not "should be"; it is. It's long been a crime under N.C. law, under federal law. And international law, too.

Law and order. Hardly a new or radical idea.

Neither are the calls for an investigation of Aero. They've been raised by protests at Aero for over six years. But previously, few in the media noticed.

Even now, state officials were studiously noncommital with the UNC team. Beyond a polite welcome, it appears their response to the new report is to ignore it and pretend it never happened.

The chairman of the Johnston County commissioners also shrugged it off, saying Aero was just running a flying taxicab service.

Right: "taxis to the Dark Side, if you will," to quote a former vice president much involved with the whole shameful project.

Fortunately, media around the state did better. The UNC report made news in Raleigh, Charlotte and Winston-Salem and on several TV news shows. It even ran in Johnston County's hometown paper.

The UNC report, and the call for a state probe, also made the big time, as the subject of a major piece in the Washington Post.

Appearing in the Post made Carolina's torture connections an international story. And with each news article, the answering silence at the top in Raleigh grows louder, and more embarrassing for those who are concerned with the state's good name.

Nothing dramatic is likely to come from this spate of exposure soon. Yet report by report, brick by brick, a trail to accountability for Carolina's torture connections is being blazed and paved.

That trail may be long; heck, it's long already. And there may be twists in it – including turns toward Fort Bragg, where the infamous "torture migration" of 2002 went from here to Guantanamo and beyond.

But similar paths have been blazed in several other countries where official torture sullied a heritage of law and justice. And many of those finally reached their goal.

Turning points in these struggles typically involved high officials who broke through the wall of silence and denial and demanded the truth be found, exposed, and acted on.

Let's hope Gov. Perdue and Attorney General Cooper find the fortitude to join that distinguished company.

UNC and the media have done their part. Now it's the state's turn.

Chuck Fager is Director of Quaker House in Fayetteville.

http://fayobserver.com/articles/2012/02/26/1159804?sac=fo.opinion

Fayetteville NC *Observer* – May 13, 2012

Highway Toll "Discounts" open lid on Pandora's Box

Chuck Fager

Uh-oh, I said when I read that some area leaders are ready to sign on with putting tolls on I-95 – as long as we locals can get a "discount."

Memo to Jimmy Keefe, Rick Glazier, Elmer Floyd and other solons: Don't go there! That's like saying, "It'll be OK for Pandora to open her box, just halfway." Or, "We'll let the fox into the henhouse, but only halfway."

Bad idea. Very bad idea.

To see why, let's look at some numbers: The initial toll rates are supposed to be $20 each way, border to border. Suppose we locals get a 50 percent discount; $10 each way.

It sounds better. But that would just be an opener – as in opening a big can of worms.

The toll plan has a built-in inflation escalator, which would jack up the initial tolls by billions of dollars. In fact, the plan figures to spend about $12 billion on the highway – but expects to take in at least $30 billion in toll revenue.

Thirty billion. Out of our pockets.

Discount that, folks, if you can.

It's been rightly said that tolls on I-95 will amount to a heavy tax on the citizens of the I-95 corridor. The planners just don't want to call it that.

And why do they plan to take in $30 billion if the road work will cost "only" $12 billion?

Here's where it gets interesting. Because a search for answers led me to study what's happened to other toll roads. And the answer that popped up again and again was simple, and shocking:

The toll roads get sold off, usually to foreign corporations.

That's where all that extra toll (tax) revenue will most likely go: to some overseas companies' bottom lines.

Think I'm kidding? Check out the Indiana Turnpike (part of Interstate 90): It was sold in 2005 to a joint venture from Australia and Spain. Or the South Bay Expressway in San Diego; same deal.

It was easy enough to do. After all, putting tolls on a freeway

139

"monetizes" the road. That means it can be bought and sold, just like your mortgage.

Did somebody say "mortgage"? Wasn't there a lot of trouble about bad mortgages recently?

Funny thing: The foreign companies "bought" these U.S. roads with borrowed money – that is, mortgages. But then the Southwest Expressway in San Diego went bust. And the Indiana Turnpike's new owners are teetering on the edge. Lots of other toll road deals have had to be, um, "renegotiated" to avoid bankruptcy.

But who's on the hook if such a deal goes sour? Repeat after me: We are. Carolina taxpayers.

How do these fiascoes happen?

The basics are simple: the promoters claimed to know the future. But in fact, they didn't. Their crystal balls were a dud.

The road-planners and corporations all figured American drivers would never stop crowding their lanes and dropping ever more dollars into their toll boxes.

Didn't happen. Traffic – and toll revenue – went down, not up. The companies raised tolls repeatedly, to cover the shortfall. Didn't work.

Looking back, it seems obvious: When the crash threw millions out of work, they quit commuting. Then $4 gas made lots of us cut back on car trips, and lots more drivers, royally ticked off by ever-rising tolls, stayed off those roads entirely. Ah, 20-20 hindsight.

But that's all over, right? Tomorrow is another day, right? And NCDOT is confident its new crystal balls are way better.

Well, maybe they can't tell us if it will rain tomorrow. But they're confident they know what traffic on I-95 will be 20, even 30 years from now.

Really? There's some very colorful Sandhills slang for such ideas. I'll stick with one from my Yankee mother: malarkey.

And add an anguished appeal to our local politicos: Glazier, Keefe, Meredith, Floyd and all the others, from both parties (I'm looking at you, Senators Hagan and Burr):

Please. Put down that cup of discount Kool-Aid, now. Next, step away from that I-95 tolls can of worms. Shove it back on the shelf. Way back.

And then tell NCDOT to go back too: back to the drawing boards. Don't let them turn Interstate 95, our lifeline, into the road to disaster.

Pandora, shut that box, before it's too late!

Chuck Fager is director of Quaker House in Fayetteville and a frequent driver on I-95.

http://www.fayobserver.com/articles/2012/05/13/1177109?sac=fo.opinion

FOUR: Targets of Opportunity – Book Reviews

P. 142 – *Just War Against Terror; the Burden of American Power in a Violent World*, by Jean Bethke Elshtain. Reviewed 2003.

P. 159 – *AWOL: The Unexcused Absence of America's Upper Classes from Military service – and How It Hurts Our Country.* By Kathy Roth-Douquet and Frank Schaeffer. Reviewed 2007.

P. 161 – *Waging Peace: The Art of War for the Antiwar Movement.* Scott Ritter. Reviewed 2007.

P. 163 – *The Dark Side.* By Jane Mayer. And *Never Surrender.* By General (retired) William G. "Jerry" Boykin. Reviewed 2008.

P. 169 – *Wounded,* by Dr. Ronald Glasser: the Hidden, Sky-High Costs of the Iraq War. Reviewed April 2008.

P. 171 – *The Green Zone; The Environmental Costs of Militarism.* By Barry Sanders. Reviewed 2010.

P. 174 – *Hostage in Iraq,* by Norman Kember. *118 days: Christian Peacemaker teams Held Hostage In Iraq.* Tricia gates Brown, Editor. Reviewed 2010.

P. 183 – *To Change The World, The Irony, Tragedy, & Possibility of Christianity in the Late Modern World.* By James Davison Hunter. Reviewed 2011.

P. 191 – *Christianity & War, and Other Essays Against the Warfare State.* Laurence M. Vance. Reviewed 2012.

P. 209 – *Deep Green Resistance: Strategy to Save the Planet.* By Aric McBay, Lierre Keith & Derrick Jensen. Reviewed 2012

From *Quaker Theology* #9, Fall-Winter 2003

Just War Against Terror: The Burden of American Power In a Violent World. Jean Bethke Elshtain. New York: Basic Books, 2003. 240 pages. $23.00

Reviewed by Chuck Fager

I

First a bit of autobiography: Jean Bethke Elshtain and I were both undergraduates at Colorado State University, and late in my time there, we became acquainted. I recall with a smile a party where she, a known intellectual, amazed me by dancing wildly to the Beatles, at a time when I was still holding out against the "British Invasion" as a classical-music snob. Jean was the one who taught me better.

Later, our paths crossed again in Boston, when she was at Brandeis and I was sputtering along at Harvard. There, at some particularly low moments, she was very kind to me, and I still feel gratitude for her personal compassion in time of need.

A lot of water has gone over the dam since then. Jean, who was always headed into the academy, has had what is commonly called a "distinguished career" there, which I, not being an academic, have not followed closely. But my own path does put me in the way of books like *Just War Against Terror*, (JWAT) so I made haste to read it.

Thus it is with regret that I am obliged to report this is a dreadful book, a sub-par example of the genre called "neo-conservative," and one that I hope is not representative of her overall body of work.

II

I'm not the first to say this. Indeed JWAT has overall not fared well among the critics, as we will see below. Leaving aside the predictable kudos from the usual neo-imperial claque (e.g, Paul Berman in the New York Times, whose praise was damningly faint enough at that), even a brief online search shows it being savaged both from left and right.

I wanted, for the personal reasons stated above, to be sympathetic to an author thus besieged, but reading *Just War Against Terror* made it difficult.

The book opens by claiming Albert Camus' help in constructing a straw man image of those who doubt the wisdom of America's new imperial mission and the wars it is spawning, as fools who have "banished the word evil from their vocabularies." They are, she says, mired in a "naivete" which "can get thousands of innocents killed." (1-3) No actual people or statements are identified, but such a transparently underhanded way of painting critics of her argument with the guilt of the September 11 attacks hardly seems the way to avoid tendentiousness in the debate, not to mention responses that might become equally caustic, if less literarily pretentious.

Then she moves on explicitly to Al Queda's attacks, and is soon spending several pages denouncing any attempt to understand or even to speak of what happened in other terms than those of her outrage and calls for vengeance. Any other terms are "misdescription"(16) and are simply, as she says three times, quoting Stephen Carter, "a pile of garbage" (13, 14, 20), or somewhat more loftily, indicative of "moral nihilism." (20)

Taking any other approach is to "traffic in distortions of language that lead to contortions of moral meaning," (11) though how we are thereby to understand what the belief in "martyrdom" could teach us about their pathological worldview (a very useful step, most intelligence agencies would agree, in ferreting them out and stopping them) is not explained, and evidently not her concern.

For Elshtain, Al Queda and their attacks represent, not instruments of "mass murder" (20) but the "heart of darkness," (12) and in dealing with them, "no political solution is possible." (19) With all this scorn and ridicule as preamble, it is hard to avoid the sense that the "robust politics of democratic argument" (20) the book claims to favor flows from a well poisoned from the outset.

Such generalized demonization of critics, actual and potential, is an all-too familiar neo-conservative rhetorical strategy, which I have encountered and exposed before. (Fager: 1992) Only a few days before this review was finished, Richard Perle, a central neo-conservative figure, repeated it almost casually at a televised Hudson Institute forum on the prospects for the "Neo-conservative moment," noting that the movement's critics are "living in a fantasy world," and that they are persons in whom "visceral anti-Americanism runs deeper than any other value." There was no challenge to these comments from the audience or most of the other panelists; they are taken as established truisms by this constituency. Only the token non-neo-con panelist, Joshua Micah Marshall, voiced even a tepid dissent.

For Elshtain, this book marks a major departure from the more measured, ambivalent tone of her 1992 essay, "Just War as Politics: What the Gulf War Taught US About Contemporary American Life." (Decosse) That essay was somber, even melancholy, and declined to render a definite judgment on the 1991 war:

> . . . As we draw up the balance sheet in the matter of the Gulf War, whose effects will be felt for years to come, we must do so not only in mind of the strategic brilliance of the Desert Storm campaign, with its remarkable tote sheet "in our favor" on all counts, including combatant lives, but also in mind of malnourished Iraqi children; alongside breaking the war machine of an aggressive and despotic power. We must weigh the breaking of fundamental human relationships, some at their most fragile point, in the early weeks and months of lives as parents, especially mothers, and children were separated: in the same breath as we marvel over the peaceful taking and decent treatment of thousands of Iraqi prisoners of war, we must recount, with appropriate unease, the frenzied destruction of defenseless Iraqis on the "Highway of Death."

> The celebrations are over. The bands have played. The soldiers have marched. The confetti has fallen, creating multicolored drifts on city streets. Now is the time to get sober and to remember what St. Augustine taught: war and strife, however just the cause, stir up temptations to ravish and to devour, often in order to ensure peace. . . . de Tocqueville warned that military greatness was pleasing to the imagination of a democratic people. He feared the ephemeral but corrupting luster of such greatness. So does the just war thinker. (59, 60)

III

No such temporizing dilutes the righteous fervor of JWAT; evidently any lingering doubts were consumed in the smoke of the Twin Towers. Here all the important conclusions are made clear before the book gets to the just-war casuistry, "The Burden of American Power" that is its subtitle and Elshtain's ostensible main subject. And what of the book's version of the just war theory?

While less than twelve months old, the arguments in Just War Against Terror, (JWAT) have not worn well as a theological-ethical justification for the ongoing war. That's partly because the ink had barely dried on her elaborately anticipatory defense of the Bush regime's rationale for attacking Iraq, when this rationale evaporated in the unexpected, unfinished outcome of the actual war.

For instance, "By the time this book appears in print," she notes, ". . .we may be embarked upon the perilous course of a war against Iraq in order to force a murderous regime to disarm." (7; emphasis added.) When written, this was a faithful rendition of the line of the moment; how quaint it sounds now, only a year or so later, when the Washington regime's explanations have moved from it through warding off imminent attack by weapons of mass destruction, to eliminating the potential for such weapons, to freeing Iraqis from a murdering tyrant, to simply shrugging off questions of justification in the face of the fait accompli the occupation seems to have become. As George W. Bush said to a TV interviewer in December 2003, "So what's the difference?" (Stevenson)

But for me, what most undermines the book's staying power is something else: the fact that when all its intellectual posturing is done, all the references to old Church Fathers and new ideologues have been trotted out, the linchpin of her thesis – that America, as the "world's sole superpower," has acquired (actually, JWAT states that this right was "thrust upon it" [151]) both the right and duty to set the world straight, and has the capacity to do so – this notion is crumbling before our eyes.

Whether the US indeed has acquired any such "right" (even if phrased as a "burden") is, to say the least, debatable, even if it is expressed as guaranteeing "only" what Elshtain repeatedly calls "minimal civic peace." (46ff, 107, 187) I for one do not believe it. And whether our present level of military power gives the US government has a duty and a license to make war for this "civic peace" wherever it deems such lacking (and by her definition it is lacking in too much of the world) is likewise debatable, though here a stronger case can be made, at least for some cases such as Rwanda and Bosnia.

But even if one were to grant Elshtain's belief in this right and duty – which despite her ritualistic mantra of purported qualifying and balancing seems reliably to come out exactly where the current White House wants to go – there remains a thorny third query: Is the US really as "super" a power as she so totally believes?

IV

She approaches this question from her position as a fixture of the academic conference and issues-seminar circuit, which a casual websearch suggests she rides almost nonstop

Her knowledge base was also, it seems, immensely expanded in October of 2001, when she was among the august group of forty religious figures ushered into the Oval Office for a two-hour session with its occupant back in October of 2001. Besides yielding an evidently in-depth personal understanding of the administration's character and leadership, this meeting also appeared to be something of a spiritual epiphany for her. Either that or a groupie's dream come true; the breathless account of it written for her university colleagues leaves the reader unsure which rubric

145

is more heuristic. (Elshtain: 2001)

I come at this from a different place, not in the academy but hard by the gates of Fort Bragg, North Carolina, one of the largest and most important military bases in the so-called "war on terror." And from here this issue of capability dwarfs the others, and offers the truest, most damning measure of the hubristic illusion on which is built what JWAT – approvingly acknowledges as "imperialism.'" (166ff) I have argued that this self-assumed "mission" can be more accurately termed "messianic hegemonism" (Fager: 2003); but we'll use her term as a shorthand here.

To get at this "superpower" question, it's worth attempting some precision regarding the term, which Elshtain does not pause to define. In the strict military sense, what this now means, as I see it, is that the US war machine is able to go farther, and deliver more destructive force than any other existing military force, or combination of forces, and perhaps any other in history. It also means that few if any other militaries can effectively oppose such strikes, at least in the short term. In army jargon, the US can "break things and kill people" with unparalleled reach and efficacy. To this extent, the term "superpower" fits.

But this is only the beginning phase of exercising the "right" and "duty" of creating and enforcing "basic civic peace" in the world, or at least that much of it as the US regime chooses to notice. Installing such a "peace" in a place like, say, Iraq, also means occupying it, for an indefinite period. But unlike destruction, which has been largely technologized, occupation-cum-reconstruction takes, again to use army jargon, "boots on the ground." A great many boots.

And there's the rub. Elshtain's mission for the US is built on abstractions, hardly unusual for an academic. But occupation/pacification is a very concrete undertaking. It takes not only weapons, but many other human skills, linguistic and cultural to name but two. And what is already painfully clear is that the "world's sole superpower" is radically "un-super"and massively under-equipped for this part of the imperial mission. Woefully, even pathetically so. Moreover, as it pursues these projects, its forces are indeed vulnerable, particularly to bloody guerilla insurgencies like that now tormenting Iraq.

V

Thus, our "superpower" status, while real, is much more limited and dubious than its more enthusiastic advocates presume.

How is that possible?

It's simple, actually: the US has far too few troops and other skilled personnel for what Elshtain's soulmates at the Project for a New American Century confidently refer to as "constabulary duty," a phrase selected, no doubt, with a wink and a nod to Gilbert and Sullivan.

146

(Project) But the actual work of establishing "minimum civic peace" in Iraq is proving to be something other than a comic opera. Besides taking mounting casualties, the US forces there are also stretched to the breaking point, and beyond. (Hockstader)

One may not get much a of a sense of this at scholarly confabs in world-class hotels; but its ground-level reality is confirmed concretely every day in my work here at Quaker House. Yet one need not be a peace movement "grunt" to understand. Numerous eminent military and strategic figures who could hardly be tarred with the peacenik label have made this point analytically and cogently.

Not that the war party hasn't tried to tar them. When General Eric Shinseki, a Vietnam veteran who lost a foot in combat there, told a Congressional committee last winter that occupation of Iraq would require 500,000 troops or more, his testimony was dismissed by "a high administration official" as "bullshit from a Clintonite." (Vest)

Whatever Shinseki's political opinions might be, his numbers have gained considerable credibility since then. They were resurfaced and buttressed in November 2003 by no less a hawk than strategist Edward Luttwak. In a stinging *New York Times* analysis, aptly titled "So Few Soldiers, So Much To Do," he made a similar case. (Luttwak) And such technically civil exchanges aside, the casualty figures from Iraq underline their credibility daily.

So that's just for Iraq, which along with Afghanistan are merely the beginning of the list of societies that meet and surpass the Elshtain/neoconservative criteria for calls on US power to establish "minimal civic peace." But the plain truth is we don't have enough human beings under arms to achieve anything near that in either place. It is not even plausible, never mind realistic, without a uniformed military several times the size of our current 1.4 million force. The task becomes even more massive if one factors in the unmet demands of "homeland security," guarding vulnerable points within the US. (Tilford)

For me, this concrete test of capability throws the fantasy of new American empire, even in its most scholastically ethicized "civic peace" guise, into a cocked hat.

Why? Two reasons: One, this nation, yea even the "world's only superpower," can't afford the imperial war machine it now has in action, never mind the behemoth here envisioned.

Second, if the US did manage to raise, finance and equip the uniformed force required, doing so would turn the nation into a different, wholly militarized state, of the sort that peopled the last century's nightmares.

VI

It seemed odd to me that Elshtain does not see these clear implications of her thesis, but that is a common neoconservative blind spot. The nub of this US mission is laid out especially in her Chapter 12, "American Power and Responsibility" (161-173), and perhaps the best summary is:

> The principle I call "equal regard" underlies the Universal Declaration of Human Rights, just as it lies at the heart of our Declaration of Independence and Lincoln's matchless Gettysburg Address. But equal regard, as the American founders knew, as Lincoln understood, and as we are coming to understand, must sometimes be backed up by coercive force. This is an ideal of international justice whose time has come. Equal regard is a mixture of old norms given new urgency and new possibilities.
>
> Some will understandably query: If the claim to justice as equal regard applies to all persons without distinction, shouldn't an international body be its guarantor and enforcer? Perhaps. But in our less-than-ideal world, the one candidate to guarantee this principle is the United States, for two reasons: Equal regard is the foundation of our own polity; and we are the only superpower. (168)

Thus wrapped in the Declaration of Independence, the Gettysburg Address, and the mantle of the martyred Lincoln, this notion is supposed to be beyond question by any loyal American. But look closer: enforcing these standards, as interpreted in JWAT, on the international scene is what is now required, and the US is the only one competent, both morally and militarily, to do the enforcing.

This is a very tall order. Reading these sections of JWAT, I kept hearing the echo of Jesus in the Gospel of Luke: "For which of you, desiring to build a tower, does not first sit down and count the cost, whether he has enough to complete it? . . . Or what king, going to encounter another king in war, will not sit down first and take counsel whether he is able with ten thousand to meet him who comes against him with twenty thousand?" (14:28, 31) Elshtain twice mentions the issue of cost as a "prudential" aspect of just war thinking, but then essentially shrugs it off. (58, 173, 178)

From this base, her treatment of the just war canons, despite a pose of dispassion and independence, has a remarkably similar outcome, namely that of dismantling any potential bar it might raise to US plans for war and military dominance.

Just cause? Under the flag of establishing minimal civic order in the world, it can be whatever the US regime decides it is.

Right authority? As we saw in early 2003 at the United Nations, the US makes its own. And the US rulers, because of our superior "democratic values," have all the legitimacy they need, regardless of what any other state or body might say. Elshtain's disdain for the UN and other international institutions, a marker of the neocon ethos, is palpable. (127f;162-166)

Last resort? This now means only that non-military options need to be "explored" by the US rulers (61). For how long, one wonders – an hour? Moreover, with our adversaries, she repeats, "there is nothing to negotiate about." (61)

A reasonable chance of success? Even in the case of Afghanistan, the results in mid-2002 when JWAT was written obliged her to admit that "I cannot pronounce with any degree of certainty that this criterion has been met."(62) One doubts she could say much more at the end of 2003. But as she also notes, such judgments are "always tricky"(62), so perhaps she can be forgiven for disregarding them. This is another instance where she seems unable to see beyond the myth of American "superpower" omnipotence. One might wonder how she would rate the success of the ongoing war in Iraq; but as JWAT amounts to an advance justification of whatever happens, the answer is regrettably not much in doubt.

Imminent threat? If a possible threat could someday become imminent, that's imminent enough. (54;57f;166-173) Or to quote again the chief executive carrying out the policy, "So what difference does it make?"

Discrimination and proportionality? The mangling of the previous criteria are bad enough, but it is on these latter two points that the book's argument reaches its nadir. Elshtain is fully satisfied that,

Those of us who have studied this matter in detail, however, know that a basic norm of US military training is the combatant- noncombatant distinction the principle of discrimination. We know that American soldiers are trained to refuse to obey illegal orders under the code of restraints called the "laws of war," derived in large measure from the historic evolution of the just war tradition and its spin-offs as encoded in international conventions and arrangements.

US. military training films include generous helpings of what went wrong' in various operations. "Wrong" refers not only to US. military losses but also to operations that led to the unintentional loss of civilian life. These films ask: How can such losses be prevented in the future in a theater of war?" (21)

She also cites a senior navy officer, asserting to the *New York Times* that "With precision-guided weapons, you don't have to use as many bombs to achieve the desired effects, and using fewer weapons reduces the risk of collateral damage."(66-67) "Many agencies and groups, as well as the US military, are continually trying to get an accurate count." (120; emphasis added)

Very nice. Her confidence is touching in its self-assurance. And startling in its blatant naivete.

VII

"In our quest for answers," JWAT has admonished us, "we should not take comfort in banalities and nostrums." (180) Sound advice. But when the book turns from Augustine and medieval popes to the twenty-first century, Elshtain has somehow, despite her detailed study, and the round of academic fora, managed to remain utterly innocent of the thunderous ethical fact that during its last three major wars (Vietnam and the two Gulf conflicts), the US military has refused as a matter of stated policy to make any accounting whatever of civilian casualties in these campaigns. None. Zip.

"I don't believe you have heard me or anyone else in our leadership talk about the presence of 1,000 bodies out there, or in fact how many have been recovered,' Gen. Tommy Franks, commander of the Afghanistan operation, said Monday (March 18, 2002) at Bagram Air Base. – You know we don't do body counts.'" (Epstein)

This see-no-evil, report-no-evil policy is well-attested, and has been repeatedly criticized, to no effect, even by confirmed pro-military specialists. One was the *Washington Post*'s William Arkin, who wrote this from Afghanistan, where he was with a Human Rights Watch team investigating civilian casualties:

Throughout the Afghanistan campaign, the Pentagon asserted that the U.S. effort was the least deadly military campaign in history. The Pentagon, however, has no factual basis for which to make such a judgment and it is doing little to study or substantiate its self-congratulatory line. (Arkin, April 2002; emphasis added)

A year later, his judgment was even more blunt:

Over the past few months, I've been struck by how many times senior officers and officials have insisted that the level of civilian deaths in Afghanistan is low. This isn't a case of military secrecy where they know something we don't. The Pentagon can't say low compared to what, how low, nor if the low they describe is good enough. The U.S. military can assert all it wants that it takes "all" measures to minimize civilian harm. But until it is willing to actually study why civilians die in conflict, it is an assertion that has little credibility. (Arkin, February 2003; emphasis added.)

When Helen Thomas, the senior White House correspondent, asked the Pentagon how many Iraqis had been killed in the latest war, she was told, " They don't count. They are not important.'" She later wrote, "Remember the enemy body counts during the Vietnam War? Some of those U.S. tabulations were highly exaggerated in an effort to show gains on the battlefield.

"Well, we don't do that anymore."(Thomas)

And the *Washington Post*, in what can be considered a definitive statement on the current Iraq war, reported on April 5, 2003 that the "U.S. Has No Plans to Count Civilian Casualties." Beneath this headline was a remarkably terse statement of military defiance of Congress: "The Pentagon said yesterday that it has no plans to determine how many Iraqi civilians may have been killed or injured or suffered property damage as a result of U.S. military operations in Iraq.

"The statement followed passage Saturday of a congressional measure calling on the Bush administration to identify and provide – appropriate assistance' to Iraqi civilians for war losses." (Graham)

Numerous other corroborative citations could be included, without even a detailed study. We will only note that this stonewalling continued through December of 2003, when it was extended by Occupation authorities to the Iraqi Health Ministry, whose officials were ordered to stop keeping tallies of civilian deaths. (Jackson)

This last points toward another level of disingenuousness in such "careful discrimination" arguments. In the 1991 Iraq war, there were many public utilities destroyed with more or less precise bombing and missile attacks. Their explosions hit few civilians nearby. But then with these utilities destroyed, thousands of civilians, especially the elderly and children, died of disease and lack of basic resources. Any honest moral accounting has to include this predictable "downstream" death toll as part of its calculation of "collateral damage." Yet any such accounting would call the "discrimination" and proportionality" arguments fatally into question. Ignoring them, as the U.S. military had steadfastly done, and is also done in JWAT, is no more than the equivalent of averting one's eyes from the bodies on the side of the road from Jericho. There is every reason to believe that a similar toll is building in Iraq today. The official response? Suppress the information. The heart cries out: have they no shame?

VIII

This policy of total denial raises issues both procedural and substantive for just-war theorists. When the "world's only superpower" declines even to enter the discussion of whether its real wars live up to its stated ethical standards for warmaking, how is the calculus that can give meaning to just war thought supposed to take place? And more substantively, how can the credibility of these stated standards be

151

maintained in the face of such a policy of refusal?

My conclusion is that they cannot, and on this ground alone the just war calculus fails when applied to the U.S. war machine.

This leaves aside the abundant evidence that the best available estimates of total civilian deaths in two of these three conflicts (Vietnam, Iraq I and II) are in seven figures – evidence which, because it is perforce unofficial, can be and is shrugged off or ignored by those who advocate the new US imperium. (White) It is telling, I think, that when JWAT trumpets the purported extremity of care the US military devotes to avoiding civilian casualties, no specific or primary sources are cited in corroboration; not even the training films are identified.

But even when confronted with this data of defiance, JWAT still has an escape hatch: it has declared these civilian deaths, morally almost weightless, because they are, she has been assured, unintended:

Every civilian death is a tragedy," the book tells us, "but not every civilian death is a crime. . . . Contrast the gleeful reaction of bin Laden and his cohorts to the collapse of the twin towers with the widely broadcast apologies of America's top military leaders, including, on occasion, the chairman of the Joint Chiefs of Staff, for errant American bombs, whether in Afghanistan or elsewhere, and for any and all unintended civilian deaths. (4f)

So it appears that superior democratic values means occasionally having to say you're sorry; at least when large numbers of civilians are killed in view of the media, and otherwise assuring ingenuous academics that you're doing your best. But not having actually to account for the killing.

Further, this foreign casualty total needs to be augmented, again based on the work at my ground-level position beside a major military base: well over 500,000 US troops who survived these wars were nonetheless made their permanent victims, by Agent Orange, Gulf War Syndrome, severe PTSD, and other war maladies. (Vlahos, Arison, National Coalition for the Homeless) And while it is still relatively early in the latest Iraq war, the likely crop of its domestic victims shows signs of equally gruesome promise as well. In any honest just war calculus, these US citizen victims deserve to be counted as well, and like the Iraqis they are not here.

For this grim reality is substituted a dependence on the banalities of a few army training films, and the nostrums of unnamed naval officers assuring The New York Times that all is well. Such a record puts the book's argument for "discrimination and proportionality" almost beyond the need for further examination.

Yet one more point: JWAT insists that in the US military, "No one is encouraged, or even allowed, to call the killing of civilians – God's will' or, even worse, an act carried out in God's name."(21)

No doubt she was told so, and found words to this effect in her detailed studies, though again no source is cited. But as her confident words were being written, General William G. "Jerry" Boykin, a key figure in the Pentagon's war, was traveling the country, loudly preaching just such toxic stuff. He was doing so in uniform; but not, one supposes, at the scholarly conference the author frequents. And when he was finally exposed, his superiors snickered and did nothing. (Leiby)

Added up, these failings bring to mind another damning review of the book, at the top of the customer-feedback section of Amazon.com. The heading tells it all: "Embarrassing."

IX

Yet credit where it is due: Elshtain makes some very valid points about how widespread is the teaching of violence and hatred for US values by some Muslim groups, how oppressively most Muslim countries are governed, and how ignorant of Islam and Islamic culture most Americans are including, she is less clear to say our policymakers, and how dangerous such ignorance is. When she lays some of this American ignorance to the refusal of many in the academy to take religion seriously, there is likely no little truth in that as well.

These insights do not redeem the book, however, because they weigh just as heavily (I would say more so) against the new US imperial overreach as for it. There is plenty of evidence that the "war on terror" and the new American "burden" is as much a threat to the world's "minimal civic peace" as its protector. Moreover, despite its preoccupation with Catholic thought and papal teaching, JWAT's credibility in this regard too is steadily undermined by its blatantly tendentious and unfair treatment of Pope John Paul II – otherwise the hero of every neocon Catholic (and almost-sort-of-quasi-not-quite Catholic like JWAT's author). (Zoba)

At first blush, her regard for the Pope would seem to be limitless. She decries how the Pope was "ignored in intellectual circles" (73) when he denounced communism in the 1980s. Then early on she demands, "Whose description of September 11 am I going to trust? That of a person who disdains any distinction between combatants and noncombatants . . . or that of John Paul II," who has called these acts an "unspeakable horror." She finds this quite proper papal description so comforting that it is quoted four times (9,12,16,121).

But then JWAT, like other Romish neo-con tomes, is only too quick to distrust, and entirely ignore, John Paul's even more eloquent, and much more often repeated, condemnations of the Iraq war (both of them), as well as the "burden" of US imperialism and pre-emptive warfare that underlie it.

For that matter, in their studied rebukes, the Pope and his close advisers cited just those issues of last resort, imminence, and proportionality that have weighed so heavily here and with other critics of the book. As Catholic writers Mark and Louise Zwick succinctly put it, "John Paul II has sought to distance the Catholic Church from George Bush's idea of the manifest Christian destiny of the United States"; they also point out that Cardinal Ratzinger, the watchdog of orthodoxy, repeatedly declared that "The concept of a 'preventive war' does not appear in the Catechism of the Catholic Church." (Zwick)

The bulk of JWAT's Chapter 8, "The Pulpit Responds to Terror," is devoted to scoffing at the many statements by US religious leaders condemning the Iraq and Afghanistan wars, and the imperial doctrine they herald. But then she skims completely around the Pope's many statements making exactly the same point, noting only in passing that the pontiff is a "near-pacifist." (16) One wonders how even a non-world-class scholar could have missed them; the Holy See's website reserves an entire section for his statements on peace. (Vatican)

X

The gist of these papal misgivings is becoming clear to an increasing portion of the educated public. This perhaps accounts for why JWAT has overall fared poorly in the reviews, and here it is worth noting some of this reaction.

One striking review came from the right, by David Gordon of the "classical liberal/Austrian school" *Mises Review*. He was merciless in pointing up numerous historical and logical errors, deftly exposing JWAT's manipulation of just-war theorizing, and concluding archly that "Students cramming for a history final will be ill advised to use her works as a substitute for a diligent perusal of Cliffs Notes . . . Evidently she needs a remedial course in logic as well as several in history."

From another perspective (the "left"?), theological ethicist Stanley Hauerwas joined with Paul Griffiths to let JWAT have it with both barrels on the author's own turf, the neocon journal *First Things*, blasting it . . . "as nothing more than an uncritical justification of the ideology of America as empire. It is itself a deeply ideological work rather than one of careful and critical thought."

Then they told us how they really felt:

Put more bluntly: when America sees states organized on principles it doesn't like (this is what Elshtain means by "failed states") it should

154

remake them by force (if necessary) into states organized on principles it does like. These principles will be those of rights-based democracies with free economies that is, countries like the United States. This new imperialism means that the more a state diverges from American principles, the more pressing will be America's duty to remake it in its own image. This is a heavy burden to bear, for a moment's thought shows that a high proportion of the world's states diverge deeply and systematically from American principles. If Elshtain's program were followed, perhaps thirty or so invasions and nation-buildings on the Iraqi model would be immediately required.

So much for Elshtain's position. Kipling thought the white man's burden heavy; on Elshtain's view America's similar burden is immeasurably heavier . . . . In the end, the use of Christian language and ideas in this book is nothing more than window-dressing for a passion to impose America upon the world. It is not a book whose argument should convince Christians; it is not a book whose argument should convince anyone thoughtful; it is a book and here, out of respect for its author, we do not mince words informed by jingoistic dreams of empire. (Hauerwas)

XI

Both essays drew outraged replies from the stung reviewee: a long letter to Gordon at the *Mises Review* denounced its "snide and caustic tone," and insisted that the suggestion about a remedial course in logic "could only have been written by a crude positivist, a sexist, or both." (Which, one wonders, is the worse epithet?)

And she complained to *First Things* that, "When confronted by a review so tendentious and unfair, it is hard to know where to begin a response." Perhaps not, but she nonetheless knew how to end one, by falling back on the basic neo-conservative ad hominem reflex, clothed, as is typical here, in the words of some reputedly eminent authority. In this case it was Francis Cardinal George of Chicago, who reportedly once said "'in reference to America's radical critics that you cannot effectively criticize what you loathe.' Perhaps," Elshtain writes, "this loathing explains the sour tone of the Hauerwas and Griffiths collaboration." (Hauerwas)

Perhaps; but I doubt it. More likely it is is reaping what has been sown: Can a writer whose own book poured gall in the well of discourse not expect to find wormwood in her cup? My guess is that they were simply as able to spot a "pile of garbage" as the next person.

Elshtain leans heavily at points on Reinhold Niebuhr's critique of sentimental idealism (106-111), and it still carries much force. Yet there's little sign here of his balancing insistence on the "irony of American history," which can turn our political culture's many virtues into vices for us and risks to the world. Niebuhr supported World War II, but he opposed Vietnam; one wonders where he would come down today.

Elshtain may not be able to bear it, but the idea that America could become, may be becoming, as much a threat to the world's "minimal civic peace" as its fanatical Muslim enemies is one that deserves to be, nay must be on the table of our personal and public deliberations. Could it be that in efforts to ward off one kind of "unspeakable horror," we may tragically be preparing the way for another? Niebuhr might not have said yes, but I doubt if he would have refused to let the question be raised; such paradox and irony fits only too well with the best of his mature thought.

Neo-conservatives can demonize the question and the questioners all they want, but from here at the foot of the war machine, that appalling prospect looms larger with each passing month. With it comes the growing imperative to find another, better way to overcome terror and promote the "minimal civic peace" she seeks.

What is saddest to me about JWAT is that I am sure that if Jean Bethke Elshtain applied her skills and scholarship to the work of finding ways to prevent such an outcome, her contribution could be exceptional.

But *Just War Against Terror* is not it.

WORKS CITED

Arkin, William, "Checking on Civilian Casualties," *Washington Post*, dot.mil April 9, 2002
http://www.washingtonpost.com/ac2/wp-dyn/A13327-2002Apr8?language=printer

Arkin, William, "Not Good Enough, Mr. Rumsfeld," *Washington Post*, dot.mil , February 25, 2003.
http://www.washingtonpost.com/ac2/wp-dyn/A63267-2002Feb25

Arison, H. Lindsey III, "THE COVER-UP OF GULF WAR SYNDROME – A QUESTION OF NATIONAL INTEGRITY,"
http://www.gulfwarvets.com/arison/gws.htm

Elshtain, Jean Bethke, "An Extraordinary Discussion," *Sightings* 10/03/01   Date: Wed, 03 Oct 2001 09:50:34 -0500
http://marty-center.uchicago.edu/sightings/archive_2001/sightings-100301.shtml

Elshtain, Jean Bethke, "Just War as Politics: What the Gulf War Taught

US About Contemporary American Life," in David E. Decosse, Ed., *But Was It Just? Reflections on the Morality of the Persian Gulf War*, Doubleday, New York: 1992.

Epstein, Edward, "Success in Afghan War Hard to Gauge," *San Francisco Chronicle,* March 23, 2002.
http://www.globalsecurity.org/org/news/2002/020323-attack01.htm

Fager, Chuck, "Gulf War (1991) Books Review." Published in the *Washington City Paper*, 1992. Online at: www.afriendlyletter.com

Fager, Chuck, *A Quaker Declaration of War*, Kimo Press, 2003.

Graham, Bradley, and Morgan, Dan, "U.S. Has No Plans to Count Civilian Casualties," *Washington Post,* April 15, 2003.
http://www.washingtonpost.com/wp-dyn/articles/A26305-2003Apr14.html

Hauerwas, Stanley and Griffiths, Paul J., "War, Peace & Jean Bethke Elshtain," *First Things* 136 (October 2003): 41-47.
http://www.firstthings.com/ftissues/ft0310/articles/hauerwas.html

Hockstader, Lee, "Army Stops Many Soldiers From Quitting: Orders Extend Enlistments to Curtail Troop Shortages," *Washington Post*, December 29, 2003; Page A01.

Hudson Institute, "Is The Neoconservative Moment Over?" December 15, 2003, Washington, D.C.
http://www.hudson.org/index.cfm?fuseaction=hudson_upcoming_events&id=153 (The Perle quotes are from the C-SPAN video, which was posted briefly on the C-SPAN website.)

Jackson, Derrick Z., "U.S. Evades Blame for Iraqi Deaths," *Boston Globe*, December 12, 2003.
http://www.boston.com/news/globe/editorial_opinion/oped/articles/2003/12/12/us_evades_blame_for_iraqi_deaths?mode=PF

Leiby, Richard, "Christian Soldier: Lt. Gen. William Boykin Is Inspiring Faith in Some and Doubt in Others," *Washington Post,* November 6, 2003. page C01.
http://www.washingtonpost.com/ac2/wp-dyn/A6529-2003Nov5?language=printer

Luttwak, Edward, "So Few soldiers, So Much To Do," *New York Times,*

November 4, 2003.
http://www.nytimes.com/2003/11/04/opinion/04LUTT.html?th

National Coalition for the Homeless, "Homeless Veterans: NCH Fact Sheet #9." April 1999
http://www.nationalhomeless.org/veterans.html

Project for a New American Century, "Rebuilding America's Defenses."
http://www.newamericancentury.org/RebuildingAmericasDefenses.pdf

Stevenson, Richard W., "RememberWeapons of Mass Destruction'? For Bush, They Are a Nonissue." *New York Times* December 18, 2003.
http://www.nytimes.com/2003/12/18/politics/18PREX.html?th

Thomas, Helen, "Who's Counting the Dead in Iraq?" *The Miami Herald,* September 5, 2003.
http://www.miami.com/mld/miamiherald/news/opinion/6695128.htm

Tilford, Earl H., Jr.,"Redefining Homeland Security."
http://www.carlisle.army.mil/ssi/conf/2001/homesec.htm

Vatican, "Peace on Earth . . ." (Special section, Vatican website)
http://www.vatican.va/holy_father/special_features/peace/prayer-peace_index.html

Vlahos, Kelley Beaucar, "Many Homeless in U.S. Are Veterans," November 27, 2003
http://www.foxnews.com/story/0,2933,104184,00.html

White, Matthew, "Death Tolls for the Man-made Megadeaths of the 20th Century"   Vietnam
http://users.erols.com/mwhite28/warstatz.htm
http://users.erols.com/mwhite28/warstat2.htm#Vietnam

Zoba, Wendy Murray, "Civic Housekeeping: Jean Elshtain on Mothering and other duties," *Christian Century*, May 17, 2003.
http://www.findarticles.com/cf_dls/m1058/10_120/102140728/p1/article.jhtml

Zwick, Mark and Louise, "Pope John Paul II Calls War a Defeat for Humanity: Neoconservative Iraq Just War Theories Rejected," *Houston Catholic Worker Newspaper*, July-August 2003
http://www.cjd.org/paper/jp2war.html

AWOL: The Unexcused Absence of America's Upper Classes – from Military Service— and How It Hurts Our Country. By Kathy – Roth-Douquet and Frank Schaeffer. 248 pages, Collins 2006.

The two authors of *AWOL,* Kathy Roth-Douquet & Frank Schaeffer, – grew up as children of privilege. They don't apologize for this, nor have they left this milieu behind as adults. But along their own life paths, each took a turn that, given their heritage, they never expected: they became familiar with the military.

Their respective encounters Roth-Douquet married a Marine, and Schaeffer's son joined the Corps opened their eyes to what they now feel is a very important reality, namely that: "People like us educated, urban, in careers where you make good money, and interested in the good life, good food, travel–entire extended communities of people like us, *know nothing about the military.*"(Emphasis added.)

And in the course of time, this discovery brought them to an equally unexpected conclusion, which is the premise of the book: "We are trying to make the case here that this ignorance is not okay. .. [and] the growing gap between many civilians and the military is a bad thing."

It needs to be said here that much of the rest of their argument does not persuade me – they largely buy into the notion that since the end of World War Two, and especially since the end of the Cold War, the US: "[found] itself with unparalleled responsibilities for maintaining world order. ... Nations might complain about American 'hegemony,' but . . . whenever real trouble brewed, the cry went up on all sides: where are the Americans? Why don't they *do* something?" (Emphasis in original.)

But I mention this larger worldview only to firmly set it aside. The value of this book is not in the authors' politics (which are not, in any case, particularly reactionary), or their view of war, but rather in their crucially important, dead-on insights into culture and class, viewed across the canyon of the growing and deepening civilian-military divide.

As they put it: "The evidence is that those who serve and those who don't are looking at each other with growing uneasiness and across a widening philosophical, ideological, political, and even religious social gap."

On this I agree with them almost one hundred per cent, and would go further than they, and insist that this divide is as harmful to pacifists and other peace-minded folk as it is to anyone else, perhaps more so.

They point out that, among other indicators, "Today, the number of congressmen and congresswomen who are also veterans is only about one-third what it was a generation ago, in 1969, and it is falling fast. Only slightly more than one percent of members of Congress have a child serving." [NOTE: the percentage of vetereans in Congress has continued to fall since then.]

To which I could add similar data from extensive travels among Quakers and other settled peace folk (other than the antiwar veterans). This, my friends, is *a very serious problem*, which there is not enough space here to explore fully. But reading and reflecting on *AWOL* would be a very good way to begin.

Waging Peace: The Art of War for the Antiwar Movement. Scott Ritter.
New York: Nation Books, 175 pages, paper, $13.95.

Reviewed by Chuck Fager

I looked forward to reading this book. Since moving next door to a
major military base, I have been impressed with the idea of strategic
thinking and planning, and concerned at the lack of it in the wider peace
constituency of which Quaker House is a part.

Most peace action planning I have seen is very short-term, and
narrowly on what in military terms are tactics. And tactical thinking alone
is grossly inadequate. To quote the patron saint of this field, Sun Tzu,
"Tactics without strategy is the noise before defeat."

Scott Ritter, who was a top UN weapons inspector in Iraq after the
first Gulf War, began his career as a Marine officer. He knows his Sun
Tzu, author of The Art of War, the towering classic in this field. So I
figured his book should be an excellent way to fill this gap.

In many ways it is. Ritter's critical analysis of the peace movement is
sharp but apt: The anti-war movement lacks any notion of strategic
thinking, operational planning, or sense of sound tactics. . . . As a result,
when the anti-war movement does get it right (and on occasion it does),
the success is frittered away. . . . In short, the anti-war movement is little
more than a walk-on squad of high school football players drawing plays
in the sand, taking on the National Football League Super Bowl
Champions.

These weaknesses are the more damaging because:

America is pre-programmed for war, and unless the anti-war
movement dramatically changes the manner in which it conducts its
struggle, America will become a nation of war, for war, and defined by
war, and as such a nation that will ultimately be consumed by war.

To have a chance of changing this programming, Ritter urges above
all that peace folk need to start thinking like a warrior . . . .

"Start thinking like a warrior." I echo this in my workshops, and
neither Ritter nor I mean by it that anyone should prepare to be violent or
militaristic. Above all, it's a call to take seriously learning to think and
plan strategically. The stakes are very high.

Ritter introduces some key elements of strategic thinking and planning. But Ritter's sense of the peace movement seems weak, perhaps colored by his military background. There is no central leadership," he complains. " . . . it operates as little more than controlled chaos . . . ." True enough. And yet . . .

His proposed remedy: The anti-war movement needs to develop its own [Incident Command System] that is universally applied throughout the movement, so that an anti-war effort in Seattle, Washington operates the same as an anti-war effort in New York City, and as such can be coordinated and controlled by an overall command staff operating from Denver, Colorado.

Well, no. Such a centralized command system is impossible, and I think it would be undesirable. The variety and decentralism of the U.S. peace movement is ingrained and not always a problem   after all, the major enemies of the U.S. have a similarly decentralized character (think Al Queda). Improving our strategic abilities will come more from a spreading "viral" process of education and networking, not the establishment of some "Peace Pentagon."

I've made this case at more length in "A Quaker Declaration of War," available in print and on the Quaker House website. Yet despite its limitations, Waging Peace is an important contribution to the work of strategic education of which we are both champions.

From *Quaker Theology* #15, Winter-Spring 2008

The Dark Side, Jane Mayer. Doubleday, 395 pages.
Never Surrender, General (retired) William G. "Jerry" Boykin. Faith Works, 360 pages.

Reviewed by Chuck Fager

Since I live and work next door to Fort Bragg, North Carolina, I looked forward to these two books. From very different angles, they shine sharp spotlights on Fort Bragg and its important role in our current war. Beyond that, they illuminate much of our common landscape in the United States today, and the role of religion in it. The scene they highlight is disturbing indeed.

The first is *The Dark Side*, by the *New Yorker*'s Jane Mayer. It brings together several years of pioneering reporting on the creation of the US police state and torture system after 9-11.

Much of Mayer's narrative focuses not on North Carolina but on Washington, and in particular the machinations within the White House. One of the early outcomes of these maneuvers was the launching of what I have called the "Torture Industrial Complex." It occurred on September 16, 2002, at Ft. Bragg, hosted by the Special Operations Command. Interrogators from Guantanamo were brought to Bragg for briefings by Special Forces trainers on their SERE program–Survival-Evasion-Resistance & Escape.

In the SERE training, soldiers are subjected to supervised abusive treatment, including water-boarding, to simulate conditions they might encounter if captured. The techniques had their origins in events of the Korean War, when some US prisoners in North Korea were tortured into making false public statements about taking part in alleged US war crimes. SERE's torture techniques are reportedly applied to coerce trainees into likewise signing false confessions. It appears that almost all trainees break down and sign.

Mayer's book describes how the techniques demonstrated at the Ft. Bragg sessions then "migrated" to US military and CIA prisons at Guantanamo, Iraq, Afghanistan, and elsewhere. ("Migrated" was the term used by an internal Army investigation of the spread of abuse; "exported" seems more accurate to me, but let that go.) There they became the basis for a routine of secret interrogation-by-torture, which came to public notice first at Abu Ghraib, but has since been documented as ongoing elsewhere.

This torture regime has been condemned around the world, including in a rare public report by the International Committee of the Red Cross. Further, as Mayer shows in extensive detail, it has produced many false and recanted confessions, but little in the way of documented useful intelligence. Moreover, hundreds of people held and abused at Guantanamo for years, and thousands more at other prisons, have been ultimately released without being charged; that is, they were innocent.

Nevertheless, Mayer reports that this torture program still has the support of the White House, and it continues. This is consistent with my observations in this area, where two CIA-linked charter flight companies are expanding their facilities for clandestine flights. More than five years after the invasion of Iraq, the "torture taxi" business appears to be booming.

The other book, *Never Surrender*, is by a Special Forces insider and former commander, retired General William G. "Jerry" Boykin. In 2003 Boykin came to public notice in the US because of a series of speeches he gave at large churches, in uniform. In these, he framed the US war against Al Queda and terror as an apocalyptic religious struggle, with the US representing God against Satan. He also declared that the current US president had been installed by direct action of God.

Boykin was criticized and investigated for these statements, but was cleared of any wrongdoing and finished his career as a top pentagon planner of secret anti-terror missions. But despite the shock of the mainstream media reporters who heard them, the underlying theology of these sermons was nothing new.

Rather, they express one current reiteration of Dispensational End-Times thought, filtered through the lenses of the religious right. Boykin was raised in this thought world, and found church homes that reaffirmed it while in the military. In his account of the 2003 controversy, he says he was stunned to discover that anyone would consider such views controversial or out of the ordinary.

But this tale makes up only the bookends of *Never Surrender*. In between, after describing his youth in small-town North Carolina tobacco country, Boykin devotes most of it to re-telling with relish a number of war stories from his days as a member and leader of the super-secret Delta Force unit within the Special Forces, also based at Fort Bragg. These tales are exciting enough, and include among others the failed Iranian hostage rescue mission in 1979, the Grenada and Panama invasions, the hunt for Colombian drug lord Pablo Escobar, and the costly "Black Hawk Down" fighting in Mogadishu Somalia.

Boykin, who was wounded twice in combat, has certainly earned his spurs as a warrior. However, as he admits, his tales are limited to incidents which have already come to public notice. Most of his Delta missions are still shrouded in secrecy. This includes work with the Israelis, which is mentioned, perhaps accidentally, in a photo in the book. When a newspaper interviewer pointed out the photo, Boykin acknowledged working in Israel, but declined to say anything more about the mission.

One question which arises from reading these two books in tandem is, how much did Boykin know about the fateful "migration" of SERE torture techniques from North Carolina across the world? At the time of the 2002 interrogation conference, he was commander of the Special Warfare School at Ft. Bragg; training was his main job. And a second question follows the first: whatever his role then, what does Boykin think of the program now, six years on? How would he judge Mayer's extensive evidence that cruelty in interrogations produces many confessions, most of them false and worthless?

Boykin retired in 2007, and has revisited Fayetteville several times in the summer of 2008, promoting his book. While he did not address these questions directly, many of his comments suggest that he supports what the administration calls "enhanced interrogations" to the hilt, and would see any slackening as a defeat.

Indeed, during these visits, Boykin frequently repeated his contentions about the eschatological character of the struggle against "radical Islam," which he sees as "the gravest threat in our history," more dire than the Cold war with the Soviet Union, either World War, the Civil or Revolutionary wars.

This threat is so ultimate, he believes, because it specifically embodies the presence and work of Satan. To stop this satanic drive, he is convinced that the US has been "ordained by God" to be a "light in a world of darkness." Further, he told his church audiences that this conflict will "soon" culminate in the cataclysmic fulfillment of biblical prophecies, including the Rapture, with Israel at the center.

This is the strategic worldview which Boykin brought to the highest levels of the Pentagon in the last years of his career. And it's a worldview evidently shared by many other "operators," as these secret warriors are called. At least it was among the many who gave Boykin an enthusiastic reception at Fayetteville's Airborne & Special Operations Museum.

The main setting for his mission now is churches, like the Fayetteville megachurch where he preached twice on an August Sunday morning, in front of an enormous American flag backdrop. Both there and at the museum, people were snapping up copies of Never Surrender.

Yet, Boykin repeatedly told his audiences, to best understand his convictions, they needed to look at several other volumes besides his, of which he named five.

Taking him at his word, I obtained them all.

One books is called *Armageddon, Oil & Terror*, by end-times author

John Walvoord. It lays out a familiar scenario, based on a reading of chapters 38-39 in the biblical book of Ezekiel. The text is seen as describing our times, and pointing to a climax in a massively bloody but doomed attack on Israel by an alliance of Russia with Islamic nations.

Another is *Epicenter*, by best-selling novelist Joel Rosenberg. Rosenberg could be called the thinking man's Tim LaHaye: he has published several apocalyptic thrillers that mirror recent historical events much more closely than Lahaye's "Left Behind" series. But Epicenter is a nonfiction work that undertakes to analyze Middle Eastern tensions and predict their outcome, again using Ezekiel, plus Daniel and revelation.

The next two are ostensibly non-religious. In *America Alone*, conservative columnist Mark Steyn rails against what he sees as the weakness of Western, and especially social democratic European culture in the face of Islamic immigration and high birth rates.

Most of Europe, Steyn contends, is deep into a "demographic death spiral," performing an act of "auto-genocide." These portend "the end of the world as we know it," there and elsewhere, and its replacement by a slow-mo plunge into "societal collapse, fascist revivalism, and then the long Eurabian night."

Steyn is a churchgoer, but unlike the previous three authors he does not predict the Second Coming of Christ to set everything right at the climactic moment.

Likewise, Paul Sperry is not counting on divine intervention to stop the evil tide he detects in his book, *Infiltration*. What kind of infiltration is he talking about? This:

"Forget everything you have been told about these 'moderate' and 'mainstream' [American Muslim] leaders . . . .In reality, the Muslim establishment that publicly decries the radical fringe . . .is actually a part of it. The only difference is they use words and money instead of bombs. . . ."

Finally, Boykin spoke of Steve Coughlin, a Washington- based Defense Department analyst who he regarded as the best student of Islam inside the Beltway. But Coughlin's insider status at the Pentagon was recently challenged, according to Boykin, because his view of Islam was not "politically correct" enough.

Coughlin hasn't published a book. But his briefings of the top brass are based on a master's thesis for the National Defense Intelligence College, titled "To Our Great Detriment: Ignoring What Extremists Say about Jihad."

This thesis, which is available online, reports on Coughlin's study of the Quran and Islamic law. These persuade him that the jihadis correctly claim that their violent drive for world domination is an essential meaning of core Islamic doctrine. Thus, Coughlin insists, arguments that Islam is really a moderate, non-violent faith, which the jihadists distort and twist to evil purposes, are mistaken, deliberately deceptive, or both, and certainly dangerous.

Added together, these six works make a heady brew. Boykin writes that in the 2003 controversy over his speeches in churches, he was wrongly called "an intolerant religious bigot," who wanted to "resurrect the crusades." He indignantly rejected this view, repeating to his Fayetteville audiences that his target is jihadist extremism, which he said represents only one to three per cent of the Muslim population.

Yet that math is not reflected in his religious rhetoric, or that of his other sources: Sperry, for one, insists that so-called "moderate" Muslims are no more than a mask for extremists. Steyn hears in Islamic immigration and fecundity the death knell for the entire "Free World"; Walvoord and Rosenberg foresee a looming apocalyptic war involving Islamic nations (plus Russia) versus Israel. They also insist that this conflict is predestined by biblical prophecy; and Coughlin identifies holy war for domination as being of the essence of Islamic law and doctrine, not some bizarre deviation.

No wonder Boykin sums it all up as posing a greater danger to the Judeo-Christian "Free World" than even the Nazis or the Cold War nuclear standoff with the USSR.

The depth of this perceived danger was underlined by one other warning Boykin repeated several times: that this existentially-menacing situation is one that our political leaders, even those now at the highest levels, will not dare speak of truthfully, because of "political correctness." Indeed, his implication seemed to be that they are either dupes or fifth columnists, in on the plot.

Yet if the adequate response to such an apocalyptic threat is not a "Crusade," then what other term would be adequate? My Thesaurus does not mention many options: "Rally." "Campaign." "Movement." "War." Or – well, I suppose I should have guessed it: "Jihad."

One other response is that of the worried skeptic. It notes that careful scholars like University of Wisconsin professor Paul Boyer, in his book *When Time shall Be No More,* (Harvard University Press, 1994) have shown how biblical passages like Ezekiel 38 have been re-interpreted over many centuries as the basis of a long series of failed predictions of an imminent climax of history, with a varied cast of characters filling in for Gog and Magog.

Applying such prophecies against Islam goes back at least to 1190 AD and the Third Crusade. Its leader Richard the Lion-Hearted was assured by the monk-seer Joachim of Fiore that Saladin, the Muslim ruler of Jerusalem, was the Anti-Christ, and that Richard would defeat him. (He didn't.)

While this long history of unsuccessful "prophecy" may make some of us dubious, it has done little to dampen the popularity of such speculation.

Certainly many here in Fayetteville were listening to Boykin's clarion call. And the end-times books he cited are big sellers.

The Dark Side's conclusion is more understated, as befits the *New Yorker*'s style. Jane Mayer notes that by early 2008,

> growing numbers of former administration insiders had abandoned the government with the conviction that in waging war against terrorism, America had lost its way. Many had fought valiantly to right what they saw as a dangerously wrong turn.

But thus far, these principled conservatives have lost every major fight inside the White House.

Thus in these two books, both of which are important to understanding our current plight, we have starkly divergent and competing visions of both our recent past, and likely future: *Never Surrender*, and prepare for Armageddon; versus a careful delineation of our national slide into *The Dark Side*, with the way out as yet unclear.

The Hidden, Sky-High Costs of the Iraq War:
Care of the Wounded & Return of the Draft

When Dr. Ronald Glasser came to Fayetteville this spring, he was an angry man.

Quietly angry. Furiously soft-spoken. But outraged just the same.

Why was he upset? Almost forty years ago, he was a young army doctor, patching up soldiers wounded in Vietnam. Doing this work, he gained a great respect for the soldiers, and the doctors and nurses who fought keep them alive. The book he wrote about Vietnam, *365 Days,* is widely regarded as a classic account of that bloody ordeal.

Today, most of a career later, he is still friends with many of the officers he met then.

These officers are proud of the great advances in battlefield medicine sine the Vietnam years. But they are shocked and seething over the effects of this care in the current war. And, he insists, they are spoiling for change – change that could affect every American family.

The outrage has deepened, Glasser insisted, ever since a fateful show of bravado in the White House in the summer of 2003. It was then becoming clear that the "Mission Accomplished" claims for a seemingly victorious Iraq invasion were crumbing into the sand and blood of a determined, violent resistance: "Bring it on," was the boast.

Glasser and his friends were appalled. "He dared them to "bring it on," he says. "And that's exactly what they did."

As an indicator of his disgust, Glasser shared a quote from a report in *The Times* of London from 1920, not long after the British had helped create Iraq out of territory conquered in World War One, and were well into a long, vain occupation of their own: "How much longer," the paper asked, "are valuable lives to be sacrificed in the vain endeavour to impose upon the Arab population an elaborate and expensive administration which they never asked for and do not want?"

The British eventually gave up. Yet almost ninety years later, the same question is still being asked, despite the ever-optimistic reports about the current "surge." And as Glasser was at pains to point out, the impact of the present war goes well beyond the 4000+ battle deaths. It is these survivors, the wounded, that Glasser really came to talk about.

Wounded is also the title of Glasser's latest book, his seventh. "In Iraq the ratio of wounded to killed is sixteen to one," he contended. That's at least 64,000 seriously wounded GIs. And among them are many who are as much victims of the advanced medical technology being applied as they are of combat itself.

Glasser's book quotes an army nurse at the Twenty-eighth combat surgical Hospital in Baghdad: "We're saving more people that shouldn't be saved. We're saving severely injured people, legs, eyes, parts of brains. These injuries are horrific."

"But many of them are now being hidden inside DOD [Department of Defense] hospitals," Glasser notes. "But eventually they will be discharged, and their care will shift to the VA."

The DOD hospitals, he said, get plenty of funds, as part of the endless series of "emergency" appropriations for the war. But the VA is woefully under-funded. And according to Glasser the VA faces a crushing backlog of 400,000 claims for disability status by veterans from this and previous wars. Processing these claims takes too long, and thousands of vets die while waiting for a determination.

These delays are another target of Glasser's ire. Instead of making the vets wait for years while tracking through the claims one at a time, he urges the VA to accept all the claims when they are made, and then audit them for fraud later. He says previous VA audits have shown that fraudulent claims are only a tiny percentage,

"I get calls from church groups all the time," Glasser said, "and they're asking, 'What can we do for these wounded vets?' My answer is: Absolutely nothing. You can't deal with this by selling cookies."

"The government has been very effective at hiding the costs of the war," he said. In fact, the cost of lifetime care for these tens of thousands of grievously damaged vets he estimates at three trillion dollars. That is in addition to the two trillion-plus price tag for the Iraq war itself.

The war's cost, Glasser argues, goes beyond casualty and cost figures too. Like many other knowledgeable observers, he insists that the military as a whole has been worn down by the endless round of long deployments. He added that this view is shared by his Army friends – who are now generals in the Pentagon. One outcome that he predicts is the likely return of the draft. "We gotta have more troops. And these generals now are not willing to fall on their swords for the politicians." he has been told by pentagon officials that the Selective Service is quietly ramping up its readiness in anticipation.

Like Glasser's book *365 Days*, *Wounded* is attracting high praise. And when he spoke in Fayetteville, there were grateful veterans on hand to thank him for both.

Yet considering the hard truths the new book tells, it is no wonder Ronald Glasser, doctor and author, is angry. When the true final costs of the Iraq war are known – human, social and financial – he thinks a lot more people will be mad too.

Book Review – Quaker House *Newsletter* June 2010

The Green Zone: The Environmental Costs of Militarism.
Barry Sanders. AK Press, 2009
Reviewed by Chuck Fager

Putting together the environmental and peace movements in the U.S. would be one of the greatest advances in social change work of the past generation. But to do this requires plumbing in depth the role of the U.S. military as an environmental actor.

The military is a vast–likely the single largest–consumer of energy and other resources; a huge polluter of land, earth and water; the imperial enforcer of our oil hegemony – and a major force in shaping that very policy. We desperately need to know more about all these aspects of the military's role, in detail and with analytic skill and rigor.

We need it – and unfortunately, Barry Sanders is not the one to deliver it. His major qualification for writing *The Green Zone* is that he spent his career teaching English and the history of ideas.

What difference does this make? *The Green Zone* began as a projected series of lengthy blog pieces for the *Huffington Post,* a progressive-leaning website, in October 2007.

However, by the time the second installment appeared, the right-wing blogosphere was lit up with derisive posts pointing out numerous factual errors in Sanders's efforts to outline how much fuel and other energy resources U.S. military planes, ships and other equipment actually use. After eliciting a response from Sanders that "confuses as much as it clarifies," website proprietor Ariana Huffington killed the rest of the series.

Huffington's decision was both defensible and unfortunate. Defensible because Sanders's work does not stand up to factual scrutiny. But unfortunate in that a better course would have been to do it over, with a different team. Sanders himself said of the project,

"Sometimes, it takes a military expert to find the facts. Sometimes a chemist is needed. . . .That is why at the outset I said:

"I write as a citizen. . .as a layman, not a scientist; as an outsider from the academy, not an insider from the Pentagon.. . . I am not a mathematician, not a military person, not a trained climatologist and it would be wonderful to put together such a team and reach an absolutely authoritative version of this essay, if such a thing is even possible."

It is indeed possible for an "outsider" to the Pentagon to do related work of high quality. But expertise is indispensable for rigor and credibility.

To be sure, Sanders also pointed out, rightly, that when it comes to dealing with the military, and not only on this issue, "so much of the data that one needs to make an argument is hidden and obscure." And, "As a friend told me from the outset, one cannot take on the military in this country, without getting knocked about."

All true. But all the more reason why this project needed to be undertaken by a researcher (or better, a team) with both the requisite expertise, and the experience of being "knocked about" – and having survived in the rough-and-tumble of military policy debates.

This said, it is still the case that Sanders makes some important points. Take the matter of basic information: "Finding answers for virtually any question about the military, in general, or the war in Iraq, in particular, is not easy. Finding exact answers is next to impossible."

Partly this is simply a matter of scale: our military establishment is so vast, girdling the globe, that as one astute observer, Chalmers Johnson, put it, "the Pentagon itself may not know the answers to many of the questions"; I have no doubt this is the case.

Further, beyond the ignorance and incompetence that make good research difficult (and which it unwise to underestimate), much information about this war machine is intentionally kept secret.

For instance, I am writing this next door to Fort Bragg, North Carolina, a large and well-known installation. Much data (though not all) can be retrieved about it. But a few miles west of its far border, in the pine forests, there is another sizeable base, Camp Mackall. It is publicly known that thousands of troops train there, for the secretive Delta Force and other clandestine units. Almost nothing else about it is public information; and the army isn't telling.

Good luck making an accurate environmental or energy assessment about Camp Mackall. A researcher with enough background in Special Forces operations could work up an educated guess; but only a guess. And there are many other secret bases like Camp Mackall.

As for keeping track of the Pentagon's trillions, the situation is equally murky. Sanders says tartly that, "As taxpayers, we own stock in a nefarious corporation that cooks the books until they are well done. When they get audited, they typically tell the auditors to go to hell."

Reflecting on what he was able to learn, Sanders comes to one conclusion that may be shocking to many, but is I believe very well-founded:

"Public service announcements, advertisements, politicians, and celebrities, all with the best of intentions, urge every American to recycle and reuse . . . .Those in charge make us feel that the [global warming] crisis remains in our hands to fix or fumble. But the military numbers

172

reveal a very different, perverse truth.

"Even if every person in America decided to stop driving today, and even if every polluting factory in the country voluntarily shut down, the land and the animals and the water and the air . . .would still face a most serious assault. And, ironically, that greatest single assault on the environment, on all of us, around the globe, comes from one agency, that one agency in business to protect us from our enemies, the Armed Forces of the United States."

Lightbulbs and laundry, in short, don't cut it. All this is discernible from even the incomplete, less-than skillful research Sanders was able to undertake. And it underlines the value of assembling a team of experts to get closer to these hidden truths than he was able to. Filling in the blanks about military energy use can be done – not completely, but better. It needs to be done, if we are to be adequately equipped for doing our part in helping make "the deal" that will get us through these next dangerous decades.

From *Quaker Theology* #17, Spring-Summer 2010

Hostage In Iraq, Norman Kember. Lorimer, 2007, hardbound.
118 Days: Christian Peacemaker Teams Held Hostage in Iraq. Tricia
Gates Brown, Editor. Christian Peacemaker Teams, 2008, paper.

Reviewed by Chuck Fager

This is a bad news-good news review. Bad news first:

In US army jargon, the "Tooth-to-Tail-Ratio" describes the fact that
for every armed soldier on the Baghdad streets or in Afghan mountains,
there is a "tail" of eight to ten others, stretching back to the states, and
typically including civilians.

I thought of the "Tooth-to-Tail Ratio" often, and with chagrin, while
reading Norman Kember's sorry tale of misbegotten adventurism.
Competent military commanders know that the "tail," while cumbersome,
provides useful places for those unfit for the front line. "They also serve
who only stare at computer screens," and such.

This is said not to praise the military but to acknowledge the
underlying rationality of its organization. And this rationality casts a
sharp and unflattering light of contrast on the account at hand.

The "Christian Peacemaker Teams" (or CPT), under whose auspices
Norman Kember went to Iraq, would do well to make a careful study of
this military approach to structure. Instead, it is hard to overstate the
reckless incompetence displayed in their abetting of this frail
septuagenarian's self-indulgent fantasy of combatant tourism.

This recklessness is not an accident. CPT claims as its inspiration a
1984 speech by Ron Sider, the founder of Evangelicals for Social Action,
to a Mennonite world conference. In it Sider declared that "To rise to this
challenge of history, we need to . . . prepare to die by the thousands." In
particular, the test of real Christian peacework, he insisted, was for his
hearers to get "ready to start to die by the thousands in dramatic vigorous
new exploits for peace and justice . . . ."

Sider's speech is still posted on the CPT website at: www.cpt.org as
a kind of scripture and manifesto.

Frankly, such martyr machismo has no appeal for me. My problems
with it are theological, strategic, and practical.

Theologically, I simply don't believe that martyrdom is the test of true
Christian peacemaking. After all, when Jesus sent his disciples out
(Matthew 10:16), he told them they were like "sheep in the midst of

wolves," so they were to be "wise as serpents" as well as "harmless as doves." He did not urge them to make themselves available as wolf food. Sure, faithful peace action will sometimes entail risk, and occasionally martyrdom. But like the military, it's the mission which is primary, not the risk.

Strategically, there is simply no clear relationship between dead Christians and effective peacemaking. Both peace and war are much more complicated than that; not to mention Christianity. If "dead Christians" equaled peace, then Iraq should be fine, because in fact Christians have been "dying by the thousands" there   many of them U.S. soldiers fighting the war, and many others native Iraqis victimized by it. The simplistic, sectarian frame of the Sider/CPT approach may not be apparent to them, but it is obvious to others, and makes a hash of its moral pretensions.

And practically, CPT's attachment to this premise "on the ground," has not gone much beyond a kind of rhetorical pose: its members have not been dying even by the dozens (and thank god for that). But cases like Kember's show that the difference between "dramatic vigorous new exploits" and plain damned foolishness can sometimes be hard to discern.

In this case, Kember's whole rationale for wanting to go was cockeyed. A retired professor of Biophysics and a longtime British anti-war activist, he felt he hadn't "risked" enough for his longtime pacifism. As a Baptist, he was particularly haunted by the example of Dietrich Bonhoeffer, the German theologian who conspired against Hitler and was killed.

But here's a clue for wannabe Bonhoeffers: neither peacework–nor for that matter military operations–is primarily about risk; they are about achieving specific objectives. And any experienced army squad leader knows that soldiers who go out courting danger and excitement (scornfully called "cowboys") pose potentially fatal hazards to their entire unit and their overall mission.

Kember could have found a suitable place in the "tail" of peacework; there is plenty that's useful to do. But his acknowledged liberal guilt would not yield to such undramatic stuff: "In no way was I taking risks for my beliefs in the way that young servicemen and women in Iraq were taking risks for theirs," he wrote.

But guilt aside, there were good reasons for this disparity: Kember was in no kind of shape to be "on the front lines." In real life, combat troops train for months, or even years, for their hazardous tasks. But all Kember needed was–well, CPT as it turned out. And once he found it, the rest is history. As his book makes plain, his planned ten-day jaunt was little more than a kind of guilt-fueled danger tourism, which CPT had no business enabling.

Such lack of preparation is not unusual in that group's ranks. A few years back, I met a much younger fellow who had spent two weeks in Iraq with CPT. He was terrified most of the time, and raced back across the border to Jordan just in time to write a melodramatically callow little book about the experience.

More recently, a CPT volunteer approached me; he was packing to leave for a two-week stint in a conflict area of Colombia, and wanted my advice (and, I suspect, blessing).

To begin, I asked him questions:

Did he speak or understand Spanish? No.

Was he familiar with the players and issues in the long Colombian civil war? No.

Had he, indeed, studied guerilla warfare at all? No.

In that case, my advice was: stay home until you have a better idea of what you're getting into. Or, in gospel parlance: get some serpentine wisdom if you really want to be harmless as a dove.

Of course, he went anyway, and thank goodness came back okay. But that outcome did not diminish my skepticism.

Kember, of course, was not so lucky. He went to Baghdad in November 2005 for a similar jaunt, and was kidnaped along with three others, including Quaker Tom Fox.

They were kept til March of 2006, when rescued by SAS Commandos – all except for Tom of course, who had been taken away and murdered.

By the way, Tom Fox was a friend of mine, and I discussed his situation with him personally between his stints in Iraq. In contrast with these others, he seemed very well-informed about the dangers there; and the evidence afterward showed that he had prepared carefully to face it: he wound up his worldly affairs; he took graduate courses in peacemaking in one of the finest programs available; he studied Arabic and Islam; he gathered a support committee; etc.

Whether this was adequate in a personal sense we shall never know. But I think it's a fair judgment that Tom Fox was better prepared to face that life-threatening situation than many of the soldiers who leave Fort Bragg for Iraq. His blog posts from Iraq, which continued until a few days before his capture, are anything but simplistic. For me at least, his example wears better than some others.

Kember summarizes this information about Tom, which he learned later. The meat of the book is his inside account of their captivity. Kember earns a grudging measure of respect for admitting just how unready he was for any kind of physical privation. So much that, when the four were chained together for sleep each night, he had to be placed where he could scramble abruptly for the toilet, dragging the others along, to avoid unmentionable disasters, which were not always avoided.

Mentally he was little better prepared. He admits to once starting a row with Canadian captive James Loney over what he felt was the latter's

176

slovenly pronunciation of Loney's home town, Toronto, as "Tronno," the native version. (At least he later apologized.)

Much of this can be forgiven as due to the harsh tedium of their imprisonment. But Kember's querulousness was such that even his captors reversed their cultural deference to elders and regarded him, in his words, as "the wimp" of the lot.

Kember notes that during the empty days, there were long and vigorous discussions about CPT, particularly between Tom Fox and James Loney, the two who had been with the group longest. We have not been favored with the details of these talks, and Kember says he had no interest in them. But my suspicion is that the issue of the wisdom of the whole Iraq project was on the table. I do note that the 2008 annual report from CPT indicated that they had withdrawn from Baghdad. (More recent reports indicate they have sent a small, more experienced unit to the Kurdish region there, which is relatively less dangerous.)

Certainly peaceworkers should be thinking about how their skills and energies could be applied to ameliorating the awful situation in Iraq. But considering how much time, effort and money was expended, by both civilians like myself, and military units like the British SAS, to the end of saving the lives of these four visitors, it is more than an open question whether the benefit even comes close to matching the cost. And that's just resources; how much was Tom Fox's life worth?

Kember tells us that at one point during his captivity,

"I wrote in my captivity notebook: Once I had a nightmare that I was kidnapped and, confined, handcuffed to three others, in a small room, for weeks. I woke and it was reality.' I opened my eyes to see the dreadful truth of the room around me. I felt the handcuff on my wrist and the chain on my ankle. Why did I ever come to Iraq?"

Why indeed?

Kember didn't have much better answers after the rescue, when he was given a rough time by BBC interviewer Fergal Keane:

Can you yourself, having been back – now that you've been back some time and absorbed some of the things that have been written about you, can you see how you got up a good many peoples noses? Because they probably would have seen you, and I have to put it to you this bluntly, as a sanctimonious old buffer who went and put himself at enormous risk, put his family through hell, is then rescued by the SAS and still says they are the most violent outfit in the world and that war is wrong. Do you see how that might greatly aggravate people?

177

In the audio version, Kember's embarrassment at the weight of this indictment is clearly audible, as he replies, "Oh yes, I understand it . . . ." (http://www.bbc.co.uk/radio4/news/norman_kember_transcript.shtml)

Maybe this is now all water under the bridges of the Tigris. Yet one more item requires notice:

On arrival in Baghdad, Kember and the others were given what CPT called its "Magic Sheet," a scrap of myopic piety that was supposed to preserve them from harm by expounding their peaceful intentions. In the catalog of folly that is *Hostage In Iraq*, the "magical thinking" behind this document may be the most egregious example of all.

Again: I'm not opposed to peace projects in dangerous situations; but in planning them, I think Quakers have much to learn from the military, and much to eschew in this example. That kind of arrogant naivete could get someone killed.

And in this case, of course, it did.

It's always hard to read about Tom Fox's death, and let me never forget him and his sacrifice. That said, when it comes to our other book, *118 Days,* I want to focus on someone else. In this reading, two chapters in the book leaped out.

They were about the Canadian captive, Jim Loney, who is gay, and what his being gay meant in this life and death saga.

This was a bad news-good news situation also, but of a different sort. The good news is, of course, that Loney survived. The bad news is about what was required for that, even half a world away.

118 Days is a compilation of reports by various staff and others associated with CPT about the kidnaping; this is the "official story," or more accurately, stories. And one of the stories is about silence. Not the silence of Quaker worship, but the enforced silence of the closet.

What's clear from these pages is that if Tom Fox had not been killed, Loney's plight and its ramifications would have been a major chapter of this saga. And Like Tom's, Jim's story transcends the specifics of his kidnaping.

The two chapters which deal with this story are by Dan Hunt, who had been Jim's partner for more than ten years in 2005; and by William Payne, one of their gay friends. Payne is part of a community of LGBTs and their supporters, centered in Toronto, among whom Jim and Dan lived. The couple, like the community generally, had been publicly out for years.

The impact of these chapters grows out of the gruesomely undeniable fact that by 2005 in Iraq, gays were being hunted down and murdered, brutally and with impunity. (They still are.) Many reports have documented this ongoing reign of terror, which is one of many tragic outcomes of the US invasion and overthrow of Saddam Hussein's regime.

178

A gay Iraqi exile, Ali Hili, who launched the website Iraqi LGBT said of this:

"Homosexuality was generally tolerated under Saddam. There certainly was no danger of gay people being assassinated in the street by police. Since his overthrow, the violent persecution of gays and lesbians is commonplace. Life in Iraq now is hell for all LGBT people; no one can be openly gay and alive."

That's what was happening in November 2005, three years into the US occupation. So a few days after the kidnapping, when a Toronto TV reporter came knocking at the door where Jim and Dan lived, saying, "I'm looking for Jim Loney's partner," a housemate did not mince words:

"'If you mention in your story that Jim might be gay, whether he is or not, you'll get him killed.' It was time to be blunt," Payne writes, "and it worked."

The reporter protested, no doubt truthfully, that neither she nor her employers were homophobic. And it was no secret in Toronto that Jim and Dan were a same sex couple. But that wasn't the point; and the reporter soon backed off That incident was only a beginning. To make the silence about Jim and Dan stick, Payne notes, "our collective return to the closet began."

At first, Dan Hunt writes,

"my public disappearance seemed like an inconsequential strategic decision, one that would be easy to bear. I was responding to homophobia that was far away, in Iraq. It wasn't real. How quickly that changed."

An essentially false identity had to be constructed and then maintained:

"Publicly, Jim became known as an upstanding Christian boy and community-worker from a typical, small-town all-Canadian nuclear family. It was the only picture of him that was safe to portray. I, and everyone connected to me, including the community Jim and I began with William [Payne] in 1990, had to be erased if Jim was to have any chance of surviving."

The erasing was done in very concrete ways. Needing a photo of Jim for CPT to give the media, they settled on one taken the night before Jim left for Baghdad. "It was my favorite photo from that night," a friend recalled, Jim with his arm around Dan's shoulder, both smiling, with Jim's head tilted toward Dan's head."

But Dan had to go. He was literally cut from the photo. A CPT staffer who was there said,

"The defining moment for me as a queer woman during the crisis was when Dan's image was cut out of that loving photo . . . . I watched the process of photo editing from my desk, and cried quietly. In the days that followed I worked ferociously to protect Dan and Jim's relationship, from an already knowledgeable media. At the same time, my active role in making Dan invisible broke my heart."

Another gay man who was present when the photo was taken said he

"found something in the photo to hold onto. I noticed . . . a little red triangle in the bottom right corner, Dan's shirt. I thought, There's Dan. You're silent, you're invisible, but there's the visibility.' It was the weirdest thing. I don't know why but it comforted me to know that even though Dan was cut out of the picture – at least to the few who knew that little bit of red shirt was actually Dan. That was beautiful to me."

To be effective, this "re-closeting" and becoming invisible extended well beyond Jim and Dan.
"For the sake of Jim's safety, those who love him took great pains to reconstruct the closet walls he had so painstakingly torn down a decade ago . . ." Payne wrote. "Reversing years of closet dismantling is hard to do, but we were amazingly successful.

"Gay, lesbian and bisexual people used the gifts of their lives to do whatever could be done in a situation where there as very little to do. We are used to surviving despite the closet. Though it's not a place we want to go, we know how to craftily navigate the waters of deception when we need to protect life and limb, and we did it again for four months."

While necessary, this invisibility was a destructive burden.

"The media is very powerful," Dan wrote. "It shapes the way we view the world and the way we experience ourselves in it. Though I knew a myth was being created, it was difficult not to let the myth have the power of truth. Media coverage of the kidnapping was so intense that not being included in it began to annihilate me – especially because my behind-the-scenes experiences often paralleled my public disappearance. . . .
"When I went downtown for the vigil following Tom [Fox's] death,

I watched from a distance of a hundred yards until the vigil was well under way. The media were there and so were my friends. I did not want them to pay undue attention to me in front of the media. The myth became my reality over and over. I could not exist, therefore I did not exist."

But then it seemed to be over.

"In the end," Dan Hunt wrote, "Jim came home to all of us who love him."

Dan was there to greet him at the Toronto airport, and walked with him, finally, to face the press openly and together.

But there was a bittersweet tinge to the moment:

"I sometimes wonder," Dan wrote, "if the diminishment and debasement I endured would have been washed away in a single moment, had Jim and I held hands, walking towards the thousand cameras, when he arrived home at the airport, or if we'd embraced in front of everyone. But we didn't. It would have been unnatural for us. Our own coming out hadn't brought us that far. The terrible violence of being silenced was more dominant than the freedom we had thus far acquired.

Silence equals death.' It was the rallying cry of the queer community as it faced the AIDS crisis. It's a statement of truth. Non-recognition, disappearance, invisibility, are violence that can eradicate one's very being."

For William Payne, his chapter of *118 Days*

"is about queerness and about how the sexual orientation of one of the four CPTers kidnapped in Iraq must be seen as an intrinsic, even central part of the story." Indeed, ". . .the narrative of the hostage-taking is incomplete without an account of how homophobia played a leading role in this drama."

And in some concrete ways, even after Jim's rescue, the ordeal was not entirely over. Both Payne and Dan Hunt report that along with the jubilation following Jim's return home, there was a homophobic backlash.

This negative report is underlined by the note, "Why We Are Self-Publishing," at the front of the book: First one, and then a second church-related publishing house agreed to print this book for CPT, but both later demanded that sections about Jim and Dan be deleted. More silence, more invisibility. When CPT refused, the publishers dropped the project.

"Sadly," the CPT editors conclude, "what neither publisher seems to recognize is that their editing requirements are part of the same system of homophobia that threatened Jim's life while he was in captivity, and subsequently condemned Dan to invisibility."

My hat is off to Dan and his friends for their dedication and skill, and to CPT for standing up to this renewed call to re-closeting and silencing. It is an example that applies to issues beyond gender, and I hope others will remember and live up to it.

From *Quaker Theology*, #18, Fall-Winter 2010-2011

James Davison Hunter, *To Change the World, The Irony, Tragedy, & Possibility of Christianity in the Late Modern World.* Oxford University Press, 360 pages.

Reviewed by Chuck Fager

Quakers don't like to remember Prohibition, and the Temperance movement which birthed it. From liberals to evangelicals, I can't recall a serious discussion–and but one incident of reminiscing–about it in four decades among Friends.

Yet for several generations, outlawing the manufacture and sale of alcoholic beverages was one of the prime Quaker priorities, pretty much across the board. Lucretia Mott and Susan B. Anthony, while advocating for women's rights, also campaigned against demon rum–as did evangelical leaders like John Henry Douglas. The various factions may have had their own committees operating independently, but all aimed at a similar goal.

And in 1919, they finally achieved it. The Volstead Act amended the Constitution so that "the manufacture, sale, or transportation of intoxicating liquors within . . . the United States . . . is hereby prohibited." Alongside abolition of southern slavery, this has to stand as the high water mark of Quaker and other religious reformers' impact in the arena of American law and social policy.

So why don't Friends remember and celebrate this landmark of "social change"? Probably the biggest reason is that by 1933, Prohibition was widely deemed to be, not only a failure but disastrously counterproductive, and repealed. Who wants to remember such a humiliating fiasco? Denial is much more than a river in Egypt; such strategic forgetting is a pillar of organizational as well as individual self-esteem.

But James Davison Hunter remembers Prohibition. And in his ironically titled, To Change the World, this misbegotten crusade is cited as a model of the failure of religiously-motivated reform–not only its failure, but its larger cultural irrelevance.

For while Prohibition's end left America such enduring but unanticipated artifacts as the Mafia, it was also falling abysmally short of its prime objective, which was to reduce or eliminate the damage done by the very real plague of alcohol abuse.

That epidemic is still with us, wreaking havoc every day, almost a century after the Prohibition experiment began. Further, Volstead's bastard children live on in the various "wars" on drugs, which annually ruin tens of thousands of lives, cost us tens of billions, and have now plunged Mexico into a bloody drug war right on our doorstep. No wonder Quakers don't want to remember Prohibition, or how deeply they were invested in it. (Though of course we should remember, and ponder deeply.)

Yet Hunter's book is not about the past so much as the present, and ongoing American religious-based reform efforts. He identifies three of these, not of equal influence, but worth comparable attention: the currently pre-eminent Religious Right, the much smaller Religious Left (epitomized by *Sojourners* and its spokesman Jim Wallis), and, even smaller still, a pioneering Neo-Anabaptist trend that has attracted his attention.

Hunter is known for his pathbreaking book *Culture Wars,* which helped many of us get a better grasp on what we were up against in the 1990s. I opened his latest tome hoping to better understand our prospects ten years into the twenty-first century.

To Change the World is less a book of prophecy than of analysis. Nevertheless, Hunter spends many pages explaining why he believes none of these three religious reform movements is likely to reach their goals of "changing the world," or even changing America, particularly in the ways they say they want to.

Why not? In sum, he asserts that each of these movements, in its own way, basically misunderstands how cultures change, and thus their varying recipes are likely to fail, at best, and boomerang, at worst.

And how do cultures change? His argument here is complex and nuanced. In sum, he says they change from the top down, as rising elites challenge and change (or replace) existing ones, and then inject their new plans and values into the dense thicket of existing cultural and social institutions, changing them incrementally, overcoming resistance slowly but surely. And such change is usually not recognized until it has already happened, that is, retrospectively; in the hurly-burly of daily social jostling and struggle, it's almost impossible to see which way the river of history is "really" flowing.

His three target movements, he argues, have at best only a dim understanding of this larger process of change, each for their own reasons. For the Religious Right, the problem centers on a combination of idealist individualism which believes that "changing hearts and minds" one by one is the path to redeeming society from its state of decay—and then when that doesn't work, the mobilization of these "transformed" individuals into political forces which will install "good Christians" in positions of public power, where they will govern in a transformative

184

way. "The hope Christian conservatives place in politics is quite astonishing," Hunter writes. ". . . Political action [they believe] will return a sense of cultural ownership to Christian citizens nationwide.' . . . As the late D. James Kennedy has put it, Our job is to reclaim America for Christ, whatever the cost . . . .'"

Yet while individual change may be good for the individual, Hunter believes, that doesn't do much about the larger cultural structures and currents. Further, once the "transformed" are set marching into worldly politics, they become captive to the narrow notion that formal politics is where all the action is, which it isn't. And then become subject to all the predictable corruptions thereof, plus that special vice of the "saved," namely the conviction that their holy ends justify whatever unholy means seem necessary to achieve them in this "practical" world; which puts them on the well-worn path to religious tyranny.

The Christian Left looks to social justice more than the saving of individual souls. It cherishes the memory of Dr. Martin Luther King, and the years of activism for peace and related issues, cresting in the Vietnam years. They regard the agenda and tactics of the Religious Right with disdain as a perversion of the Gospel. Says Jim Wallis, their best-known spokesman, "I don't think Jesus' top priorities would have been a capital gains tax cut and the occupation of Iraq." Their distress has increased with the successes of their opponents.

And they fail to impress Hunter as amounting to much more than a smaller, weaker mirror image of the Right: "In its commitment to social change through politics," he concludes, " . . . in its conflation of the public with the political, in its own selective use of scripture to justify political interests, and in its confusion of theology with national interests and identity, the Christian Left (not least the Evangelical Left) imitates the Christian Right. The message is obviously different . . . but in their framework, method, and style of engagement, politically progressive Christians are very similar to their politically conservative counterparts."

To the progressives, this judgment that they are an imitation of the Right could hardly be more wounding; and even worse is its corollary that the record shows these Christian Leftists to be a pale imitation of their conservative nemeses, because it's the latter who have been winning most of the major elections for thirty years.

Against this backdrop, many readers may turn with relief to Hunter's "third force," the Neo-Anabaptists, whose guiding spirit was the late Mennonite theologian John Howard Yoder, and current guru is theologian and ethicist Stanley Hauerwas.

While the smallest of the three groupings, Hunter pronounces it "intellectually serious," which is "one reason why it has growing appeal among young Christian adults. It provides a credible, even compelling, script for those who find the account offered by the Christian conservatives distasteful if not dangerous and the narrative offered by Christian progressives unconvincing and irrelevant."

It also resembles the secular libertarian movement in its disdain for the state, though for the Neo-Anabaptists this stance is theological, based in a recognition of the larger reality of both the modern state, economy, and communications technologies as forces in themselves, "principalities and powers," in biblical terms. Similar scorn is aimed at most Christian churches: these too have been corrupted and absorbed by the fallen, corrupting powers. For the Neo-Anabaptists, as Hunter puts it, "Christianity in America, as it is believed and lived by most believers, is just not Christian enough."

The Neo-Anabaptists' stance in relation to the principalities and powers, including churches, is one of resistance, sometimes from within, sometimes from without, even if it takes mainly an intellectual form. For some it has also been embodied in a "new monasticism," of small communities that work with the poor, prisoners, or other outcasts. These groups embody an effort to lay aside the conventional political focus of both right and left, as the way of challenging the powers and their destructiveness.

For them the real challenge to the worldly "establishment," is not a newer, better establishment, but the church itself, the purified, faithful church, in the form of independent, worshiping, active communities, typically (though not necessarily) small, often persecuted, and rejecting as much of the world as is practical.

For those weary of the back and forth of conventional political jousting, even in clerical garb, the Neo-Anabaptist's views can seem fresh and radical. And they insist that their path is not one of withdrawal: "Our response to the call of discipleship not only threatens the powers of the world," one of their advocates declares, "but positively and publicly overthrows them."

Maybe. Hunter faults the Neo-Anabaptists for being naïve about the clutches of the powers and over-estimating the potential of their efforts to escape them. Indeed, such declarations as that just cited have more than a whiff of magical thinking about them; one might remark sardonically that the Pentagon, after all, is still standing. He also calls them out for being relentlessly negative, citing a characterization of their ethos as a "passive aggressive ecclesiology." He points out that such narratives of negativity ("the establishment is evil, the culture is corrupted, the church is sold out, nobody is any good except thee and me, and I'm having doubts about thee"), far from being "counter-cultural," are instead all-too typical artifacts of our culture, available in as many varieties as tee shirts with snarky slogans.

So. With the shortcomings of these various religious reform movements laid out, what does Hunter propose? How does he recommend

186

that churches work "to change the world"?

Well, in one real sense he doesn't. Instead, he describes a program of "faithful presence," which comes down to the church being the church, within and yet in tension with the larger culture. Summarized that briefly, it sounds almost like a clich,, and there were points in his exposition when this reader felt Hunter was on the brink of sliding from the profound into the banal. Certainly the "bottom line" is very modest: accompanied by what seems like a weary sigh, the book ends with a wistful hope that "by enacting shalom and seeking it on behalf of all others through the practice of faithful presence, it is possible, just possible, that [Christians and their churches] will help to make the world a little but better."

Such modesty is certainly welcome, if somewhat astringent. Religion is surely a crucial force in American culture; yet this influence is largely contextual and institutional. Within its realm, particular churches large and small are prone to exaggerated views of their overt ability to have impact on the culture.

Take, as Hunter notes, the steady advance of American acceptance of homosexuals as full persons, even able to marry. The Religious Right has a long track record of winning practically every referendum and legislative fight on the issue. Yet somehow the acceptance of gays and same sex marriage continues to spread anyway, quietly, relentlessly nullifying all the political "victories." Whatever are the real sources of this change, the Religious Right's political skills seem to have little real impact on them.

Yet this doesn't mean their actions are meaningless. Such election victories often do have effects, too often negative and unpredicted. Hunter pauses near the end of the book to underline this: "It should be clear at this point that good intentions are not enough to engage the world well. The potential for stupidity, irrationality, cruelty, and harm is just as high today as it has ever been in the past. God save us from Christians who are well-intentioned, but not wise!"

I wish he had devoted more attention to this point. His mention of Prohibition's failure did not go into the catalog of dismal long-term impacts on American society, which are far from exhausted. This case is one I wish Friends would study in depth, to gain better understanding of the pitfalls of our reforming zeal, which is undiminished, if pointed now in other directions.

Hunter also pays no concentrated attention to the militarism-entwined-with-religion that is such a major reality of American life. This is a major failing. After all, the United States has just been through a period of calamitous "rule by the saints" from 2001 to early 2009, when devotees of Christian conservative ideology controlled both the White House and Congress. In the wake of their unwisdom, we are left with two ugly and pointless wars, frenetic preparations for more, the legitimation of torture, huge holes in our civil liberties, and an economic crash of near-apocalyptic proportions. "God save us" from such Christianity regnant, indeed.

I have another bone to pick with Hunter. His focus on big-picture, top-down processes of change is largely valid. Yet he gives much too short shrift to the potential of small groups that have good ideas, tactical shrewdness and persistence. He does acknowledge the latter: "Persistence over time is essential; little of significance happens in three to five years." That's right; but there's more to it.

On numerous occasions in Quaker history, good ideas and persistence have combined to have a salutary influence on the larger world. Not always, of course: sometimes persistence has combined with bad ideas, like Prohibition, which was the wrong remedy for a real problem. Likewise, as Friends adapt to the ever-shrinking attention span of our times, even our best ideas are pursued with less and less of the needed persistence and skill.

Still, these complaints are the basis for fruitful thinking and discussion, rather than a reason to set aside Hunter's many insights and depth of historical/theological analysis. If your religion calls for changing the world, *To Change the World* is a book to reckon with.

An Excerpt From *To Change The World:*

Imagine, in this regard, a genuine "third great awakening" occurring in America, where half of the population is converted to a deep Christian faith. Unless this awakening extended to envelop the cultural gatekeepers, it would have little effect on the character of the symbols that are produced and prevail in public and private culture. And, without a fundamental restructuring of the institutions of culture formation and transmission in our society– the market, government-sponsored cultural institutions, education at all levels, advertising, entertainment, publishing, and the news media, not to mention church – revival would have a negligible long-term effect on the reconstitution of the culture. Imagine further several social reform movements surrounding, say, educational reform and family policy, becoming very well organized and funded, and on top of this, serious Christians being voted into every major office and appointed to a majority of judgeships. Legislation may be passed and judicial rulings may be properly handed down, but legal and political victories will be short-lived or pyrrhic without the broad-based legitimacy that makes the alternatives seem unthinkable.

Such is the story of one of the most powerful transatlantic social reform movements of the nineteenth and early twentieth centuries–the temperance movement. This movement failed, of course, not least because it did not and could not address the culture of restraint on which the particular interest of temperance depended. In the end, the ideal of "temperance" finally expired in derision with the repeal of the Volstead Act in 1933, the word now having disappeared from our public vocabulary. This same logic accounts for the contemporary failure of the Christian Right to stop the growth and legitimation of homosexuality, abortion, and pornography, among other concerns. The passion and earnest resolve generated by all such movements may change people and may affect com-munities and they may, for a time, change laws, but they generally will not influence the course and direction of the culture as a whole unless they are tied to larger structural changes in the culture.

Culture, at root, provides the very terms by which life is ordered. In our own culture, the inherited categories derived largely from biblical and classical sources by which we understand the most basic aspects of human life have been and are being transformed by very powerful forces over which individuals and social groups have little control, forces such as consumerism, com-munications technology, and so on. The most humane under-standings of personhood, relationships, community, time, space, freedom, obligation, material wealth, cannot be established or recovered through a five-year plan or even in a generation cer-tainly not through politics, not through social reform, and not even in and through revival. In this light, the call to this generation of Americans to repent and pray for revival to renew the values of the national culture may be welcome, but no one should be under any illusion about its capacity to fundamentally transform the present cultural order at its most rudimentary level .... All such engagement may be worthy, but if the end is to "save civilization," it most certainly is naive. By themselves or even together, evangelism, politics, and social reform, then, will fail to bring about the ends hoped for and intended.

The important qualification one must make in all of this is that even when successful, change does not always occur in the direction that people propose or with the effects for which people hope. There are almost always unintended consequences to human action, particularly at the macro-historical level and these are, often enough, tragic. The architects of the Enlightenment who understood the power of science and predicted the progressive amelioration of human suffering through it, would never have desired or predicted the development of nuclear weapons. The Protestant Reformers of the sixteenth century never would have imagined that the turn toward individual conscience and moral asceticism would have contributed to an economic system that would "act back" on the culture as a cause of secularization. Likewise, the Puritans who founded Harvard and Yale would have never expected that their schools would become strongholds of secularity. And the missionaries who brought aid to impoverished parts of the Third World would have never wished for the growing cycle of dependency they unwittingly helped foster. And so it goes. One can never quite predict where things will go.

Culture is endlessly complex and difficult, and it is highly resistant to our passion to change it, however well intentioned and heroic our efforts may be.

Christianity and War, and Other Essays Against the Warfare State.
Laurence M. Vance.
Vance Publications, Pensacola, Florida. 418 pages.

Reviewed by Chuck Fager; plus an interview with the author, and excerpts from the book

In the spring of 2011, a young soldier came to see me, at the Quaker peace project where I work. He wanted to talk about filing a Conscientious Objector (CO) claim.

Once a very enthusiastic recruit, he had been in the elite Special Forces training program. But the realities of military life had quickly disillusioned him. Raised a conservative Baptist in Texas, he said his worldview had changed so radically that—here he paused to take a deep breath: "I'm not even a Republican anymore."

Not that he was now a Democrat. Instead, when I explained that he would have to describe his current views in his CO claim letter, and show how he had arrived at them, he handed me a book he'd brought with him.

The book was *Christianity and War,* by Laurence Vance.

I don't know how the GI's CO claim turned out; like many who call or visit, he hasn't followed up. But for me, *Christianity and War* was a godsend, and a revelation.

Why? For several years I've been increasingly convinced that something which can be called "American War Christianity" (or AWC) is a key pillar of U.S. militarism. A crusading variety of fundamentalism has become pervasive in the armed forces, including the top levels, and its impact is frightening, its potential even more so.

There are books and articles that document this phenomenon: one, *With God On Our Side,* by Michael L. "Mikey" Weinstein, was a trailblazer when it appeared in 2006. Another is a paper by Air Force Col. William Millonig, "the Impact of Religious and Political Affiliation on Strategic Military Decisions and Policy Recommendations," which despite the lengthy title is concise and straightforward. These and others have been valuable to me. (Millonig's paper is online at:
 http://www.dtic.mil/cgi-bin/GetTRDoc?AD=ADA449308)

But ever since I came to an awareness of AWC, I figured that besides journalistic or sociological reports, there must also surely be some theological challengers to it. I began looking for them, to guide me in raising a specifically religious challenge to this dangerous phenomenon. Any day I expected to encounter a cadre of liberal religious thinkers who were all over it.

Not so. Yes, I have run across a number of theologians who are writing from an "anti-imperial" perspective, but the empire in question usually turns out to be the Roman (or Babylonian, if they're Old Testament types). When it comes to our current plight, their writing typically recycles cliches from such sources as National Public Radio.

Interesting, but hardly adequate. Besides which, much such "postcolonial" writing is encased in such impenetrable academic jargon that even the Air Force's bunker-busters couldn't penetrate it.

The closest thing I found to an actual theological challenge to AWC as a force today was *Wayward Christian Soldiers*, by Charles Marsh. But while Marsh effectively called out the war-mongering rhetoric of a handful of evangelical leaders on the eve of the Iraq invasion in 2003, he denied being a liberal, instead swearing fealty to Karl Barth's "neo-orthodoxy." Besides, his small book didn't go beyond the handful of targeted statements to examine the broader theological phenomenon involved.

Marsh was a bright brief candle on a dark horizon. Elsewhere among evangelicals, the voices were either uneasily equivocal, or more often entirely on board with the AWC outlook.

So when the young soldier handed me Vance's book last spring, I was still in search of an informed, vocal liberal theological opponent of AWC.

I'm still searching–for a liberal or conventionally evangelical challenger to AWC, that is. But not for an effective one; not anymore. *Christianity and War* wields a theological bat like Babe Ruth on a tear, knocking pro-war piety right out of the park. A representative affirmation:

"The love affair that many conservative, evangelical and fundamentalist Christians have with the military is an illicit affair. It is contrary to the tenor of the New Testament. It is an affront to the Savior. It is a cancer on Christianity."(254)

And again, in 2006: "it is a blight on Christianity that many of those who continue to support [former President George W.] Bush and his [Iraq] war are evangelical Christians who will support Bush until the bitter end–no matter how many more U.S. soldiers are killed, no matter how long the war continues, no matter how many more billions of dollars are wasted, and no matter what outrages the president commits against the Constitution, the rule of law, and Christianity itself." (327)

But the author, Laurence Vance, is no liberal. As he modestly puts it, "I am willing to match my Christian, Protestant, conservative, evangelical, fundamentalist, Baptist credentials up against anyone." The difference is that Vance is all these things, and a staunch Libertarian. A

Ron Paul supporter (tho the book doesn't deal with presidential politics), he names names, calls a spade a spade, and cites scripture, the Church Fathers, the Founding Fathers, Erasmus, Charles Spurgeon, and even the occasional Quaker to back up his strongly held views.

Wait–Spurgeon was a peacenik? Spurgeon, the legendary 19th century British Baptist preacher, who built the prototype of a "megachurch" that regularly gathered crowds of 5000, and who delivered at least 3561 sermons, which are still in print – he was antiwar?

Yes. Hear him, in 1857:

> The church, we affirm, can neither be preserved nor can its interests be promoted by human armies. We have all thought otherwise in our time, and have foolishly said when a fresh territory was annexed to our empire, "Ah – what a providence that England has annexed Oude," or taken to itself some other territory "Now a door is opened for the Gospel.
>
> A Christian power will necessarily encourage Christianity, and seeing that a Christian power is at the head of the Government, it will be likely that the natives will be induced to search into the authenticity of our revelation, and so great results will follow.
>
> Who can tell but that, at the point of the British bayonet, the Gospel will be carried, and that, by the edge of the true sword of valiant men, Christ's Gospel will be proclaimed?"
>
> I have said so myself; and now I know I am a fool for my pains, and that Christ's church hath been also miserably befooled; for this I will assert, and prove too, that the progress of the arms of a Christian nation is not the progress of Christianity, and that the spread of our empire, so far from being advantageous to the Gospel, I will hold, and this day proclaim, hath been hostile to it.

Vance cites other theologians and preachers from many centuries, and not a liberal in the lot. He's been making his fundamentalist antiwar case across the internet for several years, based at http://www.lewrockwell.com , a major libertarian website. Indeed, *Christianity and War* is less a treatise than a compilation of blog posts. If that fact makes its text often repetitive, it doesn't diminish the force of Vance's arguments, or the pungency with which he makes them.

There's plenty in his fiery sermonettes likely to offend the large mass of church folks of various denominations who value politeness over any point of doctrine or ethics, especially when it concerns those in their own circles. But Vance doesn't care about that. He cares about truth and the Gospel. His model is the Gallilean who ignored all advice to go easy on calling his Pharasaic opponents "hypocrites," amid much more incendiary terms. No, his vehemence will not commend this book to such "nice" folks; but Vance says he has heard from many disenchanted soldiers, who once accepted the USA=God's-licensed-killers, but have been cast into a wilderness of confusion by the lies and hypocrisies of imperial war. Many found Vance speaking truths in a way theu could understand. And it was one of them, a soldier rather than a genteel church elder or disttracted seminary professor, who brought his book to me.

Why I hadn't heard about Vance before mid-2011 probably bespeaks my share of this provincialism; and none of my liberal friends had heard of him either. Too bad for us.

But that doesn't mean Vance hasn't been heard. Oh,indeed, he has. And he has answered: Three times he repeats a list of epithets often flung at him: "Yes, I know, I am a liberal, a communist, a Quaker, a pacifist, a peacenik, a traitor, a coward, an appeaser, an America-hater, and an anti-war weenie." (p. 189; also 102, & 122)

Well, I'm here to say that Vance is NOT a Quaker; not that there's anything wrong with that. He is no pacifist either. He makes plain that he would fully support a defensive war, if the U.S. were ever invaded. Just sayin'.

Further, his book is not just a compendium of invective. Vance's biography states that he holds degrees in history and theology, as well as economics and accounting. Besides knowingthe literature of orthodox and evangelical writers against war and militarism, he is also steeped in Biblical languages. (Among his other books is one about Greek verbs in the New Testament; another deals with its prepositions. One wonders if they are as controversial in their more esoteric fields.)

It turns out, as he shows in detail, that there is actually a sizeable body of anti-military work by very orthodox, even fundamentalist authors, most of it unmentioned by the tradition's modern spokesmen, and ignored by liberals too, for other reasons. But Vance has reprinted many of these volumes, including one, *The Morality of War*, published in 1829 by a Quaker, Jonathan Dymond, which was widely circulated in its day. (Dymond's essay is now online as a free Google book.)

Christianity and War deploys the author's linguistic skills in a detailed linguistic-theological analysis of the sixth commandment, "Thou shall not kill," from Exodus 20:13 (pp. 84ff). Many recent Bible translations have rendered the text as "Thou shalt not commit murder," on the basis that some kinds of killing were not only sanctioned in the Bible but commanded by various texts.

Vance is not having it. He points out that the Hebrew term translated "kill," in the commandment is not used anywhere in the Old Testament to refer to killing in battles.(86) And he goes on to say,

Exodus 20:13: "Thou shalt not kill."God only knows how many people around the world have been killed as a direct result of

194

U.S. foreign policy. No, I am not equating the United States with Nazi Germany, Soviet Russia, or Red China. . . .[But] From the beginning of the Iraq War, I have maintained that participants in this evil war violate the express teaching of the biblical commandment against killing. Christian apologists for war say that either the commandments don't apply to the state, and therefore killing done in service for the state is permissible, or else that the sixth commandment is limited to murder, and therefore killing done in wartime is permissible. Therefore, just as Calvary covers it all, my past with its sin and shame, so the wearing of a uniform covers it all, my military service with its death and destruction. Thus, killing someone you don't know, and have never seen, in his own territory, who was no threat to anyone until the United States invaded his country, is not murder if the U.S. government says that he should be killed. No soldier is responsible for the death and destruction he inflicts in a foreign country as long as it is state-sanctioned death and destruction. I reject this ghastly statolatry.(106f)

He also takes on those "Bible believers" who defend American wars because the Bible says,"the Lord is a man of war" (Exodus 15:3):

That this is a true statement there is no question, but how this phrase justifies the United States becoming a country of war shows how warped the Christianity of some people is. (261f)

Further, as a biblical literalist, Vance acknowledges that indeed, "God commanded the nation of Israel in the Old Testament to fight against heathen nations (Judges 6:16). . ."

Then he goes right for the jugular:

but George Bush is not God, and America is not the nation of Israel . . . .God sponsored these wars, and used his chosen nation (Deuteronomy 7:11-12) to conduct them,[but] it does not follow that God sponsors American wars, or that America is God's chosen nation. It does not follow unless, of course, one is a Christian apologist for the U.S. government and its wars."(p. 126, 129)

But that is precisely what American War Christianity comes down to: the shockingly idolatrous identification of U.S. interests as being dictated by God, and treating its leaders (especially conservative presidents), as the equivalent of God. (And no, Vance does not regard Romans 13 as a "get-out-of-hell-free" card.)

Such nationalist idolatry is hardly new, nor is it an American invention. But in U.S. history its tracks go back more than two centuries, and its advocates have included many religious leaders considered "progressive" in their day. But in our time this sanctified militarism has become an evangelical-fundamentalist phenomenon, and the paper by Air Force Colonel Millonig shows how groups associated with it have intentionally and diligently colonized much of the armed forces since the Vietnam War:

> The rise of evangelicalism in today's Armed Forces can trace its roots to the Viet Nam War. Public support for the war declined steadily as the years wore on, but evangelical Christians remained generally supportive of the war throughout. Over the course of the war, they found themselves progressively more aligned with the military   a military which increasingly found itself isolated from the general population. . . .
> By the early 1970's, prayer groups, breakfasts, and luncheons became commonplace in the Pentagon. Some activities were sponsored by International Christian Leadership and others by the Christian Men of the Pentagon. An informal outreach group called Teams of Two began to increase its evangelical efforts. . . . Many General Officers actively supported the groups and even held leadership positions as these conservative Christian groups continued to grow in size. By the 1980's, nearly 20 evangelical groups held regular meetings.
> Under this supportive leadership umbrella, participation in conservative Christian groups also increased at the service academies. . . . Throughout the 1990's, a conservative Protestant shift in the chaplain corps mirrored the regular force. Since 1994, the number of Roman Catholic priests in the Air Force alone has dropped 44 percent and similar decreases exist in mainstream Protestant chaplains as well. (Millonig, 4f)

Millonig's critique of this colonization is carefully nuanced, and secular: his point is that, especially at the top, when an organization's leadership all(or mostly) share the same worldview, the resulting groupthink atmosphere leads to bad decisions. For instance, Millonig says,

> When the [G.W. Bush] Administration issued its policy of pre-emptive war in the National Security Strategy, many "mainstream" religions and nearly all Democrats rejected it, insisting pre-emptive war rejects the United Nations charter of war as a last resort and takes a unilateralist, militant approach to national security.
> Many conservative Christians however, applauded the

declaration. In a letter to President Bush, several prominent conservatives strongly endorsed the policy of pre-emptive war against Iraq as "prudent and fall(s) well within the time honored criteria of just war theory.

By now, spring of 2012, we've seen where that kind of foolishness led us; and it was from this pre-emptive cheerleaders' sector that the religious influence on military leadership has come for nearly forty years. I've called this outlook "American War Christianity"; and though I've seldom been accused of speaking too cautiously, Vance makes this phrase look mild. These people and their followers, he insists, make up the "Christian Axis of Evil." (99), adding:

> In the Church's conservative, evangelical, and fundamentalist circles and I identify loosely with all three—much of what is being said is not just wrong, it is evil, immoral, hypocritical, shameful, and more importantly, unscriptural. But the Church is also not saying enough. It is not saying enough about the defective Christianity of the president. It is not saying enough about the evils of war. It is not saying enough about our overgrown military establishment. It is not saying enough about our interventionist foreign policy. It is not saying enough about the warfare state.
>
> President Bush has mastered the art of using religious rhetoric to capture the support of gullible Christians for his aggressive, militaristic, interventionist foreign policy he terms "this great mission." (98)

He pounds this theme repeatedly. One of his most striking posts is called, "Are You A Christian Warmonger?"(27-27). With his permission, we have included this piece below. It presents the reader a quiz, or "self-assessment tool": a list of twenty pro-war cliches, (29) For those who agreed with many of these statements, Vance's "eldering" is sternly forthright.

Vance takes on just about all the biblical rationalizations one could imagine for endorsing wars and their killing, as long as they're being fought by the U.S. We already heard his take on the assertion that "Thou shalt not kill" does not apply; but what about Jesus being a bloodthirsty warrior, especially during his Second Coming battle with the Anti-Christ (Revelation 19). Vance's reply (he says he does believe in the Second Coming, but):

> The problem here is a simple one: American military officers are not surrogates for Jesus Christ. Whatever Jesus Christ did or will do has absolutely no relevance to what the U. S. military does in Iraq

or anywhere else, except, of course, in the depraved mind of a Christian warmonger. The Bible says that "in righteousness" Jesus Christ "doth judge and make war." There is nothing righteous about the actions of U.S. battlefield commanders.(132)

What? The U.S. military is not a surrogate for Jesus? Iraq isn't Armageddon? Why didn't I think of that?

"Pray for our troops," says a militant petition he saw. Vance replies to it this way:

> Yes, we should pray for the troops. We should pray that the troops come home. We should pray that the troops come home now. We should pray that the blood of not one more American soldier is shed on foreign soil. We should pray for the healing of the thousands of U.S. soldiers who have been injured in the senseless Iraq war. We should pray for an end to this unconstitutional, immoral, and unjust war. We should pray that Congress ends funding for this war. We should pray that Bush leaves office a disgraced commander in chief. We should pray that young, impressionable students are not ensnared by military recruiters. We should pray that pastors stop recommending military service to their young men (and women). We should pray that families stop supplying cannon fodder to the military. We should pray that the troops actually start defending this country instead of every other country. We should pray for a change in U.S. foreign policy that can make this all possible.

Not only that: ". . . This ideological desire to legitimize killing in war is an unholy one, and every Christian who attempts to do so should be ashamed of himself and repent "in sackcloth and ashes" (Matthew 11:21)." (86)

The upshot is that *Christianity and War* offers the most trenchant and articulate critique of American War Christianity I have seen. In ten-plus years of struggling with the impact of this phenomenon, his work stands alone.

While he's not at all a pacifist, Vance draws on Quaker sources perhaps more than he realizes. He quotes Friend Jonathan Dymond as "one young in years but old in wisdom," who was exposing the pernicious work of war propaganda in 1827:

> Another cause of our complacency with war, and therefore another cause of war itself, consists in that callousness to human misery which the custom induces. They who are shocked at a single murder on the highway, hear with indifference of the slaughter of a thousand on the field.. . .The inconsistency and disproportionateness

which has been occasioned in our sentiments of benevolence, offers a curious moral phenomenon. . . .

But perhaps the most operative cause of the popularity of war, and of the facility with which we engage in it, consists in this; that an idea of glory is attached to military exploits, and of honor to the military profession. The glories of battle, and of those who perish in it, or who return in triumph to their country, are favorite topics of declamation with the historian, the biographers, and the poet. They have told us a thousands times of dying heroes, who "resign their lives amidst the joys of conquest, and, filled with their country's glory, smile in death;" and thus every excitement that eloquence and genius can command, is employed to arouse that ambition of fame which can be gratified only at the expense of blood.(166f)

Vance also applauds "Thomas Jefferson's 'Quaker' foreign policy"; as the third president put it:

Peace has been our principle, peace is our interest, and peace has saved to the world this only plant of free and rational government now existing in it. However, therefore, we may have been reproached for pursuing our Quaker system, time will affix the stamp of wisdom on it, and the happiness and prosperity of our citizens will attest its merit. And this, I believe, is the only legitimate object of government, and the first duty of governors, and not the slaughter of men and devastation of the countries placed under their care, in pursuit of a fantastic honor, unallied to virtue or happiness . . . . (192f)

And–okay, this is a bit from left field–Vance makes much of the late-life witness of Marine General (and two-time Medal of Honor winner) Smedley D. Butler. Butler became a militant isolationist and anti-militarist activist in the 1930s. He proposed a constitutional "Amendment for Peace," which would have prohibited the American military from fighting or being based beyond a defensive zone around our coasts.

Butler believed that his amendment "would be [an] absolute guarantee to the women of America that their loved ones never would be sent overseas to be needlessly shot down in European or Asiatic or African wars that are no concern of our people."

He also reasoned that because of "our geographical position, it is all but impossible for any foreign power to muster, transport and land sufficient troops on our shores for a successful invasion." In this Butler was echoing Jefferson, who recognized that geography was one of the great advantages of the United States . . . .(404)

199

Why are we talking about a Marine general? Because Smedley Darlington Butler was the product of several Quaker families with deep Pennsylvania roots. He attended a Quaker school before enlisting in the Marines to join the Spanish-American War. And despite his valor under fire, Butler's military career persuaded him that, as he later wrote in the title of a famous booklet, "War is a Racket."(Online for free here: http://www.archive.org/details/WarIsARacket) In hailing him, Vance is again bringing forward a strongly Quaker-influenced figure.

So like it or not, Quaker peace witness has left its fingerprints on Laurence Vance's perspective. But most important is his fundamentalist Christian libertarian outlook. While he repeatedly blasts George W. Bush in these pages, he is no more fond of the many ways Barack Obama has continued most of his predecessor's pro-imperial policies. Though *Christianity and War* was published in 2005 (updated in 2008), before Obama's elevation to the White House; Vance's recent blog posts do not give Bush's successor a pass.

Yet overall Vance minimizes talk of politics outside the recent wars; his book is not a campaign screed. A look at his extensive blog posts makes clear, however, that he's a passionate partisan of the longtime libertarian standard-bearer, Rep. Ron Paul. Vance is also a southerner, and has affinities with the neo-Confederates who despise Abe Lincoln, prefer to call the Civil War by other, rebel-friendly names, wish the Confederate states had been allowed to secede, and then abolished slavery in their own good time.

These views, and many others of the libertarian platform, are deeply problematic to me, and doubtless to many others, who may be drawn to its anti-imperial and anti-militarist features. Nevertheless, Vance prudently keeps these other matters out of his 400-plus pages in *Christianity and War*, and except for taking note of them here, I'll stick to the book's themes. Those are arguments for another day, and another book.

This judgment also takes into account this reviewer's experience of watching numerous Republican presidential debates in late 2011 and early 2012. In these fora, I have heard Vance's hero, Rep. Ron Paul, repeatedly make forthright and eloquent challenges to U.S. militarist and imperial pretensions, oppose current and threatened wars, and call out presidents of both parties for perpetuating a giant military- industrial complex–and do all this in the face of boos and openly hostile crowds.

Besides offering an impressive show of personal courage and integrity, Paul's statements were the most extensive challenges to American war-mongering at the presidential campaign level in forty years–forty long years since the valiant but doomed campaign of Senator George McGovern in 1972.

I don't say Paul has converted me to libertarianism beyond its anti-militarist stance; but dammit, when he's right, he's right. And he has certainly won my respect, even admiration, for these anti-militarist convictions. And likewise, Laurence Vance hasn't turned me into a pre-millennial, dispensationalist Baptist, or made me any more sympathetic to a neo-confederate outlook. But his assault on the theological and sectarian underpinnings of American War Christianity is right on target, and an achievement that is serious and credible on many fronts. It deserves wide attention as such. It is intellectually, historically, theologically and biblically informed, and as a polemicist, his aim is true.

The book (and the blog) takes on the "Christian warmongers" on their own turf, naming names, citing sources, and demolishing every major pillar of their defense of war. After a decade of seeing this war machine close up, I remain convinced that such a deconstruction is one of the most important tasks of peace work.

Yet I know of no liberal Christian writer who has come anywhere close to a similar effort

Shame on them; shame on us. A bow to Laurence Vance, and *Christianity and War,* for going where we have feared to tread.

An Interview With Laurence Vance
Author of *Christianity and War*

QT. Please tell us something about your own background: where you were born, brought up, etc. And where you were educated; your brief bio speaks of degrees in history and theology–where did you study, and what fields did you concentrate in?

LV. I am a semi-native Floridian. I was brought up on the east coast of central Florida, lived in the navy town of Pensacola for twenty-four years, and now reside in central Florida. My theological degrees are from small Independent Baptist schools that would now probably prefer that I didn't name them. I also have degrees in history, economics, and accounting from the University of West Florida, including a master's degree in accounting. However, most of my education stems from years of reading, writing, and studying.

QT. Are you still teaching, or is your writing and publishing a full time occupation now?

LV. I no longer teach and only wish that my writing and publishing were now a full-time occupation. I write about 100 articles a year now. I could conceivably double my output if I didn't have to work to supplement my writing and publishing.

QT. Have you always been identified with the conservative Baptist tradition, or was there an evolution/conversion somewhere along the way?

LV. I was raised a Roman Catholic. After a brief period as an evangelical and then a Southern Baptist, I became an Independent Baptist and have been so for my entire adult life.

QT. Ditto for your involvement with libertarian thought and support for Ron Paul. Were you ever a Republican? (Or Democrat?)

LV. I thank God I was never a Democrat. I am ashamed to say that I was once a Republican, albeit a libertarian-leaning one. It was sometime in 1993 or 1994 that I made the acquaintance of Lew Rockwell, the founder and then president and now chairman of the Ludwig von Mises Institute, after stumbling across a Mises Institute publication called The Free Market. It was through articles in The Free Market that I was introduced to Murray Rothbard. This led me to the Rothbard-Rockwell Report and the realization that I was more of a libertarian than a conservative. I have been a diehard libertarian ever since. It was probably about ten years ago that I met Ron Paul, although I had been familiar with his great work on behalf of liberty for several years before then. Dr. Paul is one of the few members of Congress that I have ever had any respect for.

QT. Your positions on dismantling the empire and war machine are pretty clear. But what kinds of reforms/repentance would you recommend to Christian churches to free themselves of this "Christian warmongering" spirit? "Sackcloth and ashes" would be appropriate, but are there other changes called for as well?

LV. Christians need to need to demilitarize their church. To help them do so, I wrote "How to Demilitarize Your Church." Here is the condensed version.

First, they need to recognize the need to demilitarize their church by educating themselves as to the problems with the military its unnecessary size, its bloated budget, its inefficiency, its merchants-of-death contractors, its murderous mercenaries, its weapons of mass destruction, its unconstitutional mission, its inability to protect its own headquarters, its foreign interventions, its foreign occupations, its overseas bases and troop deployments – and just how much the military has pervaded all of society.

Second, stop the practices of military appreciation days, recognizing current members of the military or veterans, making unspecific and unspecified prayers for "the troops in harms way," putting "God Bless Our Troops" or "Pray for Our Troops" or "Thank a Veteran" slogans on church signs, bulletins, and websites, calling soldiers returning from overseas heroes, and the blasphemous nonsense about the troops dying for our freedoms like Christ died for our sins.

Third, Christians need to immunize their churches from the military by warning young people about the evils of "serving" in the military, never ceasing to point out although God in the Old Testament commanded the nation of Israel to fight against heathen nations, the president of the United States is not God, America is not the nation of Israel, the U.S. military is not the Lord's army, the Christian's sword is the word of God, and the only warfare the New Testament encourages the Christian to wage is against the world, the flesh, and the devil.

QT. One of your pieces, "What Happened to the Southern Baptists?" points to the radical shift in their denominational statements and behavior. But it doesn't tell us much about how and why that drastic change came about. Can you outline your own sense of what made that shift possible? And have you seen any softening of that warmongering spirit since the departure of Bush & Cheney?

LV. I believe it all has to do with the newfound admiration of Americans for the military that began after the debacle in Vietnam. On this I would highly recommend two books: Anne Loveland, *American Evangelicals and the U.S. Military 1942-1993* (LSU Press, 1996) and Andrew Bacevich, *The New American Militarism: How Americans Are Seduced by War* (Oxford, 2005). As Bacevich says: "In the aftermath of Vietnam, evangelicals came to see the military as an enclave of virtue, a place of refuge where the sacred remnant of patriotic Americans gathered and preserved American principles from extinction."

I have not seen any softening of the warmongering spirit in evangelical churches. Although some Christians may now openly criticize the Iraq War and even call for the withdrawal of U.S. troops from Afghanistan, it is all too little, too late. Adoration of the military has never abated and actually seems to have increased no matter what details come to light about atrocities committed by U.S. troops in Iraq and Afghanistan. But of course, both wars were entirely criminal from the beginning.

QT. In your view, have the deaths of Jerry Falwell, D. James Kennedy, and Bill Bright, plus the retirement of James Dobson had any measurable effect toward softening the "Christian warmonger" bloc, or are there new leaders, and others less visible to outsiders, who have taken their places?

LV. Not at all. There are always new warmongers to take their place. I think the influence of these Christians "leaders" is overstated. I'm sorry to say that many evangelicals are just incorrigible warmongers and military idolaters. Just look at how Christians in the Bible Belt are voting for Newt Gingrich (Catholic), Mitt Romney (Mormon), and Rick Santorum (Catholic) instead of Ron Paul (Protestant). The main problems they have with Paul are his views on war and foreign policy.

QT. How important do you consider the "Christian Zionist" movement spearheaded by such as John Hagee to the "Christian Warmonger" ideology and influence? And do you see its impact waxing or waning? Are there specific ways you can suggest to challenge this "crusade"?

LV. As a dispensationalist and a premillennialist, I have certain sympathies with the "Christian Zionist" movement. However, I think the warmonger spin and the constant defense of the government of Israel are completely off base. I think the movement is often blamed for having too much influence. I believe that Christian devotion to the military and American exceptionalism are a greater influence. Challenges to this "crusade" must be rooted in biblical arguments.

QT. You call out many prominent conservative evangelical figures in your book, from Charles Colson to Bill Bright and, of course, Jerry Falwell. Did any of these members of the "Christian Axis of Evil" ever respond to your critiques, either directly or indirectly?

LV. Not at all. Neither directly nor indirectly. And when their followers did respond to my critiques, it was usually just name calling (communist, liberal, pacifist, traitor), accusations ("you hate America" or "you want our troops to die"), or profanity.

QT. There are many calls today for a pre-emptive U.S. attack on Iran. If such an attack occurs, how important a role do you think the "Christian warmongers" will play in instigating and defending it? Do you have any thoughts about how these voices can be countered in advance, beyond your blog?

LV. Because all the talk about Iran usually includes Israel, Christian warmongers who think that God needs America's assistance to protect Israel would love to see a preemptive strike on Iran by the United States, Israel, or both in unison. They don't have enough influence to instigate it, but would be the biggest defenders of such a thing. These voices can be countered with the truth of what an immoral and disastrous thing a preemptive strike would be as presented at least every week at websites like Antiwar.com and LewRockwell.com and in the sane writings of conservatives like Paul Craig Roberts and Pat Buchanan.

QT. I read in the book your comment that, in addition to many replies to your blog posts calling you all kinds of terrible names such as "traitor" and, of all things, "Quaker," you had also heard from many soldiers. Overall, are the active duty GIs who have written to you more sympathetic to your views than the civilians or veterans you have hear from – or less so? (Certainly, the soldier who gave me your book liked what he had read.) If more so, on what points are they most in agreement?

LV. Most of the active duty military who have written me are sympathetic to my views. Many of them say they are getting out of the military as soon as they are able. A few have told me that they were seeking to become a conscientious objector. Soldiers seem to be most in agreement that they are not defending our freedoms and have no business fighting foreign wars.

The veterans who write me are generally very sympathetic, and especially Vietam Vets. The few veterans who write in disagreement normally just blast me with profanity and threats. But the worst abuse I get is from civilians. I know they are civilians because the military people, whether friend or foe, always identify themselves. Thankfully, the abuse has let up considerably since the wars in Afghanistan and Iraq have turned out to be such debacles.

QT. Among your sources, you cite favorably Jonathan Dymond and General Smedley Butler. Dymond was a Quaker, and Butler came from a long line of Pennsylvania Quakers on both sides; his post-military activism shows (to me, at least) a resurgence of his heritage in large measure. Are there any other Quaker sources you have drawn on? Or conversely, are their Quaker writers/figures who you have discovered pushing the "Christian warmonger" line? (One might point to Richard Nixon for the latter; yet his "Quakerism" was the next thing to a military secret, and it's hard to find any signs of its influence. But are there others?

LV. Aside from Dymond and Butler I don't recall any other Quaker sources that I have drawn on. I have always drawn on a wide variety of sources, including Catholic, Orthodox, Church of Christ, Mennonite, Presbyterian, and Baptist. Nixon was a disgrace to all Quakers for his continued fighting of the Vietnam War that he inherited from Johnson, and especially his horrendous bombing campaigns. Like the Iraq and Afghan Wars, Vietnam was criminal from the beginning. I have been called a Quaker in derision because of my anti-war views. I feel, though, that I am in good company. Thomas Jefferson, who espoused a foreign policy of peace and nonintervention, referred to his principles as "our Quaker system."

An Excerpt from *Christianity and War:*

Are You a Christian Warmonger?
Originally posted on the blog April 7, 2005

by Laurence M. Vance
Reprinted by permission

It is appalling that many defenders of the war in Iraq are Christians; it is even worse when they appeal to Scripture to excuse or justify a senseless war that has now resulted in the deaths of over 1,500 Americans and the wounding of countless thousands more.

When the president of the Ayn Rand Institute, Yaron Brook, appeared last December on The O'Reilly Factor and called for "harsher military measures in Iraq," it was disheartening to hear him advocate that the U.S. military should "be a lot more brutal," "bring this war to the civilians," and "turn Fallujah into dust." As reprehensible as these statements are, they come as no surprise since Brook is guided by Objectivism and not Christianity.

But the sad fact is that some Christian warmongers are just as militant. They consider this war to be a Christian crusade against Islam and view the thousands of dead Iraqi civilians as collateral damage. Congressman Sam Johnson (R-TX), when speaking on February 19 at Suncreek United Methodist Church in Allen, Texas, related to the congregation how he told President Bush: "Syria is the problem. Syria is where those weapons of mass destruction are, in my view. You know, I can fly an F-15, put two nukes on'em and I'll make one pass. We won't have to worry about Syria anymore." Although Johnson later claimed to be joking, it is strange that "the crowd roared with applause" instead of with laughter.

Other Christians are passive Christian warmongers. Although they don't actively participate in the war in Iraq, cherish the thought of dead Iraqis, or "joke" about nuking Muslims, they excuse, dismiss, make apologies for, and defend the war (and sometimes even the torture of prisoners and the killing of civilians) with such profound scriptural and logical assertions as "we should always obey the government," "Bush is a Christian so we should follow his leadership," or "doesn't the Bible say there is'a time of war.'"

The following test is designed for Christians of any stripe to determine to what degree, if any, that they are a Christian warmonger. These statements are based on things I have read or been told by Christians seeking to excuse or justify the war in Iraq in order to defend President Bush. The statements are not in any particular order. Each statement is designed to be answered with either "true" or "false." A "true" answer receives 1 point and a "false" answer receives no points. Add up your points and consult the scale at the bottom to obtain the results.

1. The commandment "Thou shalt not kill" (Exodus 20:13) never applies to killing in war.

2. We should follow President Bush's leadership because he is a Christian.

3. Torturing Iraqi prisoners to obtain information is okay if it saves the life of one American.

4. The command to "submit yourselves to every ordinance of man for the Lord's sake" (1 Peter 2:13) means that we should kill foreigners in their country if the government says to do so.

5. U.S. intervention in the Middle East is necessary to protect Israel from the Arabs.

6. Muslim civilians killed by the U.S. military in Iraq and Afghanistan are just collateral damage.

7. A preemptive war against Iraq is nothing to be concerned about because the Bible says there is "a time of war" (Ecclesiastes 3:8).

8. It is okay to kill Muslims in Iraq because the terrorists who kill Jews are Muslims.

9. Since the Bible says that "the powers that be are ordained of God" (Romans 13:1), we should always obey the government when it comes to war.

10. U.S. wars and interventions abroad are ultimately a good thing because they pave the way for the spread of the gospel.

11. The command to "obey magistrates" (Titus 3:1) means that it is not immoral to drop bombs on foreign countries if the government says it should be done.

12. The U.S. should take vengeance on Muslims because of the September 11th attacks.

13. A perpetual war against the Muslim world in order to fight terrorism is just because "The LORD is a man of war" (Exodus 15:3).

14. Christians can wholeheartedly participate in their government's wars since God commanded the Jews in the Old Testament to go to war.

15. Christians can proudly serve in the military in any capacity.

16. Christians can proudly serve in the CIA in any capacity.

17. The command to "obey God rather than men" (Acts 5:29) does not apply to refusing to kill for the state in a war.

18. God approves of the war in Iraq because Islam is a false religion.

19. Muslims in the Middle East hate Americans because of their Christianity, their freedoms, and their democratic values.

20. Christians in Iraq are better off now than they were under Saddam Hussein.

1 ____	2 ____	3 ____	4 ____	5 ____	6 ____	7 ____	
8 ____	9 ____	10 ____	11 ____	12 ____	13 ____	14 ____	15
____ 16 ____	17 ____	18 ____	19 ____	20 ____			
Total ____							

If you scored:

0   You are truly a man of peace.

1 4 You are not a Christian warmonger, but you may want to reevaluate some of your beliefs.

5 8 You are on your way to becoming a Christian warmonger, but there is still hope for you; repent.

9 12 You are a Christian warmonger; turn from the error of your ways.

13 16 You are a militant Christian warmonger; get right with God.

17 20 You may be a Christian but you are a crazed warmonger whose idea of Christianity is seriously defective.

First posted at
http://www.lewrockwell.com/vance/vance40.html

From *Quaker Theology* #21, Fall 2012

Deep Green Resistance: Strategy to Save the Planet, by Aric Mcbay, Lierre Keith, and Derrick Jensen. Seven Stories Press, 560 pages.

Reviewed by Chuck Fager

In early August 2012, a large Chevron oil refinery in Richmond, California was hit by an explosion and fire, disrupting production of as much as 240,000 barrels a day.

About two weeks later, at the huge Amuay refinery in Venezuela, an explosion and fire killed more than forty people, and shut down the processing of over 600,000 barrels of oil a day.

Venezuelan officials claimed that the refinery was back in operation by early September, pumping out forty percent of the previous total, with more expected as repairs continue. In California, however, industry experts said it could be months before the Chevron refinery resumes full production. By early October, gasoline prices in California were breaking records, in many places topping $5 per gallon.

Supporters of Venezuelan president Hugo Chavez, then locked in a tight race for re-election, suggested that sabotage might be involved in the Amuas blast, and pointed at the U.S. Special Forces troops operating from neighboring Colombia as prime suspects.

Maybe. But I want to point at another candidate: the Oil Industry Destruction Team, not from the American Special forces, but from the Deep Green Resistance (DGR). To wit: "In this scenario, well-organized underground militants would make coordinated attacks on energy infrastructure around the world. These would take whatever tactical form militants could muster   actions against pipelines, power lines, tankers, and refineries . . . ." (439)

Actually, I made up the "Oil Industry Destruction Team." But not the Deep Green Resistance – or their desire to blow up the oil industry's key installations. Further, while the DGR saboteurs would consider five dollar gasoline a modest success, it would only be a small step on their path. That's because their larger objective, spelled out several times in these pages, is this: "We want, in no uncertain terms, to bring down civilization." Or, as in the section on "Decisive Ecological Warfare strategy": "Goal 1: To disrupt and dismantle industrial civilization; to thereby remove the ability of the powerful to exploit the marginalized and destroy the planet."

In this "Decisive Ecological Warfare," the energy infrastructure oil, gas, coal – will provide a central set of targets. The plan is to mount enough attacks on enough critical points in the grid and associated networks that the whole network crumbles: "The overall thrust . . .would be to use selective attacks to accelerate collapse in a deliberate way, like shoving a rickety building." (433)

But wait a second. What about all the people – scores of millions in the U.S. alone – who depend on this infrastructure for their very lives?

Good question. It is posed explicitly in the book: "If we dismantle civilization, won't that kill millions of people in cities?" a reader asks, on page 422. "What about them?"

Ah, yes. Well, you see: they're part of the problem. So they, and the farms that sustain them, have to go. In a target list of "All activities that destroy living communities must cease, forever," coauthor Lierre Keith notes that: "It includes agriculture and it includes life in cities." (194) Besides, it turns out all those urban dwellers are not actually innocent after all. Co-author Derrick Jensen pronounces the verdict: "No matter what you do, your hands will be blood red. If you participate in the global economy, your hands are blood red because the global economy is murdering humans and – nonhumans the planet over." (422)

Yet even though all urbanites are guilty, we shouldn't think our authors are unmindful of the human cost of this sudden, forced collapse. We are assured that they agonize over the "wrenching ethical decisions" such attacks will raise: "If there are people between us and our targets, they are not soldiers. We can say [and they do say CF] that civilization is a war against the living world, but that does not answer the moral dilemma of putting living beings at risk. I [co-author Lierre Keith] have no answer, only an emergency the size of land, sea and sky. . . . No one who does not feel the burden of the moral risks of serious action should be making these decisions. Extremism has its own addictive thrills; violence feeds masculinity too easily, and the human heart is quite capable of justifying atrocity. And I know that decisions have to be made, life and death decisions, the decisions of the desperate." (497, 499)

So, for instance, if the Amuas explosion were the result of DGR sabotage, the perpetrators would have figured that the 40-plus people it killed were an acceptable cost in terms of "collateral damage." And in the full-on campaign of "Decisive Ecological Warfare" as envisaged by these authors (425ff), the casualty toll would amount to 40 with several zeroes added. Several.

Oops – did I forget to mention that I picked up *Deep Green Resistance* on the book table of a strongly green-oriented Yearly Meeting this past summer? The thesis and authors were entirely new to me. But once open, I couldn't shut the book; bought it and read it from cover to cover.

As a writer, I'm something of a fanatic about freedom of the press and freedom to read. So I would not propose banning books. Nevertheless, standing at the book table, turning the pages in something like a state of shock, I wondered how a Quaker bookstore manager would feel about helping disseminate the ideas and plans that *Deep Green Resistance* laid out.

I wondered because, to be strictly accurate, I had encountered many of the ideas in it before – not in a Quaker setting, but in my day job, witnessing for peace near a large U.S. military base which hosts many of the most secretive and ruthless killer units of our war machine. These units excel in exactly the skills, such as clandestine sabotage, that these authors recommend and say they are working to attract and, pardon the expression, refine in the service of destroying industrial civilization.

Having browsed at many book tables at many Quaker gatherings, I can't recall seeing – such a manifesto and textbook on one of them before. It is jarring to find, across from Woolman's *Journal*, Kelly's *Testament of Devotion*, and tracts extolling pacifism, a book which favorably referenced the Special Forces Guerrilla Warfare handbook, and the *Sabotage Manual* of the pre-CIA OSS. It hails the IRA terror campaigns, along with the French Resistance and the Algerian rebels, as models of action on their intensely felt "concern," and dispassionately analyzes the proper uses of assassination, and the necessity to "eliminate" (i.e., murder) informants, infiltrators, or those who leave the underground groups with critical identifying information.

In military terms, especially in the U.S. clandestine units, none of this is unusual; DGR's authors have done this part of their homework well. For Quakers – well, not so much. (I hope.)

Yet if you look past the surface of Quaker history, there are analogues. Who else has read of Abraham Lincoln writing to Eliza Gurney in 1864, as the Civil War raged:

> "Your people – the Friends – have had, and are having, a very great trial. On principle, and faith, opposed to both war and oppression, they can only practically oppose oppression by war. In this hard dilemma, some have chosen one horn and some the other."

And it was so: many young male Friends chose the "horn" of joining the Union army, where they saw and took part in unspeakable violence.

Or what of the Quaker magistrates who ruled Rhode island in 1675, when an Indian terror war engulfed the colony, and most of eastern New England? How were they to uphold their peace testimony while discharging their official duties to protect the citizenry at large? In that case, they did two things: they passed the first Conscientious Objection law for their brethren of "tender conscience" as to bearing arms; then they went to war, joining the campaign which won the war and destroyed much of what was left of Indian culture in their region.

In both these cases (as later in World Wars One and Two), many Friends came to believe that an imminent emergency on their very doorstep required a response which included violence – not just the force of self-defense, but the organized violence of warfare.

So let me not retreat into naivete: dealing with actual wars up close has often been difficult for otherwise dedicated Friends. Thus the question becomes: are we in such an emergency situation now, with regard to the environment? And if so, is guerrilla war aimed at destroying civilization the proper and faithful response?

In DGR, the authors' answers, of course, are Yes, and *Hell, Yes!* They make their case forcefully, in detail, and with a seemingly well-organized, coherent argument. I have to hand it to them: they take the tenor and content of much doomsday ecological rhetoric, and follow the logic out to the end, or at least, one end.

At points they almost had me nodding in agreement that it might indeed be better if nine-tenths of the world's humans would hurry up and perish in the wake of these guerrilla/saviors' intended infrastructure destruction, so the survivors could flourish quietly in the scattered, feminist-oriented, elder- governed hunter-gatherer villages that they foresee in their place. (26) There they'll follow the new religion that Lierre Keith says we must invent to replace the irredeemably sexist traditional faiths, especially the hopelessly misogynist Abrahamic religions. (160)

Almost nodding? Forgive me; that was an exaggeration for stylistic effect. Once I read through the entirely of their plans and saw where they were headed, my reaction was similar to others mentioned dismissively in passing: they were talking a "Pol Pot-styled genocide," but on a much larger scale; which they acknowledged that "the authors of this book are often accused of suggesting." (225)

The accusation has merit. If they could, these self-appointed world saviors are prepared to kill off 95 percent of humanity to impose their vision of how the remnant ought to live: they insist that "we face a decision, individually and as a resistance movement. Because a small number of people could directly target that [industrial] infrastructure; a few more, willing to persist, could potentially bring it down." (110)

Co-author Aric McBay puts it this way: "A drop in the human population is inevitable, and fewer people will die if collapse happens sooner. . . . Therefore, those of us who care about the future of the planet have to dismantle the industrial energy infrastructure as rapidly as

212

possible. We'll all have to deal with the social consequences as best we can. Besides, rapid collapse is ultimately good for humans – even if there's a partial die-off – because at least some people survive." (439) And Lierre Keith gets coy: "The authors of this book have been accused of suggesting genocide: meanwhile, the genocide is happening now." (502)

Does this make sense? Consider: life is a terminal condition; over time, the fatality rate is always one hundred percent. But if we're all going to die eventually, does that make it okay for somebody to intentionally kill you, or me, or our children, now, to achieve some anticipated future benefit?

Such early, induced deaths do happen, of course; normally, we call them murders. When they happen on an industrial scale, it's genocide. And urging the elimination of ninety to ninety-five percent of – human life by intentional action qualifies as genocide squared in my book.

But, they promise, their genocide will be better than "ours," that is, the planetary damage inflicted by the current system. And besides, remember that they promise to feel bad over the "wrenching ethical decisions" involved in carrying out their program. Indeed.

I had to get past the mind-boggling scale of this scheme, which wasn't easy, before I could respond to the underlying chain of reasoning. Once I did, however, many features of it became familiar. So familiar, in fact, they were almost hackneyed. I've lived through similar arguments, and their calamitous consequences, at least twice in my adult life.

First of all, a key premise of their program is that nothing less will or can be "effective;" all else is mere talk or escapism. And to give them their due, they present often incisive critiques of many other approaches to the environmental damage of our present course. Yet the record of their violence-based approach is not subjected to the same scrutiny.

But it needs to be: Guerrilla insurgencies often fail, with great and pointless loss of life. And where others have initially succeeded (as, for instance, in Zimbabwe, Algeria or, dare I say it, Pol Pot's Cambodia), they have often produced new regimes as destructive and repressive as (or worse than) anything that went before.

The authors' response is that, no matter how flawed their plan might be, the present course is unimaginably worse, and its future bound to be even more destructive.

But here another question comes into view: in saying that, they are claiming to know the future, at least of the current trajectory. But do they?

In this case, one can be definite: no, they don't. Nobody does, after all. And the limits of the authors' prescience are shown by the fact that when they venture into actual prediction, they run smack into the Harold Camping problem. (Camping, one will recall, was the radio preacher who put up billboards nationwide announcing Judgment Day and the End of

Time in May or October of 2011.) In DGR, they cite a confident prediction that by "2012" there will be "an epidemic of permanent blackouts [that] spreads worldwide . . . ."(42)

Well, 2012 is more than three-quarters over as this is written, and while it has seen its share of natural disasters, Judgment Day has yet to arrive, and the lights are still going on in most places that have electricity. More unsettling, this year the U.S. appears to be on its way to producing more energy rather than less. So like preacher Camping, the DGR Endtimes scenario deserves to be taken with a grain of salt. Or maybe a shaker, full.

Further, not knowing the future undercuts their forecast in another way: in many areas of the world, population is dropping even without genocidal attacks; so there may be hope for a softer landing than they envision. Similarly, technology is advancing in many areas related to energy use. Is it really impossible, unthinkable that technology, which largely got us into our current environmental fix, might be able to help us figure out how to, at least, muddle through it? Sometimes I feel pessimistic too; but not always, and who can be sure?

Next, there is the problem of the vanguard. People, the authors declare, cannot be counted on to do the right thing, either in society generally, and certainly not regarding the planet. "The vast majority of the population will do nothing," declares Keith, "unless they are led, cajoled, or forced." (26) Only the latter option will now serve, they insist, and thus they are ready to shoulder the unwelcome burden of coercion. Not that the authors plan to blow up the refineries and power grid themselves, you understand; but they expect to inspire and attract those cadres who will actually "shove the rickety building" of industrial civilization, and the billions of us living in it, over the cliff.

Moreover, they are confident that, despite the inevitable and regrettable "collateral damage," their violence will be different, and better than that of the status quo. Keith, a determined feminist, is particularly confident of this, insisting that "violence is a broad category of action; it can be wielded destructively or wisely. . . .We can build a resistance movement and a supporting culture in which atrocities are always unacceptable; in which penalties for committing them are swift and severe; in which violence is not glorified as a concept but instead understood as a specific set of actions that we may have to take up, but that we will also set down to return to our communities . . . .We need our combatants to be of impeccable character for our public image, for the efficacy of our underground cells, and for the new society we're trying to build. . . . . Only people with a distaste for violence should be allowed to use it." (83)

Well, good luck with that. After my decade of watching U.S. combat forces returning from the current wars, I've seen too many once-idealistic

214

youths of good character reduced to a state in which suicides outnumber combat deaths, rapes and domestic violence are rampant, along with drug abuse and alcoholism. Reports from other war-torn countries reinforce these observations. (The technical phrase for this, if I recall correctly, is, "War is Hell.") So count me as deeply skeptical about developing a new, civilized variety of deep green violence.

And when it comes to their scenario for "Decisive Ecological Warfare," the forecasts, while well-informed at one level, follow a path that is all-too familiar, and disastrous.

Consider the recent case of Iraq: we were confidently told that Saddam Hussein was as bad as Hitler or worse; that he certainly had WMDs and was ready to use them against us; that all nonviolent responses to his regime were hopeless or naive; that dissenters from the plan to remove him were uninformed, foolish, and/or terrorist sympathizers; that while there would be some unavoidable civilian casualties, these would be strictly minimized and the airstrikes surgical; that our troops would be greeted with cheers as liberators; and the good we would accomplish would far outweigh any harm done. Meanwhile, the war would be cheap, and quickly pay for itself.

How did it turn out? US officials and combat commanders didn't know as much about Hussein or Iraq as they thought; they completely misjudged the internal balance of forces in the country, and unleashed terrible waves of internecine bloodletting (which continue, almost ten years later); the war produced millions of refugees; the planners grossly under-estimated the war's cost, both in blood and treasure; and grossly over-estimated the US forces' ability to direct events. They lost control of the violence, and saw their idealistic pronouncements descend into the moral sewers of Abu Ghraib, Guantanamo, and black site torture prisons. And after them all have come the killer drones.

The U.S. lost the Iraq war. Thirty-five years earlier, after a decade of fighting similar in many respects, it had likewise lost the Vietnam war. It will soon lose the Afghanistan war as well.

All of which brings a new and decidedly colder light to the bedrock issue of "effectiveness." The authors insist that nothing less than an eco-war, spread across an area vastly larger than Iraq can "effectively" end human damage to the environment. They will end the damage with a new kind of feminist-informed, genteel violence, that will bring down civilization while somehow minimizing harm to the innocent. The short-term human cost, they inconsistently admit (but shrug off) will be huge; but the few survivors will thank these revolutionaries in the end.

How feasible is this plan to smash civilization with guerrilla strikes on infrastructure? Frankly, it looks to me like a steep mountain to climb. The world is a big place; there's an awful lot of infrastructure, and it's not all linked together. Much of it is also very resilient: large pieces have come back from major shocks.

The 9-11 attacks are a prime example here: yes, they dofit the small-scale covert model: a handful of fanatics did bring down the twin towers, killed more than 2000, and traumatized the nation. No question, that attack was a very big deal.

But look also at what it did NOT accomplish: 9-11 didn't crash the U.S. economy (it took our own feral financiers to do that, several years later, and not with underwear bombs, but with paper and glowing computer screens, from plush corner offices). Nor did 9-11 crush the US military, or paralyze the government; even major league baseball was only interrupted for a week.

So: 9-11 was a historic terrorist trauma, yes; but it came nowhere near shoving the US over the edge of any abyss. It suggests that bringing down civilization, even just America's flawed version of it, is a much bigger undertaking. A much bigger war.Is this really almost within the reach of "a small number of people," and needing only "a few more, willing to persist" to "bring it down." (110) Again, I doubt it.

Which raises one final query: what do the authors know of war, real war, beyond what they have read? There is no indication of direct experience among any of the three.

So let me be plain: DGR's plan is fantasy. Dangerous fantasy. And folly. But a potentially seductive folly, particularly in certain credulous corners of our society. The authors appear to be aiming their thick volume squarely at younger readers, particularly those clustered around hippie enclaves and liberal college towns. In their recounting of how the "decisive" warfare will go down, they list as centers of resistance Asheville, North Carolina; Austin, Texas; Burlington, Vermont; Eugene, Oregon; Madison, Wisconsin; Berkeley; Lawrence, Kansas; Northampton, Massachusetts; and Ithaca, new York: hip college towns all, with only one in the Ivy League. In midsummer of 2012, a DGR recruiting roadshow traveled north from Florida to Washington DC, stopping at several college towns and activist collectives, where they shared a summary of the book. The tour team was five young people, who faithfully called for the development of underground groups to bring down civilization, for our own good.

Can anything be salvaged from this DGR false gospel? Perhaps. To the extent that it contributes to the growth of what it calls "a culture of resistance" to environmental degradation, there could be some positive potential. Such "cultures of resistance" need not be part of mass death cults such as DGR envisions. Quakerism has, in time of persecution and war, sometimes performed similar functions. This history has not escaped our authors' notice: they mention Quakers several times as examples of such a resistance culture.

The attention is flattering, but caution is called for. Environmental concern is widespread among Friends today; but I urge us to clearly distinguish this concern from the genocidal pretensions and rhetoric of the DGR approach. There are practical as well as religious reasons for this.: DGR's dreams of "shoving the rickety building" of industrial civilization into collapse by sabotage and violence are not only unhinged, they are also a recipe for legal trouble, both for participants and their fellow travelers. Co-author Keith refers to the "Green Scare" (170), a series of federal indictments and trials of environmental underground activists in the western states for arson and other crimes involving animal farms, horticultural facilities, housing developments, cell phone towers and other targets. The authors expect more government crackdowns, and I believe they're quite right to do so. But if Quakers are going to face persecution, let it not be for such a crackpot scheme.

Nevertheless, I predict this book will have a long shelf life, and a spreading influence. Parts of it could make a valuable study guide even for many who can see through and set aside the grandiose illusions of their planned eco-armageddon. This would include the preponderance of liberal Friends, who subscribe to one or another of the ecological transformation schemes described and challenged in its pages. The work of understanding this "deep green" version, sifting out what's valuable in its critiques, and understanding its limits, already glimmering in the flames of the Chevron and Amuay refineries, will be a useful and enlightening exercise.

Maybe that's why the book was on the yearly meeting's book table.

Maybe.

FIVE: Sun Tzu Who? – Major Essays

Speaking Peace, Living Peace

Baltimore Yearly Meeting
In the American Civil War

Compiled & Edited by Chuck Fager
2003

Introduction: How have Quakers lived out their peace testimony in time of war? And in particular, what about wars in which they were directly caught up in the hostilities?

The Hicksite Baltimore Yearly Meeting was one such body. Its territory included many places which were to become some of the most bitterly contested battlefields of the U.S. Civil War. The following excerpts from the Baltimore minute books of 1861 to 1865 record their testimony and their trials in these years of trouble. They are presented here for purposes of remembrance and reflection in our time.

Through out this period, the yearly meeting's Discipline called upon monthly meetings to prepare answers annually to a specified set of Queries, and submit them to their superior Quarterly Meetings, which passed them on to the Yearly Meeting.

At the yearly meeting sessions these responses were brought together and summarized, The state of the Society indicated by the responses was then carefully considered. This discussion was reviewed in a Minute of Exercise. Among these Queries was the following:

"Sixth Query. Do you maintain a faithful testimony against oaths; an hireling ministry; bearing arms, training, or other military services; being concerned in any fraudulent or clandestine trade; buying or vending goods so imported, or prize goods; and against encouraging lotteries of any kinds?"

As late as 1858, the responses by Baltimore's monthly Meetings on this topic were summed up thus:

"Our testimony against a hireling ministry, oaths, military services, clandestine trade, prize goods and lotteries, appear to be generally maintained."

But a cautionary note can be found in a letter to *The Friend* of London, in 11th Month, 1859, signed "Pacificus," and which said of Friends on the eve of this contest:

"We live in a well-ordered state, where persons and property are, with rare exceptions, amply secure from the hand of violence, and in a country where the presence of a foreign enemy has not been felt for centuries. It is no trial of faith for us to abstain from the use of arms for our protection, and to refuse to engage in military service., We can scarcely, by any effort of the imagination, place ourselves in the position of those, who, in the midst of anarchy and lawlessness, feel the necessity of being always on their guard against violence, or who experience the misery of seeing their homes desolated by the invasion of a hostile army. It therefore becomes us, at the present day, while stedfastly supporting the Christian doctrines which we believe to be right, to speak with diffidence, as never having really had our principles put to the test."

Such a test was soon to come for Baltimore Yearly Meeting Friends. The minutes below describe, in their own words, how they grappled with the shock and the impact of this "desolating evil."

1861

From SUMMARY ANSWERS TO THE QUERIES

Sixth

Friends appear to be mostly careful to maintain our testimony against a hireling ministry, oaths, military service, clandestine trade, prize goods, and lotteries. Yet some deficiency is acknowledged by several of the reports to exist, in the support of our important Christian testimony against war and military services, some cases of which are under care.

Baltimore   10th Mo 30th

The Committee appointed at a former sitting to endeavor to embody some of the exercises of this Meeting, produced the following Minute, which was read and united with, viz:
During the consideration of the state of our Religious Society, as reported from the Quarterly Meetings, this Meeting has been solemnly impressed with the great responsibility that rests upon us as professors of the Christian name, that we should manifest in our life and conversation, the fruits of a Christian spirit, devoting our hearts without reserve , to the service of God.
In view of the present unhappy condition of our country, we have been reminded of the circumstances by which George Fox, and his companions

in spiritual labor, were surrounded when in a time of civil war, they ent forth as ambassadors for Christ, to proclaim and exemplify his peaceable kingdom. The false rest of the people had been broken their confidence in their spiritual guide had been shaken and finding in ceremonial observances no spiritual sustenance, they were induced to seek in the inner sanctuary of the heart, for that communion with the Father of spirits, which alone can satisfy the longings of the immortal soul.

And so we trust, when the tempest, and the earthquake, and the fire shall have passed by, that the still small voice the word of the Lord will be heard, and that many will be found who have not bowed the knee to Baal, nor kissed his image.

Even if suffering should be the portion of those who are called to labor I the cause of righteousness, to uphold, by example, the Testimonies of Truth, let us remember for our encouragement the language of our Lord, "Blessed are ye when men shall revile you, and persecute you, and shall say all manner of evil against you, falsely, for my sake: rejoice and be exceeding glad, for great is your reward in heaven." . . . We have at this time felt the necessity of digging deep, in order to secure a foundation on the rock of everlasting Truth, and may we ever bear in mind, that he only who heareth the sayings of Christ and doeth them, hath built his house on this rock, against which the winds and waves of human passion will beat in vain. . . . . .

The consideration of our important testimony against war, brought a deep exercise over the meeting, accompanied by a desire, that this righteous testimony may be faithfully maintained by our members. The times we live in call loudly on us to abstain from everything calculated to encourage this desolating evil now sweeping over our land, mingled with the wail of the widow and the orphan, and the groans of our countrymen.

We were reminded that we have fallen on troublous times in regard to the welfare of our Religious Society; for the deep interest manifested by many of our members in the contest now unhappily raging in our beloved country, may gradually alienate their minds from the peaceable principles inculcated in the precepts of Jesus, and exemplified in his life. While we cannot be indifferent spectators of things passing around us, and in which we have so deep an interest, we earnestly desire that Friends everywhere may give evidence that they are followers of the Prince of Peace that they have an abiding faith in the protecting power of our Heavenly Father, and that he will not suffer his dependent children to be tried farther than he gives ability to sustain.

The right education of our children, and their preservation from the corrupting influences too which they are too often exposed, have again claimed our attention . . . .

From the Epistle of New York Yearly Meeting, included with the

Baltimore Minutes:

Dear Friends,

The condescending goodness of the Great Head of the Church has again permitted us to meet together, at a time of great outward commotion and strife, when the war cry is heard in the land when brother is arrayed against brother in deadly strife where the children of one common Father, (the workmanship of his holy hand,) whose watchful eye never slumbers, whose ear is ever open to the cries of the poor and needy, and whose arm of power is continually stretched forth to save all who put their trust in Him, are contending together.

At a time like this, of outward agitation, we thankfully have to acknowledge a belief that all who wholly trust in this Power, will experience the truth of the declaration of the Prophet when addressing the Most High: "Thou wilt keep him in perfect peace, whose mind is staid on thee, because he trusteth in thee."

While we do not assume to interfere with other men's matters, or sit in judgment upon those not of us, to mark out their path of duty remembering the answer of the Divine Master to the question, "what shall this man do?" "if I will that he tarry until I come, what is that to thee?" follow thou me" it is with earnest and affectionate solicitude that we fervently desire that all who bear our name may rally to the standard of truth, and enlist under the banner of the Prince of Peace, who will assuredly lead us unto victory; not by the battles of the warrior, which is of confused noise and garments rolled in blood, but by that warfare which is spiritual, designed to overcome all evil, to eradicate every germ of bitterness fro the mind, and to introduce into that kingdom wherein dwelleth righteousness.

Might not the inquiry be made of us, individually, whether the perusal of the war news of the day, unless guarded against, is not calculated to excite and foster those passions in our breasts which are in direct opposition to the blessed precepts of our Saviour, as expressed in his most excellent Sermon on the Mount.

It was the declaration of the Prophet formerly, that when the judgments of the Lord are in the earth, the inhabitants thereof learn righteousness. are not his judgments now in the earth? and will he not turn and overturn until his purpose is accomplished? "I will shake not only the earth, but he heavens also," was his declaration by the mouth of his Prophet, clearly showing that all false rests will be removed, and our tent will be only place of safety. "God is our tent."

1862

From ANSWERS TO THE QUERIES

Sixth

Our testimony against a hireling ministry, oaths, military services, clandestine trade, prize goods and lotteries, appears to be generally maintained. Though three reports mention deviations, respecting military services, to some cases of which care has been extended.

Baltimore   Thirtieth of the [Tenth] Month, and 5th of the week.

The Committee appointed upon the subject at a former sitting, produced the following minute of the exercises of this Meeting, to be inserted in our Extracts for the benefits of our absent members, which was approved, viz:

The reading of the Epistles, from the several yearly Meetings with which we correspond, has brought us into near unity with our distant brethren, and has afforded to our minds confirming evidence of the unity of the Christian Church; for all who are taught of the Lord, are actuated by one spirit, even that which ascribes, Glory to God in the highest, and breathes peace on earth, and good will to men.

The sorrowful condition of our beloved country, so feelingly alluded to in those Epistles, has tended much to solemnize the Meeting, and to humble us under the considerations of our many delinquencies, as a nation and as individuals. Lively testimonies have been borne in this Meeting, not only against the horrors of war, but to the all-sufficiency of that grace which emanates from the Father of Spirits, and which will save to the uttermost all who place their trust in him.

It was clearly shown, that however ardently we may feel attached to our excellent government its preservation, or that of any civil institution, is of small importance when compared with the sublime principles of the Gospel of Christ, and the salvation of immortal souls. The disciples of the Prince of Peace can only promote the advancement of his kingdom, by obedience to his Spirit, and keeping his commandments. "Without me," he says, "ye can do nothing." "If any man will come after me, let him deny himself, take up his cross daily, and follow me." These are still the unchangeable terms of discipleship; for we cannot serve two masters; we are either conformed to this world, or transformed by the renewings of our minds.

They who have experienced the mercy and forgiveness of God, will be enabled by his grace to forgive others; and continuing under this holy influence, they will be endued with patience and confidence in him who, "ruleth in the kingdom of men, and giveth it to whomsoever he will." He sees from the beginning to the end of time, for one day with the Lord is as a thousand years, and a thousand years as one day.

Information has been received at this Meeting, that many of our members who reside in Virginia, have, during the past year, been subjected to great trials by reason of the civil war which is now desolating that portion of our country. Some of them have been arrested by the military authorities of the Southern States, and held as prisoners for a time. Among these, our beloved friend, Job Throckmorton, was one whose sufferings excited general sympathy. While on his way to attend the Monthly Meeting at Hopewell, he was arrested by the military, and with many other prisoners, who had not been bearing arms, he was subjected to fatiguing marches and great privations, which resulted in his death. His pure and blameless life was such, that we have no doubt he laid down his head in peace, and has entered in to eternal rest.

Our religious meetings in that section of the country have generally been maintained, though most of our meeting-houses have, at times, been occupied for military purposes. At Hopewell and Winchester, our members have been subjected to peculiar privations and trials, by reason of the large contending armies that have alternately occupied and despoiled that region; but the Meetings of Friends have seldom been omitted, though often held in private houses.

At Woodlawn, a branch of Alexandria Monthly Meeting, the meeting-house was, during the whole of last winter, occupied by the federal troops. The Midweek Meetings of Friends were then held in a private house; but on First days, they assembled in the meeting-house with the soldiers, who carefully prepared the house, expressed a desire that the Meetings should be kept up, and were evidently much interested in them.

At Waterford [Virginia], a part of the meeting-house was for many months, occupied by the Southern soldiers, while another part was reserved for the Meetings of Friends. The officers and some of the soldiers usually attended, behaved with decorum, and at times expressed their cordial appreciation of those seasons of deep solemnity and religious exercises. We have reason to believe Gospel of Peace and Love, at some favored seasons, was felt to flow, like a refreshing stream in a desert land.

The evidences thus afforded of the power of Divine truth, and the consolations of the Gospel of Christ, should incite us to increased diligence, that we may, through watchfulness and prayer, and unreserved obedience, fill up the measure of our duties, and obtain the rich reward of divine approbation.

While engaged in examining the condition of our religious body, an earnest desire has been felt, that we may live up to our professed principles, and faithfully maintain our religious testimonies. . . .

1863

From ANSWERS TO THE QUERIES

Sixth

Friends appear to be generally careful to bear our testimonies against a hireling ministry, oaths, clandestine prize goods and lotteries; but all the reports admit a want of faithfulness in the support of our important testimony against military services and requisitions.

Baltimore   10th Month 27, 1863

The Committee appointed at a former sitting to endeavor to embody the exercises of this Meeting whilst engaged in the consideration of the State of Society, produced the following Minute, which was approved by the Meeting, viz:

A precious solemnity has prevailed over the Meting during its several sittings, and much unity and harmony of feeling were manifested throughout. Many lively testimonies were borne during the examination of the State of Society, to the efficacy of that pure love, which is a redeeming principle in the hearts of all who yield to its benign influence, and wholly resign themselves to the Divine disposal. Many hearts were tendered and contrited under the baptizing influence of that living Gospel ministry that reached the witness in their own breasts, and much affectionate advice and tender counsel were held forth, particularly to the younger members, to come forward to the help of the fathers, in maintaining the testimonies of this people, being assured that to willing and obedient hearts, the yoke of Christ becomes easy. These were encouraged to greater faithfulness in the attendance of all our Meetings, and to unreserved dedication of heart to every feeling of duty required of them. Faithful obedience in little things leads to increased strength and greater openings, for we rarely stand still in religious experience, but are either advancing or retrograding in our course, and lamentable, indeed, is a condition of degeneracy. Let us all be awakened to increased watchfulness over ourselves and one another, and renewed concern to seek first the kingdom of heaven, and to walk answerable to the high and holy calling wherewith we are called.

Our predecessors in this Religious Society, by faithfulness to the manifestations of the Divine Power, wrought a great work in the earth, and to us is bequeathed this rich inheritance, the fruits of their labors. Shall we then let fall these great testimonies that have enlightened mankind, and modified human governments? Shall we suffer the brightness of the light of these ancient worthies to be eclipsed by our unfaithfulness? Such, alas, is to much our condition. Many deficiencies appear amongst us, and we fall far short of their primitive faithfulness. Yet such is the condescending goodness and mercy of our great heavenly Parent, that with all our frailties, He suffers not our light to be put out, but still raises up faithful standard-bearers to exalt His name in the earth.. . . .

A considerable number of our members, who live within the lines of military operations, being now in attendance with us, represent, that although they have been subjected to great trials, they have generally been preserved from personal injury, and have cause of thankfulness to the Shepherd of Israel. Two members of Fairfax Monthly Meeting [Virginia] have been arrested as hostages by the Southern troops, and so far as we know, are still held as prisoners, but measures have been taken to obtain their release, which, it is hoped, will prove successful.

On considering the condition of our beloved country, now subjected to the calamities attendant on a civil war, our hearts are affected with sorrow for the many victims who have fallen in the conflict, the many widows and orphans who mourn their bereavement, and the demoralizing effects of military service. We nevertheless hold fast our confidence in the wisdom, goodness and power of that Almighty Being, who rules in heaven and on earth, who permits the passions of men to work out their own chastisement, and brings forth, in the operations of His providence, results that cannot be foreseen by human wisdom, nor frustrated by human depravity.

The testimony to the peaceable nature of Christ's kingdom, maintained by our fathers, is still dear to our hearts, and notwithstanding the cloud of discouragement that now overshadows us, we trust the Son of Righteousness will yet arise, and the glory of the Lord be made manifest to the nations. As the Prophet saw, in the visions of light, a stone cut out without hands, which became a great mountain, and filled the whole earth, so, we believe, will the Redeemer's be established in the fullness of time, by the word of Divine Power.

In order that this precious testimony maybe advanced, there have been raised up in every age of the Christian Church, witnesses for the truth, who have often prophesied in sackcloth, or been slain for the testimony of Jesus. Such were the members of this Religious Society at its rise.

They were faithful to the civil governments under which they lived, and when they could not actively comply with laws that conflicted with their conscientious convictions, they patiently endured the penalties, until through suffering they obtained relief, and were thus made instrumental in promoting the cause of religious and civil liberty. May we be faithful in following their example, so far as they followed Christ. How instructive is the reply of the blessed Jesus to the disciple who inquired "what shall this man do?" "if I will that he tarry until I come, what is that to thee?" follow thou me." It is not our place to judge others, who may believe themselves called to pursue a different path from that in which we walk, but to follow the foot-steps of our Holy Exemplar, "who did no sin, neither was guile found in his mouth; who when he was reviled, reviled not again; when he suffered he threatened not, but committed himself to Him, that judgeth righteously."

Much solicitude and religious concern have been felt in this Meeting, that in the education of our dear children we may seek for a qualification to lead them, both by precept and example, in the way of righteousness. In order to promote this end, provision should be made for a guarded religious training at school, and suitable books for use in the family. . . .

1864

From ANSWERS TO THE QUERIES

Sixth

Our testimony against a hireling ministry, oaths, clandestine trade, prize goods, and lotteries, appears to be generally maintained. But many of our members have deviated from our precious testimony in relation to military services. Some cases of infringement thereof, are under care.

Baltimore 11th month 2d

The Committee appointed at a former sitting to endeavor to embody the exercises of the Meeting while engaged in the consideration of the state of Society, produced the following Minute, which was approved, viz:

. . . The sanguinary conflict that now rage sin our beloved country, laying waste some of its fairest scenes, bringing to an untimely grave many thousands of its inhabitants, and causing bereavement throughout the land, has called forth the expression of much sympathy for those who are suffering from this awful calamity. It has been our earnest prayer that we may not put our trust in the arm of flesh, but rather rely on the never-failing arm of Divine power, which sustained our worthy ancestors in seasons of severe suffering, made them instrumental in promoting the cause of Truth, and, in His own good time, delivered them from all their afflictions.

Our ancient testimony to the peaceable nature of Christ's kingdom, has been made more dear to our hearts, by contemplating the scenes of carnage and destruction that abound in our land. It was doubtless the intention of the Most High in sending his beloved Son into the world, to redeem mankind from the dominion of evil, to influence them by his meek example and sublime precepts, and through the guidance of his pure Spirit, to bring them into harmony and fraternal love. This happy condition was shadowed forth in the figurative language of prophecy: "The wolf shall dwell with the lamb; the leopard shall lie down with the kid, and the calf and the young lion, and the fatling together, and a little child shall lead them."

The primitive Christian church was the depository of this pure doctrine, which subsequently became obscured through the false teaching of a corrupt priesthood, and an alliance with the world; but being revived by the early Friends, the precious legacy has been transmitted to us. May we ever remember that the Truth of God can only be promoted by obedience to His Spiritual law; and placing the light upon the candlestick by a consistent example, may we keep alive the sacred flame which must spread far and wide, before the prophecy shall be fulfilled, "The kingdoms of this world are become the kingdoms of our Lord and of his Christ."

We have rejoiced in the announcement that, throughout the State of Maryland, liberty has been proclaimed to the long-oppressed descendants of Africa, and an earnest desire has been expressed in this Meeting, that we may not be unmindful of the great work yet to be accomplished, in extending to the freed people who dwell among us, the benefits of education and christian care. In contemplating the progress of our testimony against slavery, from its small beginning near the close of the 17th century, to the present day, our hearts are filled with gratitude and love to that Almighty Being who called our predecessors to labor in this cause, and led them safely along through the guidance of his grace. the prophetic language of John Woolman, written nearly one hundred years ago, has been feelingly revived among us, as being now in the process of fulfilment: "I have seen in the light of the Lord, that the day is approaching, when the man that is most wise in human policy, shall be the greatest fool; and the arm that is mighty to support injustice, shall be broken to pieces: The enemies of righteousness shall make a terrible rattle, and shall mightily torment one another; for He that is omnipotent is rising up to judgment, and will plead the cause of the oppressed; and he commanded me to open the vision."

The Christian duty of dealing with offenders in the spirit of meekness and love, has been to our minds, a subject of religious exercise, and an earnest desire is felt that at this trying season, we maybe governed by Divine wisdom, remembering that the first object to be sought, is the restoration of the diseased member to health, rather than its separation from the body.

Our Meeting this year has been unusually large, and favored with remarkable solemnity. A considerable number have attended from that section of our country where the scourge of war has exerted its desolating effects. Although great pecuniary losses have been sustained, and personal danger sometimes encountered, we have rejoiced in learning that the Meetings of Friends have been generally kept up, their lives have been preserved from the hand of violence, and amidst all their trials, they have often had cause to rejoice in the Lord.

1865

From ANSWERS TO THE QUERIES

Sixth

Friends generally appear to be careful to bear our testimony against a hireling Ministry, oaths, clandestine trade, prize goods and lotteries. But a deficiency in the faithful maintenance of our precious testimony against war and Military services, is acknowledged in all our reports.

Baltimore   11th month

The Committee appointed to prepare a minute, embodying the exercises of this Meeting, produced the following Report, which was satisfactory, viz:

On entering upon the consideration of the state of Society as portrayed in the answers to the Queries, the Meeting was brought under a solemn covering on account of the many deficiencies amongst us . . . .

We have felt it to be a cause of gratitude to the Father of all our sure mercies, that the desolations of war have been stayed in our land, while at the same time we have to lament, that so many of our precious young members, and some of more mature age, have been led to join the ranks of the warrior, disregarding the emphatic declaration of our blessed Master to His disciples, "my kingdom is not of this world, else would my servants fight." We were exhorted that while remembering the scripture injunction to "deal gently with the young man," we should not desert the glorious banner of the Prince of Peace. It was feelingly testified that the many departures from this distinguishing characteristic of the followers of our blessed Lord, as reported in the answers which have come up fro our subordinate meetings, should teach us humility, inasmuch as we are thus shown we are not all living up to our principles in this particular; hence the necessity of a return to our first love, in humble prostration before Him "who dwelleth in the high and holy place, and also with him who is of a contrite spirit, to revive the spirit of the humble, and the heart of the contrite ones."

The duty of remembering the poor, and comforting the afflicted, has claimed our serious attention. we are persuaded that the spirit of Christ will, in all ages, bring forth similar fruits; and as in the Apostles' days, no man counted aught that he had his own, but gave all to be used as any had need; so in our day, those who have abundance, should remember the afflicted and destitute, and minister liberally to their wants, thus gladdening their hearts, and causing them to glorify Him who is the Author of every blessing.

The condition of the colored people residing within our limits, has ben brought feelingly before us; and while we rejoice at their liberation from the shackles that have so long impeded their moral and intellectual advancement, we are conscious that there is yet much to do on their behalf, and a wide field open for religious labor among them. An earnest desire is felt, that we may be no less faithful in this interesting concern, than were our forefathers, who, through obedience to the Divine Monitor, became the pioneers in the great work of emancipation. . . .

The attendance of our members at this Meeting has been large, and among them are many from that section of our country which has so lately been the scene of sanguinary conflict. Since our last yearly Meeting, they have been subjected to heavy losses of property, and much anxiety of mind, by the ravages of War. Notwithstanding the perilous situation in which they have sometimes been placed, their religious meetings have been very generally kept up, their lives have been, through Divine mercy, preserved from the hand of violence, and their necessities supplied. The sympathy and aid extended to them by members of this and other Yearly Meetings, are gratefully appreciated, and have tended to strengthen the ties of brotherly love by which all the branches of our religious body are united.

From the Epistle of Philadelphia Yearly Meeting, included with the Baltimore minutes:

Dear Friends,

We are now permitted to address our distant brethren, under circumstances calculated to clothe the heart with rejoicing, although this has been overshadowed by the great grief of the Nation, for the death of our much lamented President.

the clouds of war, so fearfully dark upon our country's horizon, and which have cast their shadows upon all private and public concerns, are apparently soon to pass away.

We are again assembled to examine into the affairs of the Church, with thankful hearts to the author of all our sure mercies, that he has, in great measure, removed this awful scourge.

That we may be individually and collectively, so chastened and prepared in heart, as to do always, to all men, whatsoever we would have them do to us, and feel of a truth, that Christ's kingdom is not of this world, is the moral we should draw from the terrible calamities through which the nation has passed.

It is no new thing to hear of wars and rumors of wars, but to stand unmoved amid all commotions, is the prerogative of the redeemed and ransomed of the Lord. . . . .

A lively exercise has sprung up ion regard to the divided condition of those bearing the name of Friends. We have travailed in it with much feeling and unity. The exhibition of schisms, and divisions, among a people so nearly alike in themselves, and so widely differing from those who lay great stress on ceremonies and outward ordinances, is a stumbling block to inquirers Zionward, and a great impediment to their own usefulness among men.

We hope that the day is approaching, when there can be a coming together of a people, all professing to be led and guided by the spirit of Christ, and thus enabled so to labor, as to renew that "unity of the spirit, which is the bond of peace," that was the distinguishing characteristic of the early gathering of this people." . . . .

From the Epistle of Genesee Yearly Meeting [in western New York and southern Ontario], included with the Baltimore Yearly Meeting Minutes.

Dear Friends,

As we are again assembled in a Yearly Meeting capacity, we have been made to rejoice, in that we have been thus permitted to partake of the rich bounties with which the Lord's table is spread . . . .

While we have mourned that the spirit of war should have made its

232

inroads among us, a peace-professing people, while we have sorrowed that some of our young men should have, under the influence of the excitement around them, been induced to enter the arena of military strife, and there become the instruments of shedding the blood of their fellow men; yet we earnestly hope now, as the conflict has ceased, and as they return to their peaceful homes, they may become so convinced of the superiority of the principle of love to that of force, and that it is better to suffer wrong for a season, than to do wrong, that they may so live in the future as not only to give satisfaction to their friends, and thus be continued in the bosom of Society, but by being thus convinced by experience, of the sweeter and more hallowed influence which surrounds those who dwell under the canopy of this Divine principle, become its devoted advocates in the future.

Harvard divinity School *Alumni Bulletin* – February 2004

Up Against The Powers

When Quaker House was organized near Fort Bragg in Fayetteville, North Carolina, there were dozens of GI organizing projects near military bases around the country. It was 1969, and the antiwar movement was surging.

In 2004, thirty-five years later, Quaker House is the only one of these projects left.

What accounts for its longevity, despite such setbacks as a mysterious firebombing in 1970, admitted government spying, and many other ups and downs recorded in the project's archives?

After two years here as Quaker House Director, it's my belief that it's the Quaker basis of the project that has made the difference. That is, the Society of Friends were the ones among the tumultuous and shifting activist ranks with a religious background that could sustain a peace ministry in one of the nation's largest military towns.

What does Quaker spirituality offer for such a task?

Above all, the virtues of stubbornness and tenacity, qualities seemingly undervalued in many other theological traditions. Once Friends really sink their teeth into an issue, or as we call it a testimony, we seem to excel at producing dogged gadflies and persistent pests. It's a kind of Apostolic Succession of the Annoying, who just don't know when to give up and go away. Friends, remember, spent a century agitating against slavery in the US, and some of them almost as long crusading for women's rights (though, full disclosure: there were some doubters on this last matter for awhile). Pacifism, while popularly associated with Quakerism, is hardly universal in our ranks; but a preoccupation with ending war has been nearly so.

So it is in Fayetteville. The upheavals of the Sixties here are now but a dim memory – one preserved mainly in a special exhibit from our archives, as this counter-narrative has been otherwise expunged from local annals. Similarly, Quaker radicalism is generally less visibly exasperating, but, perhaps even more persistent and extensive.

Take, for instance, the GI Rights Hotline we're part of. Quaker House began in an effort to help dissident soldiers, mostly draftees, find legal ways out of a military they didn't support. When the draft ended in 1973, some thought that also ended the need for this free counseling service.

Not so: many of the "volunteers" find themselves the victims of false promises by bait-and-switch recruiters, and decline to suffer in silence.

More recently, with the Iraq war/occupation dragging on amid a steady trickle of US fatalities (and a much larger stream of the seriously wounded), measurable numbers of GIs are becoming dissatisfied with the war and their treatment in it, with a potential impact that could be substantial over time.

Certainly our work shows this: In 2001, our GI hotline counselors received 3128 calls from servicemembers or their families looking for help with finding a way to get out of the military. That was a record. But in two years the calls had doubled, to 6187 in 2003.

And one of our counselees just became the first visible army deserter of the Iraq war, applying for refugee status in Canada.

Another, Stephen Funk, was a Marine from California who filed for CO status, then went AWOL when it was ignored. He spoke at peace rallies during the build-up to the invasion last year, then turned himself in, was court-martialed. and sentenced to six months in the brig at isolated Camp Lejeune, a continent away from his friends and family. As he had also declared himself gay, his attorney feared for Funk's safety there.

Camp Lejeune is two hours away from Fayetteville. Funk's California attorney called Quaker House for backup. We organized a support effort that brought him more than a thousand letters from several countries, and visitors on almost every visiting day. The work paid off: he not only encountered little harassment from guards, the flood of mail also became an educational tool among fellow inmates. Funk was released in early February.

But work with servicemembers is not our only task at Quaker House. We also join other peace groups in planning public events that work to keep challenges to militarism in the public arena here and elsewhere. As this is written, we're busy working on plans for what is hoped to be the largest peace rally here since the day in May of 1970 when several thousand gathered to hear Jane Fonda.

And just as important, at least to me, we serve as a resource for our Quaker constituency, conducting workshops and retreats on peace issues, considered particularly in their religious and theological contexts. Since 2001, many Friends have questioned our peace traditions, and we have assisted many as they worked their way toward a new, deeper understanding of it.

It is a frequently-heard complaint about church-related social witness groups that they often tend to leave their church base behind in favor of basically secularized political activism. I want to minimize that hazard at Quaker House. It is amply evident to me that projects like ours are the fruit of a tree, the roots of which are sunk deep in our meetings and churches, and through them to the Church Universal.

235

From Friends we get, most mundanely, much of the donation income that keeps us afloat. But underlying that is the drive, the spiritual DNA of the Quaker charisms, especially the usefully vexatious ones mentioned earlier. Maintaining that integral connection, I conclude, requires nurturing a mutuality of service. And traveling among Quakers lifts my spirit; they got my back.

But the value of this integral connection I am seeking can be expressed in more conventional theological terms as well. Being here in Fayetteville, up close and personal with the US military machine, reminds me daily that "principalities and powers" is not just a hoary phrase from Paul; it is a dominating reality of life here – and, I would contend, American life in general, though we are generally too mesmerized by yet other powers to see it.

And if so, then the companion phrase about "spiritual warfare" is also validated: we do not work against "the troops" here, but against the spirit of the machine that enmeshes them – and us. And as an early Quaker peace statement (1661) put it, quoting and paraphrasing Paul (2 Corinthians 10:4), "Our weapons are spiritual, and not carnal, yet mighty through God, to the plucking/pulling down of the strongholds of sin and Satan, who is the author of wars, fighting, murder, and plots." When the artillery on the post rattle our windows several miles away, as they did the week this was written, this verse moves from mere homiletics to being the basis of sound strategy. Up against the worldly forces in battle array here, only grace can give us any hope of impact. And it does.

But there is more biblical validation in my work as well. One of the guiding themes of early Quaker witness was the "Lamb's war," drawing on Revelation 17:14, and this curiously incongruous image is regaining ground among Quakers today, as the situation of our nation and the world looks in many ways increasingly apocalyptic. Such an atmosphere also calls forth the underlying message of Revelation, that "they that are with him {the Lamb) are called, and chosen, and faithful," (Rev. 17:14)

These brief musings could be expanded, were I a trained theologian. But among such, the voice from my time at HDS that most resonates for me here is a suitably crochety one, that of Jacques Ellul. This cantankerous French Protestant (1912-1994) was not particularly popular on Francis Avenue in those days; I discovered him myself while here. And he has doubtless gone from neglected to forgotten by now.

But his was the flinty and often sarcastic insistence that the only chance the Church (or the churches) have to impact the world comes through them being themselves, and resisting conformity to the political and media fashions of the time. And it is this insistence which re-echoes for me frequently, and yields insight into why, among other things, Quaker House is still here when so many other, secular and political projects have come and gone. Quakers are a small sect, not especially wealthy or well-connected. But we are a people with some specific callings, one of which is to pursue peace, keeping at it in our often stumbling way – keeping at it and just – damn well not giving up. Ellul was not a Quaker; but I think he understood us, and I still gain understanding from him.

Thus, keeping an effort like Quaker House faithful to its role as a witness of this small but tenacious people is not only theologically correct, it is, to my mind, how we'll keep going for the next thirty-five years and more.

Which is likely a good thing, as there are few signs that the demand for such witness will have run out by then.

Not by a long shot

The Friends Peace Testimony Reconsidered

Prepared to accompany a workshop at the Alaska Friends Conference
November 2004

I

If Quakers are asked, Where can I find the "Quaker Peace Testimony"? where would we turn to find it?

Most of us in North America and England would pick up a book of Discipline or Faith & Practice. There the answer seems straightforward. All the many such contemporary books I have examined, from across the various branches, include the same statement, with only minor variations. Philadelphia Yearly Meeting's 1997 version of what it calls the "historic peace testimony" is typical:

"The Society of Friends has consistently held that war is contrary to the Spirit of Christ. It stated its position clearly in the Declaration to Charles II in 1660:

We utterly deny all outward wars and strife, and fightings with outward weapons, for any end, or under any pretense whatsoever. This is our testimony to the whole world . . . . The Spirit of Christ, by which we guided, is not changeable, so as once to command us from a thing as evil, and again to move us unto it; and we certainly know, and testify tot he world, that the Spirit of Christ, which leads us into all truth, will never move us to fight and war against any man with outward weapons, neither for the Kingdom of Christ nor for the Kingdoms of this world.... Therefore, we cannot learn war any more.' (F&P pp. 76f)

When I speak of reconsidering the Peace Testimony, these few sentences are the starting point. They are treated in our Disciplines as a definitive expression of this witness, one drafted by our founders, bearing the seal of history, and ratified today by Friends of all branches.

Indeed, such is the stature of these few phrases that I call them the "canonical" Peace Testimony, because they have become a kind of Quaker scripture. And this status makes them all the more ripe, indeed overripe for reconsideration.

Before this reconsideration begins, four preliminary points need to be made:

First, these sentences are only a brief excerpt from the 1660 Letter (about 110 words out of a total of 2500).

Secondly, they are not really representative of the full letter, which as we shall see is indeed much more complex and even ambiguous.

Third, to put it gently, even these excerpts are more qualified than they appear in our Disciplines. More plainly, they are presented in a way that significantly alters their actual import. Take, for instance, the opening statement: "We utterly deny all outward wars and strife . . . ." "We" however is not the beginning of that statement; in the text it actually starts like this:

"All bloody principles and practices, as to our own particulars, we utterly deny; with all outward wars and strife . . . ."

It can be argued that the phrase "as to our own particulars," is very important here, especially as a qualifier; we shall see why in a few moments. Further, what is presented as the sentence "Therefore we cannot learn war any more." is actually the beginning of a longer sentence, and occurs close to the end of the statement, three pages away. These standard excerpts, in short, have been significantly altered and misquoted.

Fourth, while the 1660 Letter is obviously ancient, it turns out that its elevation to "canonical" or scriptural status is not an ancient piece of Quaker history, but actually quite a recent development. Examining old books of Discipline, I have not found it anywhere before the 1920s. In fact, prior to that, it's hard to find any statement of a "Peace Testimony" as such. Instead, there was a testimony against war. Here's how most Yearly Meetings Disciplines put it throughout most of the 19th century, under the heading of "War" (There was no heading of "Peace"):

"Friends are exhorted faithfully to adhere to our ancient testimony against wars, and fightings, and in no way to unite with any in warlike measures, either offensive or defensive, that by the inoffensiveness of our conduct we may convincingly demonstrate ourselves to be real subjects of the Messiah's peaceful reign, and be instrumental in the promotion thereof, towards its desired completion; when, according to ancient prophecy,'the earth shall be full of the knowledge of the Lord, as the waters cover the sea; and its inhabitants shall learn war no more.'"

(There followed specific directives about loss of goods for refusal of war taxes, and avoidance of military ceremonies and the like.)

The other reference to the testimony in these books came in the Queries. Here's the one from Baltimore Yearly Meeting (Hicksite) in 1861, which was typical:

"Sixth Query. Do you maintain a faithful testimony against oaths; an hireling ministry; bearing arms, training, or other military services; being concerned in any fraudulent or clandestine trade; buying or vending goods so imported, or prize goods; and against encouraging lotteries of any kinds?"

Again, there is no mention of peace in this laundry list of miscellaneous mandates; and not "bearing arms" comes after the prohibitions on oaths and hireling ministry, suggesting that these were held to be greater evils.

Indeed, it is not until after World War One, that the 1660 (mis)quote begins appearing in books of Discipline. My own hypothesis about this sudden emergence is that it stems from a report on peace made to the first Friends World Conference in 1920, where delegates from all the branches were present, in which the quotes appeared.

In sum, what is presented as a definitive, unambiguous, and perennial statement in our current books of Faith and Practice, is on closer examination shown to be something quite different, and, I would contend, considerably more ambiguous and challenging.

III

To begin to explain why, two major features of the 1660 Letter's context need to be underlined, one textual and one historical.

The first is that the 1660 Letter is biblical through and through. This of course is typical of early Friends; but three biblical themes are particularly salient in it. They are:

1. The Peaceable Kingdom (e.g., in Micah 4)
2. The State as God's Enforcer (Romans 13:1-7)
3. Spiritual Warfare against Principalities and Powers
(2 Corinthians 10:3 - 5; Ephesians 6:10-18)

The second important contextual aspect is the Letter's historical situation: Friends in England in 1660 were a people without worldly power, facing threats of massive persecution by the authorities. The letter to Charles II hoped to ward off or mitigate this official persecution (and didn't succeed very well at that). Nevertheless it assumed and expressed attitudes about power and social order which were soon to become important to the shape and evolution of the testimony it was articulating.

Turning to the 1660 Letter itself, one passage in particular seems to me to best express the basis of what could be called 1660 Quaker pacifism. Here it is:

Therefore consider these things, ye men of understanding: for plotters, raisers of insurrections, tumultuous ones, and fighters, running with swords, clubs, staves, and pistols, one against another; these, we say, are of the world, and have their foundation from this unrighteous world, from the foundation of which the Lamb hath been slain; which Lamb hath redeemed us from this unrighteous world, and we are not of it, but are heirs of a world of which there is no end, and of a kingdom where no corruptible thing enters. (Emphasis added)

That is, while in a physical, temporal sense these Friends were still residents of England in 1660; by the work of Christ's Spirit within them, in their essential being they were living somewhere else, namely: in the peaceable kingdom, an entirely different spiritual reality. In this new community/state of being, they add, warfare is undertaken in a characteristic, qualitatively different manner:

"Our weapons are spiritual, and not carnal, yet mighty through God, to the plucking/pulling down of the strongholds of sin and Satan, who is the author of wars, fighting, murder, and plots. Our swords are broken into ploughshares, and spears into pruning-hooks, as prophesied of in Micah iv. Therefore we cannot learn war any more, neither rise up against nation or kingdom with outward weapons, though you have numbered us amongst the transgressors and plotters." (Emphasis added.)

Here we see two of the Letter's key biblical themes: the peaceable kingdom and spiritual warfare. These themes pervade another passage, which could be called the 1660 Quaker Peace Plan:

". . . [A]s for the kingdoms of this world, we cannot covet them, much less can we fight for them, but we do earnestly desire and wait, that, by the Word of God's power, and its effectual operation in the hearts of men, the kingdoms of this world may become the kingdoms of the Lord, and of his Christ; that he may rule and reign in men by his Spirit and truth; that thereby all people, out of all different judgements and professions, may be brought into love and unity with God, and one with another; and that they may all come to witness the prophet's words, who said, 'Nation shall not lift up sword against nation, neither shall they learn war any more,' Isa. ii. 4., Mic. iv. 3." (Emphasis added.)

Let's parse this out a bit: For these Friends, war will end when the Word of God's power changes enough of the hearts of men, that they will abandon physical (or carnal) warfare, and immigrate into the peaceable kingdom. The Friends' role in this process is principally to desire and wait for this transformation.

The contrast between this quietist outlook and the activist preoccupations of contemporary Friends is rather stark, and worth pausing over briefly. The modern ethos of Quaker peace witness was stated in classically concise form by Lucretia Mott in 1876:

"If we believe that war is wrong, as everyone must, then we must also believe that by proper efforts on our part it can be done away with."

This outlooks adds two new features to the received witness: First, doing away with war in our time. Few if any of the earlier statements spoke of this; they implicitly presumed war's tragic persistence, and called for Friends not to take part in it. In the 1660 Letter, the end of war is put off to a distant, likely post-historical future when "the kingdoms of this world may become the kingdoms of the Lord, and of his Christ. . . ." (This is virtually a direct quote from Revelation 11:15, which is definitely talking about the "end of history.")

The other new feature here is the stress given "proper efforts on our part." War, it seems, is a social problem like slavery, or like a disease such as smallpox. In a scientific, progressive society these plagues have been all but eradicated, and war is not essentially different; we're still just working on developing the "proper efforts," and mobilizing the necessary energy to apply them. The spirit of Quaker peace action today is, I contend, still essentially the same as that expressed by Lucretia Mott in 1876, and it is utterly different in tone and emphasis from what came before it.

But the earlier spirit and emphasis are not absent from our world today. The 1660 Letter and the later Queries remind me very much of the attitude of the stricter Amish sects. Some of these had colonies in a Pennsylvania valley near where I lived in the late 1990s. These Anabaptists carry on their lives as if they are already residents of the peaceable kingdom: they grow their crops, raise large families, trade with the "English" (i.e., non-Amish like me), attend their house church worship services, and otherwise do their best to ignore the corrupt outside world.

And one more thing: they don't do war.

In the years of the draft, their men trekked off to conscientious objector assignments in quiet droves – indeed, in much higher percentages than did draft age male Friends of those decades. While these Amish do contribute to relief projects, they are hardly peace activists; they don't show up for demonstrations; and the constant, Mott-like busyness of my Quaker meeting a few valleys away would leave them cold. If they have a peace plan at all, it would rather closely resemble that of the ancient Friends just cited, focused on "the inoffensiveness of [their] conduct" as a model and a signpost.

IV

So far, this reexamined 1660 testimony may differ in mood and expression from the excerpts in today's Disciplines, but not much in substance. But that is not the case when we consider two other excerpts, addressed specifically to the role of the rulers who were persecuting them. Let's hear them:

"Therefore in love we warn you [King Charles] for your soul's good, not to wrong the innocent, nor the babes of Christ, which he hath in his hand, which he cares for as the apple of his eye; neither seek to destroy the heritage of God, nor turn your swords backward upon such as the law was not made for, i.e., the righteous; but for sinners and transgressors, to keep them down." (Emphasis added.)

This mention of the ruler's sword is a rephrasing of Romans 13:1-4. This passage is worth repeating here in full:

"Let every person be subject to the governing authorities; for there is no authority except from God, and those authorities that exist have been instituted by God. Therefore whoever resists authority resists what God has appointed, and those who resist will incur judgment. For rulers are not a terror to good conduct, but to bad. Do you wish to have no fear of the authority? Then do what is good, and you will receive its approval; for it is God's servant for your good. But if you do what is wrong, you should be afraid, for the authority does not bear the sword in vain! It is the servant of God to execute wrath on the wrongdoer." (Emphasis added.)

This brief text is one of the most important biblical passages in Western political history, repeated down the centuries as the scriptural sanction for civil power and official use of violent force. And in the 1660 Letter, this view of it is explicitly affirmed–not once, but twice. Here it is again:

"And whereas all manner of evil hath been falsely spoken of us, we hereby speak the plain truth of our hearts, to take away the occasion of that offense; that so being innocent, we may not suffer for other men's offenses, nor be made a prey of by the wills of men for that of which we were never guilty; but in the uprightness of our hearts we may, under the power ordained of God for the punishment of evil-doers, and for the praise of them that do well, live a peaceable and godly life, in all godliness and honesty." (Emphasis added.)

The "power ordained of God for the punishment of evil-doers . . . ." Does this phraseology ring any bells for us today? It too comes out of Romans 13.

Well, so what? Do these two allusions make any difference to the Peace Testimony?

Yes, I believe they do. Certainly they did in practice. And the difference did not take long to become manifest. Only twelve years, to be more precise.

V

The 1660 Letter portrayed Friends as a meek and apolitical people: " . . .as for the kingdoms of this world," it said, "we cannot covet them, much less can we fight for them . . . ." But this sentiment evidently did not survive the passage across the Atlantic: in Rhode Island, Friends not only coveted worldly power, but achieved it. Although not founded by

Friends, the colony's annual election in 1672 produced a Quaker Governor, Deputy- Governor, and a Quaker majority in the colonial assembly. And Friends held most or much of the local political power in the colony for many years afterward.

This novel development (almost a decade before William Penn began the "Holy Experiment" in Pennsylvania) soon had the recognition and endorsement of no less a Quaker authority than the first signatory to the 1660 Letter, George Fox himself. He visited Rhode Island in 1672, attended New England Yearly Meeting there, and stayed on for several weeks afterward, the honored guest of the Quaker governor, Nicholas Easton.

In a sermon there, Fox expressed great satisfaction with the new regime: "What an honor is it that Christ should be both Priest, Prophet, Minister, Shepherd & Bishop, Councellor (sic) Leader, & Captain & Prince in your Colony," he declared. He also–as was his habit–gave them lots of concrete advice, about outlawing drunkenness, swearing, etc., and upholding their ancient liberties. (Quotes from Weddle, see below.)

But with the power of the magistrate or governing authority for upholding righteousness, there also came the issue of bearing the sword against evil-doers. This role was, remember, explicitly affirmed in the 1660 Letter. Now this sword was in Quaker hands. What were they to do with it?

For Rhode Island's new leaders, this was not an abstract question: on the one side, from the sea, there were threats of invasion by French and Dutch naval forces. On the other side, they were surrounded by forests inhabited by increasingly restive native tribes.

No mention of war by Fox in Rhode Island has been found. But in other contemporary epistles, he made clear his support for the Romans 13 stance. For instance, in a 1676 letter to Friends on the Caribbean island of Nevis, Fox wrote,

> "For if any should come to burn your house, or rob you, or come to ravish your wives or daughters, or a company should come to fire a city or town, or come to kill people; do not you watch against all such actions? And will you not watch against such evil things in the power of God in your own way? You cannot but discover such things to the magistrates, who are to punish such things; and therefore the watch is kept and set to discover such to the magistrate, that they may be punished; and if he does it not, he bears his sword in vain." (Emphasis added.)

Fortunately for the Rhode island Quaker magistrates, the naval threats did not materialize. But in the late summer of 1675, an alliance of native groups launched a massive, region-wide terror war aimed at driving white settlers from New England. This struggle, known to history as King Philip's war (after the Christian name given to its leading chieftain, whose Indian name was Metacomet.)The horrifying impact of this war, and its impact on settlers in Rhode Island and elsewhere, was powerfully evoked by the historian Meredith Baldwin Weddle, in her pathbreaking recent book, Walking In the Way of Peace, (Oxford, 2001):

> ... [T]o appreciate the moral task facing each Quaker during King Philip's War, it is essential to imagine the immensity of the danger threatening the people of New England; the fear of violence shredding all certainty and all expectations, just as sword and hatchet shredded the bodies fallen in their way..... The imminence of death alone would have been enough to shake each vulnerable settler or Indian; when death itself was dressed up in atrocity, whether real or rumored, it would be the rare person who could be sure that principle would not yield to terror or rage. For the Quaker, alone in his small house, miles perhaps from a neighbor, fear and horror faced down the ordained love for his enemies. ... To the extent that the danger and fear can be approximated from the security and predictability of modern America, to this extent no hesitation can be seen as remarkable or shameful.

(From the security and predictability of modern America? This must have been written in the good old days, of late 2000.)

What was a governing authority to do in the face of such unbridled terror? More pointedly, what was the duty of a Quaker "governing authority"?

We don't know if those Friends in office engaged in much theorizing or soul-searching. We do know that they did two things:

First, they adopted and upheld the first conscientious objector statute, exempting from militia duty those whose religious scruples forbade the bearing of arms. (We can be reasonably confident that this law was largely the product of their Quaker convictions, because as soon as non-Friends regained political control, they repealed it.)

And second, they went to war.

VI

As Weddle summarizes their course:

> "Rhode Island exiled Indians, supplied boats to the Plymouth and Massachusetts armies, blockaded Philip on Mount Hope, rescued English soldiers, provisioned and provided a safe haven for colonial troops, raised and dispatched soldiers, stored ammunition, transported troops across Narragansett Bay to battle, encouraged the mobilization and training of the

local militias, deployed gunboats, manned an official garrison, contributed troops to the final search for Philip himself – and, at last, tried and executed prisoners of war. This is scarcely the record of either a neutral government or an inactive one." (p. 170)

How did the Quaker officeholders reconcile this record with the pronouncements of the 1660 Letter? As far as Weddle's extensive research could determine, they didn't bother. But we can plausibly speculate that in their course they were attempting to make room for both their pacifist brethren who still thought they were living in Micah 4's Peaceable Kingdom, while also observing Romans 13's stern mandate for magistrates to "execute God's wrath upon wrongdoers"; after all, both of these texts were in the 1660 Letter. At this point, the Letter's phrase "as to our own particulars," which was edited out of the sentence as quoted in modern Disciplines, comes back into focus. How much different were the "particulars" of powerless, persecuted Friends in England in 1660 from the "particulars" of Friends elected to office in Rhode Island? And how much difference did such divergent "particulars" make?

Weddle did find one testimony by a group of Rhode Island Friends denouncing other unnamed Friends for abandoning their conviction of "dwelling with [Christ] in his peaceable kingdom" and returning to "that faith which stands in carnal weapons, or the arm of flesh . . . ." (p. 244) But she did not turn up any response from the authorities to this criticism.

Another authority who had no comment or complaint was George Fox, who sent an epistle to Rhode Island Friends in 1677, ten months after the war's end. In it, among other things, he cautioned the Quaker colonists against hasty marriages, and chastised a member for killing a neighbor's horses which had strayed onto his property. But amid these advices, he made no mention of the Rhode Island Quaker officials' involvement in carnal warfare; not a word.

If we consider only the familiar excerpts from the 1660 Letter, it is quite possible to look back at these official Friends in Rhode Island and join the critics who challenged their faithfulness to the peace testimony. But it is equally possible to fit them right into the Letter's text if we consider it as a whole, because it takes such a role for granted..

That is, this canonical document, far from dictating the unambiguous prohibition of all Quaker involvement in any war suggested by the widely-known excerpts from it, includes the very tensions and ambiguities, rooted in their turn in guiding texts from the Bible, which very likely gave rise to these Friends' course.

What can be learned from this fuller examination of both the 1660 Letter and this brief case study of its first application by Quakers in public power? One lesson would be to take a more critical attitude to the texts presented to us in our books of Discipline.

Another would be to disabuse ourselves of the notion, often heard today, that once upon a time there was a golden age of uncomplicated faithfulness to a clear standard of Quaker witness, which was followed by a steep decline into the moral morass of today. Early Friends may indeed have had moments and periods of exaltation, where they felt a strong sense of Christ's presence and divine favor. But they also, from early on, had to wrestle with the application of their convictions in life situations which called such certainties starkly into question, and in which people of good will followed their light and testimony to very different places.

A third lesson, the last for this essay, is that the Friends Peace Testimony has been subject to reconsideration from early on in our history, and such reexaminations continue even now. We are not thereby abandoning our Quaker heritage, but very likely engaging it in one of the deepest and most faithful ways.

If this beginning reconsideration of the "canonical" 1660 Letter, or rather the familiar but bowdlerized excerpts from it, deprives some Friends of easy answers to hard questions, and a comfortingly secure belief in the uncomplicated Quaker Good Old Days, this Friend is not sorry. They–and we–are actually better off to be shucked of such illusions, and to begin the sometimes hard but critical work of rethinking and reclaiming a peace testimony for us, and for our time.

APPENDIX: The 1660 Letter – Full text
1660
A DECLARATION FROM THE HARMLESS AND INNOCENT PEOPLE OF GOD, CALLED QUAKERS, AGAINST ALL SEDITION, PLOTTERS, AND FIGHTERS IN THE WORLD: FOR REMOVING THE GROUND OF JEALOUSY AND SUSPICION FROM MAGISTRATES AND PEOPLE CONCERNING WARS AND FIGHTINGS.

George Fox and others.

Presented to the King upon the 21st day of the 11th Month, 1660.

[EDITOR'S NOTES: This text has been broken into paragraph units for modern readers; but the text has not been otherwise altered. The text is from the 2 Volume 8th and Bicentenary Edition of Fox's *Journal,* London: Friends' Tract Association, 1891]

"OUR principle is, and our practices have always been, to seek peace and ensue it; to follow after righteousness and the knowledge of God;

seeking the good and welfare, and doing that which tends to the peace of all. We know that wars and fightings proceed from the lusts of men, as James iv. 1–3, out of which the Lord hath redeemed us, and so out of the occasion of war. The occasion of war, and war itself (wherein envious men, who are lovers of them-selves more than lovers of God lust, kill, and desire to have men's lives or estates) ariseth from lust. All bloody principles and practices, as to our own particulars, we utterly deny; with all outward wars and strife, and fightings with outward weapons, for any end, or under any pretense whatsoever; this is our testimony to the whole world.

"And whereas it is objected:

"But although you now say ' that you cannot fight, nor take up arms at all, yet if the Spirit move you, then you will change your principle, and you will sell your coat, buy a sword, and fight for the kingdom of Christ.'

"To this we answer, Christ said to Peter, 'Put up thy sword in his place;' though he had said before, he that had no sword might sell his coat and buy one (to the fulfilling of the law and the Scripture), yet after, when he had bid him put it up, he said, "he that taketh the when the sword, shall perish with the sword. And further, Christ said to Pilate, 'Thinkest thou, that I cannot now pray to my Father, and he shall presently give me more than twelve legions of angels?' And this might satisfy Peter, Luke xxii. 36, after he had put up his sword, when he said to him.'He that took it, should perish with it ;' which satisfieth us, Matt. xxvi. 51-53 And in the Revelation, it is said, 'He that kills with the sword, shall perish with the sword; and here is the faith and the patience of the saints.' And so Christ's kingdom is not of this world, therefore do not his servants fight, as he told Pilate, the magistrate, who crucified him. And did they not look upon Christ as a raiser of sedition? And did he pray, 'Forgive them?' But thus it is that we are numbered amongst transgressors, and fighters, that the Scriptures might be fulfilled.

"That the Spirit of Christ, by which we are guided, is not changeable, so as once to command us from a thing as evil, and again to move unto it; and we certainly know, and testify to the world, that the Spirit of Christ, which leads us into all truth, will never move us to fight and war against any man with outward weapons, neither for the kingdom of Christ, nor for the kingdoms of this world.

"First, Because the kingdom of Christ God will exalt, according to his promise, and cause it to grow and flourish in righteousness; 'not by might, nor by power (of outward sword), but by my Spirit, saith the Lord,' Zech. iv. 6. So those that use any weapon to fight for Christ, or for the establishing of his kingdom or government,   their spirit, principle, and practice we deny.

"Secondly, as for the kingdoms of this world, we cannot covet them, much less can we fight for them, but we do earnestly desire and wait, that, by the Word of God's power, and its effectual operation in the hearts of men, the kingdoms of this world may become the kingdoms of the Lord, and of his Christ; that he may rule and reign in men by his Spirit and truth; that thereby all people, out of all different judgements and professions, may be brought into love and unity with God, and one with another; and that they may all come to witness the prophet's words, who said,   Nation shall not lift up sword against nation, neither shall they learn war any more,' Isa. ii. 4., Mic. iv. 3.

"So we, whom the Lord hath called into the obedience of his truth, have denied wars and fightings, and cannot more learn them. This is a certain testimony unto all the world, of the truth of our hearts in this particular, that as God persuadeth every man's heart to believe, so they may receive it. For we have not, as some others, gone about with cunningly-devised fables, not. have we ever denied in practice what we have professed in principle; but in sincerity and truth, and by the word of God, have we laboured to manifest unto all men, that both we and our ways might be witnessed in the hearts of all.

"And whereas all manner of evil hath been falsely spoken of us, we hereby speak the plain truth of our hearts, to take away the occasion of that offense; that so being innocent, we may not suffer for other men's offenses, nor be made a prey of by the wills of men for that of which we were never guilty; but in the uprightness of our hearts we may, under the power ordained of God for the punishment of evil-doers, and for the praise of them that do well, live a peaceable and godly life, in all godliness and honesty. For although we have always suffered, and do now more abundantly suffer, yet we know that it is for righteousness' sake; 'for our rejoicing is this, the testimony of our consciences, that in simplicity and godly sincerity, not with fleshly wis dom, but by the grace of God, we have had our conversation in the world,' 2 Cor. i. 12, which for us is a witness for the convincing of our enemies. For this we can say to all the world, we have wronged no man, we have used no force nor violence against any man: we have been found in no plots, nor guilty of sedition. When we have been wronged, we have not sought to revenge ourselves; we have not made resistance against authority; but wherein we could not obey for conscience' sake we have suffered the most of all people in the nation. We have been counted as sheep for the slaughter, persecuted and despised, beaten, stoned, wounded, stocked, whipped, imprisoned, haled out of synagogues, cast into dungeons and noisome vaults, where many have died in bonds, shut up from our friends, denied needful sustenance for many days together, with other the like cruelties.

"And the cause of all these sufferings is not for any evil, but for things relating to the worship of our God, and in obedience to his requirings. For which cause we shall freely give up our bodies a sacrifice, rather than disobey the Lord: for we know a s the Lord hath kept us innocent, so he will plead our cause, when there is none in the earth to plead it. So we, in obedience unto his truth, do not love our lives unto death, that we may do his will, and wrong no man in our generation, but seek the goo d and peace of all men. He who hath commanded us that we shall not swear at all, Matt. v. 31, hath also commanded us that we shall not kill, Matt. v.; so that we can neither kill men, nor swear for or against them This is both our principle and practice, and has been from the beginning; so that if we suffer, as suspected to take up arms, or make war against any, it is without any ground from us; for it neither is, nor ever was in our hearts, since we owned the truth of God; neither shall we ever do it, because it is contrary to the Spirit of Christ, his doctrine, and the practices of his apostles; even contrary to him, for whom we suffer all things, and endure all things.

"And whereas men come against us with clubs, staves, drawn swords, pistols cocked, and beat, cut, and abuse us, yet we never resisted them; but to them our hair, backs, and cheeks, have been ready. It is not an honour, to manhood or nobility, to run upon harmless people, who lift not up a hand against them, with arms and weapons.

"Therefore consider these things, ye men of understanding: for plotters, raisers of insurrections, tumultuous ones, and fighters, running with swords, clubs, staves, and pistols, one against another; these, we say, are of the world, and have their foundation from this unrighteous world, from the foundation of which the Lamb hath been slain; which Lamb hath redeemed us from this unrighteous world, and we are not of it, but are heirs of a world of which there is no end, and of a kingdom where no corruptible thing enters. Our weapons are spiritual, and not carnal, yet mighty through God, to the plucking/pulling down of the strongholds of sin and Satan, who is the author of wars, fighting, murder, and plots. Our swords are broken into ploughshares, and spears into pruning-hooks, as prophesied of in Micah iv. Therefore we cannot learn war any more, neither rise up against nation or kingdom with outward weapons, though you have numbered us amongst the transgressors and plotters. The Lord knows our innocency herein, and will plead our cause with all people upon earth, at the day of their judgment, when all men shall have a reward according to their works.

"Therefore in love we warn you for your soul's good, not to wrong the innocent, nor the babes of Christ, which he hath in his hand, which he cares for as the apple of his eye; neither seek to destroy the heritage of God, nor turn your swords backward upon such as the law was not made for, i.e., the righteous; but for sinners and transgressors, to keep them down. For those are not peacemakers, nor lovers of enemies, neither can they overcome evil with good, who wrong them that are friends to you and all men, and wish your good, and the good of all people on the earth. If you oppress us, as they did the children of Israel in Egypt, and if you oppress us as they did when Christ was born, and as they did the

Christians in the primitive times; we can say, 'The Lord forgive you;' and leave the Lord to deal with you, and not revenge ourselves. If you say, as the council said to Peter and John, 'speak no more in that name;' and if you serve us, as they served the three children spoken of in Daniel, God is the same that ever he was, that lives for ever and ever, who hath the innocent in his arms.

"O, Friends! offend not the Lord and his little ones, neither afflict his people; but consider and be moderate. Do not run on hastily, but consider mercy, justice, and judgment; that is the way for you to prosper, and obtain favor of the Lord. Our meetings were stopped and broken up in the days of Oliver, under pretense of plotting against him; in the days of the Committee of Safety we were looked upon as plotters to bring in King Charles; and now our peaceable meetings are termed seditious. O! that men should lose their reason, and go contrary to their own conscience; knowing that we have suffered all things, and have been accounted plotters from the beginning, though we have declared against them both by word of mouth and printing, and are clear from any such thing! We have suffered all along, because we would not take up carnal weapons to fight, and are thus made a prey, because we are the innocent lambs of Christ, and cannot avenge ourselves! These things are left on your hearts to consider; but we are out of all those things, in the patience of the saints; and we know. as Christ said, 'He that takes the sword, shall perish with the sword;' Matt. xxvi. 52; Rev. xiii. 10.

"This is given forth from the people called Quakers, to satisfy the king and his council, and all those that have any jealousy concerning us, that all occasion of suspicion may be taken away, and our innocency cleared.

George Fox	Richard Hubberthorne
John Stubbs	Francis Howgill
Gerrard Roberts	John Bolton
Leonard Fell	Samuel Fisher Henry Fell
John Hinde	John Furley Junr.
Thomas Moore	21/11 M/1660

"Postscript. Though we are numbered amongst transgressors, and have been given up to rude, merciless men, by whom our meetings are broken up, in which we edified one another in our holy faith, and prayed together to the Lord that lives for ever, yet he is our pleader in this day. The Lord saith, 'They that feared his name spoke often together' (as in Malachi); which were as his jewels. For this cause, and no evil-doing, are we cast into holes, dungeons, houses of correction, prisons (neither old nor young being spared men nor women), and mad a prey of in the sight of all nations, under the pretense of being seditious, etc., so that all rude people run upon us to take possession. For which we say, 'The Lord forgive them that have thus done to us;' who doth, and will enable us to suffer; and never shall we lift up hand against any that thus use us; but desire the Lord may have mercy upon them, that they may consider what they have done. For how is it possible for them to requite us for the wrong they have done to us? Who to all nations have sounded us abroad as seditious, who were never found plotters against ally, since we knew the life and power of Jesus Christ manifested in us, who hath redeemed us from the world, all works of darkness, and plotters therein, by which we know the election, before the world began. So we say, the Lord have mercy upon our enemies and forgive them, for what they have done unto us!

"O! do as ye would be done by; do unto all men as you would have them do unto you; for this is the law and the prophets.
"All plots, insurrections, and riotous meetings we deny, knowing them to be of the devil, the murderer; which we in Christ, who was before they were, triumph over. And all wars and fightings with carnal weapons we deny, who have the sword of the Spirit; and all that wrong us, we leave to the Lord. This is to clear our innocency from the aspersion cast upon us, that we are seditious or plotters."

Added in the reprinting.

"COURTEOUS READER,
"This was our testimony above twenty years ago; since then we have not been found acting contrary to it, nor ever shall; for the truth, that is our guide, is unchangeable. This is now reprinted to the men of this age, many of whom were then children, and doth stand as our certain testimony against all plotting and fightings with carnal weapons. And if any by departing from the truth should do so, this is our testimony in the truth against them, and will stand over them and the truth will be clear of them."

Building Long-Term Religious Peace Witness:
16 Propositions On Strategy & Theology

Presented to an interdisciplinary seminar at the institute for Justice and Peace at Eastern Mennonite University, Harrisonburg, Virginia Spring 2005

In a paper widely circulated among Christian ethicists, "The Case for the Abolition of War in the Twenty-First Century," well-known theologian Stanley Hauerwas and his coauthors ask how war can be ended.

(Their paper is on the Web at:
http://www.rc.vt.edu/religious/pdfs/AbolitionofWar.pdf)

That's a very important question. But from where I sit, as Director of a front-line "faith-based" Quaker peace project in Fayetteville, NC, close by Ft. Bragg, it's a question that's, as they say out there, "above my pay grade."

Instead, I ask a related question, which also seems important, namely:

How can we sustain dogged and faithful peace witness until higher-ranking folks like Hauerwas get war abolished – especially if it takes a long time (as I suspect it will)?

This is the query I'd like to explore here in a preliminary way, drawing on some ideas emerging from my experience there, and nearly 40 years of other involvement in peace work. I'm writing here as a Quaker, addressing mainly other Quakers. But I hope others can find something of value here as well.

To get started, I note that many theologians, including Hauerwas, often talk about the special virtues cultivated by various traditions, and I think the history of Quaker House illustrates one of such Quaker virtue. This virtue is identified in the 18th chapter of Luke, in Jesus' parable of the poor widow who faced off against a corrupt and indifferent judge.

You'll recall that the widow kept coming back and coming back, demanding a hearing, til the judge said, "I don't fear God, and I could care less about people, but I think I'll have to give this widow some justice, or else she's going to drive me nuts." (That's from the Revised Quaker Version.)

The virtue illustrated here is the capacity of Quakers, at their best, to be a persistent and tenacious pain in the neck for the powers and principalities we resolve to bear witness to. There are many examples from our history; perhaps the most familiar is that Quakers worked to end slavery in America for a hundred years..

My reflections on such long-term, tenacious peace work, are laid out at some length in a piece, "A Quaker Declaration of War," which is online at:

www.quakerhouse.org). I'll try to reduce them here to a set of propositions, with related scripture texts, intended as a spur to further thought.

Proposition One: Paul's language about Powers & Principalities (e.g., Eph 6:12 & 2 Corinthians 10:4) are the biblical images that most fully inform my work and thought about peace witness. That is, I believe the US has come under the Power of the Spirit of War, and sunk into idolatrous worship of a blasphemous pseudo-Christian Principality of empire. These are not metaphors to me; they are daily realities.

Proposition Two: These twin Powers are increasingly intertwined, with both the military and the ruling regime. They are crucially assisted by a mass media that keeps a critical mass of the population not only distracted from seeing the Powers' machinations, but also unaware of their own blindness. This echoes the condition cited from Isaiah in Matthew 13:14: "Hear but do not understand; see and do not perceive."

Proposition Three: This threefold combination of Powers is extremely dangerous, both to the world and to those of us in the US. For instance, the elements of a police state are now in place here. The fact that they have not (yet) been deployed against the white "Christian" middle class only helps keep us quiet. (But read Milton Mayer's haunting book, They Thought They were Free, to learn about how just such people were brought quietly but relentlessly into the Nazi fold in pre-war Germany.) As a result, the Book of Revelation may now be the most chillingly relevant text of scripture today, and not (only) because of Tm LaHaye.

Proposition Four: Our situation confirms the charge of Matthew 10:16 that we're being sent like sheep into the midst of wolves, so we need to learn to be wise as serpents, and harmless as doves. In our time, I consider this charge to be the real "Great Commission."

Proposition Five: We don't get to be harmless unless we're also, and first, wise. And I contend we can learn some crucial wisdom from the children of this world, as in Luke 16:8, namely the military (the "serpents"). Their "wisdom" is particularly useful for learning to think strategically, and applying such strategic thought to our peace witness. This is part of the task of "taking counsel," like the king going to war in Luke 14:31, to see how to deploy our resources most effectively.

Proposition Six: The fact that we are ultimately engaged in a spiritual combat does not mean we can depend only on "spirituality," as in private prayer and individualized devotion, as responses. The Powers may be invisible in essence, but they drive visible institutions, and have a very concrete and bloody corporate impact in our world. Paul makes it plain that while we do not use "carnal" weapons, we are in a war and are called to battle. Thus the common tendency among many Quakers (and some other peace-oriented folks?) to flee or ignore conflict, and avoid even the language of struggle is neither helpful nor biblical or better it is neither wise nor harmless.

Proposition Seven: Developing an adequate strategic outlook can be a great help in breaking the media-driven fixation on the persons currently in the visible seats of power. They think they run the machine, and they are responsible, but the machine is much bigger than they, and when they have been replaced, it will still grind on like the malign Power it is. For us, obsessing on these persons is another way our potential for faithful, and meaningful witness is diverted, diminished, and dissipated.

Proposition Eight: The three elements of military strategic thought that apply most aptly for our peace witness are:

1. Think long term and big picture;
2. Secure your base; and
3. Training, training, training!

Proposition Nine: For the military, "thinking Long-term and big picture" involves both looking ahead and looking back; the best warriors are serious about learning from past wars, the better to win future ones. Here, among Quakers at least, our near-total ignorance of our own long and rich peace history is a major continuing weakness.

Proposition Ten: "Securing Your Base" for the military has both short-term tactical and long-term institutional aspects. For peace work, securing the base is both a spiritual and a practical challenge. It calls us both to deepen the roots of our congregations, and to build a networked infrastructure of peace projects that can sustain their witness, and if need be, serve as the current counterparts to the catacombs.

Proposition Eleven: At Ft. Bragg, the 82d Airborne Division fights wars part of the time; but they train ALL the time, at all levels, in all specialties. They do that because if they don't teach the troops how to make war, who will? Among Quakers, our "program" of "training" for spiritually rooted, institutionally sustainable peace witness is mostly a pathetic joke. If we could break free of the media spell, we could see this plight and perhaps begin devoting the undramatic effort needed to overcome it. I have the impression that Mennonites and some other peace-oriented religious groups are doing better at this.

Proposition Twelve: To begin overcoming our weaknesses. let us learn and adapt some of the central insights of military classics such as Sun Tzu's "The Art of War." For Sun Tzu, a key to battlefield success is identifying the strengths and weaknesses of each side, and then putting your strengths up against the adversary's weaknesses.

Proposition Thirteen: Following Sun Tzu, while we work on the long term tasks of base-building and learning to think long-term and big picture, there are also some useful guerilla sorties we can make. I would point to two: counter-recruiting, and challenging the "Christian" imperial false religion.

Proposition Fourteen: Counter-recruiting puts the strengths of decentralized, mainly educated church constituencies like ours up against the military's weakest point, namely its need to entice and seduce an endless supply of cannon fodder from an increasingly skeptical populace. Similar work (against the draft) made a big, if unheralded, impact during the Vietnam War. (For more on this, from a military historian, see "The Collapse of the Armed Forces," By Col. Robert Heinl at: www.chss.montclair.edu/english/furr/Vietnam/heinl.html)

Proposition Fifteen: In theory, challenging the blatant heresy of "Christian" war and empire worship should be simple. After all, it pits our strength (the gospel) against their weakness (idolatry and blasphemy). In practice, of course, taking on such a Power is not so simple. But with some imagination and courage, much could still be done. And I'll offer you my fantasy example: a line of billboards along highways in the areas most under the spell of this religion of war and empire, that read: "Who Would Jesus Torture?" and "Blessed are the Peacemakers – or Warmakers? Which version is in YOUR Bible?" with a website which gives a more detailed challenge to the pretensions of imperial "War Christianity."

What might such "guerilla billboards" accomplish?

First of all, they would be seen. In our balkanized culture, most of us spend most of our time in subcultural bubbles, seeing reflections of ourselves and hearing echoes of our accepted ideas, oblivious to alternative ways of seeing and thinking. Public highways may be one of the last remaining piece of the commons, where such bubbles can be penetrated.

Second of all, they would challenge some of the key (pre)texts of "war Christianity," and do so from within a biblical perspective. (There is good scriptural precedent for such a tactic too, in Isaiah 8:1 and especially Habakkuk 2:2)

Third, they may move an occasional passersby to think, and even question some of the false teaching they have accepted.

At least, such messages would be a start in a spiritual struggle against the idols of war and empire.

Others can undoubtedly think of better ideas.

Proposition Sixteen: But a word of caution here: Don't let tactical adventures cause us to lose sight of the overriding strategic task: to keep up our witness as long as we can, and prepare the next generations to take it up in their turn. After all: in the American Civil War, the Union armies never caught Stonewall Jackson, and Robert E. Lee was a military genius; but Lincoln and his crude crew of Sherman, Grant, Phil Sheridan and others, ultimately had the better long-term strategy, and the Union prevailed.

So this is a "quick and dirty" overview of what I call "The Hundred Year Lamb's War." This "Lamb's War" is an old Quaker motif borrowed from Revelation 17:14. And in this war, I think of Quakers as analogous to a military unit. In theological terms, this is called being a "people." A people is a group called into being by the Lord of Hosts   a phrase which after all means "the commander of the combat forces," and which occurs about 250 times in scripture and as a people given a mission and some marching orders; in our case, what Quakers call our Peace Testimony.

As Rev. 17:14 puts it, "those that are with [the Lamb's War] are chosen and faithful and true." From where I sit, though, the relevant image is less like being "chosen" in the sense of privileged and more like the military one of being drafted, summoned, conscripted. "You did not choose me," Jesus says in John 15:16, "but I chose you." To me that sounds more like a draft notice for difficult and hazardous duty than being made special and elevated; and that sense fits my experience of peace work much better.

In my view, this drafted "people" – or peoples, as there's clearly more than one–are the principal vehicles for the faithful and powerful spiritual combat of sustained peace witness.

Why do I say this? Consider North Carolina as an example: many antiwar efforts have bloomed and faded among the state's beleaguered progressives since 1969. But it's a religious one, Quaker House, that started in that year, which is still going strong after so many others have vanished. This is certainly not due to our superior character or brains. But up against the Powers, I do think we have had our invisible aids too, especially that virtue of persistence mentioned at the beginning.

That, plus grace and charism, have been enough to keep this project going, as a true "faith-based initiative," despite many weaknesses. Such projects are not models to be duplicated, but examples, useful case studies for other work that needs to be done in a similar spirit.

In sum, I certainly hope Stanley Hauerwas and the others can figure out how to eventually abolish war. In the meantime, though, I see the major task of peace work today as preparing these called peoples to take up their shares of this work, in their own characteristic fashion. Such work will be a multifaceted and multi- generational undertaking, and should be planned that way.

It will also likely bring many of us to a cross of real suffering in due course, and I'm sadly confident that none of us here will live to see the end of the work. But as William Penn wrote three hundred-plus years ago, "no Cross, No Crown."

Chuck Fager has been active in peace work since the mid-1960s, when he was a junior member of Dr. Martin Luther King Jr's staff in Alabama. Among his many books are *Selma 1965: The March That Changed the South*, and *A Quaker Declaration of War*.

For further reading:
An Ethic for Christians And Other Aliens In A Strange Land, William Stringfellow.
They Thought They Were Free: The Germans, 1933-45, Milton Mayer.

Study War Some More
(If You want to Work For Peace)

Chuck Fager
Quaker House
Spring 2010

Preface

Why a study on Quaker peace strategy?

From some current perspectives, laboring over the strategy and history of Quaker peace work is a curiosity, if not a waste of time. Larger and more influential groups are at work on these concerns, especially in Washington DC; isn't our main role is to support or join them?

While I'm all for collaboration, this study starts from a different premise, a credo: the conviction that the Religious Society of Friends is a gathered people. We are a distinct religious group because God called the early Friends together, to worship and do some particular work in some particular ways.

Quakers weren't called because we're better; we're just called. And we're still here because God is not done with us yet.

What we have named the "Peace Testimony" is a part of that work. Concern for peace is hardly unique to Friends, but in various manifestations it has long been a Quaker emphasis. Further, the history of this concern suggests that the Society has been a fertile nurturer of both new ideas and dedicated people to pursue them.

This creative potential is far from exhausted. Thus, Friends come to collaborative work, not merely as one more name on a coalition list, but as the heirs to a productive and steadfast resource that has its own integrity and dynamism.

This "Peace Testimony, however, is neither self-defining nor self-executing. We have to figure out what it means again and again, individually and as a group.

This study is a contribution to this ongoing process. It was prepared from an American standpoint, but I hope it might be useful to Friends from elsewhere as well.

One: Bible Study

Romans 13 & The Quaker Peace Testimony

Let's begin with a bit of Bible study. After all, the Bible is still very important to matters of war and peace in our world. If you're familiar with the following five verses from Paul's Epistle to the Romans in the New Testament, you already know that. If not, you may be in for a surprise:

Romans 13: 1-5

" Let every person be subject to the governing authorities; for there is no authority except from God, and those authorities that exist have been instituted by God. Therefore whoever resists authority resists what God has appointed, and those who resist will incur judgment. For rulers are not a terror to good conduct, but to bad. Do you wish to have no fear of the authority? Then do what is good, and you will receive its approval; for it is God's servant for your good. But if you do what is wrong, you should be afraid, for the authority *does not bear the sword in vain!* It is the servant of God to execute wrath on them that doeth evil. Wherefore ye must needs be subject, not only for wrath, but also for conscience sake."(Emphasis added.)

This brief text is one of the most important biblical passages in Western political history. It has been repeated down the centuries as the scriptural sanction for civil power and official use of violent force. It is regularly cited today as a justification for war, from the White House to influential preachers, as a simple web search would show.

This passage is also very important in the history of the Friends Peace Testimony.

If Friends are asked, "Where can I find the 'Quaker Peace Testimony?'" where would we turn to find it?

Most of us in North America and England would pick up a book of Discipline or Faith & Practice. There the answer seems straightforward. Almost all the recent such books I have examined, from across the various branches, include the statement, with only minor variations:

"We utterly deny all outward wars and strife, and fightings with outward weapons, for any end, or under any pretense whatsoever, this is our testimony to the whole world . . . ."

This phrase is presented as an unqualified rejection of all war. And it is offered as a direct quote from a historic letter from early Quaker leaders to King Charles II in 1660.

However, in fact this is a 20thCentury formulation, unknown in Quaker periodicals and documents before about 1920.

"As To Our Own Particulars"

The original of this statement is significantly different:

> "All bloody principles and practices, *as to our own particulars*, we utterly deny; with all outward wars and strife, and fightings with outward weapons, for any end, or under any pretense whatsoever; this is our testimony to the whole world." (Emphasis added.)

The full original statement is confined to "our own particulars," which is significantly narrower than an absolute rejection. That is, if Quakers don't do war, are they saying that no one can or should?

Not exactly. The 1660 Letter refers to the Apostle Paul's statement in Romans 13:1-5 – not once, but twice, and there it says something quite different. Here's the first one:

> "Therefore in love we warn you [King Charles] for your soul's good, not to wrong the innocent, nor the babes of Christ, which he hath in his hand, which he cares for as the apple of his eye; neither seek to destroy the heritage of God, nor turn your swords backward upon such as the law was not made for, i.e., the righteous; *but for sinners and transgressors, to keep them down.*" (Emphasis added. And note the measured character of the description of Quakers' spiritual status: they are the "apple of God's eye"; the very "heritage of God"; The "babes of Christ"; and so humble, too.)

Here is the second reference:

> "And whereas all manner of evil hath been falsely spoken of us, we hereby speak the plain truth of our hearts, to take away the occasion of that offense; that so being innocent, we may not suffer for other men's offenses, nor be made a prey of by the wills of men for that of which we were never guilty; but in the uprightness of our hearts we may, *under the power ordained of God for the punishment of evil-doers,* and for the praise of them that do well, live a peaceable and godly life, in all godliness and honesty." (Emphasis added.)

Which is to say, Quakers themselves ("as to out own particulars") declined to get involved in official violence, but they affirmed its use by the "rulers," on scriptural grounds.

261

Further, this letter is not the only place in which founding Friends affirmed this "sword-bearing" role based on the Romans passage. For instance, in a 1676 epistle to Friends on the Caribbean island of Nevis, George Fox wrote,

"if any should come to burn your house, or rob you, or come to ravish your wives or daughters, or a company should come to fire a city or town, or come to kill people; do not you watch against all such actions? And will you not watch against such evil things in the power of God in your own way? You cannot but discover such things to the magistrates, *who are to punish such things;* and therefore the watch is kept and set to *discover such to the magistrate, that they may be punished;* and if he does it not, *he bears his sword in vain."* (Emphasis added.)

There's Romans 13 yet again. And this participation in the security watch leads to another question: what would this outlook mean if Quakers moved from being "subjects" of the rulers to being "rulers" themselves? It wasn't long before this situation came to pass.

Peace Testimony – Phase Two: The Problem Of Power

The 1660 Letter portrayed Friends as a meek and apolitical people: " . . .as for the kingdoms of this world," it said, "we cannot covet them, much less can we fight for them . . . ."perhaps that was true in Restoration England in 1660. But this sentiment evidently did not survive the passage across the Atlantic: in Rhode Island, Friends not only coveted worldly power, but soon achieved it.

Although not founded by Friends, the colony's annual election in 1672 (only twelve years after the Letter to Charles II) produced a Quaker Governor, Deputy-Governor, and a Quaker majority in the colonial assembly. And Friends held most or much of the local political power in the colony for many years afterward.

George Fox visited Rhode Island that same year. In a sermon there, Fox expressed great satisfaction with the new regime: "What an honor is it that Christ should be both Priest, Prophet, Minister, Shepherd & Bishop, Councellor (sic) Leader, & Captain & Prince in your Colony," he declared. He also – as was his habit – gave them lots of concrete advice, about outlawing drunkenness, swearing, etc., and upholding their ancient liberties.

But along with the power of the magistrate or governing authority for upholding righteousness, there also came the issue of bearing the sword against evil-doers. And this aspect of the role was soon tested by fire and blood.

262

In the late summer of 1675, an alliance of native groups launched a massive, region-wide terror war aimed at driving white settlers from New England. This deadly struggle was known to history as King Philip's war (after the Christian name given to its leading chieftain, whose Indian name was Metacomet.)

The horrifying impact of this war, and its toll on settlers in Rhode Island and elsewhere, was powerfully evoked by the historian Meredith Baldwin Weddle, in her pathbreaking book, Walking In the Way of Peace (Oxford, 2001). Weddle's analysis is one of the most trenchant and truthful I have seen:

> . . . [T]o appreciate the moral task facing each Quaker during King Philip's War, it is essential to imagine the immensity of the danger threatening the people of New England; the fear of violence shredding all certainty and all expectations, just as sword and hatchet shredded the bodies fallen in their way. . . . The imminence of death alone would have been enough to shake each vulnerable settler or Indian; when death itself was dressed up in atrocity, whether real or rumored, it would be the rare person who could be sure that principle would not yield to terror or rage. For the Quaker, alone in his small house, miles perhaps from a neighbor, fear and horror faced down the ordained love for his enemies. . . . To the extent that the danger and fear can be approximated from the security and predictability of modern America, to this extent no hesitation can be seen as remarkable or shameful.

(From the security and predictability of modern America? This was written in the good old days, of late 2000.)

What was a governing authority to do in the face of such unbridled terror? More pointedly, what was the duty of a Quaker "governing authority"?

We don't know if those Friends in office engaged in much theorizing or soul-searching; no such records have turned up. We do know that they did two things:

First, in 1673, they adopted the first conscientious objector statute, exempting from militia duty those whose religious scruples forbade the bearing of arms. (We can be reasonably confident that this law was largely the product of their Quaker convictions, because as soon as non-Friends regained political control, they repealed it.)

And second, they went to war.

As Weddle summarizes their course:

> "Rhode Island exiled Indians, supplied boats to the Plymouth and Massachusetts armies, blockaded Philip on Mount Hope, rescued

English soldiers, provisioned and provided a safe haven for colonial troops, raised and dispatched soldiers, stored ammunition, transported troops across Narragansett Bay to battle, encouraged the mobilization and training of the local militias, deployed gunboats, manned an official garrison, contributed troops to the final search for Philip himself–and, at last, tried and executed prisoners of war. This is scarcely the record of either a neutral government or an inactive one." (p. 170)

The Peace Testimony: A "Great Deep"?

Reflecting on the sobering story of Quaker power confronting terror in Rhode Island, Weddle reflects on the course of Quaker pacifism with profound insight:

"The complexity of violence itself, the vast differences between cultures, both geographical and through time, the alternating periods of relative war and peace, and the influence of a shining integrity have, with underlying contradictions, rendered Quaker pacifism far less coherent than it has appeared. The major coherence, in fact, has been the persistence of a continuum of belief and behavior even when the very basis of pacifism changed. At any particular time in history one can find examples of the whole continuum of Quaker understandings –understandings about why violence was evil, the very basis of peace principles; about what kind of violence is evil; about responsibilities of government and the use of force; about weapons; and about where to draw lines to separate oneself from the violence of others. . . . The existence of a pacifist continuum reflects the fact that the renunciation of violence is a great deep, containing within it schools of sources and justifications and reefs of contradictions and requiring a tide of action and restraint. . . ."

She also notes that:

"An uncharacteristic silence in Quaker records has *veiled the complexities of Quaker pacifism.* Quaker record-keeping, historically so comprehensive, has, in the area of pacifism, been minimal. . . . When people cannot agree, *they may conceal that disagreement* for very practical reasons. Quaker recording of history was a witness of the unity of Truth for outsiders and to a degree was meant to be instructive for Quakers as well. To display the variety of approaches to issues of peace undermined the presumption of unity; it also compromised the ability of Quakers to plead that they were a special case the next time a Quaker attempted to refuse military involvement.

Even when a particular group did seem to adhere to common standards, they may have been tempted to leave any "backslidings" obscure. They were torn between two needs: recording an offense, in order to reinforce the standard, and not drawing attention to the offense, in order to avoid bringing a "reproach" upon Truth. The offender, too, needed time to repent." (Weddle, pp. 229-230. Emphasis added.)

So where does this brief historical review leave Quakers today who want to be mindful of their tradition, yet make the testimony practical for our time?

In response, two points seem worth highlighting: First, looking to early Friends for a simple, unambiguous rule of thumb doesn't work. Sorry; the history of Quaker pacifism is just not like that.

But second, this ambiguity has an upside: for one thing, it is not really a modern predicament. In fact it leaves us in fellowship with early Friends and earlier Christians, for whom Paul's advice in another passage (Philippians 2:12) applies: "Therefore, my dear friends . . . continue to work out your salvation with fear and trembling. . . ."

Fear and trembling? That doesn't sound very encouraging. But in our world of wars and rumors of war, is witnessing and working for peace supposed to be easy?

Besides, Paul wasn't finished with his counsel. To the "fear and trembling" he added, "for it is God who works in you to will and to act according to God's good purpose."

So if the task is hard, and the course not always clear, at least we're not working alone.

Questions:

1. How familiar are you with the passage from Romans 13. How significant does it seem to you? How important should it be?
2. Does the ambiguity of the 1660 Letter to Charles II change how you think about it?
3. Were the Rhode Island Quaker leaders being faithful Friends when they joined in fighting King Philip's War?
4. Suppose you were a member of the Rhode Island Assembly when the war vote came up: how would you have voted?
5. Is Meredith Weddle right that Friends have tended to gloss over differences about pacifism in our history?

TWO: What Are We Up Against?

January 2011 will mark fifty years since Dwight D. Eisenhower gave his farewell address to the nation on January 17, 1961.

In this address, the retiring president introduced the now-famous phrase "military-industrial complex" (MIC for short) into American public discourse. It's worth recalling what he said in full:

> "Until the latest of our world conflicts, the United States had no armaments industry. American makers of plowshares could, with time and as required, make swords as well. But now we can no longer risk emergency improvisation of national defense; we have been compelled to create a permanent armaments industry of vast proportions. Added to this, three and a half million men and women are directly engaged in the defense establishment. We annually spend on military security more than the net income of all United States corporations.
>
> "This conjunction of an immense military establishment and a large arms industry is new in the American experience. The total influence – economic, political, even spiritual – is felt in every city, every Statehouse, every office of the Federal government. We recognize the imperative need for this development. Yet we must not fail to comprehend its grave implications. Our toil, resources and livelihood are all involved; so is the very structure of our society.
>
> "In the councils of government, we must guard against the acquisition of unwarranted influence, whether sought or unsought, by the military-industrial complex. The potential for the disastrous rise of misplaced power exists and will persist.
>
> "We must never let the weight of this combination endanger our liberties or democratic processes. We should take nothing for granted. Only an alert and knowledgeable citizenry can compel the proper meshing of the huge industrial and military machinery of defense with our peaceful methods and goals, so that security and liberty may prosper together."

All of this is still worth pondering. But one phrase, overlooked in most discussions of this MIC concept, leaped from the page as I re-read it:

"The total influence [of the MIC] – economic, political, even spiritual – is felt in every city, every Statehouse, every office of the federal government."

The total influence ". . . even spiritual . . . ."

The military industrial complex (or MIC) a "spiritual influence"?

In my experience, absolutely. Let me try to explain why.

During the half-century since this historic speech, presidents have come and gone; political parties have waxed and waned; Secretaries of Defense have taken office and given it up; and there have been times of open war, punctuated by intervals of "peace," and covert conflicts; the economy has seen boom and bust.

Yet through it all, the size and reach of this MIC has steadily grown. The MIC is, among other things, the top consumer of oil, and a major source of mostly unregulated toxic pollution. The MIC's reach is more pervasive than ever, to the point where it has become so familiar that Americans hardly notice it, except in concentrated locations like Fort Bragg and other large military bases. Today it would be more accurate to call it the *Military- Industrial-Political-Academic-Scientific- Think-Tank- Mass-Media- Entertainment Complex.* (The "MIPASTTMMEC"? We'll stick with MIC.)

And yes, to this should be added "religious" and spiritual.

Let's look at the religious connection briefly. It has several important aspects; we will speak of three.

First is a very direct connection. The Military Religious Freedom Foundation has exposed deep involvement by a kind of crusading fundamentalism in high levels of the military services, an involvement that has many ominous implications, both for freedom of religion among servicemembers, and especially forconflicts involving Muslim populations.

Secondly and more broadly, much of American religion, especially Christianity, has adopted the conviction that the United States is God's chosen instrument to exercise the role of the planetary "sword-bearing" magistrate, charged to "rid the world of evil-doers," as the president declared in 2001. Thus these churches, some of the largest in the country, not only support but actively advocate for the projection of American military might around the world, regardless of the cost in blood and treasure, to Americans, but especially to foreigners. This is, they are sure, God's work.

And third, the MIC itself has taken on the character of an autonomous, self-propagating entity. I have compared it to a schoolyard merry-go-round, with bars pushed by interests great and small, so that it has developed so much momentum it seems to run by itself. We tend to see this motion as centered in and around Washington, and its similar political whirl. But this is much too restricted a view. The hands pushing the bars to such a high and steady pitch are reaching from a much wider area – all over the country, in truth.

I call this image the Wheel of War.

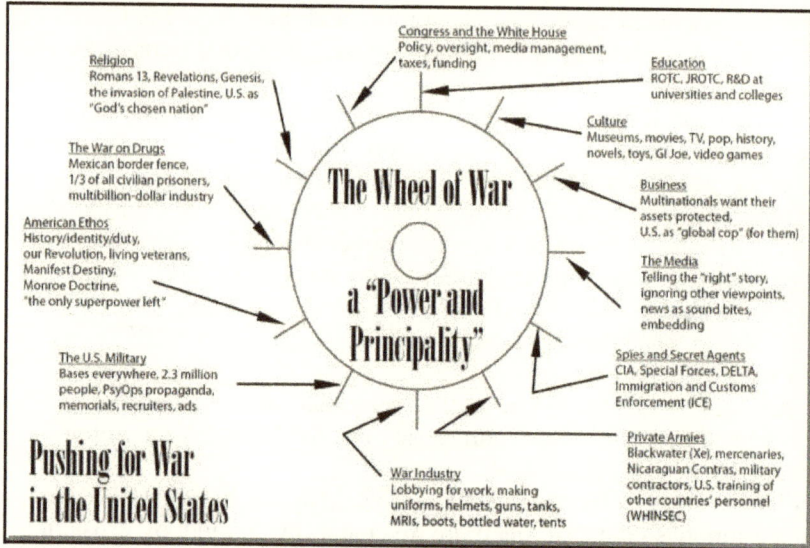

The Wheel of War

a "Power and Principality"

Pushing for War in the United States

Congress and the White House
Policy, oversight, media management, taxes, funding

Religion
Romans 13, Revelations, Genesis, the invasion of Palestine, U.S. as "God's chosen nation"

The War on Drugs
Mexican border fence, 1/3 of all civilian prisoners, multibillion-dollar industry

American Ethos
History/identity/duty, our Revolution, living veterans, Manifest Destiny, Monroe Doctrine, "the only superpower left"

The U.S. Military
Bases everywhere, 2.3 million people, PsyOps propaganda, memorials, recruiters, ads

War Industry
Lobbying for work, making uniforms, helmets, guns, tanks, MRIs, boots, bottled water, tents

Education
ROTC, JROTC, R&D at universities and colleges

Culture
Museums, movies, TV, pop, history, novels, toys, GI Joe, video games

Business
Multinationals want their assets protected, U.S. as "global cop" (for them)

The Media
Telling the "right" story, ignoring other viewpoints, news as sound bites, embedding

Spies and Secret Agents
CIA, Special Forces, DELTA, Immigration and Customs Enforcement (ICE)

Private Armies
Blackwater (Xe), mercenaries, Nicaraguan Contras, military contractors, U.S. training of other countries' personnel (WHINSEC)

Yet the most revealing description for it is one that's two millennia old, and comes from, of all people, the Apostle Paul. In several passages of his letters he speaks of "powers and principalities," by which he means disembodied spiritual powers that have concrete impact on the visible world. A spiritual influence, to repeat Eisenhower's insight.

What does this phrase, "powers and principalities" mean? Consider, as an example, Fayetteville, North Carolina: home to both Quaker house and Fort Bragg, one of the largest US army bases.

In many ways, Fayetteville is no different from any other collection of human specimens: among them are saints and sinners, happiness and tragedy. Families start, grow, and sometimes shatter there, as elsewhere. Individuals and groups are doing the best they can given their circumstances.

All this is true, but not the whole truth. The citizens of Fayetteville and Ft. Bragg are also part of larger systems, systems which have their own autonomy, momentum and identity. Together, they add up to more than the sum of their individual human components. These larger, supra-individual systems and their dynamics make up what we can call the spiritual dimension of the area.

Here is one example: since I came to Fayetteville at the end of 2001, the 82nd Airborne Division at Fort Bragg has had four – or is it five? – different commanders. Each of these men was a distinct individual, with his own personality, style, and abilities. It surprises me as an outsider how quickly they come and go; and yet the 82nd, a unit of more than fourteen thousand troops with eighty-plus years of active duty, goes on. As a unit it maintains its own "personality," its own momentum, its own "spirit."

The 82nd Airborne, I would suggest, "leads" its commanders as much as they "lead" it, if not more. It seems clear that the division would not have been seriously damaged if an enemy had captured all the generals who have passed through its headquarters since 2001; it might have stumbled briefly, but would have fought on. Its "spirit" is more important than any individual.

On a much larger scale, it seems clear the whole American militarist enterprise has developed its own over-arching "spirit," with its own dynamic and momentum. It has become an autonomous "power." The idea that it is controlled by a handful of policymakers in Washington seems less and less realistic: remember the haunting echoes of Eisenhower's farewell address: since 1961, ten presidents have occupied the White House. If changing faces in the Oval Office were enough to tame this power, it would have happened. Instead, they have come and gone, while the MIC has kept growing regardless.

In the cultures of many biblical writers, reality had two dimensions: overlapping the everyday visible world was a parallel realm of "spirit" and spirits, populated by angels and demons. These angels and demons, normally invisible to the everyday world, nonetheless interacted with and influenced it.

Moreover, somewhat like soldiers, they came in different ranks: there were low-level "privates," given minor, routine duties, such as tempting (or guarding) an individual, such as you or me. But others were like generals or even military governors, ruling vast territories or large enterprises: nations, religious cults, financial or cultural institutions, etc.

These are the "powers" and "principalities" that such as Paul of Tarsus wrote of, in his letter to the new church at Ephesus, chapter 6:12: "For we wrestle not against flesh and blood, but against principalities, against powers, against the rulers of the darkness of this world, against spiritual wickedness in high places." These spiritual beings had various names and personalities, and could rise and fall like their visible counterparts.

It is all too easy to vulgarize, mock, or simply dismiss these ideas as ancient and obsolete superstition. But one is not required to "believe" in such supernatural entities to find value in such images. Careful sociological studies could construct counterparts in secular terminology for this "powers and principalities" motif. Besides, Dwight Eisenhower, one of the most experienced warrior leaders of the last century, spoke of this "spiritual influence" of the MIC nearly fifty years before I did; and he was no myth-making sentimentalist.

Further, the concept has had much useful explanatory value for me, as Director of Quaker House, next door to Fort Bragg, in making sense of what our tiny outpost is up against. It also, as will be explained later, has

269

helped me think about how to challenge and change it.

For one thing, take Paul's associated declaration that "we do not struggle against flesh and blood" – that is, mere evil persons. This has been a crucial insight, helping me see past the fixation on individuals that I believe is a great obstacle to adequate understanding and planning for peace work. This sense is confirmed by personal experience that Fayetteville and Ft. Bragg are no more full of irredeemably evil people than is your home town.

And yet this city – like our country – is under the heel of the Spirit of War. Ft. Bragg is a key cog in the machinery of militarism. The reach is worldwide, but many of the key gears rotate back to and mesh here in eastern North Carolina.

Behind an outward semblance of ordinary existence, massive projects are hatched here for destruction, secrecy, torture, propaganda and deception, combining into a vast machinery animated by this spectral image. Although it is drawn from a two-millennium old myth, yet the Spirit of War feels as tangible and looming as the huge oak tree at the foot of the Quaker House lawn. It can be heard rumbling through the woods; its priests and acolytes carry on their rituals in the open; the faces of its sacrificial victims are regularly spat out onto the pages of our local paper.

At Ft. Bragg, for instance, more than three hundred soldiers had been killed in Iraq and Afghanistan by the end of 2009, and several thousand more gravely wounded. In addition, dozens more have killed themselves or their spouses, and an unknown but huge number bear the psychic wounds of what they have done in combat.

And what of the Iraqis, Afghans and others killed, maimed or made homeless as these troops carried out their orders? Hundreds of thousands at least. In cozier precincts, this steadily mounting toll of death can be kept at a safe, abstract distance. In Fayetteville one foregoes that luxury.

The notion and language of "Principalities and powers" were familiar to the Friends who wrote the 1660 letter to King Charles II. Indeed they cited the same passages from Paul that mention them, as here:

"Our weapons are spiritual, and not carnal," they wrote, "yet mighty through God, to the plucking/pulling down of the strongholds of sin and Satan [a paraphrase of Paul's Second Letter to the Corinthians, Chapter 10:4], who is the author of wars, fighting, murder, and plots."

The struggle against these "principalities and powers" is commonly referred to as "spiritual warfare," as evoked in these verses. What does this mean? They weren't going tomake war against powers and principalities the way one would against a physical army.

But they were called to make war. And so, I suggest, are we. In doing so there are weapons to be deployed, tactics evaluated and strategies planned. That's what we will begin to explore next.

Questions

1. Was Ike right? Is the "MIC" a "spiritual influence" in the U.S. as well as an economic or political one?
2. Does the "Wheel of War" help make sense of the "Military Industrial Complex"?
3. "Powers and principalities"? Does this idea illuminate our situation, or is it just superstitious mumbo-jumbo?
4. Is there a "Spirit of War" pervading U.S. Society?

Three: Study War Some More

When Jesus sent his disciples out, he told them (in Matthew 10:16) that they were going like sheep into the midst of wolves, so they needed to become "wise as serpents, and harmless as doves." For Quakers and other aspiring pacifists, taking on the military machine looks similarly daunting.

Further, note the order of Jesus' counsel: the disciples don't get to be harmless unless they're also, and first, wise. And I contend we can learn some crucial "wisdom" in this area from those who make it their profession, namely the military (metaphorically at least, the "serpents"; and remember, in Bible times, a serpent was not necessarily evil. Genesis 3:1: "Now the snake was wiser than any beast of the field which the Lord God had made.") Their "wisdom" is particularly useful for learning to think strategically, and applying such strategic thought to our peace witness.

Looking to the military for such "wisdom" has been more fruitful than the alternative. While the idea of war as a "principality and power" has been helpful concept to me, the corresponding biblical idea of "spiritual warfare" was initially more difficult. Not for lack of material about it; if anything, there was too much. "Spiritual warfare" is a staple of much Christian spirituality and practice, especially in pentecostalism, and there are shelves of books about it. But this body of practice has not seemed useful to me. For one thing, too much of it, as formulated by revivalist preachers, could be boiled down to two pieces of advice: Pray a lot; and send money. No doubt most f its practitioners are sincere; but it slides easily into a pose or even a scam.

I'm not against either of these. But as a basis for taking on the Spirit of War as encountered in the American military apparatus, they are no substitute for more traditional warriors' wisdom. To this end, I began exploring some military sources.

One of the first principles there is that success in war depends on strategy first. As Alfred Thayer Mahan, a renowned figure in the field put it,

"As in a building, which, however fair and beautiful the superstructure, is radically marred and imperfect if the foundation be insecure–so, if the strategy be wrong, the skill of the general on the battlefield, the valor of the soldier, the brilliancy of victory, however otherwise decisive, fail of their effect."

So where to learn of strategy? Here, amid the shelves of books available, I turned to two, one relatively new, one impossibly ancient.

The new one had the deliberately unpoetic title of MCDP 1-1, *Strategy,* and was published by the U.S. Marine Corps in 1997. It was an excellent overview, and I hereby offer a tip of this peacenik's broadbrim to its unnamed author.

But while the first yielded useful nuggets, the other was a veritable gold mine: Sun Tzu's *The Art of War,* a little book at least as old as the Bible (probably older), and treated with about equal reverence by many students of strategy. I read it online, in an edition which had all of the ancient Chinese sage's battlefield bon mots numbered like verses in scripture. This sacral aura was reinforced by the editor's charge that we not only read these verses, but savor and meditate upon them.

Although a bit fulsome, this was basically sound advice.(*The Art of War* has a big advantage over the Bible as a meditative handbook, in that it is very much shorter.) Sun Tzu's counsel to ancient generals and rulers has been adapted to serve the education of business executives and others who would wield power in environments of conflict or competition, military and otherwise. And like so many down the centuries, I found great value in it, even from the perspective of an aspiring peaceworker.

Here are some of the key insights, with a Quaker gloss:

(Caution: readers who dislike warlike language are advised that this next section contains numerous explicit references of that sort.)

Three insights from Sun Tzu seem most relevant to our work here. Let's hear his sayings, and then do some analysis:

Sun Tzu said: The good fighters of old first put themselves beyond the possibility of defeat, and then waited for an opportunity of defeating the enemy.

Hence the saying: If you know the enemy and know yourself, you need not fear the result of a hundred battles. If you know yourself but not the enemy, for every victory gained you will also suffer a defeat. If you know neither the enemy nor yourself, you will succumb in every battle.

272

You can be sure of succeeding in your attacks if you only attack weak points. You can ensure the safety of your defense if you only hold positions that cannot be attacked.

Hence that general is skillful in attack whose adversary does not know what to defend; and he is skillful in defense whose adversary does not know what to attack.

That the impact of your army may be like a grindstone dashed against an egg – this is effected by the science of weak points and strong.

The first point, If you know the enemy and know yourself, you need not fear . . . is crucial, not only in theory but in practice. In my work among Quakers and other like-minded folks, the indications are that we fall far short of adequacy here.

For instance, I often give a short quiz to these groups, putting on a blackboard two lists of names: one is a set of second-tier American generals: Stonewall Jackson, John J. Pershing, and so forth. The other is a list of Quakers who have made signal contributions to our 300-plus years of peace witness: Lewis Fry Richardson; Jonathan Dymond, and others.

A show of hands consistently discloses that most of us recognize the generals' names, even if we don't know much about them. This is due mainly to the fact of our culture being drenched in military monuments and memorials. Few among pacifist-minded Quakers have had much actual contact with the military, except for those old enough to remember the military draft, which ended almost forty years ago.

More surprising is the fact that the Quaker names are almost universally unknown among what is properly considered their own people.

(For the record, Lewis Fry Richardson was a British Quaker who singlehandedly invented the field of peace research almost a century ago; he is the Isaac Newton of that discipline. Jonathan Dymond was an early nineteenth Friend whose treatise, "An Essay On War," asserting its inconsistency with Christianity, was widely read and highly influential for many decades. And it is still online today.)

In sum, when it comes to efforts to dismantle militarism, most American Quakers know little either about the target of their labors – or of their own long heritage of such work. By Sun Tzu's standards, then, it is no surprise that one so often hears from this group complaints that their efforts too often feel hopeless, ignored and futile: of course! "If you know neither the enemy nor yourself, you will succumb in every battle."

This first point leads to the second, what Sun Tzu calls "the science of weak points and strong." Good strategic thinking for peace workers involves assessing our strengths and weaknesses, and those of the groups or forces we're up against, then finding ways of bringing our forces to bear against the other side's weaknesses. Ignorance shows its ill effects when it comes to such planning.

But the record is not all negative. Here is a positive example, from the Vietnam era: many Friends Meetings, churches and other community activist groups offered draft counseling to young men, and helped hundreds of thousands of them to avoid the military draft. This draft counseling was quiet, legal, decentralized, and little noticed by the media. Yet it made a big contribution to a serious weakening of the US military during the latter years of the Vietnam war.

From a strategic perspective, this draft counseling brought to bear many strengths of the peace constituency – a decentralized network, high verbal skills, access to local churches – on the military's major weakness: recruiting, its constant need to persuade young men to join up or submit to the draft.

Of course, there were other factors involved too; but the impact of the draft counseling movement is still an example of smart movement strategy with implications for peace work today. Too bad it is almost unknown among Quakers only a few decades later. (By contrast, the Army maintains a "Center for Army Lessons Learned" at Fort Leavenworth, Kansas, whose main task is to analyze and learn from the military's ongoing history.)

Strengths against weaknesses. Bear this mantra in mind as we move to the third of Sun Tzu's oracles:

> Sun Tzu wrote: The highest form of generalship is to foil the enemy's plans; the next best is to prevent the junction of the enemy's forces; the next in order is to attack the enemy's army in the field; [When he is already at full strength.] and the worst policy of all is to besiege walled cities. . . . The rule is, not to besiege walled cities if it can possibly be avoided . . . .

Walled cities? Do peace folks face "walled cities" in our efforts?

Yes. In my view, Washington DC is the ultimate "walled city," protected by many thick layers of institutional armor. Yet year after year it is the primary, often the sole focus of peace workers' labors. And year after year, the same complaints of futility are heard, loud or soft; and year after year, the military industrial complex keeps growing and tightening its grip upon our society.

The reasons for this are not so mysterious. After spending two years working on a Congressional staff, it seemed to me that to make things happen in Washington, a person or group needs one, or preferably more of the following items, which I call the Big Four:

274

The Big Four:

1. Big Numbers. (As in, millions of people behind you.)
2. Big Bucks. (As in millions of dollars for lobbying and campaign cash.
3. Big "Butts" (As in, high officials on whom you have some claim or hold.)
4. Big Media.

When I present this list, especially to my own Quaker constituency, I pause here and ask, "Which items on this list do WE have?"

The answer is obviously, None.

And the same goes for most other peace groups.

It is easy, if deflating, to document this conclusion. Read the accounts of the battle between the major parties for the "Catholic vote" in, say, the 2004 national election. Millions of dollars were spent, operatives fanned out across the landscape, bishops and priests were lobbied intensely, parishioners pursued and propagandized. How much time and money, was spent to bag the "Quaker vote"?

(Yes, there are moments, as during the largest peace rallies, when we have big numbers; but such moments pass.)

Again, Washington is the ultimate "walled city."Sun Tzu would smile sardonically at the strategic naivete we display in falling again and again for the mass media-fed idea that all our attention and effort should be aimed there.

If the people currently at the controls there (who are not really in control of that raging power, the Military Industrial Complex, remember) ever thought about the "peace movement" (which they don't, let's not kid ourselves)but if they did, they'd say, "Keep on doing what your doing, folks. Why?

The answer is simple: we keep putting our weaknesses up against the political system's most vigorously-defended stronghold; it's a guaranteed recipe for disempowerment and despair.

The Alternative:

Is there any hope after this realization sinks in?
YES!
But it does mean it is time to learn how to think like a warrior, think like Sun Tzu: learn and assess the strengths and weaknesses of both sides, and begin figuring out how to put our strengths into play in engagement with the other side's weaknesses.

How do we do that? We've already touched on one example, the draft counseling network of the Vietnam years. And when the sweep of Quaker peace and social witness is considered, there are many others. In fact, Quakers had undertaken many projects which have had important practical impact.Added up, they can be represented in a counter-image to the "Wheel of War" – the "Wheel of Peace." Here the momentum goes in the opposite direction – away from violence and destruction. It is not as big or as potent as the counterpart; but it is not insignificant either.

Among the examples listed there, one of my favorites is that of six housewives, sitting around a kitchen table on a farm in upstate New York in 1848, deciding to do something to improve the status of women. The Women's Rights Convention they organized in nearby Seneca Falls faced widespread ridicule in the "mass media" of the day – but it began a movement that has shaken America and the world.

Another is that of Jim Corbett, a former librarian who spent much time herding goats in the Arizona desert. One day in the 1980s, he met some refugees, fleeing from the bloody Central American wars there. Corbett's response became the seed of the Sanctuary movement, which successfully challenged the US administration which was financing the wars.

Or consider the quiet work of Friend Bayard Rustin in the mid-1950s, who along with the American Friends Service Committee made it possible for a young civil rights leader from Montgomery, Alabama travel to India to study the nonviolent action of Mahatma Gandhi. This quiet initiative helped shape the career of Martin Luther King, Jr.

It would be tempting to spend many more pages in detailed case studies of the individuals and groups who have added their "push" to this "Wheel of Peace." Such a study would be worthwhile, and encouraging, and to be comprehensive would need to include non-Quaker projects as well. Here we only have space to be suggestive.

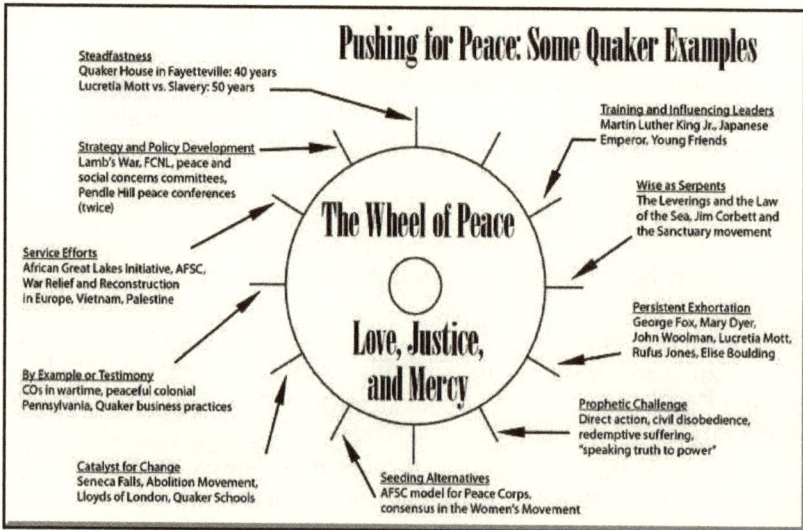

Pushing for Peace: Some Quaker Examples

The Wheel of Peace

Love, Justice, and Mercy

Steadfastness
Quaker House in Fayetteville: 40 years
Lucretia Mott vs. Slavery: 50 years

Strategy and Policy Development
Lamb's War, FCNL, peace and social concerns committees, Pendle Hill peace conferences (twice)

Service Efforts
African Great Lakes Initiative, AFSC, War Relief and Reconstruction in Europe, Vietnam, Palestine

By Example or Testimony
COs in wartime, peaceful colonial Pennsylvania, Quaker business practices

Catalyst for Change
Seneca Falls, Abolition Movement, Lloyds of London, Quaker Schools

Seeding Alternatives
AFSC model for Peace Corps, consensus in the Women's Movement

Training and Influencing Leaders
Martin Luther King Jr., Japanese Emperor, Young Friends

Wise as Serpents
The Leverings and the Law of the Sea, Jim Corbett and the Sanctuary movement

Persistent Exhortation
George Fox, Mary Dyer, John Woolman, Lucretia Mott, Rufus Jones, Elise Boulding

Prophetic Challenge
Direct action, civil disobedience, redemptive suffering, "speaking truth to power"

Besides, there's some serious homework yet to be done here: with all the campaigns and committees Friends have mounted, do we have any idea which worked well, and which didn't? And who will put for the effort to learn the military well enough to understand its strengths and weaknesses?

Such intensive learning will not be quick, easy or dramatic; but it is necessary. One feature of the best Quaker work that seems apparent even at first glance, is that its variety and creativity illustrates another of Sun Tzu's key observations about war:

> Sun Tzu wrote: In all fighting, the direct method may be used for joining battle, but indirect methods will be needed in order to secure victory.
>
> Indirect tactics, efficiently applied, are inexhaustible as Heaven and Earth, unending as the flow of rivers and streams; like the sun and moon, they end but to begin anew; like the four seasons, they pass away to return once more.

This passage is quite poetic, but rather indefinite. Beyond the needed homework, how do we apply Sun Tzu's maxims to make for better, more strategic peace action?

That comes next.

> Sun Tzu: Consequently, the art of using troops is this: When ten to the enemy's one, surround him. When five times his strength, attack him. If double his strength, divide him. If equally matched, you may engage him with some good plan. If weaker numerically, be capable of withdrawing. And if in all respects unequal, be capable of eluding him, for a small force is but booty for one more powerful if it fights recklessly.

Questions

1. What's your reaction to talking about "war" in relation to the Peace Testimony? Is it really practical to try to learn about peacemaking from the military?
2. Do we really need to know more about Quaker peace work 200 or 300 years ago to plan for peace work tomorrow?
3. Is Washington really a "walled city"? Is it wise to focus on it so much?
4. Does the "Wheel of Peace" really amount to much? Where do you find encouragement in it (if any)?

Four: The Hundred year Lamb's War

Early Friends were not shy of using "war talk." There are many references in early writings to "The Lamb' War." The term is drawn from a passage in the Book of Revelation (yes, early Friends were big on that difficult book), Chapter 17 verse 14: "These shall make war on the Lamb, and the Lamb shall overcome them: for he is Lord of lords, and King of kings: and they that are with him are called, and chosen, and faithful."For Friends, it described a struggle for peace and justice carried on both internally and out in the world.

But why speak ofthe Hundred-Year Lamb's War?

For me, the answers come from "studying war some more." And this study has more to teach about peacework than some pithy quotes from Sun Tzu. Valuable lessons can be gleaned from our current war machine as well.

To begin with, let's acknowledge what most others in the world know, that the current US military is one of the most efficient destructive forces the world has ever seen. To be sure, many things about the military, especially as a human society, are deeply flawed, even self-defeating. And the huge net of military bases the US has built may well be a burden our treasury can't afford to carry much longer. Yet when it comes to the principal mission, which is blowing up things and killing people, it still has no peer. It's not just big; it's not just costly. It's also the best in its bloody business.

How did it get that way? What has made it so effective? There are many factors involved; but I want to focus on three which, I believe, could also be applied nonviolently, to building an adequate Quaker peace witness.

1. The military thinks and plans for the long term, and with big picture strategies.

2. The military is careful to "secure its base."

3. The military makes training a top and continuing priority, at all levels. And throughout, it respects what it calls the "tooth to tail" ratio.

(One might call these "Several Habits of Highly Successful Warmakers," or maybe, "Chicken Soup for the Militarist Soul.")

Seeking A Big-Picture Strategy

Let's start with the first of these lessons, taking the long view and thinking strategically. This will take some focus, so we'll get back to the other items later.

We've already learned basics from Sun Tzu about how to begin this.

"Long term" and "big picture" are really two sides of the same coin: strategy is a way of looking ahead; but to get the "big picture," means looking back as well as forward, incorporating the past into the mix.

The importance of this two-sided effort for Friends was brought home to me when I prepared a week-long workshop on Lucretia Mott. A striking pattern emerged in her work. It went like this: Lucretia campaigned personally for an end to legal slavery in the U.S. for fifty years. (I call her Lucretia because, after reading several hundred pages of her letters and lots of other material besides, it feels like we're on a first-name basis; maybe even cousins.)

Fifty years agitating against chattel slavery – and she lived to see the end of that peculiar institution, though of course not the end of racism. I also realized that when Lucretia began her labor, Friends as a body had already been working to end slavery for the previous fifty years. While Lucretia Mott was exceptional in many ways, there were plenty of other, lesser-known Friends doing similar work.

That's a hundred years of Quaker labor on this one issue.

Or take women's rights. Lucretia personally worked on this cause, not for fifty but for sixty years – and she did not live to see its first major breakthrough, winning the right to vote. That took forty more years after her death in 1880.

There's another hundred year project.

Then we come to the issue of ending war. Lucretia crusaded for peace too. And as a very optimistic person, she believed the world was moving toward permanent peace in her day. Reading her sermons on peace today often makes my heart sink – because she's been gone for more than 120 years, and instead of progress, the world has unquestionably slid rapidly backwards on this life-or-death matter.

What does all this math add up to? Simply that the Quaker campaigns for an end to legal slavery, for peace and women's equality, were not fads or pastimes for dilettantes. They were dead-serious, hundred year projects–and in the case of war, a century was just for starters.

Obstacles to The Long View

You might think, given this recurrent pattern, that Quakers would be used to taking a long view. But by and large I believe you'd be mistaken, especially compared to how the military does it. For instance, the Pentagon is planning decades ahead, getting ready to stop even potential adversaries from challenging its supremacy. The plans may be madness and folly, but they're making them.

Moreover, the long view for them includes the past as well as the future. Each service has a cadre of professional historians, and some of them are already at work, gathering data and interviews on the latest U.S.

279

wars. They'll write thick books recounting and analyzing them in detail, comparing and contrasting them to other wars, ancient and modern. The Army's "Center for Lessons Learned" has already published numerous reports on Iraq and Afghanistan.

This self-study "feedback loop" is not new, by the way; it's a venerable tradition. The military historians' big books are not widely read outside military circles, and maybe because of that they tend to be hard-hitting and candid. That's because their purpose is not propaganda, but to help the military learn from past experience: what worked and what didn't? Which leaders and units performed well, or badly? And why or why not? All so they can do it better next time.

Makes sense, doesn't it? It's not only smart armies who do this: smart corporations, smart universities, even smart churches do too.

Now, what of Quakers–how do we compare in this area? Well, the results of my own unsystematic but ongoing research are not encouraging. We've already heard about the quiz list of Friends who did important peace work that hardly any Quakers today knows about.

That we didn't know the Quaker names didn't surprise me. After all, how many Quaker peace memorials are there?

Almost none, unless you count the Mary Dyer statues in Boston and Indiana. And the only peace museum in all of America that I know of (in 2010), is in Ohio, near Dayton. There used to be another in Chicago. I visited it once, thought it was wonderful, and wished there were more. But it closed.

By contrast, there are more than 300 war museums in the U.S. And tens of thousands of war memorials.

Think about that for a minute; 300 museums for war, 1 for peace, and none for Quaker peace work. Yet why not? There's plenty of Quaker material: Friends have been witnessing for peace in North America for more than 340 years. The records are in our archives. And there is a wealth of powerful stories: in Pennsylvania, for instance, during what William Penn called his "Holy Experiment," he and his successors managed to keep peace with the natives for seventy years, from 1680 to 1750, without an army.

No other American colony had a record that came anywhere close. (Remember Quaker Rhode Island, and King Philip's War?) But is there a museum which illustrates and celebrates this Quaker peace landmark? Or any of the others down the centuries, of which there are many? Not a chance. How many of us even know about this?

So that's one of the primary tasks: to learn how to take the long (Quaker) view and think big (Quaker) picture. And there's some work to be done to get there.

The Trap of the Media Mindset

What do many Friends have instead of a sense of our history, or a long view of our future?

Too many of us have succumbed instead to a mass media mindset. The signs of this outlook are easy to spot: a shortening attention span; a fixation on Washington and bigtime politics; urgent priorities which mirror the latest headlines; an obsession with pundit chatter; acceptance of the illusion of involvement.

A New Yorker cartoon captures it perfectly: a man on his couch, staring at the TV, says to his wife, "Watching people argue about the world situation night after night makes me feel like I'm doing something about it."

The sardonic humor hints at another common feature: an underlying sense of disempowerment.

This outlook is also highly parochial. It's almost all about us: America and Americans, with the rest of the world chronically presented in relation to our "interests." This learned self-centeredness is especially troubling in relation to war: Several million Congolese are killed in a decade-long regional war; but few Americans are among the casualties, and what do we know about it? Colombia, Chechnya, the Sudan, and many other equally horrendous wars drag on, and by and large we hardly notice.

Is this an exaggerated view of the overall mindset of too many among American Quakers? Maybe. But another poll I have frequently taken among Friends in recent years is to ask how many have been to a meeting or a protest about Iraq or Afghanistan in the past year? Consistently almost every hand goes up. The next question is, who's been to a similar meeting or protest about the Congo, or Sudan, or Colombia? Then the hands are very few.

Why is that? Can it really be that the Spirit, That of God, the beating Heart of the Universe, the Light of Christ Within, just happens to want Quakers to see the world from the same, America-centered, headline-driven perspective as the U.S. Media?

I don't believe it.

And this leads me to ask, how much of our peacework is Spirit-led, and how much of it is media-driven?

Spirit-led, versus media-driven; that's a distinction worth pondering, I think.

It's also why I very much admire those Friends who are the glaring exceptions to this rule, who like David Zarembka of St. Louis Meeting has focused on the Great Lakes region of Africa, where horrible wars and slaughter took place not long ago, and which are now off the media radar screens, where they were featured only briefly anyway. Or Newton

Garver of Buffalo, New York Meeting, who has developed an ongoing connection between US and Bolivian Friends. Or the New England Yearly Meeting Committee which has worked for years with Quakers in Cuba.

Let me come at this another way: Suppose US Army generals got the bulk of their military knowledge from daily news broadcasts, and hardly any knew who Stonewall Jackson was, and how he outsmarted the Union army, or why all of Hitler's Panzer tank divisions couldn't stop George Patton in Europe? What would happen to their brigades and battalions when they led them into battle?

The Quaker women and men I have known who were giants of peace witness, were very different from each other, but they had one important thing in common: on their issue, on their concern, they knew what the hell they were talking about. Whether it was the Law of the Sea Treaty, or how to build a sanctuary movement to save central American refugees from US covert wars, or even helping Vietnam era antiwar draftees and GIs get safely out of the country, they knew their stuff. And they didn't attain this depth and credibility from 5-minute news reports. It took work, experience, study, and time, not to mention courage, worship, and spiritual strength.

I think we all know this too, at least in the back of our minds.

The same thing goes for looking forward and thinking strategically, planning a Hundred-Year Lamb's War. Can we figure out where we want to be in twenty or fifty years, and plan realistically to get there, or at least be headed continually in the right direction? I believe that's what we are called to do.

The Elements of Strategy

What are the elements of a long-term strategy? In the military, there are several levels. At the highest level is grand strategy. US grand strategy is summed up in a document issued every four years or so, and available on the White House website: the National Security Strategy. The latest version available when this was written was prepared in 2006. In sum, its goals are to maintain American preeminence, while we remake the world, by "promoting democracy" and squashing any real or imagined rival.

In our Civil War, Abraham Lincoln settled on a grand strategy too: as I understand it, his plan was similarly straightforward: blockade the Confederate states along the coast, split them in two down the Mississippi river, and then starve or crush their forces one chunk at a time. And that's more or less how it worked out, though of course actual warfare is never that neat.

Under the umbrella of grand strategy come operational goals, the major plans for achieving the grand strategic objectives. An example of this is what Colin Powell said about Saddam Hussein's army in the first Gulf war – do you remember? he said: "First we're going to cut it off, then we're going to kill it."

We won't deal much with operational goals here, even though that's where the sexy stuff is, when some may get arrested or take other dramatic risks. They will have to be hammered out in a broad, ongoing discussion, from which an informed consensus can emerge.

I'll only note in passing that it will be a mistake to think that the most important of such goals is the next election. This essentially continuous horserace is an obsession in the media every other year, and if it becomes ours as well, then we'll still be lost in the wilderness. Instead, I hope we can begin to approach elections from the perspective of our own grand strategy, the Hundred-Year Lamb's War. Then, no matter which way they turn out, we'll find more opportunities, and sustain hope.

My Friend Lucretia Mott comes back to mind here. In the 500-plus pages of her letters that I read spanning fifty years, Lucretia only rarely referred to elections, though she was a well-informed, keen eyed, and sharp-tongued observer of public events and trends. I'm not entirely sure why she was so quiet about politics, but I suspect in large part it reflected a clear long-term perspective: she fully expected that attaining equality for women would take a lifetime of labor, and even longer.

She also understood that there were many ways of making ongoing social change, while presidents came and went. She knew her Bible, too, so no doubt she had read this verse, from Psalm 146:3 "Put not your trust in princes." Or maybe it was just that she didn't have the mass media to distract her.

For us today, I hope a concept like the Hundred-Year Lamb's War may help us see the forest behind and encompassing the electoral trees. If it's going to take at least that long to make any headway, wouldn't some grand strategic concepts help us make the most faithful use of our limited resources?

I believe so. And I believe that taking a long-term view of our witness can help us overcome the disempowering effects of walled city-centered, moment-to-moment media fixation. This doesn't mean we would give up on our beloved public radio – I'm not a fool; I know better than to ask Friends to do anything as drastic as that! But it can put the media in perspective, make them an asset for our larger work, instead of a distraction from and even a substitute for it.

Grand Strategy for The Hundred Year Lamb's War

So let's see if we can think like Lucretia. Here for your consideration are three goals which could be the grand strategy of the Hundred-Year Lamb's War, a framework for a century of practical witness:

First: To make the United States into a law-abiding member of the international community, respecting human rights both internally and externally.

Second: To move the three great monotheistic religions to a place where they conduct their rivalries without violence or bloodshed. And

Third: To make the Religious Society of Friends a meaningful player in both arenas, and one that can go the distance.

That's what The Hundred-Year Lamb's War could be about – it could serve as a Quaker counterpart and rival to the plan for a century dominated by American military might and the rival drive for a fanatic theocracy. Even partial progress toward these ends would make the world a safer place and increase our chances of surviving the clash of crusaders and their bloody visions.

Let's take a quick look at these three goals:

First, getting the US to be a law-abiding, human rights-friendly international citizen. What a concept. Was it only a few years ago that such an idea might have seemed mundane or even banal? Yes it was. But now it's downright radical, and even under the best of circumstances, it will take decades to reconstruct the major elements of international law and order that have been undermined or demolished in the recent past.

Second, peaceful rivalry among the monotheisms, Christianity, Judaism and Islam. To me this is at least as important a goal as taming the American empire, and probably more difficult. And for this, a century is likely a very short time. After all, we don't often recall that it took western Christianity about two hundred years and rivers of blood to reach a similar place internally.

Two hundred years of war to figure out that the differences between its various Christian sects could be settled in some other way than by one group exterminating another. (Even then, many of them still thought it was just fine to slaughter those other monotheists, Jews, right down to my own lifetime. And Christian-Muslim differences were whipped up into a pretext for mass slaughter in the Balkans only a few years ago. And of course, Ireland.)

This substantial but imperfect truce among most European Christians is both one of our culture's highest achievements, and yet one of its least known. Where are the peace museums celebrating the way most Western Catholics and Protestants finally learned to stop killing each other – and recalling the not insignificant Quaker role in that process?

Is this only a matter of Dead White European Male history? I don't think so. This saga – which we know so little of – could be an asset, a model– and warning – as we set out to play a part in ending the current religious warfare. And make no mistake: many of the wars and rumors of war that threaten us today and tomorrow will be religious at bottom.

Contrary to what we hear from the few surviving outposts of the "liberal" media, I don't believe the Iraq and Afghanistan wars are all about oil, or multinational corporations, though yes, these all play their part. Instead, at bottom, I hear just as much in these the echo of Romans 13: It's about God, about who gets to play God, and be the enforcer for the divine.

And then there's the third goal of the Hundred-Year Lamb's War–making the Religious Society of Friends a long-term player; which will get us to the practical part of this talk.

What would it mean to plan a Quaker peace witness on such a long-term basis?

Would deciding to be part of it make any difference when we got back home to our meetings?

Would it reorder any priorities, move us to do anything different next week, or next month?

Would it change the usual routine of following one media-hyped "crisis" or another, and fretting about the next political horserace poll, and then the one after that, and the one after that?

I believe it would. And some specifics about this impact is what's next.

Questions

1. Does the "Lamb's war" concept make sense in the 21st century?
2. Do Friends depend too much on the mass media to understand the world? Does the media set our witness priorities?
3. Which of the three Quaker "grand strategy" priorities make the most sense? Are there others that should be there instead?
4. Was Lucretia Mott right? Do we depend too much on conventional electoral politics to make the change we want to see?

———————————

Five: Getting Specific

Now we return to the other lessons I've taken from the military, starting with doing what an army in action does first, which is to secure its base.

For an armed force heading for combat, securing the base means making sure they have the supplies, the transportation, the food and bullets to fight their battles, safe places to store them, and hospitals to take care of the wounded. More broadly, back home it means keeping Congress and the public hypnotized by militarist propaganda. That's how they keep recruits signing up and megabillions in tax money flowing to the Pentagon. The US military works very hard at this side of the task. Remember those 300-plus war museums? They are not just about the past; they are also strategic investments in shaping present and future public awareness, and they pay handsome long-term dividends. They tell – and re-tell, and re-tell – a simple story: For America, war is necessary, war is righteous, war works, war is exciting, war is worth it – and war is almost painless.

What would "securing our base" mean for Friends? Let me suggest three things for starters:

First, it means build our meetings. Build them spiritually, first and foremost; and physically, and numerically. That's our base; without them we're nothing. There shouldn't be a need to expand on this imperative. While we're dealing with many concrete activities here, they are all part of spiritual warfare. Those who don't think spiritually-centered, vital Friends meetings are central to Friends' life and witness, are probably headed toward finding a spiritual home somewhere else.

Second, to this growing base of strong meetings, let us add a national network of twenty or more replicas of Quaker House.

Yes, if we're going to be mounting a Hundred-Year Lamb's War, we will need more projects like Quaker House, which have full-time, professional staff. They will be regionally controlled and supported, able to see beyond their back yard, and with sufficient support to keep them going for at least the four-plus decades that we've managed to survive in Fayetteville, as of 2010.

These projects would not be intended to replace or duplicate any existing organization. Instead, they reflect the fact that there's plenty of peace work to go around. Like the Good Book says, the fields are ripe for the harvest, so let's pray that the lord of the harvest will send laborers – and then have someplace for them to work from when they do appear.

Another reason to build these new projects is that we need to support and develop our own pool of expertise and skill, without supplanting our decentralized, lay-led meeting structures, and this is a way to do that. In my time, too many of the best activist Friends have had to go outside Quaker circles to exercise their gifts and follow their leadings, and not a few have thereby been lost to us. It's been our own homegrown Friendly brain drain.

I don't mean by this that all these projects should duplicate what we do at Quaker House in Fayetteville; not at all. Each one will have its own mission, as we do, fitted to its situation and the concerns of its sponsors. Some of them, for instance, could well be the home of peace museums; or focus on the environmental impact of militarism; or interfaith peace work; or torture accountability; or – (insert your leadings here).

And by the way, as long-term Friends projects go, the Quaker House model is a bargain: our 2010 budget is less than two hundred thousand dollars a year. So if they're well-designed, these new projects won't break our bank accounts; and anyhow, we're not a poor church.

Besides, support for these new Quaker House projects need not be all Quaker, just mostly. The remarkable interfaith religious peace constituencies brought to light by the Iraq war offer many opportunities for supportive networking, if we will only go out and get to work on it. (That's another helpful hint the military understands well, but some of our rulers – seem to have forgotten, or spurned: allies are good, especially in a long-term struggle.)

A Quaker Peace Pentagon?

Whatever their particular agendas, these new projects should all be well-networked, in touch with each other regularly for cooperation, learning and self-defense. I like the idea of an annual national Quaker Peace Conference, where those active in these projects (and similar ones) come together to share ideas and strengthen their ties (but not to pretend they're a Peace Pentagon drafting marching orders).

There have been such conferences occasionally, usually to good effect; but one wonders why they don't become a standard Quaker function. My suspicion is that the reason is that most past conferences were media-and crisis-driven. But as Lucretia Mott could have told us, peacework is an abiding assignment. But regular gatherings could help develop a consensus about plans and priorities, and help revise the long-term plans as conditions change.

Note that as Friends and meetings refocused on this base- and network-building effort, we might start missing out on some of the latest news and the urgent pull to run here and run there, trying to keep pace with this or that blip on the kaleidoscopic media radar screens. But that will be because we have better things to do. We're busy with the long-term, and acting strategically. We'll be looking at the forests, as well as the trees. We'll be working on the Hundred-Year Lamb's War, to tame and redeem the "new American century."

Building and securing our base is also closely related to the next major lesson I've taken from the military, which is the priority of training. Its relevance to Friends comes from a simple and inescapable fact: none of us reading the first edition of this study will live to see the end of this new American century.

If we're going to mount the Hundred-Year Lamb's War to bring some light into it, then from Day One we had better be about the business of training the next generations to be ready to take over for us – not least so they can fix our mistakes – because their turn will be coming soon, sooner than they think. And that training needs to be an integral – no, a central part of all our programs.

I well remember the later letters that Lucretia Mott wrote to Susan B. Anthony, Elizabeth Cady Stanton, and other founding colleagues in the women's movement. In them she spoke often and gratefully about the second generation of strong, smart young women activists who were emerging. She encouraged them, she praised them–and she quietly called on her other elder fore-mothers to give them a helping hand, and then get gracefully out of their way.

The Trouble With Osmosis

Yet here, Friends, is another area where I'm afraid we're in pretty sad shape. If you and I and most of us know so little about the rich and important history of Quaker peace witness – its failures as well as its successes–how are we supposed to improve and transmit this heritage and this work to new attenders and to our children?

One telling indication of the situation on this front for me came a couple of years ago. I asked a question to a roomful of teachers in Quaker schools – how do you teach Quakerism? The general answer – after a long, embarrassed silence – was: "Mainly by osmosis." I was tempted to ask, did they also teach math and science by osmosis? But that would have been flippant.

Or maybe not. Can we imagine an instructor at West Point or the Air Force Academy teaching navigation, or artillery – or strategy – by osmosis? No wonder their graduates are the best in their grim business.

And the military's training priorities do not stop with the academies training future generals and admirals–not at all.

The services are just as serious about training those who will be sergeants and petty officers. This fact is obvious – every day that the artillery out on Fort Bragg rattles our windows at Quaker House: the troops there only fight wars periodically. But they train all the time. In this respect, the 82nd Airborne at Fort Bragg had nothing on Lucretia Mott. May that soon come to be true of the rest of us as well!

The army also emphasizes training because they know the answer to a basic question, namely: If the 82nd Airborne doesn't prepare their own new leaders and troops, who will? The answer, of course, is nobody.

By and large, however, too many unprogrammed Friends seem to have forgotten both the answer and the question. But depending on "osmosis" doesn't cut it. If we don't train new Quakers in the past and present of Quaker worship and witness, who else will? And without that, what kind of future can either have?

Of course, we have our First day Schools. But to prepare new and young Friends to carry on the Hundred-Year Lamb's War, we'll need a lot more new and substantive Religious Ed material, and a lot more RE teachers, than we have now. And this religious education I'm imagining is not just for kids, it's not just for classrooms, and it's not just for First Days.

It will also be an integral part of the work of all active Quaker organizations. It already is, in the best of them, which have youth interns every year, as part of their ongoing work.

Good as all these are, they're not enough. In more than 40 years among Friends, I've seen too many committed young Quakers forced to go outside our ranks for the chance to learn service and to put their ideals into action. And many of them haven't been back. To sustain the Hundred-Year Lamb's War, we need to turn that around, and the sooner the better.

From Tooth To Tail

Much of that work may seem humdrum, routine, and unrelated to the exciting and scary business of war and peace as reflected through the mass media. And yes, some of these tasks may be routine, unlikely ever to show up on the news. But are such tasks part of the bigger strategic picture?

You bet they are–important parts too.

The Army understands this: it's what's behind a phrase mentioned awhile ago, the "tooth to tail" ratio. That's army-talk for the fact that for every soldier who actually fires a weapon or drops a bombs, there are up to ten more behind her or him, in a long and often humdrum line, including civilians. Most will never be noticed by the action-obsessed "embedded" war reporters, but from the long-term, strategic perspective, every link in the chain has its place.

The same goes for us. For many Friends, a role in the Hundred-Year Lamb's War may mean teaching First Day School, balancing a growing meeting's budget, deepening our worship, caring for those who are hurting or spiritually lost among us, – in other words, securing our base. Or pursuing a leading to understand, really understand Islam, or China; or North Korea.

So that's what I meant when I began by saying we need to declare war, the kind of war our tradition recognizes. I urge you to pursue this conversation about how Friends can prepare to help redeem the calamitous nuclear and environmental hubris of the American Century, and to play our part in overcoming the ancient impulse to make war for the glory of God. That's easily the work of a hundred years.

But how do we connect the Hundred Year grand strategy with the tasks of today? When we close this book and return to our meetings and everyday routines, what could we do tomorrow to help launch and advance the Hundred-Year Lamb's War?

Of course, there is no Friendly Pentagon, no broad-brimmed Chiefs of Staff to issue our marching orders – though I can't help recalling that it wasn't so long ago that Quakers did wear uniforms, and our guiding manuals were called Books of Discipline. That's a favorite military term, discipline – so these concepts may not be as alien to Quakerism as some today tend to think.

Nevertheless, Quakerism is not an army, and each of us is called to find our own leading, our own place in the tooth to tail ratio, working together with others as way opens. I think of us as more like pieces of a patchwork quilt, odd and irregular in shape, size, color and texture, but worked by the Divine Quilter, so that all our peculiarities somehow fit together the way they're supposed to.

Fortunately, the grand strategy goals of the Hundred-Year Lamb's War frame a very broad quilt. There's room under it for Friends whose pieces are concerned with women's issues, the environment, racism, or poverty. It can also cover very different styles, from inside lobbyists to outside agitators, scholars and visionaries, lone wolves and committee junkies.

So I don't think making these connections between the overall plan and the everyday will be that hard to do. Still, if this notion of a Hundred-Year Lamb's War speaks to you, but you'd feel better with a To-Do list, here are several suggestions for getting started on it, in ascending order of challenge.

First, you can write a check to your meeting –and add a zero to your usual amount.

What's the connection between that and the Hundred Year Lamb's War? Easy: it will help to secure our base. And if you don't write checks to your meeting, as I didn't for most of my early years, I suggest it's time to start.

Second, read a good book about Quaker history and witness. Not just a pamphlet or magazine article either. There's been a lot of exciting scholarship in the last twenty years, challenging many of our comfortable notions about our Quaker selves. So get one or more of these, and learn what it has to teach you.

And then, find another one. And you might also pick up the Bible – it was one of Lucretia's strongest and most reliable weapons of spiritual warfare. To do all this you might have to turn off the radio for awhile; but just for awhile. What's the connection here? It helps develop the long-term view that we need so badly.

Third, you can start a discussion/planning group in your meeting and with other meetings about the Quaker House-type project that could best serve the needs and opportunities for long-term peace work based in your area. Will it offer GI counseling? Truth In Recruitment? A peace museum? Ongoing public education? Youth work? All of the above? What alliances would help make it happen? The connections here are:

290

More base-building, and new training facilities. And you can commit to sticking with this seeking even if it takes a decade to bear concrete results. We've got a century to work with, remember.

Fourth, you could learn Arabic. It's a fundamental tool for being of use in serious peacebuilding in relation to Islam.

If Arabic isn't for you, how about Hebrew? Chinese? It's a humbling fact that learning foreign languages is one of the hardest things to get American college students to do these days. This in my view is another indicator of how far so many of us have been assimilated into the imperial outlook: everywhere Americans go today, other people learn English. It's the language of power in the new American Century.

Yet learning another group's language is the key to opening the door to true cross-cultural understanding and reconciliation. Do American Friends have the gumption to break out of that circle of privilege? It's not a matter of guilt, but simple competence.

And speaking of foreign languages, if you are truly adventurous, get started on understanding the seemingly alien tongue of conservative Christianity. As we said earlier, it is a central support of the power and principality that is the Spirit of War. Sooner or later, it's got to be challenged by people who know what they're talking about.

And – are you still with me? – Fifth, and perhaps most challenging – after you've read a couple of these meaty new books I mentioned, and done some Bible study, you can sign up to teach First Day School.

I say this especially to those in my age group, to those who taught classes back when our kids were young, to those of us who feel, "I've put in my time; I'm on parole; let me be."

But to these Friends, to us, let me repeat what the army says to such objections. If you're going to win a war, especially a long one, training doesn't get finished. Remember the question: If we don't train the next generation to take over and do better, who will?

I'm imagining a full-color poster, like the one with Uncle Sam pointing that bony finger at us, only in this one it's George Fox under his big hat, and he's saying, "I want THEE, Friend, to teach First Day School. Again."

Adding to the challenge of this call is the fact that to fulfill this part of the Hundred-Year Lamb's War objectives, you'll need a lot of material that doesn't exist yet; so you may have to research and write it, or figure out how to support someone else who can.

Remember the story line of all those war museums and memorials? "War works; war is righteous (when we make it); war is exciting; war is almost painless."

We have a different story to tell, and re-tell: "There is another and better way than war. It can work; it HAS worked; it can work again. We can make it happen." There's plenty of material for this story in

America's Quaker past and present, but it's vastly under-utilized, a lamp shamefully hid under a bushel.

So that's a quick and dirty laundry list for the opening salvoes of the Hundred Year Lamb's war. It could be longer, but that should keep some of us busy for a week or two.

Oh– I almost forgot; there's one more thing. This is for unprogrammed Friends generally, rather than as individuals: if we're going to secure our a base so it can truly sustain a century's worth of Quaker peace witness, a Hundred-Year Lamb's War, there's one other drastic change we can't avoid.

Yes, Friends, we're going to have to just give it up, and learn how to sing.

That's right, I said sing. Together.

Like the Methodists, and the evangelicals.

Why? It's no mystery: I started out as a rookie activist in the civil rights movement. And later, in my checkered career as a writer I've had jobs where there were labor unions. In both these movements, and lots of others, it's clear that when they were at their best and most powerful, music was one of their key assets, for inspiration, for morale, for courage and inspiration.

A singing church, like a singing movement, is one with hope, and with a future. So we're going to have to just bite the bullet, and get with the program.

And by the way, the military figured this one out too, a long time ago. If you are tempted to snicker at military music, you're making a mistake. It keeps the troops marching; it's done it for centuries.

Who's going to lead this change in our customs? Maybe the next generation.

But one way or another, we've got to do it, Friends.

Can't you see? There's a war on!

Questions

1. What about osmosis? Do Friends need to be more intentional about study and teaching Quakerism, to youth and newcomers?
2. What kind of regional Quaker project would you like to see created in your part of the country?
3. In the "tooth to tail" concept of peace work, where do I fit in now? Am I okay with that?
4. If a peace museum was created in our area, can you name three people or events that should be featured in it?

Postscript: Jesus Killed Mohamed.

Before we get too caught up in the specifics of the last chapter, let's recall that what's been described here is not a battle against "flesh and blood": we're facing the Spirit of War, something that encompasses much of what we can see as the MIC, but is more than the sum of the parts.

We've looked at biblical metaphors to help understand what this means. I want to do that once more, going out on a limb to quote again from that favorite book of the early Friends, Revelation. In one of its key apocalyptic visions (Chapter 13), two beasts appear that devastate the world and its people. One is more familiar: the main one with the secret name that's coded in the number 666.

But this boss-beast has a sidekick, according to the book's seer-author, John:

> "Then I saw another monster, coming out of the earth. He had two horns like a lamb, but he spoke like a dragon. He exercised all the authority of the first beast on his behalf, and made the earth and its inhabitants worship the first beast . . . . And he performed great and miraculous signs . . . . Because of the signs he was given power to do on behalf of the first beast, the second monster deceived the inhabitants of the earth. He ordered them to set up an image in honor of the beast . . . ."

Okay, this is metaphor, remember, so stay with me. The point is that the sidekick beast is the enabler and the legitimizer of the big one.

In the American context, I think of the MIC and the Spirit of War it embodies, as the 666 beast, the big kahuna. But his sidekick-enabler is critical to perpetuating the boss's power. And the enabler beast's identity is not an obscure mystic number, which preachers can haggle over indefinitely. Nope, it's plain for all who have eyes to see: It is War Christianity.

This connection has been mentioned before. It needs to be brought specifically into our strategic calculus here. That's because it relates to an idea strategists often use in battle planning, the "center of gravity."

A target's "center of gravity" is whatever is most important in making it able to defend itself. It may not have anything directly to do with weaponry; it may be a beloved symbolic leader for whom devoted followers are ready to fight to the last. Similarly, In its home society, a military establishment's "center of gravity" may not ultimately depend on guns or bombs. Rather, it can be the force which lends it the most legitimacy, which makes war and militarism worthy, honorable, deserving of support, even sacred.

After working up-close and personal for several years with the US military, I think I can point to its center of gravity. I'm convinced that the "Spirit of War" that grips our society like the Beast 666 depends for its hold more than anything else on the devotion and blessing of US War Christianity. American churches, many actively and others passively, have become tools of the Enabler beast's influence over large segments of the citizenry. As a contemporary rendering puts the verse from Revelation, "it talked the people into making an idol in the form of the beast . . . ."

There isn't space to describe this complex force in detail. It has infected Catholic as well as Protestant churches, and has a foothold in the Jewish community as well. It will require careful study as much as any other key element of the MIC. But its role is clear, and is anything but metaphorical or symbolic. It ranges from crusader infiltration of the military academies, to signs plastered on Humvees in Iraq declaring "Jesus Killed Mohamed." It is also not new – indeed, it glorified the extermination of Native Americans, upheld slavery, and blessed America's entry into the "great game" of imperialism.

In my view, real progress on two of the grand strategic goals of the Hundred-Year Lamb's War – making the U.S. Into a law-abiding nation, and promoting peaceful competition among the major monotheisms – will sooner or later major thrusts against War Christianity, as a key "center of gravity" of U.S. militarism.

Tackling the war spirit in the churches will not be easy; the struggle will be unsparing spiritual warfare that truly deserves the name. Many liberal Friends have spent much time avoiding and escaping this, and most other varieties of Christianity, becoming secular in all but name. But when push comes to shove, avoidance will not – suffice. The sooner we begin getting ready, the better.

Fall 2009 Register Now
FREEDOM
CHRISTIAN ACADEMY
A Community Christian School
at Mount Carmel Church
910.485.7777

A Scenario: Quaker Peace Conference, 2032

125 Friends gathered at the expanded Quaker Center near Santa Cruz, California. There was a lot of interest in the keynote address by the newest Nobel Peace Prize winner. But the most anticipation was felt, as usual, for the network group sessions. There staff and supporters from the member projects huddled intently sharing reports and ideas from the field, which included:

San Diego's Military Impact on the Nation's Environment (MINE) program, continues to document the calamitous environmental impact of US military operations and bases, along with war-related industrial operations, and support activism to clean up and close down theses sites. Their biggest problems continue to be the Pentagon's continued stonewalling about so-called secret facilities, its chronic use of inaccurate or misleading statistics, and the squeamishness of many mainstream green groups about taking on the military.

The Kissimmee Peace Museum, associated with Orlando Meeting, has opened a new set of exhibits, highlighting the long struggle to close down the so-called "School of the Americas," a notorious military torture school in Georgia. (Congress canceled funding for the school in 2015, after two-plus decades of activism.) The exhibit's special focus is on how the SOA Watch campaign was able to sustain its campaign for so long. The Museum's facilities are modest, but the location – a few miles from

Disney World – couldn't be better for drawing visitors.

From Indiana, the Midwest Torture Accountability Center says it is close to completing its latest action report on torture in US prisons. It has also been collaborating with the Guantanamo Torture Memorial Commission. Their proposals have been favorably received by the Cuban government as well.

The Seattle Pacific Connections program has selected its new group of interns, who will be studying Chinese, Japanese or Tagalog, and spending time in Japan, China or the Philippines, with special focus on peace and change groups there.

From Austin & Killeen, Texas, the GI Resource Center is evolving into the largest soldier's rights support project in the Southwest. Given the continuing war in Afghanistan-Pakistan, the stream of calls for help from GIs at Ft. Hood alone will keep them busy.

New York's Interfaith Committee is coordinating the logistics for the latest Abrahamic Faith Peace consultation, as part of an ongoing series.

Nashville's Volunteer Quaker House, allied with the Evangelicals for Peace Coalition, is about to launch its new billboard campaign. The theme is, "Who Would Jesus Torture?" It takes special aim at widespread southern church support for abusive treatment of US prisoners in the renewed "War on Terror."

The Delaware Valley Religious Education Action for Peace (REAP) Initiative continues to draw on the unparalleled archival resources at area Quaker colleges. This year it has produced several new booklets and videos for First Day School use, highlighting the careers of little-known Quaker activists of the past century. It has also uploaded a new monograph, evaluating the Emergency Peace Campaign of 1938-40, which attempted to keep the U.S. Out of World War Two, and came close to succeeding.

As always, there was much discussion about the two questions the network continues to face: the first was fundraising in difficult conditions, though most groups were still able to make their budgets in the past year.

The other was a review of the Grand Strategy. This year, discussion seemed to center on whether enough progress being made on capacity-building among Friends meetings and like-minded groups, to keep the Society of Friends more of "a player" in peace work. Some discussions seemed more optimistic about this than others, but energy was generally high.

Surprisingly to some observers, there was little talk about the fact that 2032 is a presidential election year. Asked about this, one Friend shrugged and said, "Yeah, I'm going to vote. But, look: The last dozen presidents were under the influence of the MIC. The next one isn't going to magically save us from it. We deal with Washington when we have to, of course. But if you ask me, the more important action is here."

A Letter To The Next Director Of Quaker House

Dear Friend,

In a few months, we'll start looking for you in earnest. My work with Quaker House will conclude by the end of November 2012. I'm relieved that the Quaker House (QH) board plans to give this search plenty of time, because frankly, I think it will be a challenge. Carrying out the QH mission is a unique and grueling task.

Here's the job description in a nutshell: as the next Director, besides managing a small non-profit, you will be called on to continue a protracted, hand-to-hand combat with the Spirit of War, operating behind the lines of one of its main strongholds, far from most Quaker bastions, and largely on your own.

Where in Quaker circles are Friends being prepared to take on such a mission? Frankly, I don't know, so the QH Board will be casting the net far and wide.

Let's break down the Director's job description a bit. Many of the routine tasks are familiar, basic to small non-profits: designing and running the prog-ram; reporting to the board; keeping the supporters informed; supervising a small staff; and of course, raising the budget.

All necessary, but not the heart of the matter.

The central skills grow out of the unique setting of Quaker House, and have a lot to do with temperament as well as actual capabilities.

Topping the list is the ability to live for extended periods outside one's cultural comfort zone (or CCZ).

It's a truism that American society has become balkanized along cultural, political, religious and other lines; more and more we hang out with people who talk and think like ourselves, we stay in our CCZ. And among these divergent "zones," no chasm is deeper or wider than that between Civilian America and Military America.

Friends, particularly liberal Quakers, are no exception to this trend; and in this particular respect, we are almost all located deep in the heartlands of the civilian side of the gap, culturally if not geographically.

This is not said to criticize, but to underline a fact: to live at Quaker House, on the doorstep of Fort Bragg, is to leave that Quaker milieu behind. In place of a pacifist heritage and a culture of civilian quiet, you'll step into the maw of the war machine: it's not only outside, but rattles the windows when you're inside. War is the main industry in this company town. Goodbye, cozy Quaker CCZ.

Is there any other domestic Quaker project that's similarly situated? Not that I'm aware of.

And the specter of war is more than a matter of uniforms or equipment; you will also have to confront the human cost of war on a daily basis. Its victims haunt the streets, fill the news columns, huddle in the bars and churches.

Speaking of churches, there are 300+ Christian congregations in the Fayetteville area, some quite large and visible. Among these, Quaker House is the only one willing to declare in public that when Jesus said, "Blessed are the peacemakers," maybe he meant it. This is said less as a point of pride than an indicator of isolation.

To be sure, it's just as possible to see and speak to the Inner Light in military folks as in any other children of God. Our motto here is "YES to the troops, NO to the wars," and as Director you will have ample opportunity to practice it. Plus there is a remnant of peace-minded folks in Fayetteville who can offer support; I have found good friends here. And Fayetteville Meeting is a tiny but tenacious Quaker bastion.

So the isolation is not total. But make no mistake: Quaker House is a mission outpost in foreign territory. So much so that you will soon find that very few Quakers from outside are prepared to venture from their CCZs to come to Fayetteville and ease your marginal status.

Indeed, there is a grim joke here, about how the distance from any of the region's established Meetings to Fayetteville must be much, much farther than that from Fayetteville to them.

Nevertheless, Quaker identity and connections are critical to QH and its mission. So if few Friends will come to you, then you will plan to go to them. Expect to spend much time on the road, especially in summer, visiting yearly meetings, monthly meetings and other gatherings.

More than spiritual support depends on these connections. They are also important to one of the Director's make-or-break practical capabilities, namely fundraising.

Apart from visits, our fundraising is mainly done on paper, via newsletters and appeals; so an effective Director will be a good writer. The internet is encroaching on print, so some web facility is also appropriate; but ink on paper will still be central to the fiscal health of QH for a long time to come.

Now, as to program: for as small an operation as we are, QH has fingers in many pies. This should be no surprise; militarism has seeped into every corner of our culture. No matter how much we do here, we can't keep up.

So as Director you'll be learning about some of the hundreds of regulations and policies involved in our GI Hotline counseling. Then there's the military recruiting apparatus to monitor. It's formidable and ubiquitous. It is abundantly financed and deploys top-flight marketing talent with great flexibility.

Recruiters also work hard – many of them too hard, in ways that put their families and even their lives at risk. Witness the four suicides in one recruiting unit in 2007-2009.

This data points up another piece of the QH workload, one we did not seek but could not escape: what we now call Violence Within the Military.

It first came to my notice as an epidemic of domestic violence, especially shocking spousal murders. In the past year or so, these have receded, but only to be replaced by a surge of soldier suicides, which in 2009 exceeded the number killed in actual combat. These and associated phenomena are military-wide, with the heaviest toll in the Army.

In addition, there is another, even more ominous side of the military centered around Ft. Bragg: what we call the Torture Industrial Complex. Most of the known "rendition" flights that carried victims to secret prisons and Guantan-amo took off from near here. The brutal and illegal "enhanced interrogation techniques" were taught here to the masters of Gitmo, and "migrated" from there to Abu Ghraib, Bagram and elsewhere. Further, several of the military's most secret and lethal units – Delta Force and the Joint Special Operations Command – are based and trained here.

As if all this isn't enough, there's one more important unit at Ft. Bragg, less colorful perhaps but very important nonetheless: the 4th Psychological Operations Group, a centerpiece of the Army's far-flung campaigns of "psychological warfare."

This unit's motto, "Words Conquer," points to a lot more than simply dropping leaflets on a battlefield urging enemy soldiers to surrender. It applies as much or more to the "homeland" as to any foreign adversary, and its principal, abiding "target" is us: the US citizenry, thee and me.

After all, Americans do not automatically start each new year resolved to spend more than half their tax money, and the lives of thousands here and abroad, to support a vast war machine: we need to be persuaded of that "necessity" and nobility, again and again.

Furthermore, when "Words Conquer" at home, the conquest depends as much on which words can be prevented from becoming part of public discourse as it does on inserting particular terms into it.

Many examples of such domestic psychological warfare could be listed here. Some of the most intensive skirmishes, however, involve issues that are close to our work: the tide of violence within the military (it must be downplayed at all times) and the programs of torture (which must never be named as such).

In my years here, this concentrated, relentless propaganda effort has had a major wearing effect. As much a course of self-deception as one of misleading others, it at once conceals, justifies and promotes the organized destruction and self-destruction that is our "military industrial complex."

And here we have named our principal adversary, and a formidable one it is: this "complex," combines reinforcing elements of massive destruction, secrecy, torture, propaganda and deception into a machinery so vast and entrenched that it seems almost to run by itself. Indeed, the most useful image or metaphor for it to me is that of the biblical "principalities and powers." That is, forces that operate within and yet behind the visible components and institutions, moving the parts and the people within them.

Those caught in this web are as person-ally virtuous, or not, as anyone else. Yet this power encompasses all their individual wills (and in large measure ours too). And it bends the whole ineluctably in the direction of war and death.

This "Spirit (or Power) of War" is a metaphor, surely, and one drawn from a two-millennium old myth. And yet, at Quaker House this "myth" feels as tangible as the huge oak tree at the foot of the front lawn. For if its mechanisms have worldwide reach, many of the key cogs mesh and grind right here in eastern North Carolina. It can be heard rumbling through the woods; its priests and acolytes carry on their rituals in the open; its sacrificial victims stare out from the pages of our local paper.

At Ft. Bragg, for instance, more than three hundred soldiers had been killed in Iraq and Afghanistan by the end of 2009, and several thousand gravely wounded. In addition, dozens more have killed themselves or their spouses, and untold numbers bear the psychic wounds of what they have done in combat.

And how many Iraqis and Afghans have been killed, maimed or made homeless as these troops carried out their orders? Hundreds of thousands at least. In the CCZs, this appalling toll of death can be kept at a safe abstract distance. In Fayetteville, the windows rattle and one foregoes that luxury.

Now we approach what has been the most challenging part of the Director's mission, which brings together all the elements previously mentioned: namely, the call to see, name, and challenge this "spirit of war." Not just once, as amid the camaraderie of a springtime Washington peace march; but day in and day out, week in and year out. Thus the job demands both tactical skill and stamina.

Stamina: one of the most glaring defects of recent US wars is the near-total ignorance of our forces, from top to bottom, of the nations and cultures they are fighting. It takes time and commitment to develop the cultural competence for effective operations in a different society.

The same goes for peace work and Quaker House: it takes time for a Director to learn the "language" of a military town; it takes time to become established as a credible actor on the local scene. In my view, this means a new Director needs to stay for at least five years, and preferably

300

longer. This is not a position for job-hoppers, or the unseasoned.

Nor, for that matter, for the faint of heart. Taking on this Spirit of War is what the same biblical texts which speak of such powers call "spiritual warfare" against them. And while this is another old metaphor, it too evokes an all-too-real combat.

In much popular religious writing, such "spiritual warfare" is typically reduced to calls for lots of prayer, and/or donations to some melodramatic preacher's ministry. Without disparaging either prayer or donations, taking on the "spirit of war" at Quaker House is a much more concrete contest. In taking it up, you will have more to learn from Sun Tzu than Pat Robertson.

I've written elsewhere of the value of studying classical military strategy and developing long-term planning and tactical agility in Quaker peace work; all this is intensified in Fayetteville. If the language, and still more the grim reality of such concepts and the struggles they signify are difficult for you, it will be advisable to look elsewhere for opportunities.

Another aspect of this strategic task is to regularly re-assess and recalibrate Quaker House's relationship to what is called the "peace movement." In 2002-3, for instance, we were happily a mere dot in a vast tide of antiwar protest. A couple of years later, QH and Fayetteville became move-ment focal points. Such occasions put dealing with police and press as additional items on the Director's skills list.

Since then we have watched this movement tide recede virtually out of sight, leaving Quaker House flashing our stubborn beacon like a lonely lighthouse across a deserted beach.

Yet if there's a lull elsewhere, QH is still plenty busy. And a broader surge may someday rise again.

Ideally, the Board hopes to pick you from among a number of highly qualified Friends. And this is where the work of finding you could get tough. There are many places to pick up the basics of non-profit management and fundraising. But when it comes to learning to live outside the CCZ, up-close-and-personal with the war machine for extended periods, I don't know where in Quaker circles such training is available.

Nevertheless, there is much about the work of the Spirit among the Society that is beyond our ken. So during the many months of seeking that lie ahead, we can hope not only that you are in fact out there, but that our paths will cross, and the unique ministry of Quaker House can continue, in a manner that upholds "the Reputation of Truth."

I look forward to welcoming you to Quaker House.

In Friendship,

Chuck Fager

SIX: The War at Home – God Is Not Mocked

Quaker House – August 2002

Reflection: Domestic Murders at Ft. Bragg   (An update follows this piece)

By Chuck Fager

There was something surreal about Fayetteville's community meeting on domestic violence on August 21, 2002. The mix of victims, civilian and Army professionals were to talk about how to prevent more domestic homicides. We were all there, of course, because seven corpses had been hauled from local homes in the space of five weeks that same summer, the deadly result of murders and suicides by military family members.

This bloody outburst brought national media attention, as well it should have. It also aborted the city of Fayetteville's latest PR campaign to change its unhappy "Fayettenam" image. But all this was muted nearly into invisibility that morning. A Colonel Tad Davis, Ft. Bragg's garrison commander, spoke, but his rhetoric was almost as hard to make out as the nametag sewn on his camouflage green uniform.

This was a "great day," he declared, in which to "come together" and "move forward" to increase "awareness" and "outreach" to "people who are hurting." Pausing to praise Fayetteville as an "All-American City," he insisted on "accountability" for people involved in "these situations " as the Army worked for "more productivity" on the "issues at hand."

He could have been talking about diabetes or drunk driving. Only when announcing a newly-scheduled seminar on post did he actually speak the "DV" words, hurrying past them to wrap up with a promise that this was not "a short-term thing." He finished to warm applause.

Most of the rest of the session was carefully focused on domestic violence away from Ft. Bragg, as a statewide problem in North Carolina, and on pleas to get more information for families at risk, about counseling and other services. The oblique character of the event was probably unavoidable; certainly spousal murders are a scourge across the state, occurring almost weekly. But that wasn't why we were there, nor did it explain the gaggle of reporters and TV cameras outside the door collaring anyone willing to call herself a victim or an expert.

Only in the back of the room, little-noticed on a literature table, was there a discordant, more revealing note: a stack of reprints from a newsletter, *Domestic Violence Report,* which presented data on the real issue, the 900-pound guerilla everyone was stepping so carefully around: the epidemic of domestic violence in the US military, and the blatant, chronic inadequacy of its responses.

One speaker could have cut through the fog of phony optimism: Deborah Tucker, who is Co-Chair of a task force on DV that was forced on the Defense Department by Congress in 1999 after earlier searing exposes of "The War At Home" on TV's *60 Minutes* and elsewhere. Tucker's task force has issued two reports which, within reams of carefully modulated bureacratese, deliver a damning indictment of systematic denial and coverup of rampant family abuse in the military. But Tucker too pulled most of her punches, offering only the mildest of criticisms, carefully wrapped in praise for the good intentions of the Pentagon brass.

As an exercise in Army damage control, the meeting was a success: I watched a uniformed officer shrug and tell a TV reporter that there was nothing special about the recent killings: "They were just an anomaly." And the *Fayetteville Observer*'s report dutifully headlined the event with a distinctly upbeat slant, portraying it as somehow marking the turning of the tide. The issue has since been receding from Fayetteville's public consciousness–at least until the next bodies turn up.

Given the institutional and cultural realities here, the meeting probably went as well as could be expected. But what was not said, and has not been acknowledged, is that the real news about this rash of killings and what it represents is–that it really isn't news at all.

in this regard, the experience of the *Fayetteville Observer* is revealing: The *Observer* has the makings of a good paper, but its coverage has a predictably ingrained pro-military bias. Thus its early stories on the killings reflected spoon-fed Army PR, with spokesmen expressing shock, bewilderment and the "just an anomaly" line.

But then something truly anomalous happened: the *Observer's* phones began to ring, and wouldn't stop. On the other end were military wives, dozens of them, spilling out gruesome tales, not only about beatings and abuse, but of a military culture that, despite PR protestations, remains deeply and systematically indifferent to their plight. The recent killings, these witnesses made plain, were just the bloody, impossible-to-ignore tip of a very large and otherwise submerged iceberg.

This outpouring must have been difficult to listen to, but the reporters, to their credit, paid attention. While the *Observer* still ignores or downplays the plentiful evidence that DV rates are much higher in the military than the civilian population, it chose not to ignore the anguished testimonials of dozens of its local neighbors.

The Army clearly hated that. It works nonstop here and elsewhere to project a wholesome, family-friendly image, for various reasons, not least as an aid to recruiting. And to be sure, many Army families are perfectly normal. But too many are in serious difficulty. Nor is this epidemic confined to "families": the *Army Times* reported on August 19 that there had also been five GI suicides on Ft. Bragg since January. A strong case could be made for adding them to the tally, but this report has not made it into the local press.

And there have been two other spousal killings this year which are likewise not included in the current tally: A female officer at nearby Pope Air Force Base was killed by her estranged husband in front of their children–but that happened in South Carolina; and in January, a woman was stalked and stabbed to death by her ex-husband in broad daylight at a restaurant–but he had been discharged from the Army a few days before, so that case doesn't "count" in their already inadequate statistics.

What accounts for this institutional tolerance of domestic violence? This is the last question the Army brass wants to have to face. And I don't blame them; it's disturbing enough to contemplate even from the outside: After all, the army is the enforcement instrument of the American body politic, that is to say, us. We pay for it, the polls say we admire it, and take pride in its skill at its assigned job of killing people and breaking things in an admittedly dangerous world.

Can we really be surprised when this violence comes home, when what is sown elsewhere is also reaped among the families who live with its professional purveyors?

Deborah Tucker's task force has come up with some constructive ideas; but even if they're adopted by the Pentagon (a big IF in the current macho administration), it isn't clear they'll get to the bottom of this ongoing plague. The more I look into it, the deeper the roots seem to go, far beyond the guarded enclosures of our military bases.

I won't pretend to have a list of ready solutions to this unfolding horror. But there's one thing I am sure of:

It is not an anomaly.

<< UPDATE: January 2003 >>
Ft. Bragg Domestic Murders: Continued

The shocking series of family homicides at Ft. Bragg in the summer of 2002, described above, has largely faded from the news. But its impact is still being felt; and there is still considerable spin being applied to the aftermath.

Two sharply differing reports were issued in the late fall of 2002 about the homicides. One came from a field investigation by an Army medical team. The other was a lengthy, probing piece in Vanity Fair magazine's December 2002 issue.

The Army report's authors took great pains to insist to the press that an anti-malarial drug called Lariam, given routinely to soldiers overseas and recently linked to numerous cases of violence, psychosis and suicide, was not a culprit in any of these cases, blaming "family stress" instead. This is curious because the actual report, which few reporters apparently read, does not at all exculpate this drug, which at least two of the killers had been taking.

By contrast, *Vanity Fair*'s Maureen Orth, an ace investigative reporter, dug up plenty of evidence casting strong suspicion on Lariam's side effects as contributing to at least one of the homicides evidence the Army team did not even look for. Why, one wonders, was the Army team so anxious to "clear" Lariam, especially when this conclusion was not supported by their own evidence?

Drugs aside, however, both reports painstakingly documented in their different ways the destructive impact of much of the army environment on families and marriages.

The military's epidemic of family abuse may have been cloaked for now by the shadows of war, but this issue has not gone away.

The *Vanity Fair* piece is not on the web. But an interview with reporter Maureen Orth about it is.

2007 - October

Domestic Violence At Ft. Bragg: A Long-Delayed Memorial

On October 1, several news shows in our part of North Carolina ran a story about a remarkable ceremony that was held in Fayetteville. It was a memorial for an army wife who was murdered by her husband. Is such a case old news here? Well, yes – from 1974, in fact. But only in 2007, thirty- three years later, was a marker placed on the victim's grave, by her daughter.

The murder victim was Beryl Mitchell, killed by her Army Green Beret husband on December 1,1974: stabbed, strangled, and dumped nude in a wooded area of Ft. Bragg.

The daughter, Christine Horne, has worked for decades to overcome the impact of that trauma. As part of that process, Home came to Fayetteville to organize a memorial for her mother and install a headstone; the fact that the ceremony took place at the beginning of Domestic Violence Awareness Month is entirely not coincidental.

The memorial was an impressive event; both the chief of police and the Cumberland County sheriff were in attendance –though the army did not respond to her invitation. The event climaxed in the release of thirty-three lavender balloons at the cemetery. A crowd of fifty-plus watched the balloons rise into the blue sky. Among them were many women, survivors of domestic violence, who showed up unannounced to be part of the witness.

And where does Quaker House fit into this story? Domestic violence is not one of our program priorities, though of course we hear about it in our counseling, and as part of the life of this community. But back in 2002, after a shocking series of seven military domestic murder-suicides here, I wrote an article in this newsletter about the aftermath of this outburst, and later placed it on our website. (It's at: http:I/quakerhouse.org/DV-Military.htm)

Which is where Christine Horne read it in mid-September, then picked up the phone and called us. She was seeking help with making the ceremony as visible as possible, particularly to help focus attention on this chronic social sickness.

And we did help her, particularly with media work, staying mainly in the background as we did so. I also enlisted the help of the Fayetteville chapter of NOW, which meets at Quaker House, and who are veteran activists on this issue.

This commemoration, while very personal, was not only about closure in Christine's life. Hardly a week goes by here now without someone voicing their apprehension about an expected increase in domestic abuse when the thousands of soldiers from Ft. Bragg, now in Iraq, return in the coming months. Is the army getting ready? Is the community? No one feels very confident.

Christine Horne has been effusive in her gratitude for our assistance. But for the past, and especially the future, I say it's the least we could do.

Quaker House

Dear Friend,

This fall in Fayetteville, "The Long War" is coming home. With your help, Quaker House will be ready for it.

Thousands of troops from the 82d Airborne Division, Fort Bragg's centerpiece unit, are returning from a long deployment in Iraq. For most, this was their second or third tour.

While families rejoice, many local observers have been holding their breath. More than 150 soldiers from the 82d have been killed, and hundreds more wounded. We've been reading about the high rates of PTSD, depression, and other problems in the ranks. Social service agencies, on and off the post, have been preparing for an outbreak of family trouble and other dangerous behavior as the combat-weary soldiers try to re-adjust.

That shoe may already be dropping: there were four murders here in the first week of November. Two GIs have been charged in one case. A soldier's wife was the victim in another.

A third incident happened out of state, but still too close for comfort: on November 5, Sgt. Steven D. Lopez shot his wife to death, then turned the gun on himself.

The murder-suicide occurred in Lovell, Wyoming. But Lopez was in the 82d Airborne, and stationed here at Ft. Bragg. In fact, he was AWOL at the time, having returned to Wyoming, by one report, to "work on his family" following grueling tours in Afghanistan and Iraq.

"After [Iraq] was when he really started having a tough time," his father said. "He volunteered for a lot of patrols, and he participated in a lot of close combat situations. He told me he had seen a lot of things that he couldn't even talk to me about."

Steven Lopez fit the profile of many war-related casualties: from a small town with high poverty rates, he enlisted after high school. He was 23, his wife Brenda, 22. The deaths made orphans of their toddlers, a son and daughter.

This is the nightmare scenario many here have long been quietly dreading. The fact that this one played out in Wyoming is cold comfort.

At Quaker House such family stresses show up in many calls to our GI Rights Hotline. These calls, by the way, are on track to hit ten thousand

310

this year (up from 8100 in 2006, which was also a record.) We had to hire a third Hotline counselor last spring to help cope with the load.

That new hire was only one of numerous cost increases for Quaker House this year. We look to you for renewed support to keep up with the surging demand for our free Hotline counseling service.

Maybe the worst part of these often tense Hotline conversations is that after all their exhausting and dangerous exertions, there's no end in sight for most of these soldiers. They can expect to be deployed overseas again soon. Why? Because this is "The Long War."

That's what national leaders call the occupations of Iraq and Afghanistan. They expect this "Long War" to last for decades, with continuing heavy costs to US troops and their families, not to mention the uncounted multitudes of dead Iraqis, Afghans – and who knows, maybe Iranians and others as well.

And yet, ever fewer here still think the war is worth it. In fact, I sometimes wonder if our peace vigils, which once were daring, are falling behind the curve. Consider:

– In August, seven sergeants from Ft. Bragg, deployed in Iraq, published an Op-Ed in the New York *Times*. They argued that the war was hopeless and should be ended, adding that they would keep doing their duty regardless.

(And so they did: within a month, two of the seven were killed in combat, and a third gravely wounded.)

– Then in October, twelve captains, all Iraq veterans, wrote a similar piece for the Washington *Post*. They even called for a return to the draft if the war was to continue.

– About the same time, a California reporter found no less than twenty recently retired generals who had broken with long tradition, to speak out about the pointless waste of US troops' lives, the devastation in Iraq, and the ruining of US credibility around the world. Among them was a former commander of the 82d Airborne.

Sergeants, captains and generals against the war? This unprecedented chorus of uniformed protest is a hard act for a few unarmed Quakers to follow. Or is it? The troops, having bravely spoken their piece, salute and follow orders. "Suck it up and drive on," is the phrase.

We don't salute. And we still have plenty to do, and we depend on you to keep doing it. Quaker House is busy at both ends of the military pipeline – the GI Hotline at one end, and our Truth In Recruiting initiative at the other– we've added to our "Sgt. Abe The Honest Recruiter" materials, and they continue to be used across the country.

Along with other efforts, this latter thrust may be working. Enlistments are down, especially among African-Americans.

How seriously is the army is taking this slide? Well, they are now offering re-enlistment bonuses of up to $150,000 (yes, you read that right?) to certain combat specialists, to keep them away from private firms like Blackwater. And new recruits can now get as much as $40,000. Recruiters will never give up.

And neither will we, with your help. And while returning troops seek rest and recovery, other war operations here are going on nonstop–especially the "torture taxi" flights taking off from the Fayetteville and nearby Smithfield airports. Two CIA shell companies, Centurion and Aero Contractors, have made hundreds of "rendition" flights from North Carolina. I've seen and identified some of the rendition planes myself.

We helped organize protests against this "Torture Industrial Complex." In late October, these reached a new level when several hundred of us gathered in Smithfield, near Aero Contractors. We were there to remember all torture victims and call for an end to US involvement in this inhuman and illegal practice.

To do so, though, we first had to face down a determined and noisy assault from right-wing counter-protesters. We did it, walking right through them to Aero's gates and festooning the fence with portraits of torture victims. It was an amazing witness.

There are other ongoing projects I could talk about– helping plan followup to the second Quaker torture conference; conducting numerous peace workshops for Meetings and other groups; outreach to Carolina's beleaguered Muslim community; and planning renovations that will put Quaker House, after 38 years, in shape for more decades of service.

Yes, we know something about long wars too.

Struggling to End Domestic Violence &Sexual Assaults in the Military

Working against domestic violence has not traditionally been a program priority for Quaker House. We already have plenty to do with the GI Rights Hotline, the succession of peace events, and Truth In Recruiting.

But living in this military community, some other issues have forced their way onto our agenda. Torture is one. And domestic violence is another.

In the summer of 2002, the first year I was here, there were seven domestic murders and suicides in as many weeks. And as we surveyed the carnage, the reality that these were but the top of an iceberg of family trouble became impossible to ignore.

So we wrote a report on that experience, here: http://quakerhouse.org/DV-Military.htm
And while sticking to our main priorities, we've still stayed mindful of the steady toll taken by this "war at home."

In early autumn 2007, Christine Horne (that's her, by the display in our dining room) read our 2002 report and called Quaker House. Her mother, Beryl Mitchell, had been murdered in 1974 by her Green Beret officer father, at Ft. Bragg, when Christine was a child.

Now, as part of her healing, she was coming to Fayetteville to pay a proper tribute to her mother, and the other victims like her. Could we help?

We did, and the resulting memorial drew extensive media and community response. (See the report in our fall Newsletter at: http://quakerhouse.org/Newsletter-10-2007.pdf.org/Newsletter-10-200 7.pdfrhouse.org/Newsletter-10-2007.pdfter-10-2007.pdf)

Unfortunately, the toll of family violence and sexual assault continues: four women soldiers have been murdered in North Carolina in the past nine months.

(Theywere; Maria Lauterbach, murdered in December 2007 at Camp lejeune; Megan Touma, killed in Fayetteville in June 2008; Holley Wimunc, an Army nurse murdered in Fayetteville in July; and Christina Smith, stabbed to death in Fayetteville in October 2008. All four were soldiers, and in all cases, male soldiers have been charged with the

313

crimes.)

And last month, our phone rang again. This time, it was from retired Army Col. Ann Wright. We knew Ann from her participation in our peace rally in 2007.

But Ann was not calling about an antiwar action. She was concerned about the murders of female soldiers. Could we help with a public action about that?

Of course. The outcome was a vigil, luncheon discussion, and wreath-laying memorial, on October 8, 2008. Again the press came out in force. The Fayetteville *Observer* hit the right note about the vigil, held outside one of the main gates to Fort Bragg:

The crowd hovering outside one of Fort Bragg's gates Wednesday was a protest of sorts.

But it was not the anti-war kind that Fayetteville sometimes sees.

This was a protest with purple ribbons and signs about soldiers killed by their husbands or boyfriends, not by insurgents.

In a way, it was a protest against the military. But not against the people who serve. Against the military culture that, the protesters argue, makes it difficult for a woman in the military to tell her commanders that her soldier husband is threatening her. Against the military bureaucracy that, the protesters think, hides sexual assault complaints and brushes victims to the side.

"I am here to say that our military must address this," said retired Army Col. Ann Wright, who served 29 years in the Army and now speaks around the country about violence against women in the service.

The response of an army press spokesman was dismissive:

Fort Bragg officials say the military's programs to prevent sexual assault and domestic abuse work.

They do? Tell that to the families of the four women who won't be coming home.

"Nothing could be further from the truth that we don't attempt to be proactive in reducing domestic violence," said Tom McCollum, a Fort Bragg spokesman.

McCollum said when soldiers and families come to Fort Bragg they are told about the different places on post they can get counseling. He said soldiers preparing to deploy are briefed about stress and domestic violence as part of the things they receive. Those same soldiers are briefed again before they return to the U.S. and again after they come home.

"They can go to our chaplains, Womack Army hospital and to the Army Community Services," McCollum said. "We are sometimes baffled why would someone do that and especially with all the help that is available? A divorce is so much easier."

Unfortunately, this statement mainly rebutted assertions that the

314

vigilers hadn't made. Ann Wright laid out the concerns in an OpEd column for the same newspaper on October 3rd:

In 2002, four Army spouses were murdered here by their military husbands after they returned from Afghanistan. But Fort Bragg, even aside from these infamous cases, has had a "disproportionately high number of domestic homicides, the highest in the country", according to "Murder in the Military," a July 20, 2008 article in this newspaper.

The sad roster of such victims stretches back over the decades. Thus we'll also be laying a wreath at the grave of Beryl Mitchell, murdered here in 1974 by her Special Forces officer husband.

Rape is a parallel plague. Veterans Administration statistics reveal that one in three women servicemembers are raped or sexually assaulted while in the military. Further, the Army's Deputy Chief of Staff of Personnel recently told Congress that of the reported rapes in the Army in 2007, ten percent were reported by male victims.

Nor are wives the only victims. In 2004 the North Carolina Child Advocacy Center issued a shocking report, "Reducing Collateral Damage on the Home Front," which showed that in a sixteen year period, the rate of fatal violence against children was twice as high in the counties around Fort Bragg and Camp Lejeune as in the rest of the state.

In short, however much the Army is doing, it isn't enough.

http://quakerhouse.blogspot.com/2008/10/struggling-to-end-domestic-violence.html

Quaker House Blog:

Sunday, October 31, 2010
The New Lavender Peace Movement??

[Fayetteville/Fort Bragg NC]– For antiwar folks and peaceniks, there was a welcome, if hidden surprise in the weekend's news.

You had to dig for it, though. It was buried in a letter about "Don't Ask Don't Tell" (DADT), which was sent in September but just surfaced in an Associated Press report out of Raleigh NC.

The letter to the president and the Pentagon was signed by 66 retired military chaplains. It urged the officials to maintain the DADT policy.

DADT has led to the expulsion of 13000-plus servicemembers since 1993, and the policy has been targeted for repeal, by the courts, Congress and the White House, and seems likely to succumb to whichever actually has the nerve to pull the trigger first.

The chaplains' letter, along with a whole cache of other pro-DADT and anti-gays-in-the-military materials, have been usefully collected on the web:
 (http://www.speakupmovement.org/church/LearnMore/Details/4081)

It was among this collection that the good news for peace folks was unearthed.

This news is not about the arguments over DADT itself; those have been pretty well laid out, to the point of tedium.

No, what caught my eye were a couple of solemn prophecies by some of these military weighties on the probably effects of DADT's repeal.

Taken together, they add up to the best news this peacenik has heard in a long time.

The first piece was in a letter from the Alliance Defense Fund, an anti-gay litigation group based in Kansas. It said, in part:

> "Historically, the values taught by chaplains-like honor, duty, self-sacrifice, courage, sexual fidelity, and complete commitment to goals and truths that are bigger than anyone person-directly supported those of the military. Perhaps the only recent example of tension between the combat arms and the chaplaincy was during the later phases of the Vietnam War, when a few chaplains aligned with pacifistic teachings were perhaps overly enthusiastic in facilitating the discharge of conscientious objectors. But a far more serious conflict will arise if homosexual

316

behavior is officially normalized by the military: For the first time in American history, the military's moral policies on sexual conduct would directly conflict with the official doctrines, moral teaching, and ethical standards of every major faith group in the chaplaincy– Christian, Jewish, and Islamic."(Emphasis added.)

Wait a minute: some chaplains during the Vietnam war were "overly enthusiastic in facilitating the discharge of conscientious objectors"? And "a few" of them were even "aligned with pacifistic teachings"???

That's news to me; tell me more!

Sure, I'm aware that there were lots of COs during Vietnam; and why not, when an immoral war and the military draft combined to bring tens of thousands of thoughtful young men up close and personal with the moral canyon that yawned between their values (such as honor and courage) and the pointless carnage they were expected to join?

So that's no surprise. But pacifistic chaplains helping them out with enthusiasm, excessive or otherwise? I want to know more about that, right now.

For the letter's authors, however, this unsubstantiated reference to troublesome peacenik chaplains is but the lead-in to the prophecy, that ending DADT will create "a far more serious conflict" within the chaplaincy corps and the military itself.

(Does it leap out at you, as it did me, that the private sexual behavior of a small segment of loyal troops is seen here as a much more serious problem than the impact of an immoral war on a much larger segment of the force, not to mention millions of innocent civilians the war left dead and maimed? But for now we can only take note of the incongruity.)

What will this ostensibly cataclysmic change mean for the DADT-free military? Here's where the prophecies come in. One is from Roy L. Bebee, a retired Navy chaplain and "Executive Director/Endorsing Agent" for the "Evangelical Free Church of America." Bebee says,

"I foresee the day when the military may have problems retaining some of its best chaplains if the repeal is approved. Furthermore, I will be reluctant to endorse chaplains to serve within an institution that embraces and affirms immoral conduct. Approximately 60-75% of all 3300+ of military chaplains and chaplain candidates align themselves with evangelical churches and their beliefs and values. Most chaplains have serious concerns for any Repeal of DADT; I represent nearly 102 of them within our endorsing body and the 1,460 sending churches."

If DADT goes, Bebee predicts, so will a sizable chunk of the two-thirds plus of chaplains who are doctrinally committed to the anti-gay version of biblical teachings. This prediction (threat?) has been echoed by some other denominations as well.

But that's not all. Next up is that largest of U.S. Protestant denominations, the Southern Baptist Convention (SBC), which last June adopted a "Keep DADT" resolution. This declaration included the assertion that if DADT goes,

"Military recruiting will be crippled because:

(1) those segments of the American population most represented in the armed services are also those segments most likely to have moral convictions against homosexual behavior,

(2) a great many of those who have served in the military since 1993 say they would not have served if required to live on intimate terms with open homosexuals,

(3) should current law be repealed, a large percentage of currently serving military personnel say they will not reenlist or will end their careers early, and

(4) should current law be repealed, many parents will not entrust their sons and daughters to superiors who require them to live on intimate terms with open homosexuals . . . ."

So there it is. If Don't Ask Don't Tell is repealed, we are advised, not only will many of the most conservative military chaplains leave, the military itself will shrivel drastically.

Now I ask you: for a peacenik, in all of this, what's not to like?

Some of us have been laboring for decades to find ways of shrinking the military, and rolling back the crusader mentality joined with biblicist homophobia that has contaminated an ever-growing chunk of the chaplaincy and officers corps.

And suddenly, here it is: kill DADT, and presto, job done, or almost.

Where anti-DADT advocates merely thought they were reaching for equality of service in a hazardous occupation, according to these Baptist and Evangelical seers, it will turn out that they were actually the vanguard who dealt the Military Industrial Complex a nearly mortal blow. What all our petitioning and mass marches and civil disobedience and tax resistance couldn't accomplish, the Lavender brigades will achieve by a stealth attack.

Well, if that's how it turns out, I say, Here's to Irony, and God bless every gay or lesbian who ever hit on a recruiter.

[Sigh.] But what these letter-writers see as a guaranteed nightmare scenario evokes a pleasant daydream that keeps me smiling – for about fifteen minutes.

Then an artillery blast out on Fort Bragg rattles the windows for the nth time today, and snaps me back awake. With that, realism sets in again.

Alas, almost all of this huffing and puffing is just that. Trust me: there will be no US military collapse if DADT goes. Nor will the chaplain corps be emptied out.

The reason none of this will happen is quite simple; in fact, it reduces to a single four-letter word:

J-O-B-S.

Chaplaincy slots are jobs. The pay is pretty good, and steady, the bennies generous; pensions beckon after as few as twenty years. And preachers, when you get past the motley of clerical garb and the jumble of doctrines, share one key ecumenical feature: they are all people who need jobs. And as too many of us have noticed, jobs are hard to come by today.

So maybe a few will toss away their chaplain's officer perks and head off to the mission fields. But I confidently predict their numbers will be few – and that for every one who leaves, many equally evangelical but currently underemployed preachers will be waiting in the wings to take their places, and paychecks.

The same goes for the troops themselves. Overwhelmingly, new recruits come from places where decent civilian jobs are scarce, a fact which happens to overlap heavily with Southern Baptist territory. Recruiters there are still exceeding their quotas this year, even with reduced budgets, given the boost of the unemployment rate.

Besides which, the Southern Baptist resolution made me laugh out loud with its prissy harumphing about "many parents will not entrust their sons and daughters" to a post-DADT military.

Do they think the army is a scout troop, or a summer Bible camp? Had no one told them that a Baptist youth of only seventeen, though unable to legally vote, drink, get a driver's or marriage license, can still enlist in the military to kill or be killed, *without* parental (or pastoral) consent? (And once in, Mom, there's no do-overs. Well, unless you want to call our GI Rights Hotline at 1-877-447-4487; then we'll talk.)

Post-DADT, the more affluent Baptist kids will go off to college, as usual. For the less affluent, unfortunately, military recruiters will still have considerable appeal, until and unless the job outlook gets a whole lot better.

As for the chances of a gay and lesbian "invasion" vanquishing a US military that no force, from the British in 1776, to Al Qaeda in 2010, has able to destroy – this scenario reads like a bad movie script, and not one from Mel Gibson. More like Mel Brooks.

Oh well; it was nice while it lasted. Back to the grind.

http://quakerhouse.blogspot.com/2010/10/new-lavender-peace-movement.html

SEVEN: Torture – The Issue We Can't Bear, and Can't Avoid

Quaker House

May 7, 2004

Dear Friend,

One afternoon this spring, with the azaleas bright and dogwoods blooming, there was a knock at the door. A lanky, nervous youth in glasses stood on the porch, and said he needed to talk.

Tom (as I'll call him) had recently returned to Fort Bragg after a year as an infantryman in Iraq. We sat down and I asked what was on his mind. He started to speak about what he had seen and been part of in the invasion. But within a few minutes this left him shaking and sobbing, unable to say more than, "This is no way for people to live."

After regaining his composure, Tom haltingly described some of what he had seen and been part of in Iraq.

What he related was very disturbing even then. But all of it, and much more, has now been confirmed and made starkly, visibly public. It's in the ugly photos from Abu Ghraib and Saddam's other, now-Americanized prisons; it's in the ongoing disclosures that pile horror upon horror.

Tom at first feared he might be going crazy under the weight of these experiences and the continuing pressures of military life. He had also been having stabbing pains in his chest, attacks severe enough to land him in the emergency room. So we turned first to the regulations about psychological and medical discharges.

But after looking over the literature, and thinking and praying about it, Tom called to say he was now clear it was the whole military system he was sick of, and instead he was writing a Conscientious Objector claim.

When he brought the draft CO letter to look over, Tom added that in the course of writing it, his chest pains had virtually disappeared. It appears that militarism was what had been "tearing him up" inside, and bearing his witness about it was the "cure."

Just this week Tom submitted his CO claim. He's now at the beginning of a difficult, months-long process. For instance, claims often get "lost." And what will happen if his claim is denied, as most are?

Whatever comes, we'll be here for him. And the others like him.

That's why we're in Fayetteville.

Best wishes for your summer,

Chuck Fager

From *The Friend,* London, England, August 8, 2008

Qpinion – Dismal predictions: a commentary on the US election

By Chuck Fager, North Carolina USA

In the US, it's the season for election predictions, so here are mine.

Not about the horse race. We all read the same polls and I have nothing to add.

And not about endorsements: make up your own minds, Friends.

Instead, this forecast is about some post-election developments, events I consider highly likely, regardless of who is inaugurated next January.

Three such developments, to be exact. First the list, and then the explanation.

One: The war-swap. We'll start getting out of the 'bad' war (Iraq) to make more room for the 'good' one (Afghanistan).

Two: A return to conscription, on the salami plan – a slice at a time, disguised as 'national service'.

Three: The torture transition: It will appear to be 'stopped', but behind the scenes will gain acceptance as a "last resort" tactic of American statecraft.

No doubt the rhythm and character of these events will differ depending on the election outcome. But that said, I still see them looming on the horizon after the campaign hoopla dissipates.

Why? Because of a maxim which sums up many years of experience, observation and study, namely: in the US, our militarism affects politics more than politics affects our militarism.

For me this principle manifested in 1964 – my first election. One candidate told us he would not send American 'boys' to Vietnam to do what those 'boys' should do for themselves, as his rival threatened.

As one of those American "boys," I said, "That's for me!" I wasn't alone: that candidate was swept into office, winning all but four states.

But within a year of his huge landslide victory, this same president had us in exactly the war he'd promised to avoid. The war lasted ten years, and it was just as bad as – nay, worse than – we had imagined.

In 2008, this principle is galloping toward re-verification in the current contest. Look closely and you will see that both candidates are in substantial agreement on each of these matters.

There's not much mystery as to why. The momentum of our military industrial complex is massive, pervasive, non-partisan – and it hates failure.

Iraq has become the template and archetype of military failure; so we are being prepared to trade it in for a promised victory in Afghanistan. This "forgotten war" has been sold much more successfully, not only to Americans but to many other governments as well.

Nevertheless, the transition will be difficult, because in truth the US combat forces are desperately over-stretched worldwide. The gap between supply and demand is huge and growing. Shifting some divisions from Iraq will hardly close the gap. The relentless demands of imperial adventurism, even without Iraq, require a massive rise in US troop strength. And both major candidates are promising such expansion.

Where will such an increase come from?

Recruiting, contractors, immigrants – none has filled the gap.

Enter the draft – renamed, repackaged and with the usual unobtrusive escape hatches for the more affluent.

As for torture, I fully expect the new president to denounce it and pledge that the US will not let it happen again.

But then I also expect we will be told that we must look ahead, there's no time for recriminations, so there will be no penalties for those who created our gulags; nor, beyond symbolism (closing Guantanamo?), will the system be dismantled or even closely examined.

In other words, this most repulsive of weapons will be put on the shelf – but kept handy for use the next time a "ticking bomb" scenario or some other temptation of power becomes irresistible. Torture will be rejected rhetorically, but accepted as precedent.

I find this last prospect the most odious on this gloomy list.

Let's hope I'm mistaken. And hey – I'm a Christian, so I do believe in miracles.

But short of that, the rule still applies: In the US, our militarism affects politics more than politics affects our militarism.

I don't see that changing this year.

QH Blog: Saturday, October 11, 2008

Good news On Torture for Psychologists, and their Clients

Among the many shocking realities that emerge as one studies the evolution of the US torture system, one of the most shocking to me was to learn of the deep, and decades-long involvement of psychologists in the process.

And not just a few obscure practitioners here and there – this roll of shame included presidents of the American Psychological Association. (An eye-opening summary of these facts is here:
 http://www.scoop.co.nz/stories/HL0807/S00253.htm)

Professor Alfred McCoy of the University of Wisconsin has also detailed the history in his indispensable book, *A Question of Torture:*
http://www.amazon.com/gp/product/0805082484/sr=1-2/qid=1223767
994/ref=olp_product_details?ie=UTF8&me=&qid=1223767994&sr=1-
2&seller=

But in late September, 2008 there was finally a piece of good news on the psychological front. This release tells the story:

American Psychological Association Members Pass Historic Ban on Psychologist Participation in U.S. Detention Facilities – Wednesday, September 17, 2008

Today, the membership of the American Psychological Association (APA) passed a referendum banning participation of APA member psychologists in U.S. detention facilities, such as Guantanamo or the CIA's secret "black sites" operating outside of or in violation of international law or the Constitution. Dan Aalbers, one of the referendum's authors, stated: "This is a decisive victory for the membership of the APA and for human rights advocates everywhere. This new policy will ensure that psychologists work for the abused and not the abusers at places like Guantanamo Bay and the CIA black sites. We expect that the APA's leadership will immediately take action to ensure that psychologists are removed from the chain of command at places where human rights are violated or said not to apply."

More on this at the blog of Stephen Soldz, a Boston

psychoanalyst who has been a strong anti-torture activist in the APA:
http://psychoanalystsopposewar.org/blog/2008/09/17/apa-members-cha
nge-associations-interrogations-policy/

http://quakerhouse.blogspot.com/2008/10/good-news-for-psychologists
-and-their.html

To End Torture, START NOW

Nov. 18, 2008

President-Elect Barack Obama, November 16, 2008: "I have said repeatedly that America doesn't torture. And I'm going to make sure that we don't torture."

To Make Sure: START NOW

START NOW is a comprehensive outline of steps toward eradicating torture from the United States government and military system:

START:

     1. S = STOP IT. Issue a presidential executive order, banning "enhanced interrogation techniques" in all U.S. agencies and facilities. Re-establish the restrictions in the Army Field Manual, apply to all military and intelligence services.
     – Follow up to see that the order is followed.
     – Identify and specifically revoke all secret memos and orders from the White House and agencies that authorize torture or inhibit investigations of torture allegations.
     – Dismantle the torture infrastructure. Close Guantanamo. Identify and close other secret detention facilities. Terminate arrangements with third countries for torture-by-proxy. Cancel contracts with Aero and other CIA torture flight front companies. Follow up with investigations to ensure compliance.
     – Preserve all relevant records, by impoundment if necessary.

     2. T = TRUTH. Find and make public the actual record of U.S. agencies and contractors relating to abuse and torture. To do so, launch investigations into allegations of torture, other war crimes, and conspiracy to commit these acts. The principal investigative focus would be the period since the beginning of 2002; but relevant earlier events will be included.
These investigations to proceed on numerous fronts, to include:
     – Inspectors General in the relevant intelligence and federal agencies;
     – The Government Accountability Office;

– The Justice Department, including independent counsels where advisable;

– Congressional hearings and probes, using subpoena power;

– Specially-created investigative bodies ("Truth Commission")

– State-level reviews into possible violations of state laws by front companies and contractors.

– Cooperate with investigations by international agencies and other governments

– Encourage journalists and independent investigators in their fact-finding efforts.

3. A = Accountability. Initiate enforcement actions for alleged war crimes and torture committed by U.S. citizens, agents or contractors. To this end:

– Rescind all exemptions for private contractors from applicable U.S. and international laws against torture and abuse.

– Convene grand juries in affected jurisdictions.

– In the military, initiate disciplinary procedures for those who took part in, gave orders for, or drafted policy guidance that permitted torture and abuse in contravention of the applicable field manuals, US laws and treaty obligations. Such procedures to begin at the top of the relevant commands.

– State officials to follow up when torture and conspiracy allegations involve violations of state laws.

4. R = Restitution/Compensation for victims of US torture, kidnaping, imprisonment without trial, and other related abuses, inflicted either directly by U.S. agents, contractors, or by proxy states. The cases of Maher Arar in Canada, who was granted $9 million in compensation by the Canadian government, and Ahmed Agiza in Sweden, of $377,000, are early examples of restitution payments.
Open US courts to such claims. Withdraw or severely restrict the doctrine of "state secrets" as a way of avoiding this litigation.

5. T = Treatment: Medical, psychological, and social welfare services to be provided to victims and their families, at government expense. This may be the one part of this program where the country is already reasonably well-prepared. A network of treatment centers for torture survivors is already in place. To meet the scale of the need, this network may require expansion.

NOW – ACTIONS:

1. NEVER let up: ending torture is a long-term project. Stay

informed about torture issues.

2. ORGANIZE: Keep the issue of torture in the public arena:

– Form or join local committees and coalitions to pursue the end-torture agenda.
– Conduct public witness: vigils demonstrations, protests
– Organize forums and conferences
– Challenge the glorification of torture in popular media
– Write letters to the editor; Op Eds, articles in local/regional media. Blog!
– Work in churches and professional groups for statements and actions to end torture.
– Press local and state officials for action at these levels

3. WORK on the government: Lobby Congress, the White House, and federal agencies to eradicate the roots and legacy of official torture

– Find supportive organizational partners among national groups; collaborate.
– Stay in touch with your US. Representatives & Senators; don't let them evade the issue.
– Monitor international efforts, support and join with them when practical.

Torture & Impunity
From *Friends Journal,* December 2008

Chuck Fager

Will government-sponsored torture remain a shocking anomaly in American public life? Or will it become an accepted precedent, one of the many tools of power in the hands of our rulers?

I believe the United States is approaching a crucial shift from the first state to the second. It can be called the "Torture Transition."

As this is written, our rulers have built Guantanamo, Abu Ghraib, a string of secret gulags, and a vast clandestine infrastructure to support them. Their inmates, who number in the thousands, have no legal protections. And as the outlines of this system of suffering has been revealed, its architects have trumpeted their open and flagrant defiance of our own laws, international treaties, and the clear majority of informed world opinion.

I spent six weeks in Europe last spring, giving talks about the need for international action to dismantle this torture system. Along the way I got a taste of just how repelled most thoughtful people on that continent are by this sordid spectacle. And while there, I came to understand better the Torture Transition and the importance of stopping it.

To be sure, each country I visited has its own shameful history of torture and abuse. Yet their reaction is not to be confused with hypocrisy. They know their own failings well enough. That's part of the reason for their dismay: they expected better from the United States, the self-proclaimed bastion of freedom and justice.

Nevertheless, most of those I spoke with were holding their breath, and still are, waiting for the rapidly approaching change of administration in Washington. Things are certain to get better then, they seem to feel: how could they possibly get worse?

I'll tell you how. Things could get worse if the U.S. makes the Torture Transition. How? The answer can be summed up in two words: "Impunity" and "Precedent."

Impunity means getting away with it. And if those who created the torture system, and those who managed it, are not held to account, they will have achieved impunity, which is now their primary goal.

And with impunity will come the transition in the nature of the torture system. It will move from being an outrageous aberration in our public order, to being an accepted part of it. It will become precedent. And with that change, all the laws and treaties against it will be worthless, dead letters.

How does this work? A homely local example will serve:

At Quaker House, in Fayetteville, North Carolina, where I work, there is a sign in the front yard that says, as you might expect, "Quaker House." It, and its predecessors, have been there for more than thirty-five years.

But this sign is in fact illegal. It openly violates local ordinances for residential neighborhoods like ours.

Nevertheless, because it's been there so long without challenge, it has become legal de facto; the technical term is that it is now "grandfathered." Fayetteville's ordinance still stands, but so does our sign. We've "gotten away with it"; our sign has achieved impunity.

The same thing could happen with torture, even though, from various reports I've seen and heard, there is a good chance that the new president will say that torture is bad, and that it will now stop.

Such an action would be good as far as it goes. But it could well mean no more than if someone took a weapon that had been used in deadly assaults, and put it away in a drawer.

It will still be there, at the ready, when – not if – the temptations of power begin to make the new ruler's hands itch to use something "more effective," when he is pushed to revisit "the dark side," and pressed to use it to head off some new version of the so-called "ticking bomb" scenario.

If we think a new president, especially one many of us might support, would never do such a thing, I suggest that is an overly optimistic view.

The weapon of torture will still be there. And next time, if the current perpetrators achieve impunity, it can be used again without hope of restraint. Torture will have been "grandfathered" into our system as surely as the sign on the Quaker House lawn.

That's the Torture Transition. And it's coming nearer, day by day.

So what are the chances for impunity? How likely is it that those responsible for the U.S. torture machinery will escape punishment?

According to Dick Marty, right now the chances are good.

Very good, in fact.

Dick Marty should know. He's the Swiss equivalent of a U.S. Senator – and the chief anti-torture investigator for The Council of Europe.

Marty produced two ground-breaking investigative reports that disclosed loads of hidden details about illegal US torture flights to and across Europe. They named Poland and Romania as the sites of similarly unlawful secret US prisons. And he charged that the UK had permitted torture flights too – a disclosure which proved correct despite initial government denials.

(These reports are now available in book form, under the title: "CIA above the law? Secret detentions and unlawful inter-state transfers of detainees in Europe," published by the Council of Europe. At $46, The book is pricey, because of the decline of the US dollar along with out international reputation. You can still find them online, though, for free, at: The Council of Europe: Marty's First Report: http://assembly.coe.int/ASP/APFeaturesManager/defaultArtSiteView.a sp?Id=468

The Council of Europe: Marty's Second report linked on this page: http://assembly.coe.int/ASP/NewsManager/EMB_NewsManagerView. asp?ID=2974)

The CIA shrugged off Marty's reports, and they got little notice in the U.S. But elsewhere they are recognized as landmarks, and haven't exactly burnished the US image abroad.

While in Europe, I sought an appointment with Dick Marty. Having done some investigative reporting myself, I wanted to pay respects to the author of such a superlative piece of work. More important, I hoped to get his candid view about the Torture Transition and what to do about it.

We met in his simply furnished office in the stunning city of Lugano, which hugs the shore of a sparkling lake in southern, Italian-speaking Switzerland. Its alpine serenity made a sharply incongruous backdrop for talk about such a grim subject.

Marty himself was informal and mild-mannered, his English limited. But his understanding of the subject was as sharp as I expected.

Without much in the way of introduction, I laid out my key query: Given what he knows, is there any way to stop the Torture transition? Or would the perpetrators skate off into the sunset on rollerblades of impunity?

(Pardon the amateur crime-fighter argot, but it fits: before Marty ran for the Swiss parliament, he was a tough prosecutor, who bested mobsters and drug barons in his home canton of Ticino, which adjoins Italy.)

Marty's response was unmistakable: "That's exactly the right question to be asking," he said.

After that, he didn't have much encouragement to offer. But he's not in the optimism business.

Sure, he agreed, torture is a crime under both international and national treaties and statutes. We don't need any new laws. But at a secret NATO meeting in Athens in late 2001, he told me, the US demanded and got assurances of impunity for its military and intelligence agencies for any actions related to the "war on terror" on their territories. Several non-NATO nations, such as Ireland, later signed on as well.

On the home front, repeated government assertions of the doctrine of "state secrets" have thus far stymied efforts even by certifiably innocent torture victims to gain any redress.

So, right now, it looks like a lost cause: tough luck torture victims. And as for us lily-livered lovers of the Bill of Rights, better luck next time.

But that's the short-term view. Marty wasn't suggesting I just go home and give up. "This will be a long work," Marty said. "It will require patience and determination."

Which means that while the current forecast for torturers may be sunny, like the weather, that can change.

How? In a lot of ways, mostly a bit at a time. Here's a scenario:

Pressure keeps building in many countries for investigations of torture. This includes the US after a new administration takes office in January 2009, driven by anti-torture groups and a growing list of their allies. Reporters keep disclosing ugly aspects of the torture structure, and the efforts of its architects to achieve impunity. Public opinion begins to shift away from support for torture.

In several other countries, these probes eventually produce legal actions: lawsuits, criminal complaints. (Reliable reports are that cases are already being prepared in several countries, to surface next January.) And maybe the next president might just decide to keep out of their way.

The American and other defendants resist and evade the actions, some successfully. But sooner or later, one or more of them makes a misstep. They travel to a country which honors an outstanding warrant, and the police are waiting.

If you think this scenario is too far-fetched, think again. Something very much like it happened in the most famous anti-impunity case so far: the arrest of former Chilean dictator Augusto Pinochet in London in October of 1998.

But to make anything like that happen in the U.S., where would such a buildup of public pressure in the US come from?

Believe it or not, the most likely place is American churches.

There are already several interchurch anti-torture coalitions at work in the U.S. Numerous monthly and yearly meetings have joined in, adopting minutes opposing torture. The Quaker Initiative to End Torture has held two conferences on the subject.

Nor are these stirrings limited to the usual liberal suspects. There's now a group called Evangelicals for Human Rights, based in

Atlanta, which has persuaded some heavy hitters in that constituency to sign on and speak out. An evangelical conference against torture is planned for Atlanta in September.

All this is encouraging. But even so, Dick Marty's sober counsel still rings in my mind. Torture is a subject that sends chills down the back for large numbers of us – and rightly so. But for too many, those chills also freeze the action response. Denial takes over; energy flows to other, less unnerving issues.

That's been the response in many churches; and thus far, Friends are no exception. It's been relatively easy for Quaker anti-torture workers to obtain minutes from meetings. But these, are merely, pardon the expression, pieces of paper. It's been much harder to gather a focused, working committee of Friends who are under the weight of this concern and carry leadings for long-term work.

Such focused groups have been the necessary nucleus of just about all the best Quaker campaigns over the centuries. We're still waiting for one to emerge in this effort.

This lag worries me. The stakes in the struggle are extremely high. If the Torture Transition comes to pass, torture will be "regularized" in American governance. Our rulers will have effectively gained the ability to declare any citizen outside the protection of the law. And they can do that from above and beyond the restraints of the law, with impunity.

Those two powers – to declare any citizen outside the law's protection, and to do so without fear of the law's restraints – are the essential components of a police state, the pillars of tyranny.

That is why I believe preventing impunity and the Torture Transition need to be top priorities for work against torture in the coming years.

The Torture Transition won't be made in one bold declaration; that would risk rebellion. Instead, it will come, as it has been coming, incrementally, step by step, camouflaged by the rhetoric of " national security," and hidden behind secrecy wherever possible.

Likewise, this transition will not be halted by any one massive act of protest, or by a single election. If impunity is stopped, it will also be bit by bit, case by case.

After all, once Augusto Pinochet yielded power in Chile in 1988, it took ten years of persistent work before Scotland Yard showed up at his door in London. Along the way, the Catholic church was a major factor in breaking through the walls of impunity he tried to build around himself and his minions.

In this kind of work, steadfast Friends can join with others to play a significant role. The early phases would not be dramatic: the gathering of an active and rooted Quaker committee; conferences, workshops and other educational efforts among Friends; building connections with other human rights groups to multiply our impact; and keeping it up for the years to come.

The two Quaker conferences on torture were an excellent start, but the work since has lagged. I hope it will soon be relaunched in the focused, ongoing way called for by the gravity of the task it faces.

When it is, I plan to send Dick Marty a postcard.

How do you say, "Patience and determination" in Italian?

QH Blog– December 6, 2008

The Rise of the Torture "Accountability Movement": New York December 4, 2008

Here's a first-cut report on "After Torture: A *Harper's* Magazine Forum on justice in the post-Bush era, held at the New York University Law School Center on Law & Security in Manhattan, December 4, 2008. I rode up on Amtrak from Fayetteville to be there.

The occasion of this forum was the publication of an article by humans rights attorney Scott Horton, "Justice After Bush," in the December 2008 issue of *Harper's* Magazine.

Key topics: An "Accountability Movement"? A special Commission? Pardon Poker playing? Opening Up Victim Lawsuits? And What can This Mean for Anti-torture activists??

The H*arper's* article is not online, but has been widely discussed. (The transcripts of an interview with Horton about the piece is online here: http://www.democracynow.org/2008/12/3/attorney_scott_horton_on_j ustice_after

In sum, Horton argues for creation of a special federal commission to investigate torture and related crimes in the past eight years, and thus lay the groundwork for later accountability actions, including prosecutions. The commission's structure and selection process would be complex, and this complexity became a point of contention, but I won't try to tease out those technicalities here.

The forum brought together a number of major players in what might be called the "accountability movement," including, besides Horton: Michael Ratner of the Center on Constitutional Rights, US Rep. Jerrold Nadler, Chair of the House Judiciary Subcommittee on the Constitution, which would have a major role in any congressional action; Retired Army general Antonio Taguba, who led the investigation o the Abu Ghraib torture scandal; Former US Rep. And prosecutor Elizabeth Holtzman; Burt Neuborne, Legal Director, Brennan Center for Justice, New York University.

Heavyweights all, but not ponderous, and all articulate.

A summary of the discussion could best begin with Neuborne,

336

because he put the accountability movement vividly in historical context. He argued that in practice, the US has had a "folding chair" attitude toward our constitution and bill of rights. Especially in times of real or perceived crisis, our rulers have "folded up" these guarantees and put them away for quieter times:

– The jailing of dissidents under the Alien & Sedition Acts in the John Adams administration (1798-1800);

– Lincoln's suspension of habeas corpus in the Civil War;

– Persecution of war critics and Conscientious Objectors during World war One; and

– The internment of Japanese-Americans in World War Two ; etc.

Moreover, those who carried out these policies of repression generally got away with it, Neuborne noted. In line with this history, such impunity is clearly what the current perpetrators expect to maintain. So the current accountability movement is among other things an effort to interrupt this long line of unhappy precedents.

To achieve such a reversal, Neuborne contended that the movement will need an overall accountability strategy, which is likely to encompass a range of initiatives. I'll say more about some ideas he mentioned later.

Special Commission: Regarding Scott Horton's special commission proposal, Michael Ratner's response was the most critical, insisting that a special prosecutor and early indictments were the most urgent priority. Jerrold Nadler, as might be expected from a member of Congress, argued that Congressional hearings were also important, and perhaps a better way to find out the hidden facts needed for further action.

Burt Neuborne was ambivalent; one the one hand, he said the record of such commissions is that they can be used to cover up the truth as much as to reveal it. But on the other hand, he recalled the work of the US Civil Rights Commission in the 1950s, when it held highly-publicized hearings in various states and cities, where both the practices and key protagonists of racism and segregation were exposed and shamed.

Such "shaming," he said, was an important non-criminal tool for accountability, and needed to be part of the accountability strategy.

And let me put in an oar here briefly: While I'm unsure about the practicality of Horton's specific commission model, I do agree with him on its purpose. It is the proper preliminary to prosecution, by getting the facts of the torture regime, making them known in an official way in the glare of the media, and thereby educating the public about the extent and depth of the lawbreaking and general evil of it all.

Call this Overcoming the "24" effect, the glamorization of torture – by US agents– in popular media over the past several years. Such a process will be needed to make prosecutions of former high officials publicly and politically acceptable. And it will take time, a few years I would guess.

I differ from Horton in that I don't want to see inquiries limited to one avenue, such as a commission. I say, let a dozen investigative flowers bloom, in Congress, a commission, the courts, inspectors general, even the states (Hello, NC Attorney General Roy Cooper? Paging Roy Cooper!) If one investigation is a whitewash, another can rinse the whitewash off.

Now, about pardons: Horton said he believes a high stakes "poker game" is underway about pardons for torturers. On the one hand are the recent statements by US Attorney General Mukasey that no pardons are needed) , because no crimes were committed by administration officials. Horton noted that it's highly improper for an Attorney General to be speaking in such a way, publicly pre-judging the merits of potential future prosecutions. So why was Mukasey doing it?

Horton thinks Mukasey and his masters are trying to goad Obama and his team into making some kind of calm-the-waters statement about letting bygones be bygones, looking forward and not backward, and ruling out prosecutions too. There have been reports that some Obama insiders are pushing just this line . Which would put Obama in the no-prosecutions camp too.

Neuborne, by the way, agreed such a move was possible. He said he had voted for Obama with pleasure – but that every president is forced to make political compromises. Thus, Neuborne said, he had also filed civil liberties lawsuits against every president since LBJ (that's forty-plus years and eight presidents, for those who forgot the math), and he fully expected to end up filing suits against the Obama administration too.

But Horton said he figured Obama for a smart poker player too, and expected him to make no clear statement at all about the possibility of prosecutions. That way, his options remain open, and he avoids taking flak about any specific plan.

There was also division among the panelists about the extent of pardons. Neuborne said he thought George W. Bush (GWB) would issue pardons before he leaves office next month, but aim them "too low," mainly at those who had actual involvement in carrying out torture programs, in the CIA, military, etc. Neuborne figured GWB would buy Mukasey's argument about higher-ups not needing pardons and would skip them. This would, Neuborne felt, be a boon to the accountability movement, by leaving high officials more vulnerable to future enforcement actions.

To Michael Ratner, this was wishful thinking. GWB will pardon everybody including himself, Ratner predicted. Horton added that he did not expect any pardons to be announced until the last possible minute, the morning of January 20 itself.

One other reason for Obama to stay cool about prosecutions and pardon talk, Horton argued, is that when the pardons come, there is likely to be a big uproar in the media and Congress, and if Obama has steered clear, all this negative attention will fall on GWB and the other conspirators.

A Brief Sidebar on Victim Lawsuits: During the Q&A, I asked Horton and Ratner about lawsuits and the "state secrets" defense. Could the Obama administration open the courts to lawsuits by victims like Khaled el Masri by simply NOT raising the "state secrets" defense? GWB has used this consistently to squash any such redress.

It seemed to me that this would be an easy thing politically for the new team–NOT doing something rather than taking some big initiative. Obviously, though, there ought to be pressure for the administration to stop raising the state secrets defense, or to sharply limit its use; and if that happens, then we can call for more victim lawsuits to be filed and supported.

To my gratification, both Horton and Ratner responded that this indeed could be done, and it WOULD open the US courts to victims. But also in response to my query, Elizabeth Holtzman, ever the prosecutor, dismissed this matter as irrelevant. Prosecuting GWB was what she felt was important. (She has even published a book on the topic.)

While I admire Holtzman's go-for-the-jugular instincts, and I'm fine with prosecuting GWB, I still think the victim lawsuits concern has much merit. For one thing, as Rep. Nadler had said earlier, torture victims need and deserve redress; that's simple justice. But for another, as these lawsuits proceed to discovery, many documents will come to light. What is learned in one case can be useful to another, and to the larger effort to get the truth which a commission, and other investigations will also be seeking. The information-gathering will be cumulative. Every revelation will help.

Now what does any of all this brilliant talk mean for those of us on the ground, in my case here in North Carolina, and the groups I work with, Quaker House and NC Stop Torture Now? Here are a few early ideas that have occurred to me; but clearly all this needs more discussion. Readers from other areas can make appropriate adjustments.

1. Add the phrase "Accountability Movement"to our action vocabulary. I'm not sure now whether someone on the panel used this phrase as such, or it just emerged; but I believe it's now "in the air." Maybe it was spoken by Karen Greenberg, the Executive Director of the Center on Law and Security at NYU, in her introduction to the panel. She did say that in her view the discussion of torture had shifted in recent

weeks from whether the US had engaged in torture, and whether that was bad, to an assumption that it had happened, it was wrong, and the issue now was HOW to institute a process of accountability for it.

I think Greenberg is right, but this shift has only begun, and I believe we can assist it, in particular by speaking about the "accountability movement," and identifying our work as part of it.

2. Join the chorus against the pardons. I hope we'll get ready to help raise hell about the pardons, to increase the pressure for an investigative response, in Congress and elsewhere. This ought to be a big opportunity.

3. Ramp up state and local-level actions. Most on the panel seemed to see only the federal courts and agencies as potential venues for the accountability movement. For such heavy hitters, that's their typical milieu. But it's not the only one. For instance, for three years now we've been productively active here protesting the presence of "torture taxi" planes used for rendition, as well as other aspects of the system , and we're not about to stop. There are many other localities where similar parts of the "Torture Industrial Complex" are located, that could likewise be targets for local and state action.

After the session, I approached Michael Ratner, identified myself as working with STN and against Aero Contractors, the NC-based CIA shell company that is the main torture taxi outfit. He knew Aero instantly – and I asked if there were any possibilities for state-level action. He expressed interest in exploring this side of possible accountability action, and I hope some collaboration will develop.

If I have one criticism of the nascent accountability movement, it is that thus far it is too Washington and New York centered. Of course, the brainpower and institutional weight of the NYU panel will be indispensable to its success. But I think they will also need active support from below as well, the sort of action being spearheaded by NC Stop Torture Now.

Addendum: Here are a couple points I didn't get to in the initial report, about the military aspect, and some legislative possibilities:

#1. Panel member Gen. Antonio Taguba. He is or should be a hero to "accountability movement" folks, not only for his pioneering probe of Abu Ghraib, which he carried out even though it meant the end of his military career, but also his clear declaration last summer of the truth of war crimes by the current administration, and a call for accountability .

He spoke at the panel on behalf of military folks, and pointed out that, however incomplete, there HAS been corrective and punitive action in the military, in response to cases of torture; upwards of 200 soldiers have been disciplined for involvement in torture, and their current orders are not to do it. (This does not apply to the CIA and other secret outfits.)

Sure, there are more soldiers, especially generals, who should face such action; when I spoke to him about this after the panel, he agreed, and mentioned a couple of names of retired generals as potential candidates for legal action.

But his point was that while some accountability action has been taken within the military, the civilian higher-ups are scrambling to avoid the same thing. He mentioned in this connection an executive order by GWB which, in the same order, declared administration officials exempt from any penalties for violating the Geneva Convention, while directing the military to follow it, or else.

He added that we are in a time of "persistent conflict" (kudos to him for NOT calling it the "war on terror") when US troops will frequently be in danger, so one of the things they deserve is a single standard of behavior and accountability, from top to bottom.

So another way of putting this would be: "Support the troops: hold civilian torturers accountable, too!" (As a slogan, that may need some work, but you get the idea.)

#2. Some legislative possibilities.

Much of this came from Rep. Nadler, and it's not entirely clear which things he DEFINITELY plans to introduce, and which ideas are in the "thinking out loud" stage.

First, Nadler repeated the point about how the new administration will come under lots of pressure from many of its "friends" and allies to leave all this accountability stuff alone. (After all, many high muckety-muck Dems are complicit to varyng degrees.) So pressure FOR accountability needs to continue. Nothing new there, but it was good to hear him say it.

As to specific proposals, here are some Nadler mentioned; keep in mind that he did not go into many technical details, and those are mostly above my pay grade anyway, so think about following up with him . And for brevity I'll refer to Nadler as "N" below:

A. Reviving the Special Prosecutor law, which lapsed after the disgraceful Ken Starr impeach Clinton fiasco. N wants to revive it with limits to prevent another unlimited Starr-type witchunt.

B. State Secrets doctrine: he wants to put limits on its use, particularly as a tool for completely shutting down court actions. N said he already had a state secrets reform bill, but didn't mention a bill number or name.

C. Pardon power: N said he plans to offer a Constitutional

341

amendment limiting the president's pardon power, especially regarding high members of the incumbent administration, and to prohibit pre-emptive pardons for persons not yet charged with a crime. Alaso, no pardons could be given in the last 6 months of an administration. There was more, that I didn't catch.

One other call for new legislation came from Elizabeth Holtzman. She noted that the War Crimes Act of 1996 made much of what the current gang did criminal. She said Gonzalez warned GWB about this in a memo that has been uncovered.

So to protect themselves, they put a section into the Military Commissions law which gutted the War Crimes act, and did so RETROACTIVELY so that everything they've done was NO LONGER A CRIME.

(Makes me wanna barf.) This section, she said, was unnoticed amid all the hubbub about habeus corpus. So Holtzman is calling on Congress to repeal that change and REINSTATE the War Crimes Act. Listening to all this legislative stuff, and weighing all the difficulties it will face, made me think favorably of the idea of shaming the perps, lawsuits, other state-level initiatives, and foreign actions as avenues for folks like us to keep exploring.

http://quakerhouse.blogspot.com/2008/12/rise-of-torture-accountability -movement.htmlSaturday,

The New President vs. Torture: Good Start. Much Yet to Be Done.

Chuck Fager

First, credit where it is due: on torture, Obama has changed the game and the momentum. His executive orders are landmarks, and their repudiation of the lawbreaking that's been going on for the past eight years is of landmark status.

But who's perfect? There are some holes in the orders; and even in the best case scenario, there's plenty more to be done. On this continuing agenda, four tasks are top priorities.

Let's check the holes first: Two stick out: a "special task force" (http://www.whitehouse.gov/the_press_office/EnsuringLawfulInterrogations/) will decide if there is to be "additional or different guidance" (e.g., exceptions to the anti-torture rules) for "departments or agencies outside the military" (e.g., the CIA and its ilk). Will this result in some kind of "Jack Bauer" loopholes? It shouldn't, but it's distinctly possible; stay tuned.

Also, Obama is evidently keeping "rendition," which means a green light to continued covert kidnapings, particularly in foreign countries.

This does not surprise me. I work next door to Fort Bragg NC, as Director of a Quaker peace project there, and we're smack in the middle of what can be called the "Torture Industrial Complex." Two reputed CIA front companies, Centurion Aviation Services in Fayetteville (http://www.quakerhouse.org/centurion-observer.htm), and Aero Contractors in nearby Smithfield

(http://www.sourcewatch.org/index.php?title=Aero_Contractors_Ltd.), have been linked to many, if not most of the "torture taxi" flights.

Over the past year, local anti-torture activists have watched both these companies expand their facilities, with more growth on the boards. So while most other sectors of the economy here are collapsing, the rendition flight industry's outlook seems quite sunny, thank you very much; Obama or no.

To be sure, we are told that future "renditions" will not include, or culminate in, torture or "black sires" imprisonment. Yet in Obama's orders, there is another exception, permitting captives to be held in foreign safe houses "on a short-term, transitory basis." (But there's no definition of "short-term" or "transitory" either.)

Thus the first priority is to keep these chinks of wiggle room from being stretched into actual loopholes.

This points us to the second major concern. How will we know if these good new policies are adhered to? More important, how will Obama know?

Take the notorious "black sites," secret CIA prisons. The one thing we know about them for sure is that they exist, because Obama has ordered them to close, along with Gitmo.

But we don't know how many of these prisons there are. We don't know where they are. And we don't know how many prisoners are being kept in them. (My guess: thousands since 2002.)

The chances are that very few people in Washington know either. Will that number include the President?

Keep in mind that we're talking about a group of people (not just the CIA, but a whole sub-culture of "OGAs" Other Government Agencies) that encompasses an undetermined number of private contractors.

Secrecy is their reason for being. Concealment and deception are basic tools of their trade. And keeping higher-ups as ignorant as possible is standard procedure, either with their superiors' connivance ("plausible deniability"), or not (Bay of Pigs).

So Quis custodiet ipsos custodes? Who will check to make sure – really sure – that all these hellholes have been shut down (and not replaced with others) and their inmates – all of them, living or (maybe more important) dead – are accounted for? The CIA? The OGAs? The contractors? Can they be trusted to clean up their mess and own up to any "issues" such as, say, war crimes?

As a practical matter, my nominee for this watchers'-watchman-and-cleanup role would be the FBI. The record as we now know it indicates that the Bureau steered clear of the torture business, hence they may be the only outfit with clean enough hands to do a reliable job.

And of course, the chance to really stick it to the arch-rival CIA after years of being sidelined would be a spur to the FBI getting as close to the bottom of this bottomless pit as may be bureacratically possible. Creative tension; checks and balances. What a concept.

Making sure torture has stopped; that's the second priority. The next is accountability. Will there be any?

At this point, the jury is still out. From my perch in the boondocks, it seems Obama is torn: on the one hand, his conscience tells him there has to be consequences for war crimes, else the ability to torture with impunity will become an established White House perk, which is intolerable.

Yet doing the necessary investigations and then even the minimum number of prosecutions will surely set off a political firestorm, which at best will be a huge distraction from the work of pulling us out of the second great depression.

Let me not discount or dismiss this dilemma. I don't blame him for hesitating. Still, while ready to cut him some slack for timing, accountability is a bullet I believe Obama must eventually bite. In the eyes of the world, it's a make-or-break question, and I think he knows that.

Numerous weighty inside-the-beltway pundits have already been pleading the case for doing nothing, and letting their governing class buddies walk. Such defenses of the indefensible are beneath contempt, and to my mind were definitively discredited by Glenn Greenwald in *Salon* here: http://www.salon.com/opinion/greenwald/2009/01/27/cohen/

Yet even a round of war crimes trials would not be the end. Imagine that the black sites had been closed; the accountability probes were complete, and at least a handful of the main perps had been shipped off to Club Fed, or perhaps even the Hague. What will remain?

The victims will remain.

Hundreds. No, thousands. And their families.

What of them? They would doubtless find a measure of vindication-by-prosecution if some infamous ex-politicians and apparatchiks wound up wearing stripes. But that would hardly be sufficient.

The victims deserve a formal apology from the US government. They need compensation – reparations, restitution, damages, pick your term. And they require treatment.

These are the practical manifestations of justice, and the last is the one area in which the US may in fact already be equipped to do its duty. Numerous centers for the treatment of torture victims are already in operation. (A directory is here: http://physiciansforhumanrights.org/asylum/resources/torture-treatment.html .) This network may need to be expanded, however, if we ever do something like justice to the scale of victimization that has been involved.

In sum: the first crucial blows have been struck against the odious and criminal "Torture Industrial Complex," and kudos to Obama for that.

Now let's continue to press him – and Congress – to make good on the necessary followups: to slam shut any creeping loopholes; ro make sure it has stopped; to get to the truth and require accountability; and to offer practical justice for the many victims and their families scarred by these atrocities.

In the past couple weeks, I've heard numerous comments to the effect that, "Thank god torture is over with; great work, Obama!"

Obama certainly has begun a great work; but those of us concerned to uproot and eradicate torture from the American system expect to be busy for awhile yet.

Quite busy.

QH Blog: - Saturday, February 21, 2009

The Torture Accountability Spectrum – A Summary of Current Views

As the first month of the new administration passes, discussion of efforts at achieving accountability for torture and other crimes is both extensive and intensive, inside and
outside of Washington. It has also gained momentum from recent polls results showing broad public support for an inquiry into possible torture and other abuses.

Here's a brief overview of the range of views on accountability, as best I've been able to determine it. While I'll not conceal my own preferences here, the purpose is not to argue for them. Rather the hope is that this sketch can help participants keep their bearings as this
rapidly-unfolding debate unfolds.

I've found four major positions on this spectrum:

First, at one end, are those we might call the "Do Nothings." They argue that no action regarding torture or war crimes should be taken. Their case appears to be based on one of two rationales: either that whatever the previous administration did was right, or at least justified; or, that it would be impossible to make a case that would convince a jury, and hence the result would only be years of divisive rancor, and thus a waste of time.

Champions of the "Do Nothing" view include some prominent figures, such as Jack Goldsmith, a former official in the Office of Legal Counsel which produced the infamous "torture memos." Of the various proposals for investigation or prosecution he says flatly, "These are all bad ideas."

Others include a distinguished father-son duo. The pere is federal appeals court judge Richard Posner, whose 2006 book, "Not A Suicide Pact, The Constitution in a Time of National Emergency," justified all the previous regime did, and more.

The fils is Eric Posner, law professor at the University of Chicago, who is convinced that no convictions would be possible, and prosecutions are unnecessary.

The second definable position could be dubbed "Investigate & Move On." Vermont Senator Patrick Leahy and retired Army General Anthony Taguba are among those who advocate for such an inquiry. The specific form and mandate of this type of probe could vary from a Congressional panel to a White House-appointed independent

347

commission. But the outcome, beyond some form of a detailed report, would specifically not include any effort at prosecutions, except possibly for perjury before the commission itself. Many nonprofit advocacy groups appear to be lining up behind this idea.

The third position is more forceful; these are the "Investigate and Then Prosecute" proposals. Rep. John Conyers, Chairman of the House Judiciary Committee, is the most visible champion of such an effort. He argues that official investigations should not rule out in advance the prosecution of those responsible for what are very serious offences. If we prosecute "petty" crimes, it would be hypocritical to fail to prosecute war crimes and torture. Scott Horton, a well-known human rights attorney, has also strongly supported this approach.

The fourth and most assertive position on the current spectrum is the call to "Prosecute Now." One way to do this would be for the US Attorney General to appoint a special prosecutor, right away, regardless of what happens on the investigation/commission front.

This is the demand of Michal Ratner, Director of the Center for Constitutional Rights, (at right) which is representing some Guantanamo prisoners. It has also been advanced by David Swanson, formerly an impeachment activist, who has a petition at Democrats.com calling for the new US Attorney General to appoint a special prosecutor immediately. (The petition had almost 43000 signatures as of February 21)

A variation of this approach is that of former prosecutor and author Vincent Bugliosi author and former prosecutor Vincent Bugliosi has made a case for prosecuting George W. Bush for murder based on taking the US into the Iraq War under false pretenses. The murder victims would be any US soldier killed in Iraq; and as murder is mainly a state offense, the charges would be brought by a local District Attorney.

Bugliosi has sent his book, "The Prosecution of George W. Bush For Murder," to all 2200 local district attorneys around the country, hoping to find one or more to bring a case. More information about this effort is at the website: http://www.prosecutegeorgebush.com/

That's the current accountability spectrum as I see it. The outcome of this debate is impossible to predict, but it does seem that momentum is building for some kind of accountability effort, and the "Do Nothing" stance is, at this point at least, losing ground.

http://quakerhouse.blogspot.com/2009/02/torture-accountability-spectrum-summary.html

QH Blog:: Tuesday, March 3, 2009

Back from the Dark Side: Hello, Johnston County– Torture Accountability Is Coming. Time to Get Ready.

I joined our partners in NC Stop Torture Now Monday night to visit with the Johnston County Commissioners at their monthly meeting. Stop Torture NOW is a terrific group, which all concerned with this issue could well learn from.

Johnston County is home to Aero Contractors, the notorious CIA front company that has been linked to many of the "torture taxi" flights called "extraordinary rendition" in official euphemistic parlance.

The report in the March 3 edition of the Clayton NC Star-News makes it sound like our mission was a failure:

"Despite impassioned pleas and warnings of irreparable damage to Johnston County's image, the county's Board of Commissioners on Monday refused to ask for an investigation of a local company accused of participating in the kidnapping and transportation of suspected terrorists to foreign countries for interrogations that allegedly include torture . . . ."

This report was entirely accurate in a journalistic sense. Yet despite the board's official refusal to act on our proposal, I came away feeling almost triumphant. That's because I felt able to read between the factual lines, and somehow take the temperature of the group before us.

And what I think I read was an underlying nervousness and unease.

That's because, while they could easily say no to us last night, there's just no question that after so many years of a cozy connection to Aero and its shadowy patrons, which has yielded many millions of dollars of income for a poor county, the ground has suddenly shifted, the winds have changed.

The Clayton Star summed up this perception well:

"Other speakers warned the commissioners that investigations currently being lobbied for in Congress could lead back to Johnston County, with dire results for this area's public image in the rest of the nation and world. "The engine of accountability is gearing up in Washington," Fayetteville resident Charles Fager said. "What we're offering you is the opportunity to get out in front of that train before it runs you over."

I'm almost certain that there were those among the Commissioners who have an increasingly ominous sense that just such unsettling changes are getting underway. In fact, a high county official approached me at the end of the session to express a kind of sotto voce agreement with this assessment.

Another hint of this came when the Chairman, Wade Stewart, who had earlier said he approved of waterboarding and thought that torture was often effective, agreed that he would take up the matter of possible future accountability actions with the U.S. Representative from that district, Robert "Bobby" Etheridge.

Members of Stop Torture Now have approached Etheridge on several occasions, trying to raise questions about Aero, and have been met with stonewalling and anger.

But if Etheridge responds to Commissioner Stewart (who said he talks with Etheridge "all the time"), the Congressman will speak of such items as:

>>the fact that the U.S. Senate is beginning hearings on a "Truth Commmission" (scheduled for Wednesday March 4);
>>the fact that the Chairman of the House Judiciary Committee, Rep. John Conyers, is also readying a plan for an investigation;
>>the fact that there is a growing stream of shocking public revelations about illegalities and torture being planned and carried out by previous high officials, many of which implicate such entities as Aero Contractors. And
>> last but hardly least, there is likely to be much more of this to come.

No one has spoken of this prospect more tellingly than U.S. Senator Sheldon Whitehouse of Rhode Island, a former prosecutor who is deeply involved in the burgeoning accountability work in Congress. Read this excerpt from his statement of February 25, 2009, announcing plans for the Senate investigation:

"We also have to brace ourselves for the realistic possibility that as some of this conduct is exposed, we and the world will find it shameful, revolting. We may have to face the prospect of looking with horror at our own country's deeds. We are optimists, we Americans; we are proud of our country. Contrition comes hard to us.

But the path back from the dark side may lead us down some unfamiliar valleys of remorse and repugnance before we can return to the light. We may have to face our fellow Americans saying to us, "No, please, tell us that we did not do that, tell us that Americans did not do that" – and we will have to explain, somehow. This is **no small thing, and not easy**; this will not be comfortable or proud; but somehow it **must be done.**" (Emphasis added.)

The engine of accountability for torture is indeed gathering steam. And it will soon have in its sights what has gone on, not only at Gitmo and Abu Ghraib, but also what has happened at Aero Contractors in Johnston County North Carolina.

I hope Bobby Etheridge will speak plainly to Wade Stewart about this. And for the good of the county they have in trust, I hope Wade Stewart and his colleagues will reconsider and get out in front of of this process while there is still time.

http://quakerhouse.blogspot.com/2009/03/hello-johnston-county-torture.html

QH Blog:
Wednesday, March 4, 2009

Accountability Curtain-Raiser: First "Truth Commission" hearing led by Sen. Leahy

Perhaps the most interesting aspect of the March 4 2009 US Senate hearing chaired by Pat Leahy on a Truth Commission (or TC), to me at least, was the preview it offered of the legal fights that are almost certain to surround the accountability movement's efforts. It also gave viewers glimpses of some of some figures who will likely be central to the upcoming battles.

The four supportive witnesses laid out arguments familiar to most of us who have been following this debate: torture and other crimes disgrace the US in the eyes of the world, make our soldiers less safe, and undermine the Constitution. They have also very likely involved actual violations of numerous existing US and international laws – i.e., crimes. We need to get the truth, all the truth.

I won't repeat these arguments in more detail here, as they are likely familiar to most readers. (The list of favorable witnesses is at the end of this post.) And a more detailed summary of the testimony and questioning is online (as of late 2013) at: http://emptywheel.firedoglake.com/2009/03/04/senate-judiciary-hearing-on-truth-commission-liveblog/ .

Much more interesting were the challenges to a TC, as laid out by the two witnesses added to the panel at the request of Republican Senators: lawyer David Rivkin and law professor Jeremy Rabkin.

Rivkin has already published an Op-Ed in the *Washington Post* blasting any "truth commission" idea as a constitutional travesty.

He has also vigorously defended the overall Bush "war on terror" approach to prisoners, insisting that "detainees in U.S. custody today enjoy the most fulsome due process procedures of any detainees or prisoners of war in human history."

Hmmm. "Fulsome"?? What does that mean?

Webster's offer an intriguing range of definitions:

1: characterized by abundance : copious. (This is probably how Rivkin meant it.)

But Webster's also offers more. "Fulsome":

2: aesthetically, morally, or generally offensive.

3: exceeding the bounds of good taste : overdone.

In line with #3 above, Rivkin fulsomely called the Leahy TC

352

proposal a "profoundly bad idea," and "a dangerous idea," He said it would involve an extra-constitutional "out-sourcing" of law enforcement functions that properly belong to regular government agencies such as the Department of Justice. He also contended that the TC's investigations would encroach upon the civil liberties and privacy of the former officials who would be investigated.

Significantly, Rivkin also asserted that the TC's work would be bad in another way: even if it did not result on prosecutions, he argued – or perhaps especially if it did not – its findings would encourage foreign prosecutors to ramp up potential criminal cases against former US officials in their countries. This risk would be the greater, he correctly noted, because some of the potential criminal charges – such as torture – are subject to claims of "universal jurisdiction" under international law.

Such foreign prosecutions, Rivkin insisted, would amount to a "soft form of rendition" for those implicated. He speaks with some knowledge in this area: besides working for the Reagan and first Bush administrations, his experience includes defending the government of Croatia against war crimes charges in the International Criminal Tribunal.

Jeremy Rabkin, the other Republican witness, is a law professor at George Mason University near Washington. As a writer he has been especially vocal in denouncing international legal efforts, as two titles of his articles suggest: "Global Criminal Justice: An Idea Whose Time Has Passed," and "The Case Against the World Court."

He declared that a Truth Commission is what a government does with war criminals when for various reasons it is unable to prosecute them. Despite Leahy's protestations that he only wants to get at the facts, Rabkin said the supporters of the TC idea see it as a forum for branding former Bush administration officials as war criminals, while leaving them no way of defending themselves, as in a real court proceeding.

Rabkin said that if there needed to be actual prosecutions, there are agencies already available to undertake the prosecutions. Congress should not be involved in setting up platforms for "shaming people."

Between the two hostile witnesses, Rivkin's points were the ones most likely to end up entangling accountability efforts in years of delaying litigation. Rabkin's main complaint, that it would be an exercise in public humiliation, is not a legal objection; shaming someone, so far as I know, is not a crime.

I expect to hear Rivkin's assertions again: that a TC would be unconstitutional and illegitimate; that its proceedings would violate the civil liberties of those called before it; that its conclusions would promote foreign meddling in matters of US law. (And behind these legalities is Rivkin's stated belief that the Bush administration did nothing wrong in its "war on terror.")

Leahy did not really debate Rivkin and Rabkin at any length.

Instead, he remarked dismissively that the largest hayloft in his home state of Vermont could not produce as many straw men as this pair had presented.

Most impressive to me at the hearing was the performance of Rhode Island Senator Sheldon Whitehouse. Whitehouse is my pick to become the star of the congressional accountability process. His statement on February 25, announcing the hearing with Leahy, was easily the most eloquent declaration on the topic I have seen from an elected official.

(His statement is still online in late 2013, at: http://www.whitehouse.senate.gov/news/speeches/whitehouse-to-fix-da mage-left-by-bush-we-must-learn-the-truth)

Whitehouse took on Rivkin and Rabkin with a combination of controlled fury and cool mockery. After dissecting what he called Rivkin's "gallery of horribles," he rebuked their fallback "everybody does it" line of defense with, "Until you know and we all know what was actually done, do not be so quick to throw other generations under the bus and assume they did worse."

We shall hear more from Whitehouse, and doubtless Rivkin too. Indeed, as the accountability process picks up momentum, I expect it will supply Rivkin and his right-wing lawyerly ilk with plenty of high-ticket billings for years to come – both, as Rivkin noted, in this country and others.

Other witnesses: Thomas Pickering, a retired career diplomat.

Admiral Lee Gunn(ret.): former Inspector general of the Navy.

John J. Farmer Jr., former Attorney general of New Jersey and Senior Counsel to the 9-11 Commission.

Frederick A. O. Schwarz, Jr. Chief Counsel at the Brennan Center for Justice and chief counsel for the Senate Select Committee to Study Governmental Operations with Respect to Intelligence Activity (1975-1976), widely known as the Church Committee.

[POSTSCRIPT: Unfortunately, this impressive "Curtain raiser" also rang down the curtain on any open Congressional examination of torture, at least through late 2013. The continuing silence has been deafening and disgraceful.]

http://quakerhouse.blogspot.com/2009/03/accountability-curtain-raiser-first.html

Torture: A Bible Study

By Chuck Fager

(From, "Patience & Determination,"
a Pamphlet from Quaker House, 2009)

I

Most biblical translators seem reluctant to write the word "torture." Yet there are places in the scriptures where softer terms read more like evasions. The spirit of torture hovers over many passages, like buzzards circling the lonely figure of Job, alone on a dung-heap.

Indeed, the entire book of Job can be seen as a meditation on the relentlessly inflicted suffering that is of the essence of torture, with Job as the archetypal torture victim. He is innocent and faithful; yet he has been stripped of everything and left bereft and in continual pain, wailing and scratching his sores.

Job's condition is not accidental. It results from an arbitrary exercise of power, without warrant, limit, or foreseeable end. Worse, as he sees clearly, its source was supposed to be the font and guarantor of justice, not its destroyer.

Yet not only translators shy away from calling such treatment what it is. Job himself confronts a claque of commentators – one is tempted to call them spin doctors – who fill pages like memos to the White House, explaining that what he is enduring is really only a new set of enhanced interrogation techniques, and anyway he must have deserved it.

The victim is not having it. These rationalizations only reinforce his sense of what's happening:

19:1 Then Job answered: 2 "How long will you torture me, and break me in pieces with words? . . . "

Only one among a score of versions in an online Bible collection (The New Living Translation) boldly renders the Hebrew here as "torture." In the King James, Job merely sniffs that the apologists "vex my soul"; the Catholic Douay-Rheims version says they "afflict" him. Others speak of "torment," which at least is closer.

But Job interrupts, at 21:6: "Know then," he continues, "that God has put me in the wrong, and closed his net around me. . . ."

And when his vivid rage is momentarily spent, he begs,

21 "Have pity on me, have pity on me, O you my friends,' for the hand of God has touched me! 22 Why do you, like God, pursue me, never satisfied with my flesh?"

A searching question; and whether Job gets any real explanation of what has happened to him (I think not) has been debated by Bible students ever since the book appeared.

Further, Job's cries for relief and vindication are more than an individual lament. For those with ears to hear, they echo as loudly for us today as they ever have down the centuries.

II

There is torture in the New Testament as well. And here again, translators typically shy away from rendering the term. This is harder to understand in the gospels, because the Greek term used there unambiguously refers to torture as we think of it today.

This specificity should not be surprising; torture was a frequent feature of life and "justice" in Jesus' world. When demons confront him, for instance, they are expecting it:

Matthew 8:28 "When Jesus came to the other side, to the country of the Gadarenes, two demoniacs coming out of the tombs met him. They were so fierce that no one could pass that way. 29 Suddenly they shouted, "What have you to do with us, Son of God? Have you come here to [torture] us before the time?"

Luke 8:27: 27 As Jesus stepped out on land (from the sea of Galilee), a man of the city who had demons met him. . . . 28 When he saw Jesus, he fell down before him and shouted at the top of his voice, "What have you to do with me, Jesus, Son of the Most High God? I beg you, do not torture me." (Jesus didn't torture him, but did banish the man's demons.)

For that matter, the scourging of Jesus (Matthew 27:26; Mark 15:15) certainly qualifies; and what else was crucifixion but execution by extended, public torture?

So again, torture was a feature of Jesus' world, though he did not inflict it. Small wonder then, that when his followers were trying to consolidate their movement after his death, it turns up in a list of general exhortations in the Epistle to the Hebrews:

Hebrews 13:3 "Remember those who are in prison, as though you were in prison with them; those who are being tortured, as though you yourselves were being tortured."

As with Job, though, only one translation of Hebrews in twenty (The New Revised Standard Version) ventures to say it plain. While the Greek term here is different from that in the gospels, and less exact, it still refers to excruciating suffering inflicted as part of persecution. This is clear enough from an earlier verse from the same epistle,

Hebrews 11:37 "The [early martyrs] were stoned to death, they were sawn in two, they were killed by the sword; they went about in skins of sheep and goats, destitute, persecuted, [tortured] . . . ."

Here the typical rendering is "tormented." yet isn't it a plausible argument that being sawn in two would be somewhat more than "tormenting"?

The earlier, more explicit term reappears in one more New Testament book, Revelation. The most vivid passage, in Chapter Nine, recounts a vision that for some readers at least, evokes surreal parallels with the more repulsive abuses of our own day, especially when carried out by those charged with upholding law and justice:

Revelation 9:1-12:
1 "And the fifth angel blew his trumpet, and I saw a star that had fallen from heaven to earth, and he was given the key to the shaft of the bottomless pit;

2 he opened the shaft of the bottomless pit, and from the shaft rose smoke like the smoke of a great furnace, and the sun and the air were darkened with the smoke from the shaft.

3 Then from the smoke came locusts on the earth, and they were given authority like the authority of scorpions of the earth.

4 They were told not to damage the grass of the earth or any green growth or any tree, but only those people who do not have the seal of God on their foreheads.

5 They were allowed to torture them for five months, but not to kill them, and their torture was like the torture of a scorpion when it stings someone.

6 And in those days people will seek death but will not find it; they will long to die, but death will flee from them.

7 In appearance the locusts were like horses equipped for battle. On their heads were what looked like crowns of gold; their faces were like human faces, 8 their hair like women's hair, and their teeth like lions' teeth;

9 they had scales like iron breastplates, and the noise of their wings was like the noise of many chariots with horses rushing into battle.

10 They have tails like scorpions, with stingers, and in their tails is their power to harm people for five months.

11 They have as king over them the angel of the bottomless pit; his name in Hebrew is Abaddon, and in Greek he is called Apollyon. The first woe has passed. There are still two woes to come."

Would that this woe were the worst, but there is one more passage to contemplate. It is one of the repeated climaxes of the same book, describing the wrath of divine judgement:

Revelation 14:9 "Then another angel, a third, followed them, crying with a loud voice, 'Those who worship the beast and its image, and receive a mark on their foreheads or on their hands,

10 they will also drink the wine of God's wrath, poured unmixed into the cup of his anger, and they will be tortured with fire and sulfur in the presence of the holy angels and in the presence of the Lamb.

11 And the smoke of their torture goes up forever and ever. There is no rest day or night for those who worship the beast and its image and for anyone who receives the mark of its name.'"

Such passages have long been a burden to those who can't see the justice in applying an infinite punishment for the limited evil that even the most fiendish humans can do. Nor are these doubts eased by the pious admonition of verse 12 that "Here is a call for the endurance of the saints, those who keep the commandments of God and hold fast to the faith of Jesus."

Perhaps that's why translators prefer "torment" to torture here, although there is no real ambiguity in the underlying Greek. Who wants to think about the worst human torturer in history being subjected to even a worse torture, unendingly, as an endless quasi-pornographic spectacle for the angels and the Lamb, the Lamb who represents the One who is supposed to combine justice with mercy?

I doubt there are many who want to contemplate such a scenario. And for those who were forced to, like Job, perhaps the best response was his:

21 "Have pity on me, have pity on me, O you my friends,' for the hand of God has touched me!"

Have pity, yes. But remember, as Hebrews charges us. Remember, and then act to banish the demons.

February 2010

Torture Accountability Scorecard:
The New Administration's
Very Disappointing Record

Quaker House worked with NC Stop Torture Now (NCSTN) to prepare a Scorecard for the new administration's record on ending torture and pursuing accountability for alleged war crimes in current US conflicts.

Like many others, we welcomed the new team in Washington with high hopes for a clear end to the widely reported abuses, and strong steps to ensure such acts would not recur.

One year later, however the record falls well short of the standards of law, both domestic and international.

The NCSTN Scorecard lists three notable positive achievements: the order to end torture; the order to close the CIA's "black sites" secret prisons; and the release of some government memos regarding torture policies.

Unfortunately, the record on the other side is much longer. The Scorecard lists thirteen issues on which the administration has failed to follow through on pledges, or even worse, upheld pro-torture policies and practice.

These include the failure to close the Guantanamo detention center; continued opposition to legal challenges by torture victims; continued withholding of crucial torture documents and photographs; obstruction of torture investigations by other governments; and, regrettably, much more.

The scorecard includes a statement by the President of Lithuania, regarding an investigation of two CIA "black site" prisons there: "If this is true, Lithuania has to clean up, accept responsibility, apologize, and promise that it will never happen again." No such standards, regrettably, are yet in view in the United States.

The complete Scorecard is available online here: http://www.ncstoptorturenow.net/PDF_Archives/ScorecardOnTorture20100201.pdf

Quaker House Blog: Thursday, April 7, 2011

A New Stage in Local Work Against Torture

I've mentioned here before, I think, about how I've been visiting and bearing witness at the monthly Johnston County Commission meetings here in North Carolina, for more than two years now.

Their Johnston County airport is home to Aero Contractors, of "torture taxi" infamy. More on Aero here. (The company is still going strong BTW.)

This is a very conservative area, and the Commissioners are all Republicans, who usually run without opposition.

Well, something remarkable has happened there, and it came into clear focus during and after last Monday's meeting with the Johnston County Commissioners (JCC).

A colleague who has been there often with me agreed that we seem to have reached a new stage there, which should offer some new opportunities, and perhaps this "case study" could be of some use to other accountability workers in other parts of the country.

The nub of it is that after two-plus years of monthly visits and careful, polite but pointed colloquies, we appear to have established a high degree of rapport there. Such that when I came in last Monday, some of the commissioners smiled and called me by name, and made cordial small talk. And when the time came to speak, they were both interested and friendly. None seemed to bridle at my clear statements against torture and the JC connections to it.

At the end, it was as if we were leaving a party with old friends. (Actually, it was a bit dis-orienting.)

One Commissioner, who has in the past been very hostile, even said that he had decided the Afghan war was awful and the US should bring all the troops home now and that he was ready to "be a pacifist like Fager."

I think this comment was somewhat in jest (but not entirely: it was sparked by his mention of the awful killings in the wake of the Quran burning in Florida. He didn't seem able to decide which was more awful.) Yet this came from a former Commission Chairman who once told us torture was just fine (as long as the US did it), and that he loved to watch the torture-porn TV series "24."

One other telling statement was from the current Chairman, that if "we gave them something they could do something about, they don't mind acting and doing."

I think this is important because they used to say they WOULDN'T do anything about this, period, no matter what. And while what the Chairman said could be partly another form of an old excuse, I think there's more involved: suppose some of them have heard our cries, and have come to feel that torture IS wrong, and something bad MIGHT be happening at their Johnston County airport?? What in practical terms could they do about it?

The answer is not as easy as it might seem from our perspective ("Investigate Aero!" has been our refrain.) That's because as a practical matter, the county airport largely runs itself, makes its own money. AND it deals with agencies (Aero/CIA) which dwarf the resources of the JCC, and could produce instant blowback if the JCC tried to mess with them directly.

So I sensed a certain subtext to the comment, almost a plea, maybe like this: "We really have much less power than you think, even in our own county; so what else might we do?"

Considering how effective the Torture Establishment has been in closing down the courts, stopping the White House from closing Gitmo or pursuing any accountability, etc., etc., such a sotto voce plea seems quite credible to me.

If some at JCC are starting to question the rightness of torture and Aero's involvement, they must also be feeling trapped: the power structure of which they are a relatively minor, low-level part, is committed, all the way to the top, to upholding the torture system. This is true informally as well as officially: the big local churches, the area banks, all their political cronies, the people they socialize with, have all accepted it. So if our two-plus years of preaching has sown any doubts, how do they get out of this web, this quicksand?

Please don't anybody think I am suggesting that we now give the JCC a pass because they have recently been cordial and friendly to me. Not at all. It's just that we're now at a place where it seems we could present ideas and get a real hearing, and have a real conversation about them. And we've been asked for some options to our traditional "investigate Aero" slogan; so let's step up. (And BTW, I'm still all FOR getting Aero investigated, one way or another.)

They have also shown that they can step outside the box, at least a little. Last month I was at the March JCC meeting, but did not get to speak, because the room and the hallway outside was jammed solid with NRA supporters, up in arms (figuratively, this time) because the JCC was considering a very minor restriction on how close to homes people could fire their weapons.

I stood outside and heard all the stuff about the Second Amendment and fighting crime and the first step toward tyranny, yada yada, some of it from some pretty creepy-looking folks. But after listening carefully and making some adjustments, the Commission faced them down and adopted the restriction unanimously.

During these two-plus years, the visits were often uncomfortable for me; the Commissioners were hostile for a long time. More than once I was angrily denounced by other local folks, and once came close to getting beat up.

That seems to have changed, at least with the Commission members. So in this more open environment, what else can we as accountability activists think of to suggest to them? It looks like a new opportunity is open. How do we make the most of it?

And are there other local authorities where some kind of ongoing witness of dialogue could be undertaken?

http://quakerhouse.blogspot.com/2011/04/new-stage-in-local-work-aga inst-torture.html

Torture Accountability: A Difficult Spring

It's been a long hard spring for those seeking accountability for US torture. On March 5, I made my usual monthly visit to the Johnston County NC Commission meeting. There I delivered a printed torture update, and a brief, earnest plea that the Commissioners investigate the ample evidence of complicity in war crimes by the CIA front "torture taxi" company at their county airport. And to hear once more their calm refusal to do any such thing.

That evening's session was unremarkable, except that it marked the third anniversary of this witness. Three years there was no celebration, unless you count the Mexican restaurant supper afterwards. There was a resolve to continue it as long as possible, or until the Commissioners, who otherwise deal mainly with zoning permits for small businesses or housing developments, decide to pay attention. This latter outcome still seems unlikely. But I remember that it took more than twenty years to crack the walls of impunity around the Pinochet regime's torture in Chile. Longer than that in some other countries in my lifetime.

Almost everywhere else one looked, the news was even more gloomy: On April 29, former CIA counter-terror chief Jose Rodriguez was interviewed on national TV, promoting his CIA-approved new book, *Hard Measures,* which sings the praises of torture, and made claims – extensively rebutted by other experts that torture was what tracked down Osama Bin Laden.

For me, the most memorable exchange in that interview came early, when CBS' Lesley Stahl, noted that, "you were getting pressure from Congress and the White House to take the gloves off. Did you go to the dark side?"

JOSE RODRIGUEZ: Well, the dark side, that's what we do.
LESLEY STAHL: You are the dark side.
JOSE RODRIGUEZ: We are the dark side

That last was probably the most accurate statement Rodriguez made on the air.

Then only a few days later, on May 2, the federal appeals court in San Francisco voted 10 to 1 to make John Yoo, one of the main authors of the infamous "torture memos" for the White House, immune from any legal action, even by victims of the torture his memos admittedly attempted to justify.

And then over the next weekend, military commission trials attempted to open at Guantanamo. Lawyers assigned to the defense side for the prisoners on trial, denounced the proceedings as "a rigged game." Some of the defendants in these "trials" may well be what are known as "high-value detainees," that is, terrorists. But they are also almost certainly victims of torture and other abuses which would, in any constitutional American legal trial, would have the government's evidence thrown out as hopelessly tainted. So, out go the constitution and our values.

The only good news on this front comes from much farther overseas. In Poland, the former head of the country's intelligence services has been charged with war crimes for helping the U.S. set up and run a "black site" prison there.

We're encouraged by the Polish investigation. As something of an echo, we've produced a new postcard to send to the White House calling for an investigation. Readers who want some – for themselves or their meetings should write Quaker House and ask; no charge.

A counterpart to the postcard is a new compact poster for bulletin boards.

Both of these are also meant – to remind us that the quest to end torture involves remembering what has happened, and speaking up, even when it feels like our voices are lost in the wilderness of public and official indifference.

"This is a long work," I was told in 2008 by Dick Marty, a Swiss senator. He conducted the pioneering investigations which lifted the veil on the black sites and the torture flights that filled them. "It requires patience and determination."

That was four years ago; it's still early.

EIGHT: Talk Is Cheap – Presentations

A Quaker Declaration of War

Adapted from a presentation at
Illinois Yearly Meeting of Friends
7th Month 30, 2003

Friends, I want to ask you to consider joining me in a Declaration of War.

Not a shooting war; we have plenty of those, and that's part of the problem. Instead, I invite you to declare the Lamb's War, the Hundred-Year Lamb's War.

The Lamb's War is an ancient Quaker term, referring to a struggle for peace and justice carried on both internally and out in the world. (Those who are uncomfortable with this biblical phrase can think of it as a New Century of Peace Work.) And why the Hundred-Year Lamb's War?

Consider the direction of our country and its role in the world. Those in power in Washington have set the United States on a course to run the world, not for a year or two, but for a very long time. Indeed, the "manifesto" for this grandiose project came from a group calling itself the Project for a New American Century. Century. Not decade.

That vision has now been codified by the White House in the National Security Strategy of the United States, an official document which makes it formal policy to maintain American world supremacy by force and eliminate all actual or potential rivals to U.S. power, while remaking the world in our image, regardless of such niceties as the desires of the people, international law, or even the rules of war.

You probably know all this, but it bears repeating. It's not easy to figure what to call this drive. I think something like "messianic hegemonism" is the most precise; but that's a mouthful, and I'll just call it imperialism for short.

By whatever name, it's a crackpot scheme, full of grave hazards for the world. It's also increasingly clear that it's not compatible with either genuine democracy or civil liberties. So we have seen in the past months the unabashed construction of a thick wall of secrecy around formerly open corridors of power, while at the same time huge holes have been driven through what used to be the Bill of Rights.

Further, the enormous financial costs of this plan cannot be borne without deep damage to both our economy and our already inadequate social safety nets. That much is already obvious. And it's not all: I predict that if this plan goes forward for many more years, the military draft will be back too. Right now, the top Pentagon and White House officials, most of them draft dodgers themselves, don't want this, and I believe they mean it.

But we're already seeing that the far-flung frontiers of this new American empire can't be policed for very long without many more troops under arms than we now have. It just can't be done. A return to conscription would bring back a form of involuntary servitude which was once regarded, rightly, as one of the deepest government invasions of our personal liberties as free citizens.

Many of us hope that with the next election there could be a regime change in Washington, and a shift of direction. I share those hopes. But even in the best case, it seems clear to me that cleaning up the damage and rebuilding will be the work of many years. Besides, my own political aspirations are tempered by bitter experience: in my lifetime more than one new presidency has begun with lofty goals and ended in shattered dreams, done in by deception and betrayal. The Psalmist spoke wisely when he urged: "Put not your trust in princes." (Ps.146:3)

You know all this too. And I think you know something else: that as hazardous and misguided as our regime's crusade is, there are other crusaders out there as well, people who think it would be a great stroke for the glory of God, to kill you, and me, and all our children, right now, even if it meant killing themselves in the process.

For the glory of God. Not for oil; not for political power; not for money. The glory of God. Since that terrible Tuesday morning which none of us will ever forget, I've gotten to where I can more or less live with most of the memories; but this part of it, that all the mass killing was done for the glory of God, still leaves me shaken.

So let me be clear: just because people in the Pentagon and the White House are paranoid, doesn't mean there aren't other people who are out to get us; because some of them are, and they're armed and dangerous.

The question that haunts me in the face of all this has probably been haunting you too, namely: What can we do about it?

That's the question I want to address here, and I want to do so as one Quaker speaking to other Quakers, along with some other like-minded folks. Why am I being so sectarian about this? Doesn't the threat of religious war and the American drive for empire threaten those outside our little circle of Friends?

Of course it does, and I'm not ignoring the larger world. But my focus is on Friends because it is an article of my faith that the Religious Society of Friends has been gathered by God as a people to do a particular piece of work in the larger, mysterious divine plan for mending the world. And it's by discerning our particular work and pursuing it faithfully that we'll make our best and most important contribution to the larger world. Our piece may not be the biggest, or the flashiest. It's not better than any other; but it is important, and above all it is OURS. It is our calling, and we dare not neglect it, or try to trade it in for somebody else's.

This piece of work we usually refer to as our Peace testimony. The phrase describes a current that runs like a deep river through our 350-year history. But this river of testimony is a wandering stream, with many twists and turns. It's not a self-defining witness; it's our task, in worship and study and struggle, to discern its direction and call for us in each new era in which we find ourselves.

A major part of this ongoing discernment is the work of answering the question of what to do. My answer is that it's time for us to declare war, the Hundred-Year Lamb's War.

I say this as a Friend who for the past nineteen months has been living in Fayetteville, NC, close by Fort Bragg, one of the larger and more important military bases.

As Director of Quaker House there, my job has put me up close and personal with the U.S. war machine. And from that continuing experience, I've come to some unexpected conclusions: I think that much of what Quakers need to know today, for peace witness in the New American Century, we can best learn from, of all unlikely groups, the U.S. military.

That's right: believe it or not, I think the war machine has much to teach us about peacework, maybe even the most important things for our time. Let me explain why:

To begin with, let's acknowledge what most others in the world know, that the current U.S. war machine is one of the most superbly efficient destructive forces the world has ever seen. To be sure, many things about the military, especially as a human society, are deeply flawed, even self-defeating. But when it comes to its principal mission, which is blowing up things and killing people, it simply has no peer. It's not just big; it's not just costly. It's also the best in its bloody business.

How did it get that way? What has made it so effective? There are many factors going into this performance; but I want to focus on three which, I believe, could also be applied nonviolently, to building an adequate Quaker peace witness:

1. The military thinks and plans for the long term, and with big picture strategies.

2. The military is careful to "secure its base."

3. The military makes training a top and continuing priority, at all levels. And throughout, it respects what it calls the "tooth to tail" ratio.

Each of these characteristics could, I believe, be a major asset to

Quaker peace witness. And in each of them, I also believe, the Society of Friends today falls far short of its potential, and what is called for by the situation we confront.

Let's start with the first of these lessons, taking the long view and thinking strategically. These are really two sides of the same coin: strategy is a way of looking ahead; and taking the long view incorporates the past into that process.

The importance of this two-sided process for Friends was brought home to me last spring, preparing for a week-long workshop on Lucretia Mott. During this study, I began to notice a striking pattern in her work. Lucretia worked for an end to legal slavery in the U.S. for fifty years. (I call her Lucretia because, after reading several hundred pages of her letters and lots of other material besides, it feels like we're on a first-name basis.)

Fifty years working against chattel slavery and she lived to see the end of that peculiar institution, though of course not the end of racism. And when Lucretia began this labor, Friends as a body had already been working to end slavery for the previous fifty years. That's a hundred years of Quaker labor on this one issue.

Or take women's rights. Lucretia personally worked on this cause, not for fifty, but for sixty years and she did not live to see its first major breakthrough, winning the right to vote. That took forty more years after her death in 1880. There's another hundred-year project.

Then we come to the issue of ending war. Lucretia worked on this too. And as a very optimistic person, she believed the world was making progress toward permanent peace in her day. But reading her sermons on peace now often makes my heart sink – because she's been gone for more than 120 years, and instead of progress, the world has unquestionably slid rapidly backwards on this life-or-death matter.

What does all this math add up to? Simply that the Quaker testimonies for an end to legal slavery, for peace and women's equality were not fads or pastimes for dilettantes. They were dead-serious, hundred year projects and in the case of war, a century was just for starters.

You might think, given this recurrent pattern, that Quakers would be used to taking a long view. But by and large I believe you'd be mistaken, especially if you saw how the military does it. For instance, we've already seen that the military is thinking in terms of an "American century." They're planning decades ahead, getting ready to stop even potential adversaries from challenging its supremacy. The plans may be madness and folly, but they're making them.

But the long view for them also includes the past as well as the future. Each service has a corps of professional historians, and it's a sure bet that some of them are already at work in Iraq, gathering data and interviews on the latest U.S. war. They'll write thick books recounting and analyzing it in detail, comparing and contrasting it to other wars, ancient and modern.

This is a venerable tradition. Their big books are not widely read outside military circles, and maybe because of that they tend to be hard-hitting and candid. Their purpose is not propaganda, but to help the military learn what worked and what didn't, which leaders and units performed well or badly, and why or why not all so they can do it better next time. There is even, at Fort Leavenworth, Kansas, a Center for Army Lessons Learned. Makes sense, doesn't it?

Now, how do Quakers compare in this area? My own unsystematic but ongoing research is not encouraging. Here's a typical case: in the summer of 2003 I gave a short quiz to a group of about 30 active Friends. I wrote three lists of names on the blackboard: one list was of some moderately notable American generals; the second was of some central figures in Quaker peace witness. I'll get to the third list in a minute.

The names on the first list, the generals, were familiar, at least vaguely, to many of us. This didn't surprise me; after all, the military has built or helped stock more than 300 military museums in this country, plus many more war memorials. When we moved to the list of Quaker names, almost nobody recognized any of them. One name on the list was Lewis Fry Richardson the Quaker who invented the field of peace research; he's the Isaac Newton of that field. Nobody there had heard of him.

That we didn't know the Quaker names didn't surprise me either; Friends have been witnessing for peace in this country for more than 340 years. There are a handful of books about it. But how many Quaker peace memorials are there?

Almost none, unless you count the Mary Dyer statues. And the only peace museum in the U.S. that I know of, is in Chicago. I visited it once, thought it was wonderful, and wished there were more.

Think about that for a minute; 300 for war, 1 for peace, and none for Quaker peace work. But why not? There's plenty of Quaker material: in Pennsylvania, for instance, during what William Penn called his "Holy Experiment," he and his successors managed to keep peace with the natives for seventy years, from 1680 to 1750, without an army. No other American colony had a record that came anywhere close. But is there a museum which illustrates and celebrates this Quaker peace landmark? Or any of the others down the centuries, of which there are many? Not a chance. How many of us even know about this?

So what do we Friends have instead of a sense of our history, or a long view of our future?

That's where the third list in the blackboard quiz came in. It turned out all of us knew all the names on that list. Here are only three: Bob Edwards, Scott Simon, Susan Stamberg. In other words and this is a demographic characteristic I've verified lots of times with unprogrammed Quaker groups instead of a common history, we have a common radio network; today we're not Hicksites or Orthodox anymore; we're the National Public Radio (NPR) Quakers.

What's my knock on this? After all, I too listen to NPR, almost every day. It's simply this: when we're more familiar with broadcast personalities than we are with our own heritage and its implications, then too many of us are caught up in a media culture that reinforces in us an atomized, moment-to-moment, ahistorical kind of consciousness which is the very antithesis of a long-term view and coherent strategizing.

What's the result of being so "embedded" in this media culture? It's not only that it purveys lots of misinformation and lies. It also dissipates our attention, helps scatter and diffuse our energy, and narrows our horizons.

Some of us may think we're beyond that because we take in "Talk of the Nation" instead of Rush Limbaugh. (For readers unfamiliar with these names: "Talk of the Nation" is a prominent program on NPR, while Rush Limbaugh is the most well-known of the conservative radio talk show hosts; my research suggests few unprogrammed Friends listen to the latter, while many attend to the former.) But my Friends, that's like thinking we're not part of the petroleum economy because we drive our Volvos and Odysseys instead of Hummers.

Who are we kidding? A preoccupation with the media, even the best, trains us to see an ever-changing parade of trees, while missing the forests, or the earth beneath them. And the American mass media, yes even NPR and PBS, are also extremely parochial. It's almost all about us: America and Americans, the rest of the world is chronically presented in relation to us.

This learned self-centeredness is especially troubling in relation to war: Several million Congolese have been killed in a decade-long civil war; but few Americans are among the casualties, and what do we know about it? The Liberian civil war has gone on for years; but this summer it's on the screen, because the U.S. embassy was shelled. Colombia, Chechnya, and many other equally horrendous wars drag on, and by and large we hardly notice.

Is this an exaggerated view of the overall state of American Quaker consciousness? Maybe. But another poll I frequently take among Friends is to ask how many in a group have been to a meeting or a protest about Iraq in the past year, and consistently almost every hand goes up. Then I ask who's been to a similar meeting or protest about the Congo, or Sudan, or Colombia, and the hands are very few.

Why is that? Can it really be that the Spirit, That of God, the

Light of Christ Within, wants Quakers to see the world from this same, media-driven America-centered perspective? I don't believe it. And this leads me to ask, how much of our peacework is Spirit-led, and how much of it is media-driven?

Spirit-led, versus media-driven; that's a distinction worth pondering, I think. It's also why I very much admire those Friends who are the glaring exceptions to this rule, who like David Zarembka of St. Louis has focused on the Great Lakes region of Africa, where horrible wars and slaughter took place not long ago, and which are now off the media radar screens, where they were featured only briefly anyway.

When so many of us end up knowing more about "All Things Considered" than about what worked and what didn't in Friends' epic struggle against slavery, or the other long term Quaker testimonies, I fear we've traded in a precious birthright for a collection of the coffee mugs and tote bags given out during NPR fundraising campaigns.

Let me come at this another way: Suppose the U.S. Army's generals got the bulk of their military knowledge from daily news broadcasts, and hardly any of them knew who Stonewall Jackson was, and how he outsmarted the Union army, or why all of Hitler's Panzer tank divisions couldn't stop George Patton in Europe? What would happen to their brigades and battalions when these men led them into battle?

Similarly, if we don't work diligently and deliberately to overcome that atomizing media conditioning, as Quaker peace workers we're cooked. The only "Lamb's War" we'll be good for is a Hundred-MINUTE Lamb's War, if that.

The Quaker women and men I have known who were giants of peace witness, were very different from each other, but they had one important thing in common: on their issue, on their concern, they knew what they were talking about. Whether it was the Law of the Sea Treaty, or how to build a sanctuary movement to save central American refugees from the Reagan administration's covert wars, or even advising antiwar GIs on how to get safely out of the country, they knew their stuff. And they didn't attain this depth and credibility from 5-minute news reports. It took work, experience, study, and time, not to mention courage, worship, and spiritual strength.

The same thing goes for looking forward and thinking strategically, planning a Hundred-Year Lamb's War. Can we figure out where we want to be in twenty or fifty years, and plan realistically to get there, or at least be headed continually in the right direction? I believe that's what we are called to do.

To this end, along with reading Lucretia Mott's letters this spring, I also read a Marine Corps strategy manual. I wanted to begin to get a sense of what this kind of thinking might mean. And one thing it means is setting several levels of goals, based on realistic analyses of ourselves and our history, our strengths, weaknesses, and various other factors and doing the same thing with our adversaries.

At the highest level, this yields grand strategy. That's what we saw in the White House National Security Strategy: to maintain American preeminence, while we remake the world, by squashing any real or imagined rival. For Lincoln in the Civil War, as I understand it, the grand strategy was similarly straightforward: blockade the Confederate states along the coast, split them in two down the Mississippi river, and then starve or crush their forces one chunk at a time. And that's more or less how it worked out, though of course real wars are never that neat.

Under the umbrella of grand strategy come operational goals, the major plans for achieving the grand strategic objectives. An example of this is what Colin Powell said about Saddam Hussein's army in the first Gulf war do you remember? he said: "First we're going to cut it off, then we're going to kill it."

I won't have much to say much about our own operational goals here, even though that's where the sexy stuff is, when some get arrested or take other dramatic risks. I'm going to pass by all that, mainly for lack of time, and out of respect for the limits of your ability to sit and listen to me talk. They will have to be hammered out in a broad, ongoing discussion, from which an informed consensus can emerge.

I'll only note in passing that it will be a mistake to think that the most important of such goals is the next election. This essentially continuous horserace will increasingly be an obsession in the media for the next year or so, and if it becomes ours as well, then we'll still be lost in the wilderness. Instead, I hope we can begin to approach that election from the perspective of a Hundred-Year Lamb's War. Then, no matter which way it turns out, we'll find more opportunities, and sustain hope.

My Friend Lucretia Mott comes back to mind here. Lucretia only rarely referred to elections in the many letters and sermons I read. I suspect that's because she fully expected that attaining equality for women would take a lifetime of labor, and even longer. She was also clear that there were many ways of making social change, while presidents came and went. And she knew her Bible, too, so no doubt the Psalmist's verse about not putting our trust in princes was familiar to her For us today, I hope a concept like the Hundred-Year Lamb's War may help us see the forest behind and encompassing the electoral trees. If it's going to take at least that long to make any headway, I believe some grand strategic concepts can help us make the most faithful use of our limited resources.

And I believe that taking a long-term view of our witness can help us overcome the disempowering effects of the moment-to-moment media fixation. It can put the media in perspective, making them an asset for our larger work, instead of a distraction from and even a substitute for it.

So let's see if we can think like Lucretia for a few minutes. I want to offer for your consideration three goals which could form the over-arching strategic basis of the Hundred-Year Lamb's War, a framework for a century of work:

First: To make the United States into a law-abiding member of the international community, one that respects human rights both internally and externally.

Second: To move the three great monotheistic religions to a place where they conduct their rivalries without violence or bloodshed. And

Third: To make the Religious Society of Friends a meaningful player in both arenas, one that can go the distance.

The Hundred-Year Lamb's War could serve as a Quaker counterpart and alternative to the plan for a century dominated by American military might and the rival drive for a fanatic theocracy. Even partial progress toward these ends would make the world a safer place and increase our chances of surviving the clash of crusaders and their bloody visions.

Let's take a quick look at these three goals:

First, getting the U.S. to be a law-abiding, human rights-friendly international citizen. Only a few years ago such an idea might have seemed a foregone conclusion, even redundant. But now it's downright radical, and even under the best of circumstances, it will take decades to reconstruct the major elements of international law and order that have been undermined or demolished in the recent past.

Second, peaceful rivalry among the monotheisms, Christianity, Judaism and Islam. To me this is at least as important a goal as taming the American empire, and probably more difficult. And for this, a century is likely a very short time. After all, we don't often recall that it took western Christianity about three hundred years and rivers of blood to reach a similar place internally.

Three hundred years of war to figure out that the differences between its various Christian sects could be settled in some other way than by one group exterminating another. (Even then, many of them still thought it was just fine to slaughter other monotheists, such as Jews and Muslims, right down to our own time.)

This substantial if imperfect truce among most European Christians is both one of our culture's highest achievements, and one of its least known. Where are the peace museums celebrating the way most Western Catholics and Protestants finally learned to stop killing each other and recalling the significant Quaker role in that process?

This saga, which we know so little of, could be an asset, a model, and warning as we set out to play a part in ending the current religious warfare. And make no mistake: many of the wars and rumors of war that threaten us today and tomorrow will be religious at bottom.

Here I differ from many of my more left-wing colleagues,

because I don't think it's all about oil, or Halliburton and other multinational corporations, though yes, these all play their parts. It's about God, and who gets to play God, and be the enforcer for the divine.

And then there's the third goal of the Hundred-Year Lamb's War: making the Religious Society of Friends a long-term player.

What would it mean to plan a Quaker peace witness on such a long-term basis?

Would deciding to be part of it make any difference when we got back home to our meetings?

Would it reorder any priorities, lead us to do something different next week, or next month?

Would it change the usual routine of following one media-hyped "crisis" after another, and fixating on the endless horesrace of electoral politics?

I believe it could make a difference. And the way to approach those differences is to consider the other two lessons I've taken from the military, starting with doing what an army in action does first, which is to secure its base.

For an armed force heading into combat, securing the base means making sure they have the supplies, the transportation, the food and bullets to fight their battles, safe places to store them, and hospitals to take care of the wounded. More broadly, it means keeping Congress and the public hypnotized by militarist propaganda, that's how they keep recruits signing up and mega-billions in tax money flowing to the Pentagon.

Remember those 300-plus war museums? They are not just about the past; they are also strategic investments in shaping present and future public awareness, and they pay handsome long-term dividends. They tell and re-tell, and re-tell a simple story: For America, war is necessary, war works, war is exciting, war is worth it, and war is almost painless.

What would "securing our base" mean for Friends? Let me suggest three things for starters:

First, it means build our meetings. Build them spiritually, first and foremost; and physically, and numerically. That's our base; without them we're nothing..

Second, to this growing base of strong meetings, let us add a national network of twenty or more replicas of Quaker House. If we're going to be mounting a Hundred-Year Lamb's War, we will need more projects like Quaker House, which have fulltime, professional staff. They will be regionally controlled, but able to see beyond their back yard, and with sufficient support to keep them going for at least the 35 years that we've managed to survive in Fayetteville.

These projects would reflect the fact that there's plenty of peace work to be done. As the Bible says, the fields are ripe for the harvest, so let's pray that the Lord of the harvest will send laborers and then have someplace for them to work from when they do appear.

Another reason to build these new projects is that we need to support and develop our own pool of expertise and skill, without supplanting our decentralized, lay-led meeting structures, and this is a way to do that. In my time, too many of the best activist Friends have had to go elsewhere to exercise their gifts and follow their leadings, and not a few have thereby been lost to us. It's been our own homegrown Quaker brain drain.

Each of these new projects will have its own mission, as we do, fitted to its situation and the concerns of its sponsors. Some could well be the homes of peace museums. But whatever their particular agendas, these new projects should all be well-networked, in touch with each other regularly for cooperation, learning and self-defense. If they're well-designed, these new projects won't break our bank accounts; and anyway, we're not a poor church.

Support for these new projects need not be all Quaker, just mostly. The remarkable religious peace movement brought to light by the latest Iraq war offers many new opportunities for supportive networking, if we will only go out and get to work on it. (That's another helpful hint that the military understands well, but our government evidently does not: allies are good, especially in a long-term struggle.)

Building and securing our base is also closely related to the third major lesson I've taken from the military, which is the priority of training. If we're going to mount the Hundred -Year Lamb's War, then from Day One we had better be about the business of training the next generations to be ready to take over for us, not least so they can fix our mistakes, because their turn will be coming soon. That training needs to be a central part of all our programs.

I well remember the later letters that Lucretia Mott wrote to Susan B. Anthony, Elizabeth Cady Stanton, and other founding colleagues in the women's movement. In them she spoke often and gratefully about the second generation of strong, smart young women activists who were emerging. She encouraged them, she praised them and she quietly called on her other elder fore-mothers to give them a helping hand, and then get gracefully out of their way.

Yet here, Friends, is another area where I'm afraid we're in pretty sad shape. If most of us know so little about the rich and important history of Quaker peace witness, its failures as well as its successes, how are we supposed to improve and transmit this heritage and this work to new attenders and to our children?

One telling indication of the situation on this front for me came a couple of years ago. I asked a question to a roomful of teachers in Quaker schools, "How do you teach Quakerism? The general answer, after a long, embarrassed silence, was: "Mainly by osmosis." I was tempted to ask if they also taught math and science by osmosis; but that would have been flippant.

Or maybe not. Can we imagine an instructor at West Point or the Air Force Academy teaching navigation, or artillery, or strategy, by osmosis? No wonder their graduates are the best in their business. And military's training priorities do not stop with the academies training future generals and admirals. Not at all.

The services are just as serious about training those who will be sergeants and petty officers. This fact is obvious to me every day that the artillery out on Fort Bragg rattles our windows at Quaker House: the troops there only fight wars occasionally. But they train all the time. In this respect, the 82d Airborne at Fort Bragg had nothing on Lucretia Mott. May that soon come to be true of the rest of us as well!

The army emphasizes training because they know the answer to a basic question, namely: If they don't prepare their own new leaders and troops, who will? The answer, of course, is nobody.

By and large, however, too many unprogrammed Friends (I speak here of my own branch; pastoral Friends can judge themselves) seem to have forgotten both the answer and the question. But if we don't train new Quakers in the past and present of Quaker worship and witness, who will? And without that, what kind of future can either have?

To prepare new and young Friends to carry on the Hundred-Year Lamb's War, we'll need a lot more original and substantive Religious Education material, and a lot more teachers, than we have now. And this religious education I'm imagining is not just for kids, it's not just for classrooms, and it's not just for First Days.

It will also be an integral part of the work of all active Quaker organizations. It already is, in the best of them: FCNL and the Quaker UN Office and Pendle Hill have youth interns every year, as part of their ongoing work. And I can't neglect to mention the unique Quaker Leadership Scholars Program at Guilford College.

Good as all these are, they're not enough. In close to 40 years among Friends, I've seen too many committed young Quakers forced to go outside our ranks for the chance to learn service and to put their ideals into action. And many of them haven't come back. To sustain the Hundred-Year Lamb's War, we need to turn that around, and the sooner the better.

Much of that work may seem humdrum, routine, and unrelated to the exciting and scary business of war and peace as reflected through the mass media. And yes, routine some of these tasks may be, unlikely ever to show up on the news. But are such tasks part of the bigger strategic picture? You bet they are! Important parts too.

The Army understands this: it's what's behind a phrase I mentioned awhile ago, the "tooth to tail" ratio. That's army-talk for the fact that for every soldier who actually fires a weapon or drops a bomb, there are ten to twelve more behind her or him, in a long and often humdrum line. Most will never be noticed by the action-obsessed "embedded" war reporters, but from the long-term, strategic perspective, every link in the chain has its place.

The same goes for us. For many Friends, a role in the Hundred-Year Lamb's War may mean teaching First Day School, balancing a growing meeting's budget, deepening our worship, caring for those who are hurting or spiritually lost among us; in other words, securing our base. Or pursuing a leading to really understand, say, Islam.

So that's what I meant when I began by saying we need to declare war, the kind of war our tradition recognizes. I urge you to pursue this conversation about how Friends can prepare to help redeem the calamitous nuclear hubris of the American Century, and to play our part in overcoming the ancient impulse to make war for the glory of God. That's easily the work of a hundred years.

But how do we connect the Hundred Year grand strategy with the tasks of today? What could we do today to help launch and advance the Hundred-Year Lamb's War?

Of course, there is no Friendly Pentagon, no broad-brimmed Chiefs of Staff to issue our marching orders though I can't help recalling that it wasn't so long ago that Quakers did wear uniforms, and our guiding handbooks were called Books of Discipline, which is a favorite military term, so these concepts may not be as alien to Quakerism as some today tend to think. Nevertheless, Quakerism is not an army, and each of us is called to find our own leading, our own place in the tooth-to-tail ratio, working together with others as way opens. I think of us as pieces of a patchwork quilt, odd and irregular in shape, size, color and texture, but worked by the Divine Quilter, so that all our peculiarities somehow fit together the way they're supposed to.

Fortunately, the goals of the Hundred-Year Lamb's War provide a very broad quilt. There's room under it for Friends whose pieces are concerned with women's issues, the environment, racism, or poverty. It can also cover very different styles, from inside lobbyists to outside agitators, scholars and visionaries, lone wolves and committee junkies.

So I don't think making these connections between the overall plan and the everyday will be that hard to do. Still, if this notion of a Hundred-Year Lamb's War speaks to you, but you'd feel better with a To-Do list, here are several suggestions for getting started on it, in ascending order of challenge.

First, you can write a check to your meeting and add a zero to your usual amount. What's the connection between that and the Hundred Year Lamb's War? Easy: it will help to secure our base. And if you don't write checks to your meeting, as I didn't for most of my early years among Friends, I suggest it's time to start.

Second, read a good book about Quaker history and witness. I don't mean some pamphlet or magazine article either. There's been a lot of exciting scholarship in the last twenty years, challenging many of our comfortable notions about our Quaker selves. So get one or more of these, and learn what it has to teach you.

And then, find another one. And you might also pick up the Bible; it was one of Lucretia's strongest and most reliable weapons of spiritual warfare. To do all this you might have to turn off the radio for awhile; but just for awhile. What's the connection here? It helps develop the long-term view that we need so badly.

Third, you can start a discussion/planning group in your meeting and with other meetings about the Quaker House-type project that could best serve the needs and opportunities for long-term peace work in your area. Will it offer GI counseling? Counter-recruitment? A peace museum? Ongoing public education? Youth work? All of the above? What alliances would help make it happen? The connections here are: More base-building, and new training facilities. And you can commit to sticking with this seeking even if it takes a decade to bear concrete results. We've got a century to work with, remember.

Fourth, you could learn Arabic. It's a fundamental tool for being of use in serious peacebuilding in relation to Islam.

Or, how about Hebrew? It's a humbling fact that learning foreign languages is one of the hardest things to get American college students to do these days. This in my view is another indicator of how far so many of us have been assimilated into the imperial outlook: everywhere Americans go today, other people learn English. It's the language of power in the new American Century. Yet learning another group's language is the key to opening the door to true cross-cultural understanding and reconciliation. Do American Friends in particular have the gumption to break out of that circle of privilege? It's not a matter of guilt, but simple competence.

Fifth, and perhaps most challenging, after you've read a couple of these meaty new books I mentioned, and done some Bible study, you can sign up to teach First Day School.

Adding to the challenge of this call is the fact that to fulfill this part of the Hundred-Year Lamb's War objectives, you'll need a lot of material that doesn't exist yet; so you may have to research and write it, or figure out how to support someone else who can.

Remember the message of all those war museums and memorials? "War works; war is exciting; war is almost painless." We have a different story to tell, and re-tell: "There is another and better way than war. It can work; it HAS worked; it can work again. We can make it happen." There's plenty of material for the telling of this story in America's

Quaker past and present, but it's vastly under-utilized, a lamp shamefully hid under a bushel.

Oh I almost forgot; there's one more thing. This is for unprogrammed Friends generally, rather than as individuals: if we're going to secure our a base so it can truly sustain a century's worth of Quaker peace witness, a Hundred-Year Lamb's War, there's one other drastic change we can't avoid.

Yes, Friends, we're going to have to just give it up, and learn how to sing.

That's right, I said sing. Together.

Like the Methodists, and the evangelicals.

Why? It's no mystery: I was a rookie activist in the civil rights movement. And later, I've had jobs where there were labor unions. In both these movements, and lots of others, when they were at their best and most powerful, music was one of their key assets, for inspiration, for morale, for courage and inspiration.

A singing church, like a singing movement, has hope, and a future. So we're going to have to just bite the bullet, and get with the program.

And by the way, the military figured this one out too, a long time ago. If you are tempted to snicker at military music, you're making a mistake. It keeps the troops marching; it's done it for centuries.

I'm not the one, by the way, to lead this change in our customs. That's for others, and maybe the next generation.

But one way or another, we've got to do it, Friends.

Can't you see? There's a war on!

Jeremiah & Jeremy
A Sermon by Chuck Fager

New Garden Friends Meeting, Greensboro NC, First Month 11, 2004

I'm thinking about prophecy today, prophecy and its fulfillment.

As best I understand it, biblical prophecy was not always simply a matter of foretelling the future. Another indicator of the depth hidden in these texts was how they could illuminate situations and events in times other than those they were ostensibly aimed at. So a scripture could be prophetically "fulfilled" by a future event coming to pass as had been predicted. But it could also be fulfilled when a passage from centuries before fit and brought light and understanding into later events and situations, quite apart from matters of simple prediction.

That is, there were truths in scripture whose truthfulness could transcend their specific time and intention, and do this more than once

Thus in the Fourth Chapter of Luke (verses 14-21), when Jesus was handed the scroll in the Nazareth synagogue, he read that the spirit of the lord was upon him, and he had been anointed to preach good news to the poor and deliverance to the captives. And then he told the congregation that this scripture had been fulfilled in their hearing.

One perspective on the passage he quoted, from the 61st chapter of Isaiah, is that it was pure prediction, a foretelling of Jesus's mission hundreds of years later. Yet the message does not say that someone will be anointed someday; the prophet who received and wrote it down claimed that the spirit was upon him, right then, that he, Isaiah, was anointed. This good news was to be announced not only in Jesus' time; Isaiah was to declare it too, right then and there.

So when that scripture was later "fulfilled" in Jesus reading, it was not the first time it had "come to pass"; nor should it be the last. I believe it reasonable to think this prophecy could be fulfilled again: no one would replace Jesus, but others could be, as he was, and Isaiah before him, anointed to announce good news of God's favor and liberation.

In the same way, I'm remembering another prophecy, which includes an image that has stayed with me for many years, and has become more meaningful especially in the last several months in my work at Quaker House near Fort Bragg.

It's from Jeremiah, chapter 32, verses 6-15. It comes after Jeremiah, who was a reluctant prophet to stat with, had been thrown into prison for announcing the imminent ruin of Jerusalem and the captivity of its people. King Zedekiah was treating Jeremiah like an enemy combatant, as if he was an agent of his enemies the Babylonians.

This was a bum rap – which didn't make much difference then, as for many it hasn't now. Jeremiah's own statements make clear that it was just as devastating to him, a birthright Israelite, to announce the destruction of his homeland as it was for Zedekiah to hear it.

While he was in prison, no doubt wondering if he'd ever get the Israelite equivalent of due process, he had what appeared to be an oracle from God. But the message was not a grand vision of salvation, or even destruction; instead, this revelation seemed to involve, of all things, a real estate deal. The word came to Jeremiah that his uncle's son would visit him and want him to buy a piece of land, which Jeremiah had inherited an option on.

And sure enough, the uncle's son showed up with news of the option, and so Jeremiah decided that this word must indeed be from God. So he bought the field and, was careful to complete all the needed paperwork, assemble the required witnesses, and weigh out the pieces of silver to pay for it, to make sure it was all legal and official.

He then had his secretary Baruch put the deed in a sealed urn and bury it to keep it safe. And all this went on just as an enemy army was surrounding and bearing down on the capital, shortly to destroy it and make all such transactions worthless and void–just as he himself had predicted.

Yet for Jeremiah the prophetic meaning of this action was made clear (32:15):

"For thus saith the LORD of hosts, the God of Israel; Houses and fields and vineyards shall be possessed again in this land." (and v. 43 adds) that "fields shall be bought in this land whereof ye say, It is desolate, without man or beast."

For Jeremiah this message and the commercial ritual became prophetic signs that although his nation, his people faced total disruption of their lives, and loss of life for many, and then exile and captivity for the survivors – yet they also had a divine promise was that someday, they would return and, at least for a time, be able to enjoy the ordinary, even mundane elements of peaceful life.

I said this passage had long stuck with me and become even more meaningful in recent months. Here's how: I know four families at Fort Bragg, each of whom has had to face the disruption of having a spouse sent into combat in Iraq. None of them believes in this war; all were facing the great stress of at least short-term disruption of their families, while one member risked death or the debilitating wounds of modern war.

Three of them are there now. They are not pacifists; each would fight to defend their country from attack or imminent threat. But that's not what they see happening in Iraq, and they don't believe the occupation is worth the lives of their buddies, the Iraqis, or themselves.

Every day when I pick up the Fayetteville *Observer,* I hold my breath before reading the casualty list, wondering if it will include names I recognize. These are not my blood relatives; but they're brothers and sisters. They are my neighbors, in a very concrete biblical sense. They are men caught in a war they don't support, conditioned to obey orders, trying to see their duty and do it and yet somehow keep body and mind and conscience together in a place and time that threatens all of these. And if I hold my breath, what must their wives and children be going through?

The fourth family took a different course. The husband spent six miserable months in Afghanistan last year. He came back last summer, safe and sound, but with a broader conviction than the others, that the whole program of war was misdirected and posed as much a danger to our homeland as it does to that of the Iraqis and others. He filed a Conscientious Objector claim, but to no avail. Over the months since his return, his sense of the immorality and absurdity of the whole military venture only strengthened.

So when orders came in December that his unit was sending troops to Iraq, and his name was on the deployment list, it presented not only a crisis of risk to him, his wife and their toddler son. It was also a crisis of conscience.

The troops from that unit left for Iraq this past week; they must be there by now. But this soldier was not among them. One night the phone rang and I learned that he and his family had left the country, and are seeking refuge in another land, probably never to return. They left almost all their possessions behind, and are literally starting new lives.

This is a story familiar to those who remember the Vietnam War; it's also a story that should be familiar to readers of Jeremiah, because he too left his homeland and ended his days, so far as we know, as a refugee in Egypt.

If there is a word of prophetic comfort for these families, for me it comes in this account of the assurance to Jeremiah that despite the coming perils and devastation, yet someday these would be overcome, they would have an end. The exiles or their descendants would return, and once again there would be in the land the ordinary things that make up the warp and woof of peaceful common life: homes, families, vineyards, even the routines of commerce.

This, the routine. the everyday, all that which we normally think we can take for granted, was shown to Jeremiah to be signs of God's favor, and a ground for hope.

I'm no prophet, and I don't know when this passage of hope and peace will or can be fulfilled for these four families, or for the hundred and forty thousand others in this country who face similar perils. Or, for that matter, for the millions of Iraqis, among whom the disruption of life is so much more general and near-total.

But it has been fulfilled before; it has come to pass before, and it can be fulfilled again. Its achievement would also mean the fulfillment of yet another scripture passage that resonates for me today, from Psalm 107, verses 4-8:

They wandered in the wilderness in a solitary way; they found no city to dwell in. Hungry and thirsty, their soul fainted in them. Then they cried unto the LORD in their trouble, and he delivered them out of their distresses. And he led them forth by the right way, that they might go to a city of habitation. Let them thank the LORD for his goodness, and for his wonderful works for humankind!

That can't come soon enough, for any of them, for any of us, and that is my prayer this morning.

My prayer and my hope, and the basis for continuing witness.

Using the Weapons of the Weak

A Message by Chuck Fager, at the Quaker Conference on Torture,
Guilford College, Greensboro NC June 3, 2006

Friends, time is short, and torture is long, so I'm going to talk fast
. . . .

I want to start with the Bible, specifically a parable – a parable of
Quakerism. It's from the beginning of Chapter 18 of the Gospel of Luke.
I'm sure you're all familiar with it – this is a religious crowd, right? Piece
of cake.

Well, to refresh our recollection, the parable tells of an unjust
judge, who neither feared God nor had any regard for people, and a
widow, who had nothing but her voice, and came into his courtroom. The
widow came and she cried out to the judge, "Give me justice! Give me
justice!" But the unjust judge ignored her.

Now the text is very terse here, but the social context is not hard
to fill in: Chances are the widow's back was against the wall. Chances are
she was in court because some greedy relative or landlord was trying to
steal the inheritance from her dead husband, which was probably all she
had to live on. Yet her case at first seems hopeless, because we're told
straight up that the deck is stacked, the fix is in, and the judge is crooked.
How is he crooked? He's likely on the take, selling his rulings to the
highest bidder.

But this widow doesn't give up. She keeps coming back, again
and again, and cries out to the judge, and to anyone else who will listen,
"Give me justice! Give me justice!"

What was she doing? Consider: she was a woman alone, in a
society where such women were the very archetype of powerlessness and
weakness. If she loses her case, she'll probably starve to death – and
starvation was common in those days. So this was a life and death
struggle, and in it she made use of all she had, that is, the weapons of the
weak, and the powers of the powerless.

What are these weapons of the weak? What are these powers? I
group them under the initials TVA, for Tenacity, Veracity, and Audacity.

The widow is tenacious – she keeps coming back, she won't give
up. And when she cries out, she's speaking not only of her own case, but
also reminding the judge – and the watching and listening public – of his
sacred duty: he's supposed to be upholding the Law of Moses, the law of
God. For centuries, this Torah had echoed for faithful Jews with
Deuteronomy's stern command to Israel's judges, 16:19 "Do not pervert

385

justice or show partiality. Do not accept a bribe . . .justice, and only justice shall you pursue."

So with her cries the widow is not just making a private complaint – she's also speaking ancient truth, reminding the Israelite public, as well as the judge, that there is an authentic, a holy tradition of justice in her society, and that it's being blatantly and shamelessly perverted here. So her cries are also an exposé, a kind of committed feminist journalism. They shine a spotlight, or at least a penlight, of veracity into the fog the judge uses to conceal his dirty deeds.

And she is audacious – in her patriarchal world women were expected to keep quiet, especially in the public sphere. The courts were men's turf, and litigation was men's business. But she refuses to go along with this custom. She breaks the mold; she thinks, and acts, outside the box.

And eventually she wins, she gets a chance at survival. This is a limited victory – she doesn't convert the judge – he's still crooked; and she doesn't overturn the corrupt system of which he's a part. But she wears him out, harasses and embarrasses him, until he decides he'll have to give her what she's due, if only to get her off his back.

For a text that's only five verses long, there's a lot of meaning packed into this parable. In fact, as I said, I find in it a model for Quaker social witness, and particularly for the work we are now beginning on torture. Why is it a model? I think there are two reasons.

First of all, because in the face of the forces that are establishing torture as an accepted instrument of policy, we too are among the powerless. We – and our votes – don't count. This realization is very important, and not an easy one for Americans. It maybe especially uncomfortable for us here, because looking around, I see that most of us here are white, middle class, and pretty liberal to left-liberal in outlook.

As such, I suspect that many of us have been to diversity sessions and anti-racism workshops, where we've heard a lot about white privilege, and might even be feeling a bit guilty about all that privilege we are told we enjoy.

But how we name things is important, Friends, and here I think we need to be careful. I find the phrase "comforts" more helpful than "privilege." Whites like us have more creature comforts than many others in our society. We benefit from various preferences that are culpably connected with a past and presence of racism and oppression. That's true enough.

But the term "privilege" connotes to me a connection to power, and this is where the term falls short. Because in relation to those who are truly in power today, especially where torture is concerned, I contend that even the wealthiest and most comfortable among us here is essentially without power. We too are among the powerless.

In fact, almost all Americans are now without real power, or access to power, in this matter, and most others relating to peace and war. Not only are we without real power, we've also lost most of the rights we once thought we had. What's left is mainly pretense and illusion. And of course, creature comforts.

So our powerlessness may be more comfortable than some others, but it's powerlessness still. If any of you are inclined to doubt this estimate, I propose a little experiment to test it out:

When you get home on Monday, call the office of your senator, or Member of Congress, and ask for an appointment to discuss torture with her or him, face to face, for half an hour. Call again the next Monday and every Monday, and see how long it takes for an appointment to happen.

I suggest it will take a long time. In fact, I have here a check for $100, drawn on my personal account, made out to QUIT. I'll give it to QUIT's Treasurer as soon as someone here can verify that you have spent fifteen minutes face-to-face with your Senator or Member of Congress talking about torture as U.S. policy.

One condition: I'm talking here about actual power-holders; so Democrats don't count. And you know what? I think I'm going to get to keep this check for a long time.

So if Quakers trying to end torture are among the comfortably weak and powerless, I suggest that if we're to have any hope of success, we set out to learn from the widow of Luke 18 and deploy the weapons of the weak. That's the second reason the widow's story is a model for us. And what are these weapons? Remember the initials: TVA

Tenacity, Veracity, and Audacity.

If you look at the history of serious Quaker social witness, that's what you will find. Take slavery: we worked against it in the US tenaciously, for a hundred years. It wasn't a fad or a fashion. And in those generations of struggle, Quakers kept telling the truth, that slavery was an abomination before God and man. And they did this in many ways, some as audacious as Lucretia Mott facing down mobs with her eloquence, and others daring to start the Underground Railroad – and they had the audacity to run that railroad right through this campus, by the way.

There are other examples – but that's the past. What about now? What does TVA mean for Quaker work against torture?

I can be very concrete. Tenacity means that we prepare for a struggle that we expect to last longer than most of us in this room will live. To do that, as we return home tomorrow, we will need to keep our ears open, especially our inward ear, the one that hears the insistent whispers of the Spirit.

We need to keep that inward ear open, because some among us will are going to start hearing some insistent whispers of calling:

One among us will hear a calling to start a newsletter about the work of ending torture – because we'll get nowhere if we don't keep in touch.

And someone else will hear a whispered call to raise funds for QUIT's ongoing work, because there will be bills to pay. Another Friend will hear a whisper about going out to network actively with other groups that are building a larger anti-torture movement, because we can't possibly do this on our own.

The whispers to several more will be to form a committee to begin planning the next QUIT conference, in a year or two, in order to keep up the momentum and enlarge the network.

This is tenacity: building a small but sturdy infrastructure that can support ongoing Quaker work, and connect it to the larger struggle. If it doesn't happen, if some among us don't hear those whispers and respond to them – then that makes us tourists here, and torture an activist fad, and shame on us. But I think we'll be listening.

As for Veracity, it means continuing to educate ourselves in an ongoing way about the ugly truths of torture, and the growing opportunities to end it. I'm very serious about this educational task, and feel obliged to sound a warning here: if most of what we knew about torture before this weekend came from the news media, Friends, we are not yet well-informed – even if we get all our news from NPR. (Or for that matter, from Fox News.)

News reports are just the beginning, and too many, even in prestigious outlets, are not to be trusted. Learning the hard truths of torture will require digging deeper, doing hard work And as we become more versed, we are called to spread this information. The basics of veracity here, the roots of the matter, are elemental – not elementary, not simple, but basic: they are that torture is immoral, torture is inhuman, it is rarely effective, and torture defiles the law and debases a culture. Like the widow's cries, these truths cannot be repeated often or loudly enough.

And then Audacity: imagination and creativity are crucial. As current examples, I'm grateful for the presence of Lady Liberty outside this building, and the presence among us of some of those who have been protesting the CIA torture flights that have been taking off from right here in North Carolina. There is a "torture industrial complex" that has been surreptitiously created in our society, and a key part of our work will be to name and expose it, and give it no rest. We can't hope to do this unless we can bring imagination and creativity to bear on the truth, the information we gather.

I can't overstate how important such creativity is to our hopes of long-term impact. When we began planning this conference last year, I told the other committee members that I wouldn't put in all the work that it would entail, and I wouldn't spend a weekend sitting here, if what we were going to be told would boil down to telling us to write to Congress again.

Of course, we can't ignore Washington. But I say to you today, the salvation of this country from the curse of torture is a force that will *end up* in Washington, it will not begin there. It will come from the sparks lit by those in the far corners of this land, who have imagination and daring.

I'm talking about the spirit of six Quaker housewives in Seneca Falls New York, who started a revolution for women around their kitchen table. I'm talking about Rosa Parks, on a shabby bus in Montgomery. I'm talking about Cindy Sheehan, crouched in a ditch in rural Texas. I'm talking about Martin Luther King Jr., crossing a rusty bridge in Selma, Alabama. And I'm talking about Bernadette O'Neill, a teenager who you'll hear from later today, who risked arrest in Johnston County, two hours east of here, to challenge CIA torture flights.

That's the audacity that will set the wheels of change will turning, wheels that will roll across this country and rumble into Washington, until torture is driven from the land.

I won't pretend that the weapons of the weak, and the powers of the powerless, will bring quick or easy results. But I can make a prediction. As we sit here today, there is not an anti-torture movement in America. There are some dedicated anti-torture activists, and we've met some of them. But there isn't a national anti-torture movement. Not yet.

But here's my prediction: by the end of this year, and even by the end of this summer, there WILL be such a movement. It is being created even as we speak, and taking form almost right before our eyes. It is not just here, but in a dozen other rooms, filled with members of other churches, mosques, and synagogues.

Quakers are not the center of this movement, or its leaders. But today those of us in this room are literally on the leading edge of this campaign as it is comes into being, and our role in it can be crucial – if we will take this opportunity and run with it.

To play that role, let us remember Luke's widow, and her cries for justice. Let's seize the powers of the powerless and put them to work. And let us remember those three silly initials that can point us in the way we are to go: TVA.

Can you say them with me can we Quakers do something as radical as a little call and response?

What's This? ("T!") What's it stand For? "TENACITY!" (Can't hear you!)

What's This? ("V") The V For? "VERACITY!"

And this one?("A!") "AUDACITY!"

All right – now be radical again and give yourselves a hand.

Thank you.

"American War Christianity"

Presentation to North Carolina Yearly Meeting of Quakers (FUM), September 4, 2010, for which 2010 was the "Year of Peace."

Chuck Fager, Quaker House Fayetteville/Ft. Bragg NC

I've been hearing about many kinds of "peace" here: peace with God; inner peace; peace in the family, peace at school, and at work. Even peace in the church.

These are all valuable, but I'll leave them to others. I'm here to talk about peace as an end to war, and by war I mean large-scale organized violence between nations or population groups. That's the kind of peace we work for at Quaker House, which is next door to Fort Bragg. And that's the kind of war that Fort Bragg and many other institutions in North Carolina are devoted to.

It's also the kind of war that we were just told by the White House is coming to an end in Iraq. If it really is ending, I thank God for that, because from almost any vantage point, that war was a horrible and enormous waste of blood and treasure that achieved little if anything.

Consider this quick list of the costs. First for the U.S.:

-4400+ troops killed;

-60000 troops seriously wounded;

-Many hundreds more US troops dead by suicide, breaking all previous records;

-Many more damaged in mind and spirit;

-A $3 trillion dollar price tag, money robbed from our children and grandchildren, from the poor and the sick.

-The war saw torture used and legitimized by the U.S. Government.

-The war made us less safe, as torture and the war helped recruit thousands of new insurgents.

-It's undermined our military, where suicides are at record levels.

But what about Iraq? Yes, Saddam Hussein is dead . . .

- But so are up to a million Iraqi civilians.
- Five million Iraqis are homeless refugees.
- Iraqi women have seen their freedoms drastically restricted.
- Unemployment is between forty and sixty per cent.
- There is no functioning Iraqi government, as of late 2010.

- Most of the professions – doctors, professors and others – have been decimated, by murder and forced exile.

- Iraq's ancient Christian communities have been ravaged by killings and many driven from their homes.

- Continuing terror bombings and attacks kill hundreds of Iraqis every month.

How did this disastrous war come to pass? And what about the ongoing war in Afghanistan, which has no better prospects? Or the repeated calls for a war with Iran?

Many forces brought these wars about – we can point to politicians, large corporations, and our consumerist lust for oil; they're all part of it.

Yet my eight years of work at Quaker House next door to Ft. Bragg have convinced me that there is another crucial factor, a key pillar in the American Temple of War, that's almost never identified and needs to be, especially if we hope to change it.

That pillar is what I call American War Christianity.

American War Christianity is the conviction that the U.S. Is God's chosen instrument to bear the sword against evildoers, and thereby advance the gospel wherever we decide it needs to be forcibly planted.

This church's Jesus is the Prince of War, not peace; its gospel message is not to love your enemies, but to hate and kill them, including their children. Its Christ is the avenger of Revelation, galloping toward Armageddon with blood up to the bridles of the horses.

American War Christianity is found all across the nation. But it has especially deep roots in the southern white Protestant churches. And it manifests in two main forms. One is through loud pronouncements of wrath on America's designated enemies, while glorying in the righteous violence of our armed forces. We heard such talk leading up to the Iraq war from the likes of Charles Stanley of Atlanta; Jerry Falwell and Pat Robertson of Virginia; and to every Tarheel's continuing shame, Franklin Graham of North Carolina. (The southern accents are not a coincidence.)

But such noisy effusions are only the tip of the War Christianity iceberg. Its other and more basic expression was seen in thousands of churches, and takes the quieter form of "going along." The features are familiar: the US flag in the sanctuary; special Fourth of July and other patriotic services; "supporting the troops" by going along with whatever they have been sent to do.

And by staying well away from anyone or any group that raises questions – and not raising questions ourselves – at least not so anyone can hear.

In the case of Iraq, this meant ignoring the worldwide chorus of Christians, including evangelicals, who pleaded for the U.S. not to start this war. Yes, it meant going along, or as Paul put it, being conformed.

While this passive side of American War Christianity is less visible than the Robertsons and the Grahams, it is ultimately more important. Politicians come and go; but the war machine remains – and so do the churches that bless it. They add fuel to its fire; they grease its wheels, lubricate the cogs and help keep the whole bloody apparatus turning, year in and year out. And again, while this belief can be found also in the north and among Catholics and people of color, its homeland and stronghold have long been among the southern white Protestant churches.

Of course, this war cult does talk of peace, but almost always in personal or tribal terms – inner peace or peace in the family or church. But this peace slides off when a uniform goes on; it stops at the U.S. Border. And it doesn't extend to people who are called "illegal immigrants," or who might be suspected of possibly sympathizing with anyone on the terrorist lists.

So I'm grateful to see North Carolina Quakers designate 2010 as "The Year of Peace." This is a perfect time to "seek peace and pursue it," by naming this idolatry of war, in both its active and passive forms.

It's a perfect time to start facing it, calling it out, questioning it, challenging it, breaking its hold. And what better place for this kind of a revival to break out than in North Carolina?

– North Carolina, where much of the shame that is American torture had its genesis;

– North Carolina, which was recently self-proclaimed as the most war-friendly state of all on billboards beside all its major highways.

– And North Carolina, where Quakers have carried a Peace Testimony for more than 300 years. This witness has had its heroes; yet too often it has been treated as if it was a military secret, under deep cover. Or like a family heirloom, in a glass case, too delicate to touch, its mechanism rusty and irrelevant to today's world.

But it IS relevant. And it is about more than inner peace. It has also and always been about naming and banishing the Spirit of War, real-world wars like Iraq and Afghanistan.

So let us reclaim this testimony, put it to work again, to help us see American War Christianity for the heresy that it is, for the blight upon the land and its churches that it has been.

Let's give these churches back to the Prince of Peace, the one who said "Blessed are the peacemakers," not the warmakers. This may be a difficult task, but our work at Quaker House has made clear how urgent such a revival is. And if it starts in North Carolina, let's work to see that it doesn't end there.

Opening Address - MIC@ 50 Conference, January, 2011
Fifty Years of the Military Industrial Complex!

Why I Shouldn't Like Ike; But Do Anyway

It's easy to think of reasons to trash Dwight Eisenhower.

For one thing, he was a segregationist; he enforced it in the Army, and disliked the Supreme Court's 1954 Brown decision.

For another, he approved several nasty covert CIA wars and coups (Iran, Guatemala, plus the beginnings of Vietnam, etc.) We're still dealing with the fallout from some of them (I'm looking at you, mullahs.)

For a third he was–well, he was just so . . . so 1950s. (I grew up in that decade, and couldn't get out of it fast enough.)

But on the other hand . . . .

There are a couple BIG reasons why I cut him some slack.

A lot of slack, actually.

First, there's this item about World War Three. How it did NOT happen on his watch.

But here's the thing: it almost did. Not from a Russian attack, either–but because of bomb-happy US generals, like Curtis E. LeMay. (Now there's a piece of work; look him up if you want a cheap hair-raising thrill that doesn't involve sex.)

LeMay was in command of the B-52 nuclear bombers, and was itching to turn them loose on the USSR (Yes, if you've seen Stanley Kubrick's movie "Dr. Strangelove," that's who they're talking about. If you haven't watched the movie, it's time.)

But Ike put LeMay and his ilk in a shiny brass cage, and kept the whole thing under wraps.

When I found this out (years later, in the Ike biographies), I realized with a shiver that I (and by extension my kids and grandkids) are all survivors of this nuclear war that wasn't.

That goes for most of the rest of you too. But here I'm just talking about my reactions; and any way I slice it, avoiding incineration comes up as a biggie.

The other BIG thing didn't look like much at the time. It only took about two minutes.

It was part of Ike's Farewell Address, fifty years ago on January 17, 1961.

It was his warning, totally out of the blue, that something called the Military Industrial Complex was growing in our society like a cancer, and that if we didn't watch out, it would take over, and that would be bad.

On Jan. 17th 2011, it will be the 50th anniversary of that warning. And it turns out Ike was absolutely right. The MIC was growing. IS growing. And it has taken over. And that's bad.

In fact, work at Quaker House has convinced me that the MIC is the real driving force behind American militarism. Presidents and generals come and go; wars begin, end, and start again; through it all, the MIC stays, and keeps growing.

Prophetic is the word typically used for such utterances. The word is thrown around a lot; but you don't come across the real deal all that often, and it can turn up in pretty unlikely places. In this case, in a few words from a balding, superannuated soldier who was heading out the door, to practically universal relief.

As part of paying tribute to Ike for this genuine prophecy, Quaker House has organized this weekend conference on the implications of this grim prophecy that has come true, in spades. Here we only have space for a few tidbits. There's lots more on the conference website: www.mic-at-50.net.

There's one other thing Ike said, though I'm not so sure of the date:

"The problem in defense is how far you can go without destroying from within what you are trying to defend from without."

That's the problem, all right. And on this anniversary weekend, we will labor to get a handle on it.

NINE: Paying Dues

Chuck Fager on the Bill O'Reilly Show, Fox TV News:
The O'Quaker Factor – Foiling Faux News's Fake Exposé

From: www.afriendlyletter.com
Posted on February 25, 2005

I. The Prelude

It's true. Out of the blue, a week or so ago, the O'Reilly show on Fox News called. They wanted me to come on and talk about what we do at Quaker House, with special reference to the case of Jeremy Hinzman, a soldier who left for Canada with his family in December 2003.

The request was both puzzling and daunting. Puzzling because there was no "news peg," as we journalists say, for the inquiry. Jeremy left North Carolina more than a year ago. He had had a hearing before the Canadian immigration agency in early December, almost three months ago. But no decision had been announced, and I made plain to the Fox producer that I had no expertise in Canadian law and would not pundificate thereon.

So I fretted about it for a day or so, then figured, why not? It was a chance to speak for peace to a very large audience, and NOT be preaching to the choir. The date was set: Wednesday February 23.

It would be risky, though. O'Reilly is known for ambushing and bullying guests. So I spent a lot of time over a long weekend preparing, or trying to: thinking up talking points, working to boil them down to quick sound bytes, trying to anticipate assaultive questions.

Then the day came. A white stretch limo pulled up outside Quaker House, to take me to the studio in Raleigh for taping. The limo was a triumph of tacky, a four-wheel slice of Las Vegas: strip lighting inside that changed rainbow colors, a cutout mirror on the long ceiling, with tiny embedded lights mimicking the night sky; a TV and bar (but BYOB; only water and soda in the cooler).

Living Large . . . for a few miles

Sitting in it, I felt like I'd just won the Elvis Impersonator Contest, Over-60 Division. Or was having a fantasy flashback to the junior prom blowout I never had. Whatever.

We arrived early, and spent an hour cooling our heels in a

conference room, with nothing to watch but an hour of Fox "News." It was a sobering and revealing experience: in that hour, about 45 minutes was devoted to a fawning celebration of the visit by the person in the White House to Germany, Mains and Wiesbaden, to be specific.

Half of that time the focus was on the presidential side-trip to an army base in mid Germany. This was standard fare, with troops in desert camo arrayed around Himself like the photo backdrop that they were. Then there flashed on the screen an interminable series of platitudinous quotes from the speech (E.g., Your Sacrifices Have Accomplished Much; More hard Work Lies Ahead; We Will Always Remember The Fallen; and other equally moving bon mots.)

As this teleprompter tirade unrolled, the video behind it soon shifted to long shots of enormous naval formations, long lines of big warships steaming urgently – well, somewhere, and firing rockets, big guns, and other weapons at – well something.

This seemed very curious, but my grasp of German geography is somewhat tenuous, and it wasn't til I got home that I was able to verify that Mainz and Weisbaden are in central Germany many many kilometers from any chunk of ocean.

In sum, Fox "News" was running a twenty-minute political infomercial. I'd call it a campaign ad, except that the campaign is over. Isn't it?

Then we were led into the studio, where I was fitted with an earphone and parked in a chair in front of a bookcase featuring the works of Mark Twain on its shelves. (A good choice, by the way; Twain was a dedicated and eloquent anti-imperialist. There's even a whole website devoted to his anti-imperial writings.)

Thru this earpiece I was obliged to listen closely to the first half-hour of O'Reilly's show, as we didn't know when he'd call on me. He opened by continuing his witchunt against controversial academic Ward Churchill. Churchill has made disparaging comments about some of the victims in the Twin Towers attacks.

As I listened, however, my sense of the brouhaha changed, and became much more somber: I realized that Churchill is but a convenient tool, a club; the real target here is the university campus as a place where dissent is, or at least used to be, tolerated or even encouraged. That became clear in the show's first segment, in which he ranted less against Churchill, but rather aimed his invective at the University of Hawaii, which recently brought Churchill in to make a speech.

This insight was reinforced by the next segment, in which he brought in Michael Faughnan, whose brother died in the Twin Towers, and who recently (Feb. 16) published an open letter to Churchill challenging his views and suggesting that they talk about their differences.

397

The interview with Faughnan was remarkable: Faughnan said he had heard from Churchill, to the effect that he would be interested in some dialogue about this, and Faughnan said he was prepared to talk, to see if mutual understanding and perhaps some rapprochement might be possible.

This was a remarkably open and gracious attitude on Faughnan's part; he could have been a Quaker, or even a Christian. (Caution: irony alert.)

But once Faughnan said that, O'Reilly spent the rest of the interview demanding that he abandon this irenic posture and refuse to speak or have any other contact with Churchill. By now, the point of this assault was clear: it was not Churchill, but the idea of open dissent that had to be squashed. Faughnan, to his credit, calmly persisted that he was willing to try dialogue with Churchill, whether O'Reilly liked it or not.

As is his habit, O'Reilly said to him, "I'll give you the last word, sir," then interrupted and hectored him one last time.

All this, I repeat, was going on inside my ear, while I was sitting in a small chair staring into the blank round eye of a camera, awaiting my turn. Then it came.

II. The Transcript

O'Reilly: Unresolved Problem segment tonight [Title Window: "Unresolved Problem"]
As you may know, reports say at least four American military deserters have fled to Canada hoping for asylum there.

[New title window: Canadian Flag and text: "Deserter Haven?"]
We are keeping an eye on the situation, as the Canadian government will have to decide what to do shortly.
[New image: CEF] Joining us now from Raleigh, North Carolina is Chuck Fager, the Director of Quaker House. Mr. Fager counseled one of the deserters, Army private Jeremy Hinzman.
[Split screen images: O'Reilly and Fager side by side]

An update on Hinzman: the Canadian government ruled that his defense that Iraq is an illegal war did not apply and he will not be able to use that. We believe that Hinzman will be sent back to the USA soon.

[Comment: Such a return is unlikely. Hearings and appeals on Jeremy's application for refugee status could take years, even if he loses every round. And afterward, he could seek refuge in a third country.]

[O'Reilly addresses Fager]:

Now when Hinzman came in to talk to you, he was already in the army, right, Mr. Fager? And what did you tell him?

Fager: We told him what we told everybody else, that we offered to give them good information [Video of Jeremy pushing his son in a stroller down a snowy street in Toronto] about discharge regulations and regulations like Conscientious Objection rules, and we encouraged them to examine their situation and clarify their values and to find out what their commitments and values were [Scene change back to Fager] and to stand for those commitments. In his case, it was quite clear to him that he was not going to take part in an immoral and unchristian war and he made the choice that we stand behind.

O'Reilly: [split screen, O'Reilly-Fager] Okay, did you ask him why he enlisted in the military in the first place?

Fager: We talked about that some. He, like so many others that we have talked to, felt he had made an immature and mistaken decision, and one that he did not understand the implications of fully until after he had made it, and it was on the basis of re-examining those situations that he came to much more clarity about his own personal and family values, and moral values, and those personal and moral values and his clear understanding that he was asked to take part in an immoral and unchristian war led him to take the action that he did.

O'Reilly: Okay, now you understand within the armed forces there is a Conscientious Objector policy where you can do, you know, see a guy like you –

Fager: We understand that very well, we to talk to people –

O'Reilly: Right.

Fager: – about that all the time.

O'Reilly: Right. So you don't have to desert, you can go in and say, as you did, you know, my conscience now dictates that I can't kill people, or what ever it may be –

Fager. He filed such an application. It was turned down.

O'Reilly: Okay.

Fager: That was not –

O'Reilly: [Split screen O'Reilly-Fager] Now. Perhaps he's a charlatan–

Fager: – that was not the end of his conscience.

O'Reilly: Perhaps he's a charlatan. Perhaps he's a coward. Perhaps he's a guy who wanted to go into a military to get the benefits–

[Back to video, a repeat of Jeremy pushing stroller]

– and then when it came crunch time, he wasn't willing to fight for his country. Isn't that a possibility, sir?

Fager: That may be your opinion, sir. I believe it's completely mistaken. I know him to be a man of honor, a man of courage, and a man of deep moral convictions.

O'Reilly: And how do you know that?

[Back to Fager onscreen]

Fager: I knew him and worked with him over the course of almost two years, while he was in and out of Fayetteville and Ft. Bragg, which is where we're located, while he was considering all the issues that were involved.

O'Reilly: Now, do you feel that anybody who participates in the Iraq war is doing something immoral?

Fager: Not necessarily. We ask and invite people to clarify and follow their conscience.

[Switch to scene of US troops in combat gear, carrying weapons and walking down unidentified streets.]

And that's what we do. We do not preach to people. We don't call them, they call us. We do have convictions about the war, sir, and we're quite clear about what those convictions are.

O'Reilly: No, no Quakers historically are pacifist and don't like war. And we understand that, everybody understands that,

[Back to split screen O'Reilly-Fager]

– and I think it's respected. Many of the –

Fager: Many of the people who call us are people who are in the military and who examine the issues, they are in tough situations. There are many thousands of families who are being put through tremendous strain by this immoral and unchristian war–

O'Reilly: Well that's what happens in war, sir. You know, I mean, don't give me any tremendous strain business, these people are defending the United States of America, they have enlisted in a voluntary capacity to do that, and when the going gets tough, some people run to the Quakers. And there you are for their service.

Fager: Many people are being kept in the military past their due date by these stop-loss policies –

O'Reilly: That's up to, that's up to the legal system to adjudicate, sir. And it's certain we have a system that does that. My last question for you is this: How would you defend yourself against Al Queda, should Al Queda actually step up their operations into the Unites States, against your facility in Raleigh? How would you defend yourself?

[Switch to Fager only onscreen]

Fager: Well sir, we're not in Raleigh we're in Fayetteville, near Ft. Bragg. And we would defend ourselves the way we have for the last 36 years. We would follow the teachings of Jesus. You know that Jesus ended up on a cross. But his followers are still around, and the empire that put him on that cross is lost in the dust of history.

O'Reilly: All right, but you –

Fager: And that's what I believe is going to happen now.

[Back to split screen O'Reilly-Fager]

400

O'Reilly: But you wouldn't take up arms against Al Queda?

[Back to Fager only onscreen]

Fager: We do not have weapons in our house, and I do not think that we would do that. That would be my aspiration and my value.

[Back to split screen, O'Reilly-Fager]

O'Reilly: And you're entitled to it in the Unites States of America. And you know what? Guys died for your ability to do that. Mr. Fager, thank you for coming on, we appreciate it very much. When we come right back . . . .

[End of Interview]

But don't miss the Postscript

POSTSCRIPT:

An hour or so later, the stretch limo dropped us at the corner (Hillside avenue is a dead-end, not built for limos, and the vehicle would have had to back up all the way to the beginning of – the street to get out.) Emails were pouring into the in-box.

Sic Transit Gloria

Most were supportive. But a phone voicemail called me a "fat ineffective dumbass," and an email from Chicago declared: "I have lost all respect for your group and will no longer give you the benefit of the doubt in respect to you shirking your responsibility in supporting the country that has given you the platform to voice such dissent."

Then there was an email from a Friend in New York, with the URL for the O'Reilly program's daily webpage, which has a lineup of the day's topics.

On the page was this item:

<< Then, a Quaker institution in North Carolina is helping U.S. soldiers desert... We'll have a report. >>

(Don't go looking for it, because it's been replaced. I did save the page onto my hard drive, tho.)

Reflecting on this note, I finally, with a start, understood the underlying agenda of the interview. There was no real news "peg" for it, no new development in Jeremy's case. Instead, its point was supposed to be: "outing" Quaker house as a den of unpatriotic treachery, a school for desertion.

Such a slur could paint cross hairs on Quaker House. It fit quite well with the dynamic of his attack on universities that are willing to hear Ward Churchill and other dissenters.

But something had gone wrong. This "report" never got presented, and the "outing" didn't happen, except in the innuendo of their subtitles and the repeated video of Jeremy and the stroller. But that was not much.

No doubt this outcome was in part due to the fact that they had not a shred of evidence for the promised "report." But lack of facts has not been known to stop Fox News and O'Reilly before.

So what was it? My commanding spiritual presence? <joke> A stab of conscience on the part of a producer? (We can always hope.) A spiritual covering generated by the many Friends who wrote to say they were holding me in the Light?

I like this last. And I wonder if, given O'Reilly's own words, it also enabled that old Quaker chestnut, The Reputation of Truth, to succeed in standing up, not for me but for Itself. It managed to force from O'Reilly an expression of "respect," even if couched in the passive voice.

Nonetheless, I fired off an email of protest about this seamy insinuation. One hardly expects that Fox & Co. will repent and change their ways; but at least it's in the record. It follows:

February 25, 2005
Email to: oreilly@foxnews.com
Subject: Objection

To the O'Reilly program Host & Staff:

Following my appearance on the O'Reilly program on February 23, a friend sent me the following item on the show webpage, at this URL:
http://www.foxnews.com/story/0,2933,135164,00.html

<< Then, a Quaker institution in North Carolina is helping U.S. soldiers desert... We'll have a report. >>

This statement is FALSE on two counts:

1. We are not "helping U.S. soldiers desert." And

2. There was NO such "report" on the February 23 show. No such allegation of "helping U.S. soldiers desert" was made. Rather, to the contrary: I affirmed that we do not encourage soldiers to desert, but to clarify and follow their conscience, and that truthful declaration was unchallenged.

I strongly object to this false and unsupported statement that was posted about Quaker House.

Chuck Fager, Director
Quaker House, Fayetteville NC
www.quakerhouse.org

[I received no reply.]

From *Tom Fox Was My Friend. Yours, Too.* Kimo Press, 2006.

Introduction

I

John Stephens called me with the news: Tom Fox and three other members of the Christian peacemaker Teams' group in Baghdad had been kidnaped. In the summer of 2005 John was an intern at Quaker House in Fayetteville, North Carolina, where I am Director. When he was applying for an internship, I asked him for a letter of reference; the reference came by email from Tom Fox, in Baghdad.

John describes in his essay how he knew Tom. I met Tom in the early 1990s at Langley Hill Friends meeting in McLean, Virginia, where we were both members. I didn't know him especially well, but his children were the same ages as my younger two, and the four of them grew up in that meeting, conspiring to torment a generation of First Day School teachers, on many a weekend morning. Tom was also very kind to me at some moments of personal need.

Tom's path to Iraq and an ignominious death was straightforward. We talked about it in August, 2005 when I saw him for the final time.

It was at the annual sessions of Baltimore Yearly Meeting, our regional Quaker conference, in Harrisonburg Virginia.

Spiritually, Baltimore Yearly Meeting had long been home to both of us. The body operates three summer camps, and Tom had been active with them, serving as cook at one. He had also been a "Friendly Adult Presence" (or FAP) with the yearly meeting's youth group, even filling in as interim youth staffperson for a period. At the yearly meeting sessions, he frequently worked with the children's program. Indeed, if it had not been for his leading toward CPT and Iraq, any biography of Tom would have been much more about youth work than peace witness as such.

When we met in Harrisonburg in 2005, Tom was between tours in Iraq, and we shared a meal and did some catching up.

We talked first about kids, as older dads will do. His Andrew and Kassie, my Guli and Asa, are in their twenties now, scattered across the continent, but still in touch. A few years back, our sons started a Quaker Hip Hop group called the Friendly Gangstaz Committee. The band caused quite a stir in our small, staid Quaker world, with its startling, shouted renditions of well-worn hymns like "Simple Gifts." Tom and I chuckled ruefully about that.

We also talked about work. From that same faith community, Tom and I had traveled somewhat parallel paths, trying to be true to the meaning of texts like, "Blessed are the peacemakers,"(Matthew 5:9) and "seek peace and pursue it."(Proverbs 34:14)

How do you "pursue peace" in a violent world? My own seeking had led, after a series of conventional jobs, to Fayetteville and Quaker House, a long-standing peace project hard by Fort Bragg, one of the largest U.S. military bases.

Tom had grown up in Chattanooga, Tennessee, then did twenty years in the Marine band in Washington DC, playing bass clarinet – about as unmilitary a soldier as one could feature. He began attending Friends meetings during this time. After the Marine band, he became a baker and manager at a growing health food supermarket. He was good at this, and his bosses wanted him to move up in management.

But Tom heard a "different drummer," especially after September 11, 2001. With a war on, he felt called to "pursue peace" in a concrete way. After much prayer and reflection, he joined the Christian Peacemaker Teams (CPT).

CPT sets out to bring the "weapons of the spirit" into the front lines of conflict, places where death and life are but a hair's breadth apart. Tom's first assignment took him to Iraq. For a respite, he visited the Occupied Territories of Palestine.

This was dangerous work, in a region where conflicts seem hopelessly intractable. Tom stuck with it. Then, as the Iraq occupation shifted from the foolish illusion of "mission accomplished" to the grinding facts of guerilla and civil war, he headed back there.

After Tom was kidnaped, along with Canadians James Loney and Harmeet Sooden, and British pacifist Norman Kember, conservative radio host Rush Limbaugh sneered that "part of me likes this," because, "I like any time a bunch of leftist feel-good hand-wringers are shown reality."

What's striking in this comment is not only the mean-spiritedness, but also the ignorance. Tom certainly knew the reality of Baghdad's dangers, firsthand. He talked frankly about them over that last August supper. Tom was calm but clear about it: kidnaping, torture, murder were daily fare on all sides there. How could he be so offhand about it?

I don't know, except to say: that was Tom.

Illusions? Not in CPT. It was a CPT team, after all, that brought the first reports about the abuses at Abu Ghraib prison to reporter Seymour Hersh. They had also seen other humanitarian workers kidnaped and some killed.

But there's more to it than simply experience. The Christian Peacemaker Teams take their identity seriously. Their namesake, after all, was another unarmed troublemaker in an occupied country, who was tortured and then suffered an ignominious public execution. One other phrase that comes to mind is Matthew 10:24: "The disciple is not above his master, nor the servant above his lord."

II

But such quotations roll too easily off the tongue. When John Stephens called about the kidnaping, I wanted Tom and his colleagues released, safely, and NOW. But what, John and I asked each other, could we do to help free them?

We kept coming back to this question in the next few days – and we were not the only ones – as a deadline for the captives' execution approached. Experts in crisis situations advised informally that the best approach was to raise the prisoners' public profile, and seek as much public outcry for their safety as possible. That would raise the political cost for the kidnapers of harming or killing them. There were no guarantees, we understood that. But it was an alternative to blind panic or paralysis.

Talking this over with John on the evening of December 1, an idea surfaced: what about creating a website and an online petition for their release? John is an experienced webweaver, and such is the accessibility of the internet that within two hours, www.freethecaptivesnow.org was up and running, with a petition and links to public statements calling for the release of the four captives.

For the first several days of December, there was a growing international chorus of such statements, even from very militant Muslim groups, supporting the CPT workers and their release. Our online petition, along with another, soon gathered more than 50,000 signatures from around the world. There were vigils and rallies. While we were terrified for our friends, the swelling response made this an exciting period.

But after December 8, when the second deadline for executing Tom and the others passed, momentum shifted. The flurry of statements died down; news reports dwindled and became routine; and from Baghdad there was ominous silence about our friends, amid the noise and cries of civil war. For John and me, at our website, frantic effort to beat a deadline was replaced by keeping a vigil.

Every night of those thirteen weeks, either he or I would scan dozens of wire service reports for news of Tom and the others, and post what we found: with only a few exceptions, the news was "no news." The exceptions were when the gloomy videos of the four – and then, on March 7, 2006 the three, minus Tom – were released. On March 10 came the dispatch we dreaded most: confirmation of Tom's murder. (Early reports that he had been tortured were not confirmed by a later autopsy.) The

406

only relief from this loss appeared on March 23, when the other three captives were freed.

Who killed Tom? And why? Few other than the ones who pulled the trigger know the truth, and one wonders how much even they understand. Speculation abounds, of course, with many of my more left-leaning friends imagining a CIA-sponsored conspiracy to silence these noisy pacifist dissenters. Yet from the reading and interviews I have done, however, the most likely guess seems much more mundanely sordid: it was all about money.

The videos showing Tom and the others were issued by a previously unknown group, "the Swords of Righteousness Brigades." This name is very likely a fake, a cover for a criminal gang, which simply kidnaped them for ransom. There is, as John and I learned while keeping our vigil, a sizeable kidnaping industry in Iraq. Many Iraqis have been thus abducted for profit, as well as citizens of numerous other countries.

James Loney felt the ransom was wanted to help finance the guerilla insurgency. Many other observers feel that while the kidnapers are Muslims, and many have likely suffered from the invasion and occupation, these crimes appear to be only loosely connected to religious or political grievances. Rather, they are more a specimen of organized crime in a devastated and lawless society.

From this "profit-seeking" perspective, taking CPT team members was not a particularly good "investment": the group has pledged not to pay, and not to ask anyone else to. Moreover, none of the four had a personal fortune to plunder. But the gang likely figured that regardless of such brave declarations, given enough pressure, someone would eventually cave in and pay. (Harmeet Sooden later told a New Zealand press conference that he suspected a ransom had been paid for him and the other survivors, despite vehement government denials.)

But if the kidnapers were after money, why kill Tom? There are a number of hypotheses:

One, to show the friends and supporters of the other three that the kidnapers meant business. Some other hostage killings – for instance, that of longtime relief worker Margaret Hassan, an Iraqi citizen originally from Ireland – were evidently staged to show recalcitrant governments that ransom demands were life and death matters.

Or two: because Tom was an American, and as a veteran had a US military ID card, he was a certified "enemy," and one for whom the US government would not pay. That made him worthled and disposable.

Or three: if the kidnapers couldn't get ransom from Tom's family or government, maybe they recouped something by selling Tom to another Iraqi insurgent gang, one willing to pay for the privilege of shooting a military-identified American. (It is all-too easy to imagine their derision at his protests that he was a musician, not a fighter.)

Again, no one knows, but these are plausible explanations for the inexplicable.

With Tom's death and the freeing of Jim Loney, Norman Kember and Harmeet Sooden, our www.freethecaptivesnow.org website morphed into a memorial and an archive, and we wound up our nightly vigil. I felt more than a little guilty about moving on, as the daily discipline of focusing on Iraq's ongoing agony had brought home in cruel detail how many thousands more men and women there were being kidnaped, held, tortured, and some killed, by factions from all sides, amid a bloody confusion of agendas.

With Tom gone, and the other CPTers free, I was abandoning these legions, to return to some semblance of everyday routine. In truth, I can only hang my head and cite the Qur'an, Surra 4:110: "And whoever does evil or wrongs himself but afterwards seeks Allah's forgiveness, he will find Allah Oft-forgiving, Most merciful."

III

Yet Tom's story does not stop there. In the founding saga from which his CPT team took its marching orders, death was a tragedy, but not the end of the drama. Further, Tom was a Quaker, and in this tradition "be patterns, be examples," and "let your life preach" are among our oldest and most venerable mandates. Moreover, in our yearly meeting, my role has recently been in the religious education end, particularly with adults.

Thus while this small book is a memorial and a tribute, it is meant primarily for study and reflection. Rather, it attempts to follow these Friendly injunctions, and continue Tom's story as a well of patterns and examples. I believe he would recognize and approve such a project. Indeed, for the epigraph of his blog-journal, Tom used a paraphrase of the quote from which these mottos are taken.

Thus in the following pages, various persons reflect on passages from Tom's writings, or their memories and impressions of him, and offer comments on the patterns and examples of this remarkable, foreshortened life.

The views and affiliations here are diverse, and a few entries are unfriendly, even harsh. The latter were included because what they express is also part of the story, and the teaching. But hearing and learning even from the scoffers is part of our calling. Easy or not, everything here is meant as a prod to this process which is as religious as it is pedagogical. Tom alluded to this in a sermon to a Mennonite congregation between trips to the Middle East: "We did a lot of listening in Iraq with CPT, and the stories we heard were not always easy to hear."

'Walk cheerfully" is another Quaker motto. Tom was naturally cheerful. But even he had to struggle to maintain this outlook in Iraq. On

August 30, 2005 he was struck by a quote from Elizabeth Blackwell: "I must have something in life which will fill this vacuum and prevent this sad wearing away of the heart."

"This was the quote today in my planner," Tom wrote, "as I considered the tragedies both great and small, personal and global we are all dealing with. . . . The only 'something in my life' I can hold onto is to do what little I can to bring about the creation of the Peaceable Realm of God. It is my sense that such a realm will always have natural disasters. It is the 'man-made' disasters that we are called upon to bring to an end."

Tom sought to hold on to hope wherever he was. This was a difficult task in the regions where he chose to work. Of one rare encouraging incident, in Palestine, he recalled, "Here was a seed that can take root. Here were people working through their anger and coming out the other side committed to peace. Here were people listening to their hearts and listening to each other. Here a tiny part of the Peaceable Realm was created. Here was the justice of God taking shape."

Can that also happen here?

– Chuck Fager,
Quaker House
Fayetteville North Carolina

Quaker House Gets the
"Fox Nation-Swift Boat" Treatment from Fox News

February 21, 2011

Chuck Fager

*Background: So, what do you think? Should I be hung, along with
the Mayor of Fayetteville? Used for live ammo target practice? Tried for
treason? Or merely dressed in a clown suit and forced to run a gauntlet
of enraged, spitting Vietnam Veterans?*

All these unappetizing suggestions (and more) were part of an
outpouring of outrage by a cohort of Vietnam Veterans, in response to a
news article on January 20 in the Fayetteville *Observer*, which reported
on my suggestion, one of several others, that some movies featuring
actress Jane Fonda be included in a film series planned for this
November. The film series will be part of a ten-day set of observances
called "Heroes Homecoming"
(www.heroeshomecoming.com)
Getting the "Swift Boat" treatment is a new and unpleasant
experience for us here at Quaker House. Some of the comments made
were politely critical. But many more were vivid and virulent. A number
of these blog comments are included in a companion PDF, as are related
documents, so others can see what is involved.
Two months earlier, in November 2010, the Mayor of
Fayetteville, Tony Chavonne, had quietly invited Quaker House to be part
of this series of events. He said it was because our peace witness, and the
larger GI antiwar movement, is "part of the story" of Fayetteville and
Vietnam, and even if it was a minority view locally, should have a place
in the panoply of events.
I cautioned him then that our involvement was likely to be
controversial, because we would be obliged to tell this story as truthfully
as possible. Our motto remains, "YES to the Troops, NO to the Wars,"
and our commitment is to serve the soldiers and families who call our GI
Rights Hotline as faithfully as we can. That's what we've done since
1969. He assured me that would not be a problem.
Yet in the Vietnam years, much of the antiwar action in
Fayetteville was frankly anti-military: active duty soldiers organized an
antiwar group on Fort Bragg; then started a rabble-rousing underground

410

GI paper called Bragg Briefs. Officers here published a signed anti-war ad in the local daily, then gathered many more officer-signers for a larger version in the Washington Post. There were protest marches downtown, and peace rallies in the park, and more – even demands for a GI labor union.

And in that turbulent time, Jane Fonda also had a part: she visited Fayetteville three times during the Vietnam years, and was enthusiastically received. In 1971, when she readied a touring show of radical music and dissenting skits to take to bases all the way to Vietnam, the tour kicked off its run here in Fayetteville, to standing room crowds.

Later on many veterans turned against Fonda, and their feelings still run high. But what's done was done: her visits here are part of the local story. Not the main story, I thought; only a small part. (That view seems now to have been mistaken.)

Still, suggesting the showing of a film she starred in such as "Coming Home," even though it won six Academy Awards, was too much for some of the more hardline veterans.

And one thing led to another: by Monday Jan. 24, the story, much distorted, was going viral in the rightwing blogosphere. As you will see below, the version of it on the "Fox Nation" website has thus far evoked well over a thousand mostly angry, often violent comments. Many denounced Quaker House for daring to intrude on the "Heroes Homecoming," and condemned the Mayor for inviting us, wrongly attributing the Fonda suggestion to him. The lurid punishments listed above were among a number of proposed responses to such temerity.

Shortly before this summary was initially written, on February 2, 2011, the Mayor posted a brief video statement on his website, apologizing for any hurt feelings and promising the program would be "100 per cent" devoted to welcoming and thanking Vietnam Veterans. Where that left the invitation to Quaker House quickly became clear; we were soon un-invited.

I still shake my head at the Mayor's naivete. It turns out that while he grew up in Fayetteville, he was younger than the Vietnam generation, and had no real exposure to turmoil of those years. I also wonder if my years of diligent effort at Quaker House to make all our peace vigils and rallies steadfastly nonviolent and respectful toward the troops while challenging the wars,could have backfired in this case, by leading him to think the reaction to our presence would be likewise measured and civil. Really, as mayor he should have known these elements of the population better. I knew they were out there; why didn't he?

Personally, I am doubtful that the Quaker Hosue side of the Vietnam story around Fort Bragg will be able to be told in a public forum here until most of the members of this generation have passed from the scene. [And as it turned out, the "Heroes Homecoming" events took place without any involvement or comment from us.]

This is sad, because after all, ever since its beginning in 1969, Quaker House has welcomed soldiers home too. As our Hotline Counselor Steve Woolford put it in an email to our Board members,

> "By no means did all the veterans returning home from Vietnam personally support the US mission there. Many vets came back highly critical and swelled the ranks of the anti-war movement which many falsely claim was so inhospitable to veterans. Consequently Quaker House was a clear part of these particular veterans being welcomed home. Welcomed home to a saner life and a saner world that made sense to them amidst the betrayal they saw in the government and society at large which had forced them to conduct the inhumane war. Without the witness and truth speaking of groups like Quaker House some vets would have felt a harder time coming home. They would have felt even more isolated in a world that couldn't embrace their own opposition to war which they discovered in themselves through firsthand experience amidst the combat."

I still admire the mayor's original idea of trying to encompass the broader, still-conflicted story of Fayetteville during the Vietnam War in the city where it happened. But neither I nor Quaker House is interested in reopening old wounds; we don't live in the past of the 1960s. Yet these recent events confirm novelist William Faulkner's observation that the past is not dead; it isn't even the past.

Thirty-six years after the Vietnam War ended, it is still very much with us. And in Fayetteville, have 36 years been enough for the community to figure out how to talk about it? Today the answer appears to be No.

Below is the "Fox Nation" version. Note the false headline (the Mayor did NO such thing); and the inflammatory photo of Fonda in North Vietnam. Note also the 1400+ comments. This story went viral in a few hours. The following pages include a few of the virulent reader comments. In a companion PDF file, we captured eleven pages of Google search results from February 2, 2011, showing how widely the distorted story had spread.

FOX★NATION

Mayor 'Honoring' Vets with Jane Fonda Anti-War Films

Swift-Boating Quaker House   Part 2

Hate & Threats A Compilation

Some blog reader comments (from the Fayetteville NC *Observer* & Fox Nation websites).
As of February 21, 2011 there were at least 1500 such comments.

Note: Some Contain very strong language.

The one OpEd piece for the Fayetteville *Observer* that spoke up for Quaker House is included as well

Fox Nation:
http://nation.foxnews.com/culture/2011/01/24/mayor-honoring-vets-jan

e-fonda-anti-war-films

Vince
Disgraceful is an accurate description.
I've tried to like the mayor as someone younger and forward looking that the past mayors. but he is proving to be another flaming liberal.
What the heck would make anyone think this was a good idea.
I think this story will go national and give the city of Fayetteville ANOTHER black eye.
Way to go Tony.

Jrose
I'rn glad the event isnt until November. Thats long enough to squash this.
Good luck Quaker House. Youre gonna need it.

Chicken Little
I'd like to thank Mayor Chavonne for inviting his rat, un-American cohorts to the party. He's made the task of getting him out of office a lot easier. The first stupid idea of naming a enemy city as a sister to Fayetteville might have been dismissed as ignorance on his part. This invitation to a pack of traitors that despise our country and our military, past and present, has shown everyone that loves America and respects the brave man and women who serve it exactly where he stands.
Chavonne, the best thing you can do is resign right now. If you don't and you want to learn how we in the military felt on returning to the hostile crowds of Communists that greeted us, just show your face at the celebration. No, there will be no violence but I guarantee you that there will be a huge turnout of military and ex military noisily telling you how they feel about traitors like you.

Clowns Watcher
Sure hope they have a parade. Then all the war spitters, war protesters, Jane Fonders, Quaker Housers, draft dodgers, Bill Clintoners, Cassius Clayers, even the Westboro Baptist Churchgoers, etc.s can dress up as clowns and march)on ly them and their kind) in the parade.
All Vietnam Veterans can be invited to line the parade route on the upwind side and expectorate downwind on all the clowns as they pass by in the parade. It is hoped especially that Jane, Bill, and Cassius will accept the mayors invitation to dress as clowns and march in the parade. Most Vietnam Veterans I know will enjoy the spitting
BUT
EVEN THAT WILL NOT MAKE AMENDS FOR WHAT WAS DONE TO THEM WHEN THEY RETURNED HOME. Is that a big red nose I seem to see on Jane, Bill, and Cassius?!! Let the parade begin!!!

opakaR says:
frag the bastard and fond a too

bitterclinger says:
January 24, 2011 at 1:21 pm
Its a celebration designated to honor vets for their service.
Huh. Sounds like it's designed to rub their faces in commie garbage.

Tricky Dick says:
January 24, 2011 at 1:26pm
Him and Hanoi Jane should be hanging from the end of a rope.

obama's fault
You know what would look good on Hanoi Jane? ME! With a pair of
brass knuckles....

g ken.weaver
She would be real hot if she got what she deserved. They should burn her
at the stake very very slowly. Make Kerry watch and then do the same to
him but even slower!

Moshe Ben Avram says:
Mountain Lawyer said it right. As one of the last GI's to leave Vietnam
in 1973 after several tours, we left knowing we never lost the war. The
goddamn politicians and the leftists in this country threw South Vietnam
under the bus and lost it for them. But, be that as it may, also as a veteran
of the 82nd Airborne and one time habitee of Ft. Bragg, all I can say is
there will be blood in the streets if these asshats do this. As for Jane
Fonda, if I was the last man on earth and she the last woman, say hello to
extinction for the human race as I would end up killing the bitch on
general principal.

Abe Froman

I see the mayor get criticized a lot, but in many instances he's stuck
between a rock and a hard place.

Maybe he is as stupid as people say he is.

I don't know what it's like for the 'nam vets. Personally, I have more
respect for the taliban/AQ soldier who faces me on the field of battle than

415

I have for some reporter or hippie activist. They may use cowardly tactics, but in the face of US military might, it's their only recourse.

The group calls themselves the "Quaker House," but were formed by atheists and communists backed by the USSR in the '60s as a means to subvert the USA.

If these people were actually religious Qakers with a belief system, that would be one thing, but they are, in fact, subversives who undermine everything American.

Where's a sucide bomber when you really need one?

A Brief Interlude: The one OpEd speaking on behalf of Quaker House. (Followed by more reader comments):

Originally published on Monday, February 14, 2011 in the Opinion category.

Whole Vietnam story still left untold

By Debbie Liebers

Fayetteville - Oh my, what a lot of ugly baloney has been spread about the possibility of including something about anti-Vietnam War dissent and protests in the November Vietnam veterans homecoming.

The original idea, about including the story of dissent in those years, was a good one. I was here in Fayetteville in those years and joined many peace protests. All of us who protested were American patriots who wanted to save our country from a terrible mistake.

In those days, most of the other protesters were soldiers, including many who were just back from Vietnam. Their national group, Vietnam Veterans Against the War, is still going strong, almost 40 years later.

They weren't strangers or enemies–they were our brothers, our uncles and cousins, our boyfriends, our people.

That's right. In Fayetteville, the main antiwar protest energy came from soldiers who had seen firsthand what an awful war Vietnam was. The same thing happened at a lot of bases around the country.

Here, there were marches. They started "Bragg Briefs," a GI underground paper, and Haymarket Square, a GI coffeehouse. A group of

416

officers signed an ad in this paper against the war. Some soldiers even tried to organize a GI union–right here in Fayetteville.

Yes, there was plenty of antiwar action here in those days, coming from the troops themselves. It's a part of the story that needs to be told and considered, and it hasn't been.

All this trash talk about the Quaker House should just stop. It was anti-war soldiers asking for help that got Quaker House started, not the other way around. Quaker House has served soldiers and welcomed them home from wars ever since, in its own peace-loving way.

Getting the facts

And what a pack of lies has been spread about the mayor. Let's tell the truth for once: he never suggested showing movies by that Hollywood actress whose name you can't even mention safely. And he never asked people to make antiwar demonstrations part of the November events. The Quaker House wasn't planning any protests, either.

God help us, nobody invited Westboro Baptist Church. That's just slimy. People–get your facts straight. That awful group is not nor has it ever been a part of the peace movement.

Those were Fox News lies, spread all over the nation, and if they had any shame, they'd apologize to the mayor, Chuck Fager and all of us.

All the mayor wanted to do was have a fuller story told about Fayetteville and Vietnam. A good idea. But evidently that can't be done yet. What a shame.

Unfair judgment

Part of the shame of it is that once all the reflex slogans have been shouted, there's a lot we could agree on: Did Vietnam veterans get messed over by our society during and after the war? We all know they did Agent Orange, PTSD, homelessness, suicides, you name it.

And yes, some of the protesters back then did some stupid, even hateful things. I'm sorry for that, and they've learned better. Have you seen the signs at our recent peace vigils? They say "Yes to the troops, no to the wars." And we mean it.

Lots of us meant it during Vietnam, too. Don't judge all of us by the obnoxious things a few did. That Hollywood actress doesn't speak for us.

And let's face it: American society at large still has a bad conscience about the Vietnam War, from the White House and Congress on down. It's the veterans who have had to bear the brunt of that. It's not right; it's not fair. Vietnam is what it is (was) and you cannot change history.

It's not finished. Evidently, the mayor hoped the homecoming could take a small step toward healing some of that. The Quaker House was willing to go along. Really now, was that such a crime? Good grief, to read Fox and the blogs, you would think it was pure treason.

But the truth is out there, of proud Americans serving our country by protesting a bad war–in Fayetteville, next to Fort Bragg. And lots of them were soldiers. I wonder if I'll live to see that story told, and any real healing in Fayetteville, my hometown.

That's something that would make us truly an All-American city.

And by the way–I am what a patriotic American looks like.

Debbie Liebers, a community activist, lives in Fayetteville.

Fox & Observer reader comments continued:

January 24, 2011 at 1:15 pm
My email to the mayor:
I am not one of your taxpayer constituents so you probably care less about my thoughts. However, your intention to "honor" vets by telling Hanoi Janes side is a disgusting, back-stabbing, underhanded, leftist attempt to demonize those who served our country with true honor! This would be an embarrassment to you, the city of Fayetteville, this great nation and those who served and serve today!

Former Fayetteville Resident says:
I grew up in Fayetteville during the Vietnam war and I still have family living there and I can assure you that most of its residents DO NOT support this ridiculous idea as a celebration, it is more like an INSULT to the honorable men and women who fought in this and every other war. The only thing that Jane POS!!!) Fonda and that stupid (POS !!!) mayor are good for is live round drills as part of the CELEBRATION !!!! I think that would be the best finally the event could possibly have!!!!!

datruth36 says:
Ironically, most everyone in NC calls that hellhole Fayette Nam. And though Ft. Bragg may be in Cumberland Co., it's a ways down the road from that cesspool. I know of a few areas there I'd like to drop Ms. Hanoi Jane off and see if she survives (she won't). Mayor Chavonne: Fuuuuuuckyou.

skydiver says:

418

As someone who trained at Bragg, and knew the whore houses and bars well in Fayetteville before being sent to nam, I can asure you that there were no sister city with the rummies or anti war protesters there! If there had been, they would have disappeared in the swamps that make up a large part, of that part of the world. Gator bait!!!

Jane Fonda, I can't even see straight when her name is brought up! Anyway, her and the mayor deserve the worst kind of death, traitors to the USA and all veterans from nam, as well as all era' of war! She continues to spit on the graves of those that gave all! Not to forget the wounded both physical and mental!

I hope to live to the day, when a few of my brothers and I can ride to her grave site and shit on it! Once and for all this traitors bitch can be out of our lives!

T21i4 says:

skyd iver:

"I hope to live to the day, when a few of my brothers and I can ride to her grave site and shit on it! Once and for all this traitors bitch can be out of our lives!"

Let me know if you get the chance, I'l be more than happy to provide you all with a HUGE meal before you go! Just my lil contribution.

Paul

@Chuck Fager. I suspect you are reading this so please read my comments too.

Mr. Fager, you and I are alike in one way but differ in another. First, we both hate war. I absolutely loath it for I have seen it. At that point, we can say we are alike, but I, unlike you, detest those who would destroy my country and our way of life, which incidently gives freedom to you too. I would gladly stand up and if necessary give it all to keep it that way. I served in Vietnam and I am proud of it for what I saw on the other side was pure evil.

On the otherhand, you and those like you, see nothing that is worth fighting for and that is OK. Those of us who wore the uniform would not want your belief tramped upon in any way, for this is America, the freest country in the world. However, by protesting in the way you did, you did give aid and comfort to the enemy and great pain to those who honorably and bravely served in that war. Your attendance, IN ANY WAY WHATSOEVER, during the proposed festivities would simply be an act of opening old wounds and rubbing salt in them. I cannot understand why you would want to do that for this event is simply saying, you guys are

419

OK. The war may have been a bummer, but you are OK. Why even come?

The whole community knows who you are, what you do, and what those like you stand for. We even see that you now are giving aid and comfort to the new enemy, militant Islam.

Now with that said, stay away from this event and have the courage to stand up and say publically that you will. Then and only then will this controversy end.

By the way, unlike you, I went to Vietnam as a volunteer. I saw what you did not. The communists were violent, brutal, and totalitarian. You supported their effort and encouraged their violence againt innocents. In my opinion, you and the whole anti-war movement have blood on your hands, especially with regard to Cambodia.

2/11/2011 11:19:03 AM

Paul
I have a great idea for the event and it should please the vets and cause them to come in droves from all over the nation.

Keep the invitation to Mr. Fager open, provided he demonstrates history only one time during the event.

He could go down to the Market House and react the event that took place outside of Secretary of Defense Robert McNamera's office at the Pentagon on 2 November 1965! There, Norman Morrison, a devout Quaker with his infant daughter Emily in arms, poured gasoline over himself and the child, and lit a match.

Fortunately, a "baby killer", as the protesters used to call soldiers, witnessed what what happening and LTC Charles S. Johnson snatched the child from the fire and saved her life. Meanwshile, Mr. Morrison turned into a crispy critter to aid and abet the enemy.

Mr. Fager could reenact the event exactly as Morrison did. He could play Morriso and hold Jane Fonda in his arms to play the role of the child! I'll certainly would attend the event and I bet it would be well attended by cheering veterans. However, I don't think LTC Johnson should attend.

How about it, Chuckie? Plan it and I'll bet you and Hanoi Jane won't even have to buy the gas or matches!

Paul ~ MACV, 65/4th ID 67/MACV 71 (To all my brothers........Welcome Home, Bros!)
2/15/2011 10:56:53 AM"

Paul
I thought this whole event was to welcome home veterans?

I love how the supporters of Fager and his ilk are treating this event. The roaches of the sixties are again coming out from under the remnants of the decaying buildings on Hay St.

Colonel Curl's letter is spot on. Brave men and women went to Vietnam to serve in a war which they believed was against the international expansion of communism. They were opposed by acts of treason back home and even today, when someone proposes their welcome, the rave that the other side must be present to show how wrong the our men were.

During the war, other men like Fager remained behind and for various reasons, ranging from cowardliness to a vaguely masked belief in the communist cause.

Clearly, the peace movement was not about peace. It never even once protested the communist effort and violence, in fact they marched with the flag of the other side on our streets and cheered it on with shouts of, "Ho, Ho, Ho Chi Minh, the NLF is gonna win!"

Not once did I ever see a demonstration against in front of a Soviet or Chinese Communist embassy anywhere in the world. When the fall finally came, the Fager types celebrated. They claimed Jane Fonda saved our lives and that peace had come. Peace? Nonsense for the communist murdering went on after the war just like it did during the war. The the torture began, "Reeducation" camps opened, and the Killing Fields of Cambodia took place. Not only did the so-call peace advocates never demonstrate in from of a Soviet or Chinese embassy during the war, they never lifted a finger to protest the atrocities which took place after the fall of Saigon. Where were you, Chuckie, when that was going on?

Fager now goes on to says, ""It is time we realized we lost the war." Oh? Wrong pronoun, Chuckie! YOU side won the final victory, although not militarily as some Viet Cong sympathizers still try to lie about.

421

Colonel Curl is right. Our military fought and stacked the enemy like cord wood, but the efforts of the other side (i.e. Fager and those who speak on his behalf)plus the liberals of Congress betrayed the South Vietnamese and ensured the final fall. Yes, blood is on Fager's hands, but unfortunately not on his conscience anymore that it was on the conscience of supporters of Hitler, Stalin or Mao.

I am delighted to see comments like those who decry my urging of Fager to as the monk who set himself ablaze in Saigon. No, I would not personally incite violence against Chuckie, (I have to laugh at the analogy to a lynching. So tres chic to try an play a race card here.) No, I wouldn't burn him nor lynch him, but I'd certainly loan him the match if he wanted reenact that piece of history and with a smile on my face I would quote Robert Duvall by saying, "I love the smell of napalm in the morning."

No. I advocate no violence and never have, but this shows the depth of feeling I and other Viet vets have toward those who I believe are traitors and aided the enemy while brave Americans were in the field fighting and dying at the hands of communists.

As the so-called peace demonstrators hated our military in the 60's, they again come out like roaches to support Fager and at a time when the community wants to honor the bravery of its Vietnam vets.

Mark my word. There will be those who will line the streets on any parade and shout "baby killer." Perhaps they can even sing the Internationale if the Star Spangled Banner is played.

2/19/2011 1:01:53 PM

Paul
I thought this whole event was to welcome home veterans?

I love how the supporters of Fager and his ilk are treating this event. The roaches of the sixties are again coming out from under the remnants of the decaying buildings on Hay St.

Colonel Curl's letter is spot on. Brave men and women went to Vietnam to serve in a war which they believed was against the international expansion of communism. They were opposed by acts of treason back home and even today, when someone proposes their welcome, the rave that the other side must be present to show how wrong the our men were.

During the war, other men like Fager remained behind and for various reasons, ranging from cowardliness to a vaguely masked belief in the communist cause.

Clearly, the peace movement was not about peace. It never even once protested the communist effort and violence, in fact they marched with the flag of the other side on our streets and cheered it on with shouts of, "Ho, Ho, Ho Chi Minh, the NLF is gonna win!"

Not once did I ever see a demonstration against in front of a Soviet or Chinese Communist embassy anywhere in the world. When the fall finally came, the Fager types celebrated. They claimed Jane Fonda saved our lives and that peace had come. Peace? Nonsense for the communist murdering went on after the war just like it did during the war. The the torture began, "Reeducation" camps opened, and the Killing Fields of Cambodia took place. Not only did the so-call peace advocates never demonstrate in from of a Soviet or Chinese embassy during the war, they never lifted a finger to protest the atrocities which took place after the fall of Saigon. Where were you, Chuckie, when that was going on?

Fager now goes on to says, ""It is time we realized we lost the war." Oh? Wrong pronoun, Chuckie! YOU side won the final victory, although not militarily as some Viet Cong sympathizers still try to lie about.

Colonel Curl is right. Our military fought and stacked the enemy like cord wood, but the efforts of the other side (i.e. Fager and those who speak on his behalf)plus the liberals of Congress betrayed the South Vietnamese and ensured the final fall. Yes, blood is on Fager's hands, but unfortunately not on his conscience anymore that it was on the conscience of supporters of Hitler, Stalin or Mao.

I am delighted to see comments like those who decry my urging of Fager to as the monk who set himself ablaze in Saigon. No, I would not personally incite violence against Chuckie, (I have to laugh at the analogy to a lynching. So tres chic to try an play a race card here.) No, I wouldn't burn him nor lynch him, but I'd certainly loan him the match if he wanted reenact that piece of history and with a smile on my face I would quote Robert Duvall by saying, "I love the smell of napalm in the morning."

No. I advocate no violence and never have, but this shows the depth of feeling I and other Viet vets have toward those who I believe are traitors and aided the enemy while brave Americans were in the field fighting and dying at the hands of communists.

As the so-called peace demonstrators hated our military in the 60's, they again come out like roaches to support Fager and at a time when the community wants to honor the bravery of its Vietnam vets.

Mark my word. There will be those who will line the streets on any parade and shout "baby killer." Perhaps they can even sing the Internationale if the Star Spangled Banner is played.

2/19/2011 1:01:53 PM

Shannon:

Fager, this is not celebrating a war, it is to celebrate the military that actually made it home. You should not be so narrow-minded as to take that from them. I am thankful for the ones that made it home and is equally thankful for those that didn't. I, for one, am glad that one particular Vietnam Veteran made it home or else I wouldn't be here. My daddy is a Vietnam Veteran, and proud of it and I am proud of him.

You and people like you may have made them feel inferior to you over the past 40 years, and now it seems as if they are putting you in your place. If you don't like it, please feel free to escape the ridicule by moving to a more peaceful country...or a deserted island. There is no greater country than the United States of America. Our country gained its independence from Britain through war and we have been fighting to keep our independence ever since. Appreciate it or keep your mouth shut about war...

2/12/2011 10:52:55 AM

TL
Fayetteville's slogan is "Hometown Heroes". I see now they support people like Westboro Baptist Church, Jane Fonda, communist countries and other radical groups.

Mr Chavonne please run for mayor again so we can replace you with a real leader and embarass you in the process. The same way you have been a thorn in our side. Maybe Ronnie Mitchell will give you a job.

Mayor Chavonne: we know where your lips have been. Would you kiss your mother with those lips now?

1/23/2011 9:57:28 AM

MikeP
I take it Mayor Tony Chavonne is going to invite the KKK and Skin Heads to speak, and put up their art for Black History month here?

2/12/2011 5:03:06 PM
Report abuse

DEFENDOR

Dear Mr. MikeP:

What message of absolute truth does the KKK and Skin Heads represent? Your desperate attempt at an analogy was...desperate. Do you REALLY know any group of blacks that would cower in fear of the KKK and Skinheads? Do you know ANY black people?

2/12/2011 5:19:07 PM

Report abuse

MikeP

I'm not your Dear. Their message of absolute truth would represent just about the same as quacker house and protestor would on any day that was to Honor Veterans. Which would be to dishonor them at all costs, and get noticed in the media. After that trying to see how much money they can collect which after all is their main goal.

2/12/2011 5:45:24 PM

PA Professor:

When is the Fayetteville Observer going to follow its own rules of use for these forums? We have a poster who constantly accuses the military of being mindless killing machines and taking pleasure in it, and accuses another poster of taking mental health medication.

Hey Mr. Editor, do the rules only apply to some?

As for the Quaker House, they should be prosecuted for their past crimes of providing aid and comfort to enemies of the state (the most notorious

425

being Jane Fonda, who should be under the jail). They have no place in any event relating to the military. I hope that they have the decency to stay home.

And the question of where they get their funding is indeed a good one. I'm sure they are a 501 c(3) "charity" and collect money from individuals who are either ill informed, or who quite honestly hate their country. This group goes far beyond a conscience objector group. COs (real ones, not those minted in foreign countries for the purpose of bringing this country down) have in the past found ways to serve their country and not engage in direct combat. This group does not fit that description. THey are anti-American to the core.

Mr. Fager, please stay home, and ponder the damage that you have done in the past (and present) to soldiers who have honorably served their country. And if your own conscience ever starts to bother you, try making amends to those soldiers who you have been responsible for damaging so cruelly. The Jesus that I love and worship would call you to this action.

2/12/2011 7:26:50 PM

February 19, 2011 Letter to the Editor:
Accept consequences for past activism

I have to get this off my chest. I hope it might help you and your readers understand why we Vietnam veterans hold Chuck Fager and "peace activists" in such contempt.
Fager says, "It is time we realized we lost the war." This from a man who did everything in his power to make sure we lost it. This from a man who did not believe that preserving an independent, non-communist South Vietnam was a worthy national goal. This from a man who condemned not just 58,000 of us soldiers to death, but hundreds of thousands of Vietnamese, Cambodians and Laotians to death. He has blood on his hands. He may have meant well, but by not caring about the consequences of his actions, he became a disastrous fool.
Could the outcome of the war have been different? Absolutely! There is simply no question about it. All you have to do is look at facts, not the media propaganda. Start with "A Better War" by Louis Sorley. Examine his research. Look at realities: The American military did its job. The war was "won." Congress reneged on its promises and sold out. Chuck Fager and his ilk had sapped our national will. No money, no Army. No Army, no South Vietnam.
So don't expect us to be happy about him showing up at an event that's supposed to be about saying "thanks" for what we sacrificed for in the

426

name of the United States of America.

Retired Col. Dick Curl, Pinehurst

Knox Overstreet III
Fix it? Nothing easier. Kick out that communist mayor and his communist friends. Let them move to Vietnam and live in our communist sister city.

I'll tell you one thing, if those communists remain on the schedule there will be veterans from here and all over the country to protest. Best plan on additional parking for a lot of buses and lots more porta-potties because we're sending the word of this proposed atrocity to veteran's organizations all over the country.
2/15/2011 8:32:25 AM

MikeP
This has been, and will always be a Military City. Everyone here to include the quacker house and protestors make their living off the Military.

As this is to honor Viet Nam Veterans any idea of having or inviting the protestors is an insult. These are the same ones that stuffed mail boxes of family homes of those deployed, and called them names when they came home.

It hasn't stopped in all these years, and the lies, slander and propaganda is continuing to be broadcasted by them. Along with them making money off of us doing so. If allowed or not they will yell it's their first amendment right to cause a disurbance at this event if they want. Of course they will want police protection while doing so.

I don't believe they have a right. It would be the same as allowing the KKK or Skin Heads to a Martin Luther King Jr. Parade Down Town. It wouldn't be allowed.
2/15/2011 7:20:24 PM

TEN: Smudged Glasses – Squinting Into a Murky Future

Survival & Resistance
A Message from Quaker House
Fayetteville/Ft. Bragg, NC

Third Month 2006

Quakerism was born in a time of revolutionary upheaval. Yet it learned how to survive when the revolution failed and was followed by decades of persecution.

I sometimes hear Quakers waxing nostalgic about recovering the fire and fervor of "early Friends."

This longing is understandable. In my view, beyond the fire and fervor, the best things to recover from "early Friends" are the toughness and determination that brought the body through the years of repression.

This communal history looms large today because we are in an increasingly similar plight, facing an all-but established police state, repressive within and truculent without. The grim details are described daily, if ever more faintly, in the remaining dissident media outlets here. While many Americans recoil, the majority shrug and submit.

Unlike early Friends, we are not being singled out–but we are not exempt either. The process is more sweeping and sinister now. Its essence was best described fifty years ago, by Friend Milton Mayer, in *They Thought They Were Free*. Mayer showed in calm, harrowing detail how ordinary, virtuous 1930s Germans were seamlessly reduced from citizens to subjects, cogs in the Nazi machinery.

One of the most telling features of this malevolent transformation was that for most, all it entailed was doing nothing. As Mayer put it: "the rest of the seventy million Germans, apart from the million or so who operated the whole machinery of Nazism, had nothing to do except not to interfere."

Or as one of his German friends confessed, in abject shame: "Suddenly, it all comes down at once. You see what you are, what you have done, or, more accurately, what you haven't done (for that was all that was required of most of us: that we do nothing)."

"Doing nothing" does not mean cowering in a corner, but rather, focusing fixedly on daily life: family, job, religion, entertainments, even quiet political hand-wringing. All while being careful "not to interfere."

By tracking how this tsunami of evil quietly engulfed so many "good people," Milton Mayer became one of the most truly prophetic

430

Quaker voices of the last century.

This discernment defines the elements of the task now before us. We can also learn of it from the costly but fruitful ordeals that overwhelmed Friends after their first upsurge. The heroes who endured the "sufferings," and even wrested from them a real measure of freedom they are our examples.

The watchwords for such a time of trial are two: Survival and Resistance, and they are offered here as a motto for our life and witness today, and for many tomorrows.

"Survival" does not yet mean preserving our physical lives. Rather, it means thwarting the soul-consuming program of compliant denial and submission starkly charted by Milton Mayer. Thus our first duty is to find the courage to banish illusion and face our plight, clear-eyed. This is a daily task.

"Resistance" means being faithful to this undeceived awareness, becoming "wise as serpents and harmless as doves," persistently refusing "to do nothing": challenging, undermining, and igniting sparks of liberation in what George Fox called "this thick night."

Yet this summons to "survival and resistance," is not simply a call to the barricades, or even to more activism. There will be much of that, still. But the early Friends' experiences suggest–as does Mayer's book – that to be enduring, its wellspring will come from within, more than without. Deepening our own personal and communal spiritual roots, making them our "strongholds"– these are the deepest "action" priorities.

There are sound theological reasons for this emphasis, but just as powerful practical ones too: when the new police state (or its enemies) begins to target Friends, and those with whom we are culpably connected, it is these "strongholds" that we will be forced to fall back on. They will become our ultimate redoubt, our basic line of defense, or we will have nothing.

Until recently, Friends' mainly middle class status has seemed to protect us–not because we are strong, but because the rulers think us weak, gullible, easily intimidated, incapable of interfering. However, they are wrong about us. Quakers, after all, pioneered the making of steel, and in their early crucible, Friends learned steely resolve, doggedness, and courage. With God's help, we can survive and resist again, and our witness can again have impact.

Indeed, a few of the rulers' minions have begun to glimpse this subversive potential, as shown by the reports of spying on Quaker witness. There will be more of that. And in due time, if some persist in refusing the demand to do nothing, surveillance can be followed by more stringent measures.

So: Survival and Resistance. That is our call. Early Friends rose to it, and left us models and warnings. Our recent prophets have shown us that such a time of trial could come to us again. And so it has.

To take up this challenge, here are two suggestions: First, Read Milton Mayer's book. Discuss it at your meeting. Then move to "A Quaker Declaration of War," at the Quaker House website. Keep reading, keep talking, keep centering. The leadings will come.

Friends, the impending struggle will be long and costly. Let us set to work, then, to make it fruitful as well.

Chuck Fager, Director
Quaker House

QH Blog:

Tuesday, October 21, 2008

Lots of Bad News

Maybe you've seen the items cited below, but they could easily be overlooked among all the hullabaloo of the [presidential] campaign.

All of them relate to the military situation that the new president will confront as of January 20.

And all of them, in my view, are gloomy clouds on the new administration's horizon. They point to an American future likely to be marked by more war and a bigger military.

How so? Let's take a look:

First, from Congressional Quarterly comes news that

Pentagon officials have prepared a new estimate for defense spending that is $450 billion more over the next five years than previously announced figures.

The new estimate, which the Pentagon plans to release shortly before President Bush leaves office, would serve as a marker for the new president and is meant to place pressure on him to either drastically increase the size of the defense budget or defend any reluctance to do so, according to several former senior budget officials who are close to the discussions.

Experts note that releasing such documents in the twilight of an administration is a well-worn tactic, and that incoming presidents often disregard such guidance in order to pursue their own priorities.

"Pursue their own priorities." Sure he will. But these priorities will be pressed from several directions, all pointing toward more war and a bigger military.

One example came last spring, when a retiring army general told Congress about the size and condition of our army. Here's part of what he testified, as reported in the *New Yorker:*

General Richard A. Cody graduated from West Point in 1972, flew helicopters, ascended to command the storied 101st Airborne Division, and then, toward the end of his career, settled into management; now, at fifty-seven, he wears four stars as the Army Vice-Chief of Staff. This summer, he will retire from military service.

[In April], the General appeared before the Senate Armed Services Committee and testified that this method of engineering has failed. "Today's Army is out of balance," Cody said. He continued: "The current demand for our forces in Iraq and Afghanistan exceeds the sustainable supply, and limits our ability to provide ready forces for other contingencies. . . . Soldiers, families, support systems and equipment are stretched and stressed. . . . Overall, our readiness is being consumed as fast as we build it. If unaddressed, this lack of balance poses a significant risk to the all-volunteer force and degrades the Army's ability to make a timely response to other contingencies."

Cody spoke last spring. Last week [October 14], his estimate was echoed by a batch of strategic consultants. The Christian Science Monitor's Gordon Lubold had that story:

Is US fighting force big enough?

Washington - American's armed forces are growing bigger to reduce the strains from seven years of war, but if the US is confronting an era of "persistent conflict," as some experts believe, it will need an even bigger military.

A larger military could more easily conduct military and nation-building operations around the world. But whether the American public has the appetite to pursue and pay for such a foreign-policy agenda, especially after more than five years of an unpopular war in Iraq, is far from clear.

The Army currently has about 540,000 active-duty soldiers and is expected to attain its goal of 547,000 by 2011. The Marine Corps, also tapped to expand, should top 202,000 within the next couple of years. The total American force – including active-duty, reserve, and guard – is about 2.2 million.

John Nagl, a counterinsurgency expert and a retired Army officer, says in coming years the Army should grow to 750,000 and the Marine Corps to 250,000. Demand for troops is already high, and it won't abate anytime soon even if substantial numbers of troops return from Iraq, he recently said at the Center for a New American Security, a think tank in Washington.

Meanwhile, the top US commander in Afghanistan has asked for more American troops that the US simply can't produce until more leave Iraq.

"We don't have enough brigades to fight – that is an inconvertible fact," says Mr. Nagl.

If the US is to remain a superpower in a world in which weak nations, not strong ones, are the big threats, then it must expand its forces so it won't again enter a conflict using too few troops, as it did in Iraq, say other experts. America must stay engaged in nations with weak or nonexistent governments to prevent extremism from taking root and threatening the US.

"This is not a prediction of conflicts to come, but a recognition

434

that the potential for stabilization and reconstruction missions remains high," writes Fred Kagan, a senior fellow at the conservative American Enterprise Institute, a think tank here, in a book he co-wrote called *Ground Truth*. Mr. Kagan and Thomas Donnelly argue for a total force of about 2.8 million, which includes an active Army of about 800,000 and a Marine Corps of about 200,000.

"We may not want these missions, but they might be thrust upon us; and they certainly might appear to a future president as the least-bad outcome," Kagan writes.

Where are all these additional troops supposed to come from? Recruiters haven't been having an easy time in recent years, despite huge budgets for ads and signup bonuses

But not to worry. Now they've gained a crucial ally, as a Pentagon bigwig explained to Robert Burns, military writer for the Associated Press:

For military, bad economy aids recruiting

WASHINGTON—The tough economy could make it easier to sign up soldiers.

Fewer civilian jobs mean less competition for military recruiters.

"We do benefit when things look less positive in civil society," David Chu, the Pentagon's personnel chief, told a news conference Friday. "I don't have the Dow Jones banner running up behind me here this morning, but that is a situation where more people are willing to give us a chance."

For several years, as the Army in particular struggled to meet its recruiting needs, military officials have cited a strong economy as one obstacle to attracting young people looking at their employment options. It is one reason that over the past year the Army and Marine Corps felt compelled to pay more than $600 million, combined, in bonuses and other financial incentives to entice recruits.

Another negative factor: Parents and others who influence the decisions of enlistment-age men and women have, since the outset of the Iraq war, become less inclined to recommend military service.

In announcing that the Army, Marine Corps, Navy and Air Force all met their recruiting goals for the budget year ended Sept. 30, Chu said the economic downturn offers new possibilities for recruiters.

"What more difficult economic times give us, I think, is an opening to make our case to people (potential enlistees) that we might not otherwise have," Chu said. "And if we make our case, I think we can be successful."

The military needs any break it can get on recruiting, particularly since it is in the midst of a push to substantially increase the size of the nation's ground forces—a decision driven by an urgent need to reduce the strain on troops and their families from repeated deployments to Iraq.

And one more item. Here are snippets from some reports that will be delivered to the new occupant of the Oval Office about rising military challenges, as leaked to McClatchy Newspapers:

A new National Intelligence Estimate concludes that Pakistan is "on the edge."

Washington - A growing al Qaida-backed insurgency, combined with the Pakistani army's reluctance to launch an all-out crackdown, political infighting and energy and food shortages are plunging America's key ally in the war on terror deeper into turmoil and violence, says a soon-to-be completed U.S. intelligence assessment.

A U.S. official who participated in drafting the top secret National Intelligence Estimate said it portrays the situation in Pakistan as "very bad." Another official called the draft "very bleak," and said it describes Pakistan as being "on the edge."

The first official summarized the estimate's conclusions about the state of Pakistan as: "no money, no energy, no government."

Six U.S. officials who helped draft or are aware of the document's findings confirmed them to McClatchy on the condition of anonymity because NIEs are top secret and are restricted to the president, senior officials and members of Congress. An NIE's conclusions reflect the consensus of all 16 U.S. intelligence agencies.

The NIE on Pakistan, along with others being prepared on Afghanistan and Iraq, will underpin a "strategic assessment" of the situation that Army Gen. David Petraeus, who's about to take command of all U.S. forces in the region, has requested. The aim of the assessment - seven years after the U.S. sent troops into Afghanistan - is to determine whether a U.S. presence in the region can be effective and if so what U.S. strategy should be.

The findings also are intended to support the Bush administration's effort to recommend the resources the next president will need for Iraq, Afghanistan and Pakistan at a time the economic crisis is straining the Treasury and inflating the federal budget deficit.

The Afghanistan estimate warns that additional American troops are urgently needed there and that Islamic extremists who enjoy safe haven in Pakistan pose a growing threat to the U.S.-backed government of Afghan Prime Minister Hamid Karzai.

The Iraq NIE is more cautious about the prospects for stability there than the Bush administration and either John McCain or Barack Obama have been, and it raises serious questions about whether the U.S. will be able to redeploy a significant number of troops from Iraq to Afghanistan anytime soon.

Together, the three NIEs suggest that without significant and swift progress on all three fronts – which they suggest is uncertain at best – the U.S. could find itself facing a growing threat from al Qaida and other Islamic extremist groups, said one of the officials.

So where does this leave the US as we look ahead to a new year and a new administration?

Facing a need for more troops – and not just a few more, but hundreds of thousands. Recruiters are counting on the coming depression to fill the ranks. Will it be enough?

And what will all these additional troops face? How about:

Trouble in Iraq. Big trouble in Afghanistan. And the threat of even bigger trouble in Pakistan. (And Iran? Russia? Don't ask.)

I don't know about you, but here at Quaker House, this data indicates that we'll continue to be busy.

http://quakerhouse.blogspot.com/2008/10/lots-of-bad-news.html

QH Blog: – Monday, March 23, 2009

Understatement of the Day. The Month. The Year.

Iraq Civil War Goes On . . . .

From an AP Dispatch today, March 23, 2009:

US officials said earlier this month that Iraq was experiencing its lowest levels of violence since 2003.
But since then there have been several major bombings.
The AP dispatch told of a suicide bombing in Diyala province, which killed 25. earlier, in the Abu Ghraib district, another bombing killed 8. And, AP added–
Another attack in Abu Ghraib on 10 March killed 33 people.
In the same week, more than 30 people died in an attack on a police recruitment centre and another 10 were killed in an explosion at a cattle market in Babel province.

http://quakerhouse.blogspot.com/2009/03/understatement-of-day-month-year.html

QH Blog:
Wednesday, February 24, 2010

Two Toms In The *Times* On Torments in Iraq

Tom Friedman, the globe-trotting, incessantly name-dropping NY Times columnist, who was a big cheerleader for the US Iraq invasion. Now, after his latest hobnob with various poohbahs there, he's worried. From his Feb. 24 column:

"Alas," he writes, "some seven years after the U.S. toppled Saddam's government, a few weeks before Iraq's second democratic national election, and in advance of the pullout of American forces, this question still has not been answered. Will Iraq's new politics triumph over its cultural divides, or will its cultural/sectarian divides sink its fledgling democracy? We still don't know."

This question arises, he says, because "we gave Iraqis a chance to do something no other Arab people have ever had a chance to do: freely write their own social contract on how they would like to rule themselves and live together."

To be sure, we "gave" the Iraqis that "chance" to be like us unbidden, under a rain of bombs and artillery shells, and at the cost of a million or so civilians dead, several millions made homeless, a civil war there, the legitimization of torture here, and a few other bumps in the road.

What does one call this in Friedman-speak? "Tough-love philanthropy" maybe? How hollow this kind of commentary must ring in the ears of so many of its putative "beneficiaries"!

I see the situation a bit differently, with the help of Scripture, specifically the harsh words of the prophet Hosea 8:7. In Iraq the US has amply "sown the wind," but in typical American fashion, are hoping we can yet avoid "reaping the whirlwind" there, by sliding out, having our victory parades, re-electing whoever is in power here, and then forget the whole thing – before the bloody consequences of this orgy of destruction become too obvious.

This is more cynical than Friedman would cop to, but it's not that far from what he is hoping for. Yet he's very worried that the whole thing will blow up first.

And he's not alone. Tom Ricks, former ace Washington Post

439

reporter, shared similar anxieties on the same OpEd page the day before, on Feb. 23:

In 2006 Ricks published "Fiasco," one of the best, most honest, and hence most disturbing books about the manifold early horrors of the Iraq invasion/occupation. But honest reporting of a disaster didn't make Ricks an antiwar activist, and since then he has come to feel that the occupation might turn out better than anyone imagined.

Or maybe worse.

His OpEd piece in the *New York Times* was a plea for US forces to stay there longer. Ricks is worried about the pace at which the current administration is withdrawing US troops from Iraq

His main fear, similar to but more starkly stated than Friedman's, is that, "An Iraqi civil war would likely be a three- or four-sided affair, with the Shiites breaking into pro- and anti-Iranian factions. It could also easily metastasize into a regional war." Further, he fears that "A regional war in the middle of the world's oil patch could shake the global economy to its foundations and make the current recession look mild."

So he hopes the administration will keep 50,000-plus US troops there, essentially indefinitely, to stave off this outcome until   u n t i l what? Until a miracle happens, I guess.

Nevertheless, the real kicker in his piece comes very near the end:

"The best argument against keeping troops in Iraq," he says, "is the one some American military officers make, which is that a civil war is inevitable, and that by staying all we are doing is postponing it. That may be so, but I don't think it is worth gambling to find out."

But evading this "gamble" means keeping a major US troop force there indefinitely, as in generations.

I too wish I knew a way for the US to escape these awful consequences of our illegal and immoral invasion of that country. But I don't. Sooner or later those chickens will be coming home to roost. But like Ricks, I think they will look a lot more like buzzards.

God forgive us for this monumental folly, which is still unfolding.

http://quakerhouse.blogspot.com/2010/02/two-toms-in-times-on-torme
nts-in-iraq.html

Mission Impossible: Keeping Up With the Invisible War(s)

It's not easy doing peace work in the United States today.

Recent polls indicate that Americans dislike the Afghanistan war as many as 53-56 per cent oppose it in the latest surveys. Yet the same polls show that citizen attention to the wars is low, lagging far behind domestic concerns such as jobs, health care, government debt and fear of terror attacks inside the US.

From our vantage point, this public indifference has helped usher in the age of the invisible wars. That is to say, the wars have become largely invisible to the general public here.

This invisibility is fed in part by sheer weariness–the Afghan conflict is almost nine years old.

But it has also been carefully cultivated:

Much of the killing is now done by unmanned drone flights, which we only hear about later, or not at all, and don't see.

More killing is done by covert units, working primarily under the uber-secretive, Ft. Bragg-based Joint Special Operations Command, alongside what may be equal or even larger numbers of unaccountable "private" contractors.

While the bulk of these covert attacks take place in Afghanistan, there are also targets in Pakistan, Iraq, Iran, and many other countries, which receive almost no attention. The previous administration declared that the "battlefield" in the "war on terror," was the whole world; the targets could be anyone. The current administration has shelved the "war on terror" meme, but retained the unlimited reach of its "righteous" violence.

US casualties, while rising in Afghanistan, are still lower than at the height of the Iraq insurgency. Reports of these deaths are scattered across the nation, mainly in smaller, less visible communities.

Media coverage of the war is limited and censored. The report in Rolling Stone that cost general Stanley McChrystal his job was a rare exception; and even that focused on talk among officers rather than firsthand reporting on the killing and destruction.

– The Guantanamo prison camp remains open, as does a "secret" black site facility in Afghanistan. There are persistent and credible reports that prisoner abuse has continued.

– Military recruiting funds have been cut more than ten percent for 2010, while – quotas are the same. That's because the jobs crash pushed recruiting to a 36-year high in 2009. With no real relief in sight, the unemployment "stimulus" to enlistments will likely continue.

– Meanwhile, the overall budget for war is still growing, despite the economic crash.

– Organized antiwar actions are anemic, sparsely attended, and off the media radar. (The Gaza flotilla notably excepted; but at what terrible cost?)

Civil liberties continue to erode. A US Supreme Court decision on June 21 upheld the "material support" provisions of the Patriot Act, permitting the government – to prosecute groups advocating or training for nonviolence if their work involves designated "terrorist" groups. (But wait a minute: what groups need nonviolence training more than those which have used violence?)

That is, it could now be a crime for Quaker House to send a letter to Hamas in Gaza, urging them to cease their armed struggle and adopt nonviolence, and offering the resources on our website to that end. (Note to Homeland Security: we have sent no such letter.)

Former President Jimmy Carter said that this decision:

"actually threatens our work and the work of many other peacemaking organizations that must interact directly with groups that have engaged in violence. The vague language of the law leaves us wondering if we will be prosecuted for our work to promote peace and freedom."

We're still working, as you will see here. But no question: times are tough.

A Troubling Vista: The US vs Canada as seen from Ireland – December 2010

On a bright but cold afternoon in December, 2010, I took a serious blow to the ego, and what's left of my cultural pride. It probably did me good, but – I'm still rubbing the sore spot: like a bruise that just won't heal.

It started out fine, when I got off a bus not far from Waterford, Ireland, just in time for an interview.

I was in Ireland winding up a trip in support of torture accountability work. Some weeks earlier, an enterprising Irish student of TV production named Cormac had tracked me down on the net. He had discovered that in 1967 I was part of a large antiwar protest in Buffalo New York, where we walked across the Canadian border near Niagara Falls, and asked if i remembered it.

Sure, I remembered. We were carrying medical supplies for Canadian Quakers to distribute among wounded civilians on all sides of the Vietnam War; my stash was a packet of band-aids.

It was illegal for Americans to do this, under something called the Trading With The Enemy Act. So our border walk was open civil disobedience, and we were prepared to be arrested.

But we weren't. I didn't recall publishing anything about this protest, one of many from those years; so how did Cormac, who emailed me from Ireland, know about it, and why was he interested?

Turns out there was an Irishman named George Lennon living near Buffalo at the time. He joined the border protest and noted it in his diary.

Now, 43 years later, Cormac and two classmates were making a postmortem documentary about George Lennon, based on this diary. Surfing for material, they found one mention of the Buffalo border protest: turns out it was by yours truly, buried in a talk to a Canadian group of Quakers, back in 1997, which I had since uploaded to an obscure web page.

Which once more goes to show the marvels of the internet, the glory of google, yada yada.

Well, I told Cormac I didn't know George Lennon, but could describe the border walk. And perhaps even better, I was headed for Ireland in December, so we could talk about it live, on camera.

Which is what we did, in the coastal town of Dungarvan: Cormac, his crew of Katie & Nicola, and me. It was sunny but we all shivered in an icy wind off the Celtic Sea. As the camera rolled I did my best to talk telegenically about somebody I'd once almost, but not quite, crossed paths with.

As soon as we were done we headed straight for the nearest pub, and warmth. There we talked about life and work and all that until the next bus came and I had to head off to Waterford to catch a train.

I don't think I was with these three for more than two hours. But the conversation has stayed with me ever since. And that brief encounter is what I really want to talk about here.

First off, the three: Cormac, Nicola and Katie embody the spirit of what was formerly called the Celtic Tiger: bright, appealing, energetic and devoted to their craft. They had an unforced friendliness that is almost proverbially Irish.

They were also caught in the collapse of the Tiger and its overheated economy. The financial news from Ireland then was bad (and hasn't gotten better since, even with a new government). The unemployment figures were (and are) especially gloomy.

Which naturally had me asking, what they were going to do when they finished school? Surely TV production jobs in Ireland were few and far between?

True, they said, but they weren't daunted. "We'll just go somewhere else," they told me. After all, emigration, temporary or permanent, is almost as ancient an Irish tradition as the cloverleaf, including, for that matter, many of my own ancestors. All three had relatives abroad, mainly in the States, as they called it, or Canada.

Well then, I said, surely their prime destination had to be New York or LA, the world centers for TV production, right?

That's when the blow came. Nope, I was told, with those cheery grins, they were thinking of Canada. Especially Vancouver.

What? Canada over the US for aspiring video and movie types? And Western Canada? I mean, I hear the scenery there is great, and the winters are milder. But we're talking video and cinema. They were kidding, right?

They weren't. We only had time to get started on this before my bus arrived, and I climbed aboard and sat back to ruminate on this startling bit of news.

I've been ruminating ever since. Okay, so I've learned that B.C. is the third largest movie center in North America, after New York and LA. But even so; who wants to aim at being Number Three?

But the more I ruminated, the more I tried putting myself in the place of Cormac and his colleagues, the more an eerie hollow feeling grew that they had figured out something I as an American, and maybe

444

many others like me, hadn't noticed, even though it was right there in front of our faces.

What's that? Call it the Emigrant's Homeland Comparison Shopping List. That is, if I was Cormac, gazing from Dungarvan across the Atlantic, how would these two adjoining alternate homelands stack up?

I had plenty of time to ponder this query on the flight back to the States a few days later. By the time we were passing Greenland, pondering had turned to brooding: the blows to my cultural pride kept on coming.

Keep in mind I'm a typical American boy, raised to presume that the USA is Number One, the place to which the "huddled Masses" of the world naturally yearn to go, right?

But as I mulled and pulled together some data this presumption got shakier and shakier.

Let's tick off some of it:

In November of 2010, just before my visit to Ireland, the Canadian unemployment rate was two points lower than that in the US.

And as for opportunity, income inequality in Canada is much narrower than in the US.

What about the soundness of the economy? The US spent trillions bailing out crooked but too-big-to-fail banks, which are still crooked and rickety.

By contrast, how much did Canada, which also has lots of big banks, spend on bailouts? – Nothing. Not a dime; not a single loonie. Seems they have some regulations the US doesn't, which kept their banks from crashing. Oh, but their banks still make profits. Hmmm.

Then there's support for the arts; Canada is far ahead of the US, even in these hard times.

Soon enough I was turning to non-cultural matters: I doubt Cormac and Katie and Nicola think much about getting sick; they had that young and invulnerable glow that I remember well enough.

But if they do get sick, or hurt, there's no contest: Canada wins by a mile. Compared to the Canadian system (which has its flaws) the vaunted US "health reform" is a joke. A deadly joke.

Then there's crime. In Canada, violent crime has been rising – but the rates, even in their big multi-cultural cities, are so much lower than comparable US cities that the difference is mind-boggling. When filmmaker Michael Moore, in "Bowling for Columbine," walked down a Canadian street opening the unlocked doors on houses, there was some exaggeration in the seen – but not that much.

Sociologists have been puzzling over that huge discrepancy for years, without a clear explanation. But I have one to put in the mix: the fact that Canada isn't running an Empire, and hasn't invaded any countries lately. (Yeah, I know, their governments, especially the current

445

one, have often been loyal lapdogs for US imperial ventures, and British ones before that. But it's still not the same.)

Here's the formula: Empire & war abroad stoke violence and crime at home; or, in technical terms, we reap what we sow.

For that matter, one other item I just learned about is that there's no Fox News up there, a fact that galls their right-wingers. Seems there's a Canadian regulation forbidding "news" programs from telling blatant untruths. That wouldn't fly down in First Amendment land; but maybe there's an upside in less mind pollution.

And did I mention that while the Canadian immigration process can be bureaucratic and complex, US procedures are now worse, and have become both maddening, institutionally demeaning, and counter-productive? Besides, Canada is still smart enough to see skilled young newcomers as assets to their economy. The US used to do this, but the brain drain of bright foreign techies from Silicon Valley and other innovation centers shows how we're determined to cripple ourselves, and doing a good job.

By the time the plane landed in Philadelphia, reflecting on this depressing laundry list had put me into a definite funk.

But buck up, I told myself, Canada's not perfect; it's no Shangri-La. Consider the downside:

Higher taxes; no question about that.

More winter.

Hockey. (Though some say the sport is their substitute for war, which would justify it, if true.)

An excess of political correctness; Canadians can drive you crazy that way.

Ditto for the no-Fox-News thing; there's more censorship up there.

Yet, even after considering this other side, I can see how Cormac and his friends would head north when they get to this side of the pond rather than going to LA. And I still am really bummed to have to face up to the truth of that. I'm an American after all, I guess.

But there's always hope: maybe if they strike it big in Vancouver, then they can go south: they can afford the California health insurance rates, get a house with adequate security systems, including their own squad of Blackwater goons; then they can spend their time doing lunch and secretly voting Republican.

Yeah, that sounds like a plan. So good luck to them. Cormac, Nicola and Katie, you're great, you three, and it was a pleasure to meet you, even if it did leave my American ego battered and reeling.

But one bit of advice, guys: even after you make it to Malibu, keep your main stash in a Canadian bank. I mean, you never know, eh?

Today's Military & "Spiritual Remediation"
Can That New-Time Army "Religion" Save Lives?
And: What Is Killing The Fort Bragg Babies?

By Chuck Fager

I admit it: my first reaction to the military's new "Comprehensive Soldier Fitness" (CSF) program was eye-rolling. There they go again, putting more band-aids on a cancer.

But after a closer look, I can at least appreciate the CSF's goals. As is well-known, the military, especially the Army, has big internal problems: more GI suicides than combat deaths over the past two years; plus waves of violence within their ranks, involving dom-estic homicide and abuse, rampant sexual harassment, and other violence against soldiers and civilians.

The army itself, in the order launching the CSF program, said as much: "THE UNITED STATES AND ITS ARMY ARE IN THE EIGHTH YEAR OF WAR. OPERATIONAL DEMANDS HAVE PLACED TREMENDOUS STRESS ON SOLDIERS, FAMILIES AND ARMY CIVILIANS TO THE EXTENT THAT THE ARMY IS AT A POINT OF IMBALANCE GIVEN THE MISSIONS REQUIRED AND THE RESOURCES AVAILABLE." (Their caps.)

"Imbalance"; a carefully-chosen word. "Broken" is what one hears more often from less restrained observers. After a flurry of high-level reports and public relations damage control, the CSF is the major response.

And it is a controversial one. In the logo shown here, the silhouette of a soldier in the lower left partially obscures the program's most hotly-disputed aspect, the "spiritual" part of "fitness."

"Spiritual"? Doesn't that mean "religious"? Not necessarily. Lots of Americans nowadays, including many Quakers, say they are "spiritual but not religious"; up to 30 percent in some polls.

But when it comes to "spiritual" vs "religious," the army is not an accurate cross-section of public sentiment. The CSF was heavily influenced by the chaplains corps, which is also involved in administering it. And since the Vietnam War, the chaplains corps has been steadily taking on a more evangelical, even fundamentalist character. This change reflects both push and pull: liberal religious groups effectively abandoned the military, while evangelical churches, with a more favorable view of

US warmaking, were happy to fill in. One of the largest chaplain training programs today is at the late Jerry Falwell's Liberty University.

The CSF takes shape as a series of questionnaires soldiers fill out when they return from deployments. These are essentially diagnostic instruments, aimed at identifying troops who are at risk for various problems, above all domestic violence or suicide. And when a GI's score falls into the "at-risk" range, she or he is tapped for "remediation," a kind of group counseling.

Special attention has been drawn to the CSF's "Spiritual Remediation" program, as laid out in a detailed guide, which has been unofficially published online.

This program has to walk a narrow line. After all, it is illegal and unconstitutional for the military to promote religion, and especially any particular religion.

Further, in recent years there have been several noisy controversies over officially-sanctioned, even coercive proselytization of soldiers, which have repeatedly embarrassed the Pentagon. Such stealth evangelism is a predictable outgrowth of the fundamentalist cast of the chaplain corps, and the steady colonization of the military's upper ranks by their brethren. For these groups, evangelism is the top priority, it starts at home and the US military is seen as an excellent vehicle for spreading their message. Further, skepticism about separation of church and state is endemic.

But pushback on these issues has been growing, spearheaded by a new group, the Military Religious Freedom Foundation. MRFF has been filing lawsuits and drawing media attention to such incidents with considerable success.

Recently soldiers who are atheists and humanists have been especially vocal in their objections to CSF, and the larger context from which it came. At Fort Bragg, Sgt, Justin Griffith scorned the "Spiritual Fitness" effort as a "vacuous smoke screen for religion in the military... . The whole program," he insists, "is ripe and ready for abuse."

Griffith is a proud soldier; he is also a proud atheist. And he understands the overall point of CSF. "It is a noble cause.," Griffith told a reporter. "They are trying to track and prevent suicide and PTSD; they just need to fix the implementation. There are four parts: Spiritual, Social, Family, and Emotional. Three of them are grounded in reality. But they need to remove the spirituality piece. The results of this test are a huge slap in the face to someone like me a committed soldier who is nonreligious."

While he also insists that most feedback he gets from other soldiers is positive, that doesn't apply to the higher ups. "The big stuff that's coming down from the top, that's different. There are existing rules in place that are being violated systematically. . . . It's epidemic, and I find it outrageous. The amount of money being spent by American citizens to support Evangelical proselytizing activities is substantial. The smokescreen about spiritual fitness having nothing to do with proselytizing is just that smoke."

As this struggle continues, here are some excerpts from the "Spiritual Remediation" module, so you can begin to make your own judgment. If all the church-and-state issues were resolved, should the army be in the business of promoting "spiritual Fitness"? The problem of violence in the military is frighteningly real. Is this part of the remedy?

More on MRFF at: www.militaryreligiousfreedom.org
Spiritual Remediation Module:

http://www.militaryatheists.org/resources/CSF_Spirituality_Remediation.pdf

---

What Is Killing The Babies Of Fort Bragg?

It is a genuine mystery, the solution to which has eluded several agencies and hundreds of tests. The army can't explain it, but can't deny it either: since February 2007, twelve infants have died in on-base housing at Fort Bragg, three of them in the same house.

Army criminal investigators say an extensive probe produced no evidence of abuse or foul play. In a couple of the children, signs of infections were found, which could have made them cases of SIDS, or Sudden Infant Death Syndrome. But for the rest, including the three in one house, the cause or causes remain unknown.

The possibility of environmental contamination, such as outgassing from drywall or toxins from mold, has been explored by several agencies, including the Consumer Product Safety Commission (CPSC). They say they found little if any risk from these factors.

A giant private housing development company, Picerne Military Housing, manages all family housing on Fort Bragg, more than 6000 units. Picerne won a fifty-year management contract at Bragg in 2002.

Post officials insist Bragg's housing is safe, and that the number of unexplained infant deaths on Bragg is not out of the ordinary for a community of its size. "(Infant) deaths occur here as often as they would in a similar-sized town," Col. Kevin Arata, a Fort Bragg spokesman said.

Others were not mollified by this comment or the inconclusive investigations. The independent investigative journalistic group ProPublica found experts in toxicology who said the wrong kinds of tests were done by the CPSC on the drywall in the houses "The idea that they are skating around this and not doing the obvious measurement is very troubling," Michael Shaw, vice president of Interscan Corp. and a member of a voluntary standards committee for drywall manufacturers told ProPublica.

David M. Abramson, a professor at Columbia University's school of public health, said "The odds of three babies dying in a short order in the same house without an underlying condition of some sort, it's very unlikely. It's enormously unlikely. Common sense would dictate there's something common in the environmental exposure."

Illnesses involving toxic-contaminated drywall, particularly from China, have become public issues after large numbers of temporary shelters containing the material were sent to New Orleans after Hurricane Katrina. Lawsuits have produced large settlements there and elsewhere.

An initial CPSC field report said the house where three children died showed numerous signs of toxic drywall contamination. The final CPSC report said there was no such evidence.

"I felt betrayed, honestly," Spc. Nathanael Duke told Propublica. His son Gabriel died in 2010. "I trusted the CPSC as an independent agency to bring the truth out and clearly that didn't happen."

The army said it is finished with all its tests and investigations, except for wrapping up the two most recent cases.

But many servicemembers who reacted to the Propublica report were not satisfied.

"I am a career military officer and I love the Army," wrote J. Cogbill, "but in this case I think the Fort Bragg officials are trying to cover themselves and not doing what is best for the troops and their community."

Link to Propublica articles on contaminated drywall:
http://www.propublica.org/series/tainted-drywall

New Directors for Quaker House Designated:
Changeover Set for December 2012

After a search process that lasted two years and ranged across the US and beyond, the Quaker House board found the successors to Director Chuck Fager right across the table.

Steve and Lynn Newsom, of Charlotte NC Friends Meeting, had represented their Meeting on the board for several years. In addition, as part of Chapel Hill Meeting in 1969, Lynn was a member of the first board that came together to rent a house in Fayetteville and launch the project. While teaching art for more than thirty years, she has also been a peace activist, and an involved Friend in meetings in Ohio and North Carolina.

Steve has been a peace activist too, and he's a veteran who was once stationed at Fort Bragg. He's also been an accountant and run his own remodeling service.

Steve & Lynn will be visiting Quaker House through the summer and fall, "learning the ropes" from current Director Chuck Fager, who is completing his eleventh year of service, and looking toward retirement.

Steve & Lynn are also eager to visit Meetings to get acquainted with the Friends who have been the bedrock of support for Quaker House during its 43 years of peace witness.

"Quaker House has been a unique and satisfying opportunity to serve Friends," Chuck Fager said. "Even with the Iraq occupation 'over,' and Afghanistan drawing down, there's still plenty for us to do. The GI Hotline, for instance, is taking calls at a pace we haven't seen since 2008. The pressures for a new war with Iran are mounting. The legacy of torture, which is right in our backyard, has yet to be addressed. Violence within the military is at record levels. And war spending is at an all-time high too.

"So Lynn and Steve will have a full plate. And once they take the helm in December, I'm looking forward to some rest and reflection, and then some new opportunities. For one thing, there's a lot of writing I've had to put off due to the demands of our mission. And then there are grandchildren too."

Quaker House

May 16, 2012

Dear Friend,

The Wars Come Home: This spring, many issues came together for us: same sex marriage, domestic violence, bullying, racial profiling, and even highway privatization. With them came broadened contacts and collaboration with other groups in our area.

But what's all this got to do with war and peace?

Lots. Next door to Fort Bragg, just about everything is connected.

Here's how: the wars are supposed to be over, or winding down. The president pronounced the end of the Iraq war at Fort Bragg. The troops there were supposed to be home for Christmas.

Many were. But many others weren't. It seemed as if they got off one plane from Baghdad, caught their breath, then climbed aboard another headed for Afghanistan.

As these headlines show, soldiers from Ft. Bragg have been killed there every week this year, sometimes more than one. This is happening as public support for, and interest in the war have sunk almost out of sight. And there's little doubt the troops don't believe in it anymore than the rest of us do.

Yet the killing grinds on, and in ugly ways: almost every week we learn of Afghan soldiers or police turning their weapons on US "allies," with deadly results.

The reaction is just as repulsive: those troops recently photographed holding up body parts from suicide bombings were from Ft. Bragg.

Nor is the impact on unit morale much better: GI suicides are still at record levels. Eight soldiers who hazed and bullied an Asian-American soldier into killing himself in Afghanistan will soon be put on trial here.

As we've said before, the wars come home with these worn out, brutalized, often wounded troops. This reality connects with domestic violence: the counseling services at Fort Bragg are overwhelmed and understaffed. So is the family shelter in the city. The "Warrior Transition Unit" where many wounded troops are assigned, is a nest of dissension and scandal.

With domestic violence comes hazing and bullying for younger people. Tensions are already high among Fayetteville's African American

452

population, over a police scandal centered on an obvious pattern of profiling and harassing black drivers. At Quaker House we're working to promote inter-racial collaboration about this.

And they're not the only targets. Despite the end of "Don't Ask Don't Tell," LGBT persons, actual or presumed, remain in the crosshairs.

These attitudes reached a climax of sorts with the landslide vote in early May for an anti-same sex marriage amendment in North Carolina. The tally was ten points higher here than statewide.

One local Baptist preacher, a retired Army sergeant who graduated from Jerry Falwell's Liberty University, drew national attention with a videotaped antigay sermon that went viral. He shouted at his audience to "squash like a cockroach" the merest hint of non-standard gender behavior even in toddlers. His bellowing drew visible protests, which we helped with. But his message was by no means unusual.

Then there is our GI Rights Hotline. Calls declined a bit in the winter. But by April they had climbed to the highest level in four years. In mid-May, when this was written, they were still coming in at the same heavy pace.

Many callers are seeking discharge as Conscientious Objectors. But that isn't their only concern:

"Many of those who have enlisted never would have done so if they could have found other work," our counselors Steve and Lenore report. "They did not join because they strongly identified with serving in the military, they just had no other way to provide for their families.

"This'poverty draft' remains in effect and many people trying to get out would not be in the military were it not for the financial crisis.

"This situation is also changing. Currently the army is cutting its numbers by 140,000. The military feels it can be choosier and will no longer act as the employer of last resort. We are already seeing an increase in calls from people being forced out, often for minor disciplinary infractions, resulting in loss of benefits." There seems no question but the Pentagon is trying to avoid paying for the human costs of the wars.

So besides coping with PTSD, traumatic brain injuries and other war traumas, many who were driven to enlist by the threat of unemployment and loss of income now find that specter looming over them at Fort Bragg.

Which is where privatization comes in. The state has announced plans to put tolls on I-95, the only interstate road near here. Once tolled, the highway would be sold, probably to a foreign company. Tolls would start at $20 each way across the state, and increase each year. The planners figure they could take in $30 billion that way, mostly in profits.

With over a hundred thousand troops and family members at Fort Bragg, the biggest chunk of this toll burden would be carried by them. On top of everything else.

Protests against this scheme are starting, and we're in on it. I'm thinking of a bumper sticker: "Support the Troops: Stop the Tolls." At least we'll know what it means. It also has appeal across lines of color, religion and even class all of which we need here this spring, badly.

Peace,

Chuck Fager

PS. Has the threat of war with Iran receded? It's not in the media every day anymore, but it sure doesn't feel like we're out of the woods yet.

Difficult Homecoming

At Fort Bragg last December, the president declared the "end" of the Iraq war. As far as an active army unit presence goes, that was true. But in the more local sense, the war continues: the war at home.

As the last troops returned to Fort Bragg, we waited, holding our breath, for the shoe to drop: when large numbers of soldiers return from extended combat deployments, there is usually a wave of trouble, especially domestic trouble.

At first, though, it was quiet. Christmas, and then New Year, came and went, still quiet.

But then the shoe dropped: On January 14, firefighters were called to an apartment complex in Fayetteville. Looking for the fire, they knocked on doors. But at one, the man inside shot at them. The firemen retreated, but the man inside then pinned down police in a shootout and standoff that lasted four hours before they finally blew down his door and captured him.

Turns out the shooter was a three-time Afghan veteran with traumatic brain injury and heavy PTSD. He was apparently triggered into flashbacks by the firefighters' knocking – thought he was back in "the Sandbox," and the Taliban was coming for him.

He was also in the "Warrior Transition Battalion," the unit where wounded GIs are parked while their cases are sorted out – or not. That battalion has been under investigation after numerous complaints by soldiers there about abuse and neglect by superiors, plus overmedication with anti-depressants and other potent meds. Such units at Camp Lejeune, Fort Drum, and other bases have also been probed due to similar complaints.

It's been downhill ever since. Between April 10 and 12 an Army doctor killed his ex-girlfriend here, then drove to New Jersey, fatally ambushed another doctor, then killed himself as police closed in. On the 14th, a young woman soldier went to a karaoke bar, then vanished. She was still missing nearly a month later, when this was written; there's more, but you get the idea. Reports from Fort Bragg's social services indicate that their caseloads are backed up and short-staffed. The Fayetteville women's shelter is overcrowded and turning abuse victims away, many of them military families fleeing domestic violence among them. The war is not ended; it has come home.

Meanwhile, the other end of the war continues: soldiers from Ft. Bragg have been killed in Afghanistan at the rate of two or three per week all year. The president's plan to "wind down" the war sounds like it includes keeping several thousand troops there, mostly from the secretive special forces.

This "winding-down-but-staying-indefinitely" stance is the more ironic in light of the continued collapse of public support. A Washington Post-ABC poll in mid-April showed that even most Republicans now say they are fed up with the Afghan war. At Quaker House, we're waiting for a call from the local GOP, asking for help in organizing an elephant-led "Bring Them Home Now" vigil downtown.

We'll be there on the double. But the phone hasn't rung for that yet; and meantime, the war at home rages on, with no end in sight.

Drone Warfare Comes to Fort Bragg: An Exclusive Report

Is a drone warfare base being built at Fort Bragg?

I believe so, and will explain why below. But first, I need to talk a bit about talking:

Reporting on drone warfare soon takes journalists, not to mention citizens, through the looking glass and – pardon the mixed metaphor– into a world of 1984-type doublespeak.

Consider: US officials, from the President down, have frequently talked about drone warfare, up to and including bragging about their use in eliminating various "high value" targets, including the claim in mid-September that they had killed the Number Two leader of Al Queda. A google search will turn up dozens of such statements.

Yet in any "official" or "legal" terms, US officials refuse to admit that the drone warfare force even exists, never mind that it is being used for actual warfare. Many of the highest officials have talked openly about it – yet it's still a "secret," until and unless they say it isn't.

This talking-but-not-"talking" stance creates many anomalies, as it is apparently meant to do. Most important, it has enabled the government to fend off, thus far, all efforts to subject the drone war to any outside scrutiny, especially legal review. Many outsiders, from human rights groups to UN officials, have tried to initiate such a review. None has yet succeeded.

The ACLU, for instance, has filed FOIA requests for CIA files about drones, but the Agency says it can neither confirm or deny the existence of the program, or any records about it. The ACLU then went to court, and submitted a thick sheaf of public statements by CIA and White House officials about the drone war. The shrugging response was, in effect, all that was just "talk," not actual information.

(By contrast, in 1979, when then-Director Bill Sholar asked for the CIA files on Quaker House, the Agency replied that it did have some, but refused to release them. Those were the days . . . .)

The drone war is a major part of the current secret wars. Their use is also intensely controversial: civilian casualties, targeted assassinations, and not least, the way the "talking-is-not-really-talking" stance further erodes the accountability of the US government and its war machine to te public, Congress, and the courts?

For Quaker House, most of these questions have been, as they say in the army, "above our pay grade," involving international forums and distant courtrooms that we only read about. But in the past few months, the one about secrets that aren't really "secret" has come home to Fayetteville, when we stumbled on the drone base at Fort Bragg.

The first "disclosure" was most likely an accident. On May 10, 2012, Congressman Mike McIntyre, whose district includes part of Fayetteville, issued a press release trumpeting his success in getting $198 million in new funding for Ft. Bragg approved by the House Armed Services Committee.

Such releases are routine from Capitol Hill, and I usually ignore them: more money for war; what else is new?

But glancing over the list, three items leaped out:

Fort Bragg–

Aerial Gunnery Range, $42 million
Infrastructure funding, $30 million
Unmanned Aerial Vehicle Complex, $26 million

The third one was the key. "Unmanned Aerial Vehicle" (UAV) = drones. "Complex" what could also be called a base.

So a UAV "Complex." The other two were less certainly drone-related, but fit the frame: An Aerial Gunnery Range. Fort Bragg already has dozens and dozens of firing ranges; but for pistols, rifles, machines guns or artillery, that is, for weapons fired from the ground. An Aerial Gunnery Range: a place for airborne vehicles to practice firing missiles at targets on the ground. Fort Bragg has some helicopters, but not fighter planes. But killer drones fly and shoot at targets on the ground.

So that list got my attention. But it wasn't decisive; I needed corroboration.

Very well, where would that come from? Two avenues occurred to me: a new UAV "Complex" would need personnel: "operators" (which is what UAV "pilots" are called) and techies. Was anyone hiring them for Fort Bragg?

Google had the answer: Yes. The National Guard has posted job notices for UAV operators at Bragg twice this summer, in June, and again in late August. Why the National Guard? Because several national Guard units have been converted to drone operations.

But that wasn't all. A drone operation, I learned, is very labor intensive: most drone flights are about spying, and each spy drone sends back enormous amounts of data, especially what's called Full Motion Video (or FMV). All that "flood of data", as the New York Times called it, requires elaborate computer systems to manage. And sure enough, a company called Bosh Global Services is looking for systems engineers and several other technical specialists who will be tasked to "support Unmanned Aerial Vehicle (UAV) operations" at Ft. Bragg.

(No, I'd never heard of Bosh Global either. But its website lists its motto is "Transforming Unmanned Operations." It was formerly known as UAV Communications Inc.; and its mission states that "BOSH specializes in unmanned systems-related operations and technology services." It might as well have been called Drones R Us.)

Once the computers are up and running, bringing in that "flood of data" from the drones and their Full Motion Video (FMV) cameras, the machines can only do so much with it; ultimately, data has to be processed and analyzed by human beings. Many human beings. And sure enough, the Celestar Corporation said it "has an IMMEDIATE NEED and is actively searching for FMV Imagery System Specialists," to work at Fort Bragg.

But such analysts must be scarce. So more will have to be trained, most likely from within the Army's ranks. Thus, a current posting by the CGI group Inc., is searching for an "Geoint Analyst Instructor," to do just that, develop and teach courses at Fort Bragg. (Geoint, by the way, stands for Geospatial intelligence; more on that in a moment).

Did I mention that applicants for all these jobs must have or get a Top Secret "or higher" security clearance?

Now let's summarize: Congress is allocating money for a drone "Complex" at Ft. Bragg, probably including a target range. The National Guard is hiring UAV operators to be stationed there. Outside contractors are scrambling to find engineers to build and run the computer systems; analysts to sort out the copious drone data; and an instructor to train more analysts, all at Fort Bragg. And while I found this information on open websites, it's all being done at a "Top secret" level, or higher, as part of a drone war that the government officially refuses to acknowledge even exists.

When this report was written, there had not been a word about any of this in the Fayetteville Observer, normally a pretty good newspaper. I attribute that silence mainly to the battering the paper has taken from the crash and the continuing depression: its pages and staff have shrunk, along with the enterprise capacity it once had.

This media silence is unfortunate. Drones, like other aircraft, bring hazards: they sometimes carry explosives, and can crash. Some reports suggest they crash a lot. What new risks are the residents of Fayetteville and other communities around Fort Bragg being exposed to as this drone "complex" expands?

Drones are a key part of what's called "Geospatial intelligence," "Geoint" for short. It is the combination of images from drones, satellites and other airborne sources, supplemented by "spatial" information such as maps, all as the information base for making military decisions (e.g., raiding bin Laden's hideout). Geoint is considered by many in the military to be "transforming" the shape and direction of war-making, initially by the U.S., but increasingly by many other nations.

The technology and extent of Geoint has evolved and grown enormously since September 11, 2001. As part of its rapid expansion, in 2004 the field achieved what seems to be the military industrial complex's ultimate seal of approval: its own intelligence arm, The National Geospacial Intelligence Agency, NGA for short.

With a new $2 billion dollar headquarters complex on Fort Belvoir, Virginia, around 16000 employees, and a classified budget, NGA joins the roster of more than a dozen covert agencies. It report-edly supplied "critical information," likely drawn from drone, satellite and other sources, for the mission that killed Osama Bin Laden.

Somehow, I'd never heard of NGA before; but its existence is not a secret; it's even on Wikipedia.

For that matter, it is hardly a surprise to find drone warfare taking root at Fort Bragg: it's a key military installation, hosting some of the most secretive and deadly US military units. Yet this development should not go unremarked. For one thing, this is where war is going. For another, the morality of drone warfare is fiercely contested. In addition, recent polls show that in much of the world the US drone war is extremely unpopular.

And not least, the "hidden in plain sight" character of the drone war has serious implications for our legal and constitutional order. As ACLU privacy attorney Nathan Wessler recently put it:

"Senior U.S. officials, including President Obama and former CIA director Leon Panetta, have repeatedly spoken publicly in defense of the drone program. Countless unnamed government officials have also discussed the program in the press. Yet, when the ACLU and others have sought transparency about the legal basis for drone strikes, the number and identity of casualties . . . the government has stonewalled. The United States even persists with the incredible claim that it cannot confirm or deny whether the CIA operates a drone program, despite numerous statements by government officials confirming CIA drone strikes. The U.S. government is trying to have it both ways – publicity about drone strikes when it is politically advantageous, but secrecy when the drone program is subject to criticism. That is simply untenable in a democracy."

But is it really untenable? Day by day, such unaccountable secrecy seems more like business as usual.

460

Quaker House

November 30, 2012

Dear Friend,

Post-Election Jitters: Did you heave a sigh of relief when the election was over? We did. And not just because we were sick of attack ads, emails and robocalls. (But that, too.)

Even more, it was great to be rid of the plan to shower an extra $2 trillion dollars on the war machine. And all the talk about bombing Iran, trade war with China, getting stuck in Syria, and bringing back torture.

Besides, around Fort Bragg any post-election euphoria has already dissipated. That's because as the cheering died away and the smoke cleared, anyone with open eyes could see the hard truth: election or no election, it was war as usual here.

What's been going on behind the wall of campaign noise? Here's a sample:

− Remember Afghanistan? Ten soldiers from Ft. Bragg were killed in the five weeks preceding election day. Nine in Afghanistan, including one woman, and one from "undisclosed causes" in Florida. (Another GI suicide? The Army says it's "investigating," which is usually the last the public ever hears about them.)

− The drone attacks keep happening, as the deadly "unmanned vehicles" keep up their raids, from Fort Bragg and elsewhere.

− Combat in Syria and Gaza-Israel is spreading, with more calls for US involvement. (And don't forget Iran.)

There's more too, and all of it means steady work for us. If there's continuity amid change in Washington, the same is true at Quaker House.

The change: Chuck Fager is retiring, after eleven grueling years. The continuity: Steve and Lynn Newsom are moving in to take up the reins. And our ace GI Rights Hotline counselors, Lenore Yarger and Steve Woolford, are staying put, helping soldiers to find their way to personal peace.

− Another major story here, rarely spoken of plainly, also has nationwide ramifications. As the local chamber of commerce president put it recently: "Hurricane Sequestration" is headed for Fayetteville . . . and if it hits, "We all stand to take a pretty big haircut."

A hurricane giving haircuts? Go figure. Mangled metaphors

461

aside, "sequestration" refers to automatic cuts in federal funds set to begin on January 3, 2013. They're part of what's being called "The Fiscal Cliff." Several hundred billion dollars of these cuts would come from the war budget.

Now, here at Quaker House, that prospect makes us smile. But it has defense contractors around Fort Bragg (and the country) in a state of near panic, lobbying furiously to stop it.

And truthfully, we're not expecting that "Hurricane Sequestration" will really leave the war contractors shorn and shivering. After all, even without the un-asked for $2 trillion bonus, the war budget is at a record high, and set to increase in the next few years.

It's the other side of "The Fiscal Cliff" that really has us worried: the bulk of those automatic cuts will actually come from civilian federal programs, including big chunks from education, housing, and other human needs efforts. And if the war lobbyists succeed in stopping the defense cuts, these civilian "haircuts" will have to shave much deeper.

Even more ominous, sequestration is the curtain-raiser and prototype for what's being called a "Grand Bargain." That will supposedly lower the federal deficit by several trillion dollars while preserving a "strong military." We see that plan as a very bad "Bargain." Why? Because of a simple fact we tried to drive home a year ago when Occupy Wall Street was riding high.

Remember? It's a stark choice We can maintain the war budget, and keep military contractors booming and hairy around Fort Bragg and other bases. Or we can have a decent national safety net, Social Security, Medicare, school and college aid, and help for veterans.

We can't afford both. And the "Bargain" plans are much too protective of the war budget. It's the civilians, the middle class and the poor, who will be taking the real haircuts.

So at Quaker House, we're raising the alarm about this again, because the "Grand Bargain" scheme and its stark choices are bearing down and taking aim at the national safety net, like – well, like a hurricane waving giant barber shears. Or a missile-bearing drone.

This is on top of our continuing work with soldiers and their families, who are still calling our GI rights Hotline number at a rate of more than 200 per month. Plus our reminders about accountability for the torture of past years, to head off future attempts to bring it back, like the one we just dodged in the election.

Also our efforts to pierce "The Great Forgetting" about the expanding secret drone wars, being trained for and expanded behind the veil at Fort Bragg and other bases. And to tell the truth about the horrendous human costs being paid by our troops and their families, including an epidemic of sexual harassment and abuse.

2012 has been a tumultuous, exhausting year, militarily as well as politically. And here's something we think we've learned along the way: it's not going to let up soon. Not for the country. Not for you. And not for us.

Thank you and peace,
Steve & Lynn Newsom, & Chuck Fager

ELEVEN: Stories – You CAN Make this Stuff Up

Money for College

A Story by Chuck Fager

Copyright © 2004

I was running behind that morning, as usual.

Didn't wake up until after ten – but then, working til all hours and then sleeping in is one of the few perks you get as the head of a peace project with a one-person staff. Anyway the night before, I was trying to finish the latest Quaker House newsletter, which was supposed to be printed and in the mail within a week. I might make that deadline, might not. More late nights would probably be needed for that one.

Stumbling back from the bathroom, still rubbing my eyes, I remembered that this was Wednesday, and our peace vigil downtown was scheduled for noon. Usually it's at five, but a Canadian TV crew was going to be in town just this morning, and they asked if we could switch the time.

Damn – that meant I had to update my sign, and do it quick. So I was even more behind than I thought. Breakfast could wait; it might turn into brunch.

The vigil sign was a fold-out thing, white cardboard. On the left panel it read, "Yes to the Troops!" and on the right "No to the War!" To do peace work in an army town like Fayetteville, you have to start by saying something positive about the troops to have any chance of being heard at all. Some people won't believe you anyway, but you still have to say it.

In the middle panel of the sign were two six-inch squares, outlined in heavy black marker. Each square contained a number: on the left, the total of US GIs killed in Iraq as of last week. On the right: the total for this week.

To update, I drew the numbers on smaller squares of paper and taped them in. The sign was looking a little battered, since it was almost a year old; when I started, the death toll was about 250. It was due to pass a thousand any time now.

The numbers come off a website, and from checking the daily paper.

The paper. It was outside, on the lawn. I headed for the front door.

466

Then the phone rang. The cordless was on the dining room table. I snatched it up and kept going. "This is Quaker House," I murmured, trying to sound professional and alert.

"Chuck– it's Hank!" He sounded excited, though there was static in the connection. Probably a cell phone, that most modern means of disrupting communication.

"Good morning, Corporal," I said, trotting down the steps, "how goes the battle on the northern front?" The paper was on the grass, its plastic wrapper wet with dew.

"Forget the army," he said, almost shouting. "It's Jenny, she had the baby, last night. A boy!"

"Fabulous," I shouted back. I picked up the paper and turned back to the house. "A boy, eh? You're naming him after me, right?"

Hank laughed. "In your dreams, you egotist! We're naming him John, after Jenny's father."

"Oh well," I said, in mock disappointment, "the next one for sure. And how is Jenny? How did it go? Oh – and where ARE you now, anyway?"

"Jenny's fine," he said. "Labor was about twelve hours, not bad for the first one, they tell me. And we're in Vancouver. Hey, it's beautiful out here, man, You should come visit."

"Right," I said, "I'll book a flight, as soon as I raise some money. And for sure when your immigration hearing comes up." I dropped the paper on the dining table and headed for the office, where the vigil sign lived.

Gotta multi-task here, I thought, talk and update the sign at the same time; the clock is ticking. "And speaking of hearings," I said to Hank, "what's the word from the Canadian Immigration people – do you have a hearing date yet?"

"My lawyer says it will be six weeks, max," he answered. Then, "Jeez, was it only that long ago that you and Hostetter and me were eating burgers with Jonah Lapp?"

He was right. "Yep," I said. "Feels like six years, tho."

"No kidding," he said, through louder static, then his voice dropped a notch. "You heard from Hostetter?"

"Not since that email last month," I bellowed, into the buzz. "Remember? All it said was, 'Iraq sucks. Baghdad sucks. The army sucks. And worst of all, it doesn't look like anyone can stop the Yankees from going to the World Series this year.' Which means he was fine."

But the static had faded halfway through this recitation, and I finished it talking to a dead connection.

Cell phones. I bet the army uses them in its torture chambers in the Abu Ghraib prison.

He'll call back, I figured, if not right now, in a few days.

Unfolding the vigil sign, I carefully peeled off the sheets with the old numbers, and moved the "This Week" total to the "Last Week," square; the tape was still sticky enough to hold it. Now for today's total. The website I checked yesterday said 997. I drew the numbers with the wide black marker, big enough to be seen from across the street or a passing car, and taped the square in the larger box.

But then I thought: maybe better double-check. My memory is bad for numbers. I moved toward the dining room where the paper lay, and remembered that Thursday evening six weeks ago when Hank and Hostetter sat around this same table, two soldiers talking about their orders to go to Iraq, and wondering what to do.

Jenny had been there too, at first, her blond hair pulled back in a cute french braid kind of way. Her huge pregnant belly made her middle look like an over-inflated balloon. I could see tension in her expression, but overall she seemed very calm.

Hostetter and Hank, though, were not calm. They all looked so young, I thought. Hank and Hostetter had been good buddies since high school in Indiana. Hostetter's first name was John too, I realized, though he always went by his last.

Neither of their families could afford college, so they enlisted together, and managed to end up in the same unit at Ft. Bragg. And they had both realized how big a mistake they had made– the army was not like what the recruiters had told them, and the Iraq war didn't smell right. That's how I knew them: they came to Quaker House, for help in figuring out what to do.

Now their battalion, the 504th of the 82d airborne Division, had received its orders: they were to leave for combat duty in Iraq in less than a week.

"I'm not going," Hostetter said, rubbing one hand nervously over his nearly clean-shaven paratrooper's haircut. "I don't believe in it. The whole war is based on a pack of lies."

"But what about your college money, man?" Hank asked. "That $40,000 was really why we signed up. If you don't go, it's gone. You ready to kiss it off now?"

"What good will it be if I come back in a box?" Hostetter retorted. "Or minus my eyes, or legs? Not to mention with killing Iraqis on my conscience?"

"But the odds are in our favor," Hank said. "Look at the numbers: 135,000 troops. Six hundred casualties, a few thousand wounded. That means nine out of ten come back in one piece. So you get through it, get back, wait out your time, pick up the college money and you're outta here. That's what I'm gonna do."

Hostetter shook his head. "But it's wrong, man. Why get killed over this war? Why kill Iraqis over it? This war is stupid. Pointless."

"Sure," Hank agreed. "But we signed up for it. Nobody put a gun to our heads." He looked at me. "What do you think, Chuck?" he asked. "You're the GI counselor here. Counsel us."

I sighed, feeling vastly inadequate. They both looked so young, I thought again.

At Quaker House we talked all the time to soldiers who want out of the military; that's our job. But it's one thing to tell people about army rules and regulations, and procedures and paperwork, and quite another to sit with soldiers faced with going into combat. They were taking risks I didn't have to take. It was their lives, and their decisions. This was a moment to tread very carefully. I needed some counseling myself.

So after considering the question for a few seconds, I tried to duck. I turned to Hostetter: "Have you talked about this with Jonah Lapp?"

Jonah Lapp, Carolina's activist Mennonite, in his mid-sixties, also originally from Indiana. These days he spent half his time in Israel/Palestine, dodging bullets with the Christian Peace Teams; otherwise he was in Greensboro, organizing a peace-oriented religious community.

Hostetter had told me he had a Mennonite background, with many relatives who had been conscientious objectors and others who were veterans. So I'd taken him to hear Lapp speak a few weeks earlier, after he returned from the West Bank.

"No, haven't talked to him," Hostetter said. "But that's an idea. Do you think – ?"

"Got his number right here," I said, reaching for the phone.

I was lucky; Lapp answered. When he heard what was up, he didn't hesitate.

"I was gonna have a prayer meeting here tonight," he said. "But that can wait. Meet me at the Five Star Diner in Sanford, soon as you can get there. Find a booth in the back."

Sanford is about halfway between Fayetteville and Greensboro. We dropped Jenny off at their apartment, and the three of us sped up highway 87, a road that cuts right across Fort Bragg. We paid no attention to the rolls of shiny razor wire that lined the highway there, glinting in the streetlights, protecting the post from terrorists who so far had not bothered to arrive.

I thought we drove pretty fast, but Lapp drove faster: he was waiting in the diner. He was conspicuous in the booth, with his long gray beard, black suspenders and a battered straw hat pushed back on his sunburned forehead made him. He was sipping a glass of lemonade.

"The cheeseburgers are good here," he said. "I'll buy; a big church in Elkhart just sent a nice fat check for our peace community, so I'm taking a break from my vegetarian simple living." He smirked. "Don't tell my wife, okay?"

We chuckled and sat down. Over the burgers, the options were soon clear. "The way I see it," Jonah told the GIs, "you two have three options: One, go to Iraq, and try to get through it. Two, refuse to go and resist. Three, go AWOL. Take off and stay underground, maybe leave the country."

They nodded, but didn't say anything. I was embarrassed at how relieved I felt that my personal options didn't boil down to those three.

"Now if it was me," Lapp continued, "I'd take number two: refuse orders, and let the chips fall." He glanced at me. "They'd get court-martialed, right?"

I nodded. "Maybe with jail time," I said, "but probably only a few months. Then a discharge." That would be my preference too, I thought.

Of course, it wasn't our preferences that mattered.

"But if we refuse, or go AWOL, we lose the college money," Hank put in.

Lapp raised his eyebrows and sipped the last of his lemonade. "College money," he murmured. "Yes, war is hell." He thought for a moment. "Well, what about filing to be conscientious objectors?"

Now Hank sighed. "We tried that," he said. "I put in six months ago. They laughed at me, and turned it down."

It was true. I had worked with Hank on his CO application; it had looked strong to me, but not, evidently, to the 82d Airborne.

Hostetter sniffed. "I put mine in two months ago," he said. "Asked them about it just last week, right before the orders came down." His voice rose. "They said they never got it. The freakin' liars!"

I raised a hand, to quiet him. We didn't know who might be listening.

"And," Hostetter continued more quietly, "I don't much like the idea of jail."

Hank shook his head. "Yeah– and AWOL – how would you live? You'd have to leave the country. And who would take in a deserter? If they catch you, can't you get shot for being a deserter in wartime?"

"Well," I put in, "that's still on the books. But nobody's been executed for desertion since World War Two. And –" my voice trailed off. Was that data supposed to make them feel better?

"When is your unit set to leave for Iraq?" Lapp asked.

"The 504th ships out Tuesday," Hank answered.

"Four days," Lapp mused. "Not much time."

The discussion was pretty much left there, unfinished, like the last few ketchup-soaked french fries on our plates. Jonah and I reminded Hank and Hostetter that the decision was theirs, and we'd support them in whatever they decided, in any way we could. I said the words anyway, but I wasn't sure what they might mean in actual fact.

Tuesday came and went, though, with no word from either of them. Calls to Hank's apartment only reached their voice mail message; Hostetter didn't have a phone. It was Wednesday night when the cell phone chirped, and it was Jenny. As soon as she was sure it was me on the line, she handed the phone to Hank.

"You're where??" I shouted a minute later. "Montreal? Canada? Jesus."

Hank spoke fast. He said he and Jenny had talked late into the night after he got home from the diner; much of their talk was about their baby, and its future. And when they woke up the next morning, Friday, they both knew what they had to do. Hank had the weekend off; he didn't have to report for final pre-deployment processing until Monday.

As soon as it was dark, they stuffed their most precious and useful belongings into their old Honda, left the rest behind, and headed northwest: first to Jenny's folks in Asheville, in western North Carolina, and then angling northwest through Ohio, to Detroit. There they crossed the border to Windsor Ontario early Sunday morning. Bleary-eyed but otherwise looking like any of the thousands of tourists that head for the big casino there every day, they were out of the country before the army ever knew they were gone.

"Montreal is great," Hank said. "The signs here are all in French; but people mostly know English."

"Yeah," I said, "merci beaucoup. But what are you going to do?"

"Glad you mentioned that," he said. "I think we need some help. Do you have Jonah Lapp's number handy?"

Two hours later, Jonah called. "Meet me at the diner at 5," was all he said, and before I could ask what for, he was gone.

He sat in the same booth, sipping lemonade again, but sweat was shining on his red forehead under the pushed-back straw hat. I said, "have you heard from Hank?" but he held up his hand, shook his head, and instead asked if I knew anything about a theologian named Jacques Ellul.

"Who?" I asked. What did this have to do anything?

"Ellul was French," Jonah said. "One of the best minds of the last century. He did especially fine work in a paper on Acts 5:29. You ought to read it sometime."

What the hell is he talking about, I wondered, feeling irritated. Did he really get me all the way up here on a moment's notice to talk about some theologian I've never heard of?

But as he said this, Jonah pushed a folded piece of paper across the table toward me, and then gestured for me to stuff it in my shirt pocket. "Let's have a cheeseburger," he said. "And can you buy this time?"

Headed home an hour later, I pulled into a gas station and opened the piece of paper. On it was a phone number with a 514 area code, the name "Moses," and the sentence, "Ask him about translating the paper by Jacques Ellul on Acts 5:29." That was all.

As soon as I walked through the door at Quaker House, I went to my desk and opened the phone book: as I expected, the 514 area code was for Montreal. Then I pulled a Bible from the shelf, and looked up the verse, Acts 5:29:

"But Peter and the apostles answered, 'We must obey God rather than man.'"

I closed the book. It made sense now. The note and the verse were code: a signal to someone in Montreal, who might or might not be named Moses, or maybe Jacques, to help Hank and Jenny find a place to land in Canada. Jonah was old enough to have friends who went up there in the Vietnam years to dodge the draft. Maybe he even helped smuggle them over the border, and still had contacts with sympathetic Canadians.

All this was guesswork, as it was meant to be. The only thing I knew for sure was a phone number in area code 514; and fortunately, I have a bad memory for numbers.

Jenny called not long afterward. I read her what Lapp had written. She thanked me and quickly rang off. Then I tore up the note, and flushed the pieces down the toilet.

The next time I heard from them, Hank had found a lawyer and had asked the Canadian government for refugee status. "It's a long shot," he admitted. "They say the US is a democratic country, abides by human rights and international laws, doesn't persecute its citizens, so Americans don't have to be refugees, and they don't give us refugee status."

"The US, Law abiding?" I shouted. "Except for an occasional illegal war, eh?"

Well, no use venting at Hank about it; after all, once upon a time the Canadian policy had been pretty much correct. "So what will you do when they decide you can't stay?" My voice was tight, nervous. If he was deported back to the states, the MPs would be waiting for him at the border, handcuffs jingling.

Hank was either nonchalant, or faking it very well. "Then we'll try Sweden, or somewhere else," he said.

Christ, I thought. That thin northern air has made him light-headed. He and Jenny will be international homeless persons; hell, they already are. But at least he's safe for now; nobody's trying to blow him up with a car bomb.

The first email from Hostetter came a couple weeks later. It was short. "Hey," it read, "I figured I'll play the odds, keep my head down and get through this, grab the college money. So far, so good, we're mostly in camp out in the desert; can't say where, but at least it isn't Baghdad. Did I mention that the desert sucks? What's up with Hank?"

That had been it, til the second one, which I had repeated to Hank as the phone connection faded.

I spied the morning paper, on the dining table where I dropped it. I pulled off the plastic wrapper and unfolded it.

The headline was below the fold, only two columns wide: "504th paratrooper is latest Bragg casualty in Iraq roadside bomb attack." There was a small head shot, but my eyes slid past it to focus on a single word in the lead paragraph: Hostetter.

I dropped into a chair as if someone had punched me in the stomach, hunched over, eyes closed, head in my hands. I felt out of breath.

The phone rang. It was Hank, I knew it, trying the connection again.

I opened my eyes long enough to see the name again, and focus for a second on the photo.

And I let the phone ring; the voicemail would get it.

I'll call Hank back tomorrow, I thought. Or maybe next week. Let him sit with baby John, and Jenny, and the intoxicating northern air in peace for a few more days. And I'll have to call Jonah Lapp too.

But now, it was almost time for the vigil, and before leaving I had to revise the number in the "This Week" list again.

I have a poor memory for numbers, but this was one update I'd remember: changing it from 997 to 998.

Comfort Food

The large sign in the lawn in front of the old red brick building read:

"U.S. MARINE CORPS, CAMP ELIZABETH BRIG.
NO PHOTOGRAPHS ALLOWED."

I stopped the car right in front of it, rolled down the window, slipped the digital camera from my pocket and took a couple of quick pictures. I hoped they'd also show the razor wire coiled along the edges of the tall fence around one end of the building. A few of the blades flashed in the late winter sunlight, the only bright color in the scene..

What, I wondered, would happen to all that wire when the battle of Armageddon began? Would it melt? Would one of the brick walls crumble so the prisoners could walk out and join in the struggle? These were questions that Steve Colt, the marine I'd come to visit, could answer for me.

Taking those illicit pictures was one of only two infractions of the Brig's many jailhouse rules that I allowed myself, however. The camera stayed in the car, along with all the coins, cell phone, and almost everything else in my pockets, except my driver's license and car keys.

Inside, the guard who signed me in took these and hung them on a small hook, in trade for a large plastic Visitors pass to clip on my shirt. Then he waved me through the airport-style metal detector, and I joined the line to pass through the two big metal doors into the cell block.

Standing in line, I knew I'd gotten away again with my other rules violation – in my pants pocket was a small all-plastic ball point pen, a model the metal detector didn't notice. With it I could scribble a brief note if necessary, to hang on to some key bit of information from a prisoner, that was otherwise too easily forgotten. No notebooks were permitted, so I usually wrote these notes on my upper forearm, where a shirtsleeve would cover them.

Otherwise, I was a model brig visitor, never complaining about their endless rules, always dressing as respectably as I ever do, and calling all the guards "Sir."

The word sprang to my lips again when Chaplain Eckerd came out of the big barred door and nodded at me. "Afternoon, sir," I barked.

I had met Eckerd at Steve Colt's conscientious objector hearing four months earlier, where Eckerd was supposed to sit as an impartial witness, but had come across more like a prosecutor. The chaplain clearly didn't think much of Steve Colt and the Church of the Lamb Triumphant that he'd joined.

Not that I thought much of it either, really. Its doctrines seemed like a mishmash of apocalyptic fundamentalism, with a generous dose of cultist paranoia stirred in. They actually insisted that they weren't regular religious pacifists, because they were willing to fight for Jesus, the Lamb of God, when he came back to win the battle of Armageddon against Satan and his demonic armies.

That battle, they were sure, was coming very soon, and they were the True Witnesses to this truth. In the meantime, while they could join an army, they couldn't fight for any country or human government. So when Steve converted, he asked the marines for a noncombatant job. And he called us for advice.

"I'm not afraid of danger or death," his letter had said.

"I'm willing to go to Iraq, and clear mines or do whatever other hazardous work my superiors may direct," he had told the hearing officer, a captain. I was sitting beside him as his representative, something like a lawyer.

"But you won't carry a rifle," said the captain, while Chaplain Eckerd had looked on skeptically.

"Sir," Steve had said, "my church teaches that I can't carry a weapon or kill anyone for any human authority. Only at the direct command of Jesus Christ, when He returns as the Lamb Triumphant, can I take up arms."

Eckerd had spoken then. "What about Romans 13?" he asked, pulling out the warrior's favorite Bible passage, about how the state is God's designated enforcer, bearing the sword as a terror to evildoers.

But Steve was ready. "Sir," he had said, "that passage applies in normal times, when the world is rightly ordered. But in these last days, the world is under the power of Satan, including its human governments. So Romans 13 gives way to Revelation 13, where the beast 666 is revealed as Mystery Babylon. They're all under the anti-Christ, and doomed to fall at Armageddon."

At this the captain had glanced over at Eckerd.. The chaplain had said nothing, but frowned and shook his head.

Then the captain had looked at me. "Do you all at Quaker House support this kind of thing?" he had asked.

I was ready too. "Sir," I had said evenly, "we support conscience.

And I believe Lance Corporal Colt is sincere in his conscientious beliefs."

The captain was not impressed.

A week later the marines rejected Steve's request. The company commander ordered him to report for weapons training with his rifle. Steve snapped to attention, saluted smartly, then quietly refused.

And so here he was, spending a year behind those big clanging metal doors. Jail didn't seem to bother Steve much. He evidently regarded the brig as one large church meeting, and lost no opportunity to preach his end-times gospel among the two hundred other inmates. After three months inside, he admitted that he hadn't made any actual converts yet. But many were listening, he insisted to me, and at least one new prisoner seemed to be seriously considering joining up.

The big door rattled open again, and it was my turn to go through, wait for the second door to buzz and swing back, and then I was inside.

A long hallway was to my left, down to the open bays where the prisoners slept, unless they were being held in one of the isolation cells. A door almost directly across from me opened into the brig cafeteria. There prisoners in orange or gray jumpsuits huddled with visitors around large metal picnic style tables that were bolted to the floor.

Steve was already there, his tall lean figure unmistakable even among the anonymous jail outfits. And he wasn't alone. His pastor Jose was there, along with two large church ladies, dressed in their Sunday best. The pastor was talking. Steve grinned and waved an arm when he saw me. I shook hands all around and sat down.

After the usual pleasantries, and the standard questions about how he was doing, were the guards treating him okay and such, Steve said Jose had been giving them a lesson, and I listened.

Jose was slender and intense, with wire spectacles giving his boyish face a scholarly aspect. He spoke intently, urgently, befitting his subject. He was on message as always, explaining how the war in Iraq, which he said was soon to spread, had been foretold in the Bible, and was really the work of Satan loose in the world. Presidents, prime ministers, generals and terrorists only thought they were in charge, he insisted, mentioning verses from the books of Daniel, Ezekiel and Revelation, in rapid-fire sequence.

I couldn't keep up with his Bible quotes, but the general outline was familiar by now. When he repeated the punch line that all these "wars and rumors of war" were signs of Armageddon approaching, both Steve and the two ladies nodded vigorously. And I did too, a little. From inside this place, Jose's dire forecast didn't seem nearly as implausible as it did outside.

Jose had moved on to talk of "the abomination of desolation," when Steve interrupted. Leaning toward me, he spoke in a low tone.

"There's been a sign of this right here in the brig," he said, and tapped the table with a long finger. Glancing down, I saw he was pointing to my left, but with his hand on the table, so the gesture wouldn't be noticed outside our group. "Yes," he whispered. "Over there."

The others seemed to know who he was referring to and didn't move. So I moved slowly around, bending to scratch an imaginary itch, and scanned the room.

Two tables over, a prisoner sat silently while two women wearing scarves grasped his hands. They weren't speaking, but I could see tears glistening on their cheeks, and then the one nearest me lifted a hand to wipe her eyes.

"It's Rashid," Steve whispered. "He's in my unit. His bunk is right next to mine." I scratched again, and saw that Rashid sat stiffly, his face expressionless, hardly seeming to notice the sobbing women.

Now Jose picked up the story. "He can hardly sleep at night, so he tells Steve things when he's laying awake. Rashid's an American Muslim, a Marine. But in Iraq they suspected him of being a spy for al Queda." His voice dropped to a whisper. "He was arrested and taken to Abu Ghraib prison. Tortured in ways that left no marks – no sleep, blindfolded all the time, loud music while they made him stand all night. They even brought in dogs."

"The terrorists in Iraq do the same things to their prisoners," Steve said, "or worse. Both sides act crazy. That's how we know it's all satanic. And Rashid told me the guards there enjoyed it. The worst one was a sergeant they called Shorty. When they heard the other guards say Shorty was coming, he knew it was about to get really bad."

"But wait a minute," I objected. "If they think he's a spy, why is he sitting there, instead of in the isolation cells, or at Guantanamo, or some secret prison?"

Jose raised a finger. "That's the thing," he said. "Rashid is on his way out. Sure, he confessed to all kinds of things in Abu Ghraib. Who wouldn't? But his family hired a good lawyer, who raised cain and proved he wasn't a spy. So they dropped all the charges. Rashid is just here waiting for his final paperwork. He's one of the lucky ones."

"Yeah, lucky," Steve sounded sarcastic. "But he's been here three weeks, and his paperwork still hasn't come through."

"Wow," I said. "They owe him an apology. At least."

Steve snickered. "The marines don't apologize.'Suck it up and drive on,' that's their motto. Anyway, Rashid doesn't need an apology. He needs somebody to give him back his life, his sanity. That's what the torture took from him." He looked at me, his normally open face suddenly grim. "And where does he go to get that?"

Jose glanced at his watch; visiting time was running out. "What we can do for Rashid right now is to offer prayer," he said. "Ask God to ease Rashid's suffering, and to give us the courage to be True Witnesses when the hour comes, which won't be long." He looked down and closed his eyes. "Let us join hands and pray," he intoned.

The others followed suit, with some shuffling of legs under the big table. I reached for Steve's hand, and gazed down at the table. While Jose murmured I stole another glance at Rashid. He was still there, slumped back in the chair now. The women were speaking now, but he didn't seem to notice.

As I came out of the second big door, eager to retrieve my car keys and escape into the "free world" again, Chaplain Eckerd was there, and he pointed at me. "Fager," he said, "can I see you a minute?"

I followed him across the waiting room, down a hall to a small office. The chaplain pointed at a file on his desk. "I know you work with a lot of men who are in trouble," he said, "and I'd like your perspective on a new case I've got. Strictly unofficial, of course."

I shrugged. "I'm no therapist," I said. "So my opinion is worth every penny you paid for it."

Eckerd was leafing through the file,. Then he stood up, walked around the desk and behind me. As I turned he opened what looked like a closet door and walked in, beckoning me to follow.

It wasn't a closet, but rather a small darkened booth, with a large window in the wall, ad two folding chairs. On the other side, a prisoner in a gray jumpsuit sat at a table, listening as a sergeant talked and looked through another file folder. Their voices were just barely audible through an unseen speaker, and I couldn't make out what they were saying.

"His name is Atkins," the chaplain said quietly. "He was on deployment in Iraq when they picked him up. MPs found enough Oxy-Contin in his duffel bag to keep his whole company stoned for a week. He's up on intent to sell, and could get some hard time."

"What's his version?" I asked.

"He says he wasn't going to sell it. He planned to take it all, to kill himself."

"What for?"

The chaplain gave me a sidelong glance. "He was an interrogator. Abu Ghraib and some other places. Says he has nightmares that won't stop, especially about the coercive interrogation sessions–"

I interrupted. "Don't you mean torture?" Military jargon like that offends me. "That's what ought to be a crime."

Eckerd grimaced; I suspected he didn't entirely disagree. "Maybe it should be a crime," he said, "but it isn't. It's war. It's just what happens. Plenty of guys in here have done the same things, or worse. But that's not why they're here. At least not directly."

I wanted to argue, but stopped myself. This wasn't the time or place. "What do you want my opinion about?" I said.

Eckerd peered through the glass. "Is Atkins safe to put in the

478

general population? He's been in isolation for two weeks and he wants out. No history of violence, but we were worried he might harm himself. I'm ready to recommend it, but I wanted an outside perspective. Again, strictly off the record." He reached for a knob under the window and turned up the sound.

"– One more question," the sergeant was saying. "Where did you get the Oxy-Contin?"

The prisoner sighed. His eyes were deep-set, almost sunken. His skin was pale. "I've already answered this a dozen times," he said. "I made friends with the medic, figured out the combination to the door, then snuck into the supply room when he was at chow."

The sergeant slapped the file folder shut and stood up. "Okay, I think we're done here," he said. He glanced over his shoulder. "Corporal, take this prisoner back to his cell."

A burly marine stepped up behind him. Beside me, chaplain Eckerd leaned forward and spoke into a microphone I hadn't noticed in the dark, his finger on a button. "Sergeant," he barked, "I think he can go to the open bays now. Collect his gear and move him down there."

The sergeant stiffened at this disembodied voice. "Yes sir," he said, not looking at the window. Then he left the room.

The guard stayed behind. As the prisoner stood up, showing shackled wrists, a phone rang in Eckerd's office, and he got up. The guard put a hand on Atkins' shoulder. His grip was firm, it seemed to me, but not unfriendly. "Come on, Shorty," he said.. "You've been promoted."

"Wait!" I said, jumping up from my chair. But Eckerd wasn't there, and the microphone was off again. I hurried into the office and started to speak.

But Eckerd was on the phone. "That's right, sir," he said. Tomorrow morning–"

"Chaplain," I said, trying to get his attention. But he only glanced up at me briefly. Covering the phone, he said, 'Thanks, Fager," and then was focused again on the phone.

I sighed and left. "Shorty." Did it mean anything? What could I do if it did? Lots of guys in here have done worse, the chaplain had said.

It was a relief to be back in my car, headed for the main gate. And maybe I was a bit eager to be back on a civilian highway, headed home, so my foot was a bit heavy on the gas pedal, pushing the camp Elizabeth speed limit.

At least, that's what I figured when a glance in the rear view showed an MP jeep on my tail, blue lights flashing. "Oh no," I breathed. Not another ticket!"

But that wasn't it. When the MP came back from checking my drivers license his tone was apologetic, but definite. "Sir, I have to ask you to come with me."

"What?" I said. "Am I under arrest?"

"No, sir," he said. "Not yet. But you will be if you don't come voluntarily."

"Give me a minute," I pleaded, flipping open the cell phone. But Wendy didn't answer, so I left a frantic message, locked the car door, and followed the MP back to his jeep.

But we didn't go to a police station; the jeep headed straight back to the brig. A guard met the MP at the door, and the two of them escorted me down the office hall and around a couple corners, then through a door.

When the guard flipped the light switch, I gasped. It was the same interrogation room I'd been watching with the chaplain less than an hour before. The large window in the wall was dark. Who was watching me now?

"What's this about?" I demanded. The chaplain came in a moment later. His face was grave.

"The prisoner you saw here, Atkins, was attacked and stabbed in the hallway, not fifteen minutes ago," he said.

"What?!" I shouted. "What happened?"

"The other prisoners in the area were told to stand facing the hallway wall. That's procedure when a new prisoner comes in. But then one of them, Private Colt–"

"–Steve?" I asked.

"Yes," Eckerd went on. "Private Colt began shouting something about the True Witnesses, then turned and jumped on Atkins. He had a plastic shank, a homemade knife, and stuck him bad."

"Is he–" I started.

"The ambulance took him, and I don't know. Atkins was still alive when they left, but in pretty bad shape."

"That's awful," I said, still taking it in. "But what's it got to do with me?"

"You visited Colt today," Eckerd said.

I nodded, but it wasn't a question. Then it dawned on me. "You really don't think I gave him that knife?"

Eckerd was grim. "Somebody did. We don't have that kind of plastic here. And it wouldn't set off the metal detector. So a visitor brought it in and slipped it to him." He was staring straight at me. "Maybe you," he said.

"Me?! Are you–?"

The door banged open, and pastor Jose barged in, accompanied by another MP. He looked at once distraught and triumphant. "Is Steve all right?" he asked.

A guard came in behind him. "Sir," he said, "we have a fingerprint match for the knife. Got them off the Visitor pass."

When Eckerd did not reply, I realized the guard was talking past

480

him, to the darkened window. A deep voice came through the microphone: "Take him," it said.

A flash of terror cut through me. I stiffened, expecting a blow.

But the guard grabbed pastor Jose, and as his hands were being twisted behind him, he began to shout.

"Yes! I gave it to him. Torture is the sure sign of the beast's work, and it's right here. It's time for the True Witnesses of the Lamb to appear and begin the battle. I'm proud of Steve! I'm proud to be his teacher and fellow soldier! The lamb will be Triumphant!" Then they were dragging him out of the room.

An hour later they let me leave the brig, after the chaplain had filled in some missing links: The guard taking Atkins to the open unit had been deployed with him in Iraq, and knew his nickname was Shorty. He called him that while they were coming down the hallway.

"But how did the pastor know Shorty was here?"

"The guard's girlfriend had been attending services at the Lamb Triumphant church," Eckerd said. "One night after too many beers, the guard got to talking about Iraq, and let Shorty's story slip. She told the pastor, who heard it as a divine revelation, and gave Steve his orders from on high. The mixture of Armageddon preaching and Rashid's sleepless stories was too much for both of them."

I had a splitting headache. A quiet visit to a guy doing time for refusing to fight in a war. That's all I'd bargained for when I'd left home that morning. It seemed a long time ago.

The chaplain's phone rang again.

"One last question," I said.

He picked up the phone, said into it, "Hang on a minute," and gazed back at me, waiting.

"Those pills that Atkins had, " I said. "Oxy-Contins. Do you think he was really going to sell them? Or take them?"

Eckerd rubbed his chin and considered for a moment. Then he shook his head. "Atkins wasn't selling anything," he said. "He just wanted to take enough pills to make sure. I've seen it before."

He considered for another moment. "Like I said," he added, "it's not a crime, what he did in Iraq. But maybe it should be."

As soon as my car passed through the camp Elizabeth main gate, I started to tremble. The shaking kept up for twenty miles through the scrub pines and small towns. Finally I pulled into a McDonald's parking lot, turned off the ignition and just leaned back and let the trembling go through me.

It went on for another ten minutes, til my cell phone tinkled with Wendy's ring. "Hey, are you all right, honey?" she asked. "It sounded like you were getting arrested."

I wasn't sure she'd believe it. But as I repeated the story, the shakes diminished. By the time I rang off, I was able to get out of the car and walk a more or less straight line into the McDonalds men's room.

And then I couldn't hold back – I ordered a double quarter pounder with cheeses, supersize fries and two cherry pies, and wolfed down the whole god-awful mess.

As comfort food, it was pretty gross. But it beat a bottle of Oxy-Contin.

I Hate Dill Pickles

July 2007

Sara Rahman was my best friend then. And some of the best times we had were while walking home from school. We joked and laughed about everything – stuff in school, books she was reading, her dorky big brother Ahmed, even some of the sillier songs from "American Idol."

Maybe we were having too much fun. Maybe we shouldn't have gone running up to the ice cream truck that came jangling by and pulled over to the curb. But it was a warm spring Thursday, and Sara had five dollars in her pocket, a pre-birthday present from her aunt, and she loved ice cream. "Especially butter pecan," she said. "That's my very favorite."

So we did stop at the ice cream truck. No butter pecan, but they did have big cones of cookies and cream, so Sara got one of those, and bought me an Eskimo pie.

The Eskimo pie was good, but Sara's cone must have been better. Not only was it sweet and cold, but by the time we turned onto Hillside, our street, it had taken on an extra identity as a karaoke microphone. She was acting out one of the more outlandish American Idol numbers – I can't remember now if it was Haley or Sanjaya – singing into the melting ice cream and sashaying down the sidewalk.

"Watch this, Amber," Sara said, building up to a big finish. She whirled around and threw her arms out in a wide flourish. And when she did, the scoop of soft cookies and cream flew right off the top of the cone and landed splat! right on the side window of a parked white van.

Sara heard the splat and stopped to look, and we both saw a long white drip sliding down the dark glass. She turned to me, eyes wide, mouth open, ready to start giggling.

But then the van's window rolled down several inches, and a man in dark sunglasses looked out at us. "Hey, young lady," he said, "better be careful with that stuff."

Now instead of giggling, Sara squealed and we both turned and ran down the block, all the way to where our houses faced each other across the street. When we got to her place I stopped and glanced back,

483

and the van's window was closed again. We both stood by her porch for a minute, giggling and laughing and trying to catch our breath. Finally Sara said, "That was wild!"

"Yeah," I said, "if Sanjaya had tried that, he would have won for sure!"

She laughed, but before she could answer the front door banged open behind her. "Sara!" came a male voice.

It was her brother Ahmed, Mister dorkiness himself, a book in one hand: tall, skinny, clunky black-rimmed glasses. So what if he was super-smart? So what if he was going to Harvard, or at least Duke, for college? So what if he was always carrying the Quran and going off to pray? "Hurry up!" he said. "It's time to get ready to go to the center, and you've still got chores to do."

"What about YOUR chores?" Sara retorted. Did you take the trash out yet?"

"None of your business," he said. "Come on – you're going to make us late."

"All right, all right," Sara said over her shoulder, as he went back in.

"Hey," I whispered, "maybe it's better that men and women sit separately at your mosque. It means you can be far away from HIM."

Sara rolled her eyes and shrugged. "Oh, never mind Ahmed," she said.

"And why didn't you tell me about having to take off our shoes and sit on the floor there?" I said.

"There was a hole in my sock that day I visited."

"I forgot," she admitted. "But don't worry about that – nobody notices." Then she took my hand and gave me a serious look. "You'll be here Saturday for the party," she said. "Promise?" Her eyes dropped. "I think some of the girls at school are still a little –you know, weird about Muslims."

"I'll be there," I said. "But tell me something: are you going to start wearing that scarf then, like your mother, when you're twelve?"

She shook her head. "Nope, I'm not ready for the hijab. In fact, I haven't decided if I'm going to wear it at all. Muslim women don't all have to dress alike."

"Good," I said. "I like you better this way." I turned to go. "But hey – be careful with the ice cream at the party, okay? See ya!"

She giggled and waved. "I will. Two o-clock sharp!"

When I got to our side of the street, I reached out and brushed my fingers against the big old oak tree that stood at the end of our driveway. It was a reflex: I'd been doing that since I was little. This was my favorite tree, huge, old and gnarly, the bark all spotted with pale green lichens. It seemed to stand guard over our house and the whole block.

At home, Mother insisted I dig into homework before anything else, and there was a lot of it. I have a big brother too, Allen; but fortunately he's already at college, at Guilford, so I don't have to put up with him much.

But there's a downside of that too: it means I have more chores to do around the house. After dinner, my folks let me watch a video before getting back to homework. The last assignment on my list was to look up stuff for my big English paper. I was doing it on Islam, because it meant I could ask Sara and her mom more questions. But I had to have stuff from articles and books too.

I was still trying to figure out how to describe the difference between Sunnis, Shias, and Sufis when dad tapped on the door to my room. "Amber," he said, "the trash needs to go out."

I had completely forgotten. The trash truck came by early the next morning, and our big trash barrel on wheels had to be full and rolled out to the curb. "Okay, Dad," I said, and left the computer, headed for the kitchen to collect the first of the wastebaskets.

About ten minutes later, outside the back door, I dumped the last plastic bag into the trash barrel and started rolling it around to the driveway. It was just about completely dark now, but I knew the way with my eyes closed. The driveway ran into the street just past the big oak, and I parked the trash barrel right in front of it.

Brushing my hands, I heard a rolling noise somewhere behind me. I glanced around, and saw a figure pushing a similar trash barrel down Sara's driveway. Squinting, I could see it was Ahmed; maybe he'd forgotten too. I headed back toward the house.

Behind me a car's brakes squeaked, and a door slammed. I looked around again, and saw the white van, its side door open, stopped in front of Sara's. Three men hopped out of it, and even in the darkness I could see that they were wearing gloves and some kind of black masks.

Without thinking, I stepped behind the trunk of the big oak, held my breath, and then peeked carefully around it.

The men had grabbed Ahmed. The trash barrel was knocked on its side on the grass,, as one man clapped a hand over his mouth, another held his hands behind his back, and the third lifted his feet into the air. They obviously knew what they were doing.

Ahmed was squirming, but the men were strong and he could barely move, and there was no sound. In just a few seconds, the men had expertly folded his wriggling form into the van, two of them sliding in behind him. The big side door slid shut with a quiet thump, as the third man hopped into the driver's seat. Then the van sped off toward the corner, and into the night, its lights off.

The whole thing had only taken a few seconds, and no one had noticed me behind the tree. I stumbled back to the house in a kind of daze, and all I could think was: there was still an ice cream smudge on the van's window where the ice cream had landed.

My dad works for the police department. He's not a cop with a gun and uniform; he sits at a desk, doing something they call community relations. So I went to him first. He was watching baseball on TV. I must have looked strange, because he frowned when he saw me. "What's the matter, honey?" he asked

"I – they – these men– "I began, in a hoarse kind of whisper. "They – took Ahmed, they – " And then I began to cry.

Somehow I thought that when Dad went to call the office, there would soon be police cars crowded into Hillside Avenue, police radios buzzing and blue lights flashing in the shadows. But nothing like that happened. He did go across the street to talk to Sara's folks, but that was all very quiet, and I couldn't see anything through the living room window.

When he came back, I was still full of questions. "Is Sara okay?" was the first one. Dad nodded at that. But he raised a warning hand when I asked about Ahmed, and then said, more gruffly than I expected, "Amber, you need to get to bed. Don't worry, things will be all right. Go on now."

Mom spoke up. "But, George–" she started, and I could hear questions in her tone. But Dad shushed her and pointed toward their bedroom.

They closed the door, and I made a detour into the bathroom. Pretending to brush my teeth, I leaned up against the wall that faced their room, trying to listen.

I only made out a few words. "NOT kidnaped," I heard Dad insist, over Mom's murmur. "No, he was TAKEN. Different. This wasn't some random thing, Helen. They know what they're doing." Then more murmurs from Mom – I couldn't make out the words, but could hear worry, maybe even fear in her voice. Then Dad again: "Our job, Helen, is to go on as usual. We're not doing anything wrong, so we have nothing to worry about."

There was the sound of motion – one of them was coming toward the bathroom! Quickly I turned the faucet on, then flushed the toilet, went into my room, and got into bed.

I laid awake a long time, staring into the night.

The next morning, Sara didn't stop by so we could walk to school as usual. I saw her car pull out of the driveway, and guessed her mom was taking her. At school she was very quiet, and so was I.

Worse yet, by lunchtime, the rumor was spreading around the cafeteria that Ahmed had been picked up as a spy or a terrorist.

How could they have heard this, I wondered? But Kimberly from my home room whispered it all in the girl's bathroom: Sara's mom went to the office to say that Ahmed would be absent for awhile, and somebody in the office got suspicious and called a friend in the police department, who repeated what Dad had said about how "they" knew what they were doing. From there it spread like brushfire.

I walked home alone that afternoon. When I got to the house, mom was on the phone. And while I dawdled in the kitchen over a snack, it rang twice more. Mom took the phone into the living room, but I soon realized she was saying some of the same things each time. "Yes, yes, I understand. I'm sure it's hard for them, but we don't want trouble either." She listened, then sighed. "What I'd like is for things to just be as normal as they can be."

I was trying to focus on homework, and wondering if I should change the subject of my English paper, when Mom tapped on the bedroom door. "Honey," she said, "I'm heading to the market. Can you come along?" I was ready for a distraction.

Mother drove silently. But when we were looking over the stacks of packaged strawberries and heaps of apples, the feel of the fruit seemed to open her up. "I'm afraid a lot of parents are worried about having their kids go to Sara's party," she said.

"Oh, mom," I said. "That's awful."

She wouldn't look at me. "They're concerned," she said, lifting a large tomato, and gazing at it as if it was made of gold. "I guess I am too." She put down the tomato and picked up another one.

"Mom," I said, "are you telling me not to go?"

She didn't answer right away. Pushing the cart down a crowded aisle, she plucked cans of soup from a shelf, and searched for her favorite kind of whole grain instant oatmeal. Finally she said, "Amber, I know that Sara has been your best friend . . ." and then trailed off.

"Has been?" I said. "Can't she be anymore? What's happened, mom?"

Mom frowned, and examined the label on a bottle of low-sodium tomato juice. I knew perfectly well that she had seen this label a million times before.

"We just —" she started, "— we just want things to get back to normal. Can't you see that?"

I picked up a jar of dill pickles. I hate dill pickles, but needed to look at something too. "Have you said this to Mrs. Rahman?" I asked.

"Not yet."

I put down the pickle jar. "Good," I said. "Let me tell her. And"

I walked down the aisle and turned toward the frozen food section "I want to get something."

Saturday afternoon, two o-clock came and went. Dad was at the office; some kind of a meeting, he said. Mom had been reading, a mystery novel, I think. Watching from the side window out across the street, I saw that no cars stopped to drop off kids at the Rahman's house.

When I tiptoed into the living room at twenty after, Mom had fallen asleep.

That was my chance. Retreating to the kitchen, I made a stop at the refrigerator, then was silently out the back door, and down the driveway. At the curb I brushed my fingers along the rough bark of the big oak tree before crossing the street.

Mrs. Rahman answered the door, and smiled at me. "I'll get Sara," she said.

Then Sara was there. I held up a plastic bag, which had a film of condensation on the outside. "It's butter pecan," I said. "Happy birthday."

"Thank you," said Sara. She was wearing a hijab.

Superman in Shannon

Ed Connolly lifted the binoculars to his eyes, and leaned against the airport fence.

"I did a lot of this in Sinai," he said. "Kosovo too." He moved an inch to the right, so the lenses fit between the heavy fencing.

He was watching a medium size jet taxi toward the refueling dock. Through the smaller binoculars he'd loaned me, I could see the words "Evergreen International" painted on its side.

"Can you read the numbers?" Ed asked.

I squinted. The binoculars seemed to shake and tremble in my hands, jerking the plane's image up and down, no matter how hard I tried not to move. "I can make out the N," I said, "and then, let's see . . ."

I held my breath. For a brief moment, the lenses obeyed, and the numbers came into focus.

"Yes!" I shouted. "It's N-2-2-4-6-E-V." The lenses were jiggling again by the time I got all the numbers out, and the motion started to make me feel dizzy. I glanced away from the plane, at Ed.

He already had the cellphone at his ear, talking to his friend Thomas. "Can you check them now?" he said, then listened. His dark brows were furrowed under salt-and-pepper hair.

He turned in my direction, started to speak, but was stopped by something he heard. "Yes?" he said to Thomas. "That's it! I knew it. Thanks."

"What?" I asked.

"Just what we figured," Ed said. "That plane is CIA. Probably carrying cargo for one of its secret prisons. I think it's been here before. Come on." He headed for his car.

The Shannon International airport is in southwest Ireland, on the edge of the Shannon Estuary, a broad riverbed that meets the Atlantic a few dozen kilometers away.

I had read that early transatlantic airliners called Flying Boats used to splash down gracefully on these waters after their long haul across the ocean from America. I wanted to hear more about that, and other local history. In fact, we were supposed to be headed for lunch and a good long, get-acquainted chat. I especially wanted him to help me sort out some of the unpronounceable-looking Gaelic names that were under the English

489

on all the Irish road signs.

But Ed couldn't leave the airport without doing a bit of plane-spotting first. He'd been doing that ever since the Iraq war started, he said, and couldn't stop today.

And now Ed Connolly, who was as proud an Irishman as you'd want to meet, wasn't interested in talking about history, or Gaelic signs. As we got to his car another large jet skimmed down to the runway beyond us. Puffs of white smoke squirted from its wheels as they scraped the runway.

I craned my neck to follow it, but Ed shook his head. "It's just another Ryanair passenger run, like the one you came in on," he said. "We've got other business."

"I guess so," I said, watching an airport police car pulling to a stop a few yards from us. "We sure do."

Of course, Ed was parked illegally. He'd pulled over at this spot to get a better view of the taxiing Evergreen plane. I knew he'd been arrested several times here, protesting CIA flights in and out of Shannon.

Watching the uniformed cop climbing out of the patrol car made me nervous; I wasn't in Ireland to cause trouble. My mission was to give a talk about working for peace, at the Limerick Friends Meeting, and maybe do a little sightseeing. Talking, looking, taking it easy for a day or two. That was all. Getting arrested, especially as a foreigner, was not on the schedule.

But Ed was completely unintimidated by the officer's approach. In fact, he walked right up to him and launched into a speech.

"Officer, that aircraft is violating Ireland's neutrality," he said. "It's carrying supplies and personnel for the illegal and immoral US war in Iraq. And it's probably taking weapons and cargo to support the torture of thousands of innocent people. Either that or a bunch of American soldiers on one of their secret missions."This is a human rights complaint," he said. "I insist you board and search the plane at once, and seize any unauthorized persons and unlawful war materiel."

The policeman was obviously familiar with Ed. He put up his hands, waved away the paper, and took a few steps backward, as if he was the one in trouble, while Ed continued to browbeat him.

Within a minute Ed was jabbing a finger, now at the officer and now toward the CIA airplane, and saying something about international treaties and the shameful corruption of Irish politicians who let this illegal, blood-soaked traffic continue.

"All right, Mr Connolly, all right then," the policeman said helplessly. I could see that he knew Ed's charges were probably correct – and that Ed also knew the Shannon Airport police were not about to do anything about them.

"Just could you just move your vehicle now," the cop added,

"so's it won't be disrupting any traffic. Please, Mr. Connolly?"

"Okay, okay," Ed said, yielding just a bit to the matter of local public safety. We were finished there anyway. He walked to the back of his weathered Toyota.

"But you go search that plane," he called after the retreating police car, and popped the trunk, to put away the big binoculars. I came up to hand him mine.

Glancing into the trunk, I saw what looked like a costume of some sort, dark green, with a round hat on top. "What's this?" I wondered.

"My army uniform," Ed said. "Just back from the cleaners." He slammed down the lid and we moved to the front seats. "Wore it for twenty-two years," he said, peering up into the rear-view mirror and backing the car onto the roadway.

"Really?" I was curious. "Where did you serve?"

He snorted. "Where didn't we? The Irish army sent peacekeepers to Lebanon, East Timor, even Cambodia." He shook his head. "I was called back just last year, to go to Chad, in Africa."

Now he squinted down the roadway ahead. "They call it peacekeeping," he said, "but don't kid yourself, it's dangerous. You have to be able to think fast and improvise."

His cell phone beeped. "I lost some good men out there," he finished, putting the phone to his ear.

"Yes, Thomas," he barked. Then he stepped on the brake, stopping the car dead in the center of the road to concentrate. "When?" A different kind of urgency crept into his tone.

"In the hotel? Now? Why do you need me? All right. Be right there." He flipped the phone shut.

"What's this?" I wondered.

"At the airport hotel," he said, pulling the Toyota into a U-turn. "We have an immigration issue to look into."

We sped past the police car, once more on its routine rounds, toward the main terminal and the motel just behind it. "We get a lot of undocumented people in here," he said, "and some of them are escaping from some pretty bad places. Thomas and I work with Amnesty International to get them refuge here."

"Is that what the call was about?"

He nodded. "Yes, but this one is something a bit different." He grinned at me. "I think you'll be interested in it."

Shannon, although it is an international crossroads, is not that big an airport. Its hotel was more like a medium sized motel you might drive past in any middling American town. It had two wings of two levels of rooms, with restaurant and bar in the middle. Maybe there was a pool and an exercise spa, but I didn't see them.

Ed jerked to a stop in the motel lot and then was out of the car almost on the run. He headed through the lounge, up the stairway and down the hall to its right, in the west wing. I had to hustle to keep up with him.

Near the end of the hallway, at room 223, he knocked quietly on the door, three times, then after a pause, three times more. The door opened.

I followed him in, and saw nothing more exotic than a young couple: the man was thin, his hair cut so short that his scalp gleamed. The woman, a brunette with a pretty face, marred by circles of fear around her eyes.

"Are you Thomas?" the youth asked Ed.

"Close enough," Ed said. "Thomas will be here shortly. He's on his way, and asked me to stay with you til he arrives."

The youth sat down on the bed. The woman followed and huddled against him.

"Tell me about it," Ed said.

"I'm Roman Jackson," the youth said. "Sergeant Jackson, United States Army. I did two tours in Iraq. Can't go back there again."

The woman looked up. "I won't let him," she said. Her voice was quiet, but there was steel in it.

"And you are?" Ed asked.

"Cynthia," she said. "We're married."

Jackson smiled a little at this. "Yeah," he said, "as of a week ago. Outside Ramstein."

He kept talking. I'd heard of Ramstein. It's a big U.S. base in the German Rhineland. Many U.S. soldiers are sent there for a two-week break in their Iraq combat tours.

"It's closer to Iraq than the US mainland," Cynthia put in, "and they figure the soldiers won't go AWOL from there, because it's a foreign country."

But it turned out that Cynthia knew some German, and had been saving money. "When I got word that Roman was headed there, I took a flight a week ahead and met him. I knew how he was feeling." She shrugged. "This war is stupid," she said, "it's not worth dying for. It was time to get out."

The plan she described was simple: Roman had four days of leave. They rented a car, drove from Germany across France, and took the Eurostar train from Paris to London. There they caught a cheap Ryanair flight, and were in Shannon before anyone in Ramstein noticed Roman was gone.

"And now – what?" Ed asked.

"Ireland's a neutral country," Jackson said. "We figure they'll let us stay here as refugees."

Cynthia shrugged again. "It was worth a shot," she said, trying to sound light-hearted. It didn't succeed; she was scared, if determined.

I was about to make a cynical wisecrack about Irish "neutrality," when more quiet knocks came at the door.

Ed opened it. "Thomas," he said.

Thomas turned out to be a tall gangly fellow with a bushy black beard and sparkling eyes. His face looked designed for smiles, but his expression was dead-serious. "Ed," he said, "we've got a problem. There are two American MPs here. They're going through the hotel. I think they're looking for –" he pointed. "Them. Or at least him."

Cynthia clutched at her husband, holding him tighter. "He's not going back," she said.

Ed was peering with narrowed eyes, first at them, then me, then Thomas. Thomas began to speak, but Ed help up a hand. "Thinking," he said.

We were all silent for what seemed like a long time, but was probably not more than ten or fifteen seconds.

"Right, then," Ed said finally. He turned first to the couple. "Sergeant Jackson, you and your wife stay here. Thomas, you and our guest here," he pointed at me, "your job is to find those MPs and slow them down. I'm going for help."

With that he strode out of the room, and we heard his feet clattering quickly down the stairwell at the end of the hall. I stood there for a moment, uncertain what to do.

Then Thomas grabbed my arm. "Come on," he said, "let's get busy." He hurried into the hall.

Walking quickly back toward the lounge, he stoppede to look down the hallways of each wing as we got to the central stairway. When he glanced to the east at the bottom, he stopped me with an elbow to my ribs.

Peering over his shoulder, I saw two uniformed men coming down the hall toward us, pausing to knock on room doors as they came. Thomas hesitated a moment, then straightened his shoulders and walked up to them.

"Excuse me, lads," he said, with a more pronounced Irish accent than before, "but I think the bloke you're looking for is in the gym. Either there or up in his room – Number 203 I believe he said."

"Excuse me?" said one of the MPs, who was half a head taller than the other.

Thomas smirked at him. "Now then," he said with a chuckle, "there's no secrets 'round here. I heard you were lookin' for some Yank. He's been here a couple o' days, he has. Got a gal with him; a fair lass she is too."

"What was that number?" the taller MP said. I saw a nametape with "Sampson" on it above his shirt pocket.

"203," I spoke up. "Or was it 201, Thomas? Anyway, he was in the gym a few minutes ago."

MP Sampson was scowling at me. "You an American?" he said, noting my accent.

"Yep," I said, "I'm Thomas's cousin. Come back here every year to visit the ancestral sod. I have many O'Briens in my lineage, and there are lots of them around here. In fact, Bunratty castle not far from here is an old O'Brien stronghold. Have you been there?"

MP Sampson shook his head, then turned to his partner. "You check the gym, Clark, and I'll go up to the room. Call me on the cell if you spot him."

He brushed past me, while the other MP strode toward the stairs at the far end of the east wing.

"'Well, 'cousin'," said Thomas, "how about you and me get another Guinness in the lounge?"

We did head for the lounge, but not to drink, taking up posts outside the door where we could watch the hallways. And before long the MP named Clark came hurrying back, talking on his cell. We stepped inside the lounge, just out of sight, as he went past.

"Sir," I heard him say, "the gym is closed for repairs. I think we're being flim-flammed. Second floor west? Right."

"We better get back up there," Thomas whispered, and we were soon clambering up the steps at the far end of the hallway.

But the MP s were ahead of us. Just as we came into the hallway they were knocking on 223, and the door swung open.

I saw Cynthia peeking through a crack. But the MP pushed her aside and went in. We crept forward, but didn't know what to do.

"Sergeant Roman Jackson," the MP said sternly, "I have a warrant here for your arrest, for unauthorized absence and attempted desertion." There was a rustle of paper. Then he said, "Surrender your passport, Jackson, and you too, Mrs. Jackson. Clark, get the restraining cuffs on him, and then go prepare the vehicle. Bring it to the side entrance."

I heard Clark say "Yes Sir," but then someone was brushing past me, shoving Thomas and me roughly aside.

"Excuse me, Lieutenant," said a loud voice, "I'll take those if you don't mind. And Sergeant Clark, I suggest you stay right there."

What the– ? I pushed in behind Thomas, just as the MP said, "Who the hell are you?"

"Commandant Connolly, Irish Army." It was Ed, in his dark-green uniform. But he also had a white leather belt across his chest, attached to a large holster, from which a pistol butt protruded. One of his hands was on the belt, right next to the pistol. In the other he held the two American passports.

Neither of the MPs, I now noticed, had a weapon.

Ed glanced at the passports, then stuffed them into a breast pocket and retrieved a sheet of paper. "Thank you for locating this man Jackson, er, Lieutenant –"

"Sampson," the MP said.

"Very good, Sampson. We've had a notice from Ramstein via Interpol about this fugitive, and instructions to take him in."

Now Thomas spoke up."But wait a minute," he protested, "you can't –"

Ed rounded on him, eyes flashing. "That's enough from you right there," he shouted, "you and your damned interfering Amnesty do-gooders. Another word from you and I'll run you in as well. This is a military matter."

He glared at Jackson. "As for you, young man, Ireland may be small and neutral. But we have a real army here, and we know the meaning of duty and discipline. We want nothing to do with deserters and malingerers."

"That's right," Sampson murmured approvingly.

At this Jackson slumped, and Cynthia began to cry.

Ed faced the MP lieutenant again, and handed him a card. "Sampson," he said, "my instructions are to convey this man to the Curragh Camp stockade, for initial processing. That shouldn't take more than twenty-four hours, and then we'll be ready to turn him over to your men."

"Curragh Camp," said Sampson. "Where's that?"

"Not far," Ed said, and picked up a phone book on the bedside table. He shoved it at Thomas. "There's detailed road maps in there, so why don't you make yourself useful for once, and show him where it is."

Thomas looked resentful, but started paging through the book. Sampson looked over his shoulder.

"The rest of you come along," Ed commanded. "You too," he said to me. "I want a word."

Once in the hallway, he pushed us toward the stairs, and hurried down.

"What's going on?" Roman asked."

"Just shut up and move!" Ed muttered.

His Toyota was there, illegally parked as usual, with the engine idling. The four of us filled it up, and Ed sped out of the parking lot, down the airport road, then veered to the right at the first intersection.

My eyes widened when I saw the "One way – Do Not Enter" sign, but it was only for a block or two, then he turned left and abruptly pulled into an empty lot surrounded by trees.

As soon as we stopped, Ed tossed his hat in the back. "What is this?" Roman asked. "Was that uniform a fake?"

"Never," Ed snapped. "It's as real as Ireland's neutrality is supposed to be. All," he added, "except this."

He pulled out the pistol, pointed it at the windshield, and pulled the trigger.

Cynthia started to scream, but all we heard was a tinny click.

"Plastic," Ed shrugged and tossed it in the back too. "Real guns are too dangerous for grown men to play with."

Twenty minutes later, we were on the N18 highway past Ennis, headed northwest. "As soon as we get to Galway," Ed was saying, "we'll file your applications for asylum. That will put a stop to Lieutenant Sampson's mischief.

"Do you think the government will let us stay?" Cynthia asked.

"There's a fair chance," Ed said. "Thomas and his Amnesty International friends have had good luck. But if they don't, we'll find you another place, in the European Union, or one of the other neutral countries."

His cell phone was beeping. "Thomas!" Ed said, "you were magnificent." He laughed. "And did you fix up our American friends there?" Another chuckle, and he said, "Good work. We'll see you in Galway, at the usual," and shut the phone.

Ed gave Roman and Cynthia a smile. "I think your Lieutenant Sampson is in for a disappointment," he said. "It seems Thomas has given him directions, by a long and winding road, to the County Clare Central Landfill."

"But," I objected, "won't he figure that out?"

"Not for awhile," Ed said. "You see, all the signs there are in Gaelic."

Disappeared In America
A Novel of the War on Terror
Today It's Fiction. Tomorrow . . . ?

By Chuck Fager

Non-Fiction Prologue

RICHMOND, Virginia (CNN) January 8, 2003 – A federal appeals court Wednesday ruled President Bush has the authority to designate U.S. citizens as enemy combatants in military custody if they are deemed a threat to national security.

I

Murphy dropped another stack of papers on the Intelligence Chief's desk.

"About time," the Chief said briskly. "We're late with these. Anything interesting?"

"Not much," Murphy said. "The usual. Some Muslims, some fellow-travelers. They're all overdue for action, though."

"Sleeper cells?"

"Some of them. Money-launderers too. And this one–"Murphy fingered a sheet from the pile – "some so-called peacenik in Fayetteville. By Fort Bragg. Named Chuck-something. Claims he's just counseling GIs about their rights."

"Yeah, sure," the Chief grunted. He glanced at the sheet. "Guy doesn't look dangerous. Just another chunky middle-aged guy. Guess you can't tell from a picture."

"But the phone logs are full of him talking about something called the 'Lamb's War.' And baseball. Obviously a kind of code."

"'Lamb's War,' huh?" The Chief squinted at him. "Wasn't that one of the nicknames for the Muslim version of the Crusades?"

Murphy grinned. "I thought you'd remember, Chief. You're good. Damn good."

The Chief dismissed him with an impatient wave. "I gotta get these to the Boss. And you gotta get back to work, Murphy. There's a war on, you know. And not the Lamb's either."

497

II

The president was talking with Karl about baseball and the latest polls from Florida when the Chief was ushered into the oval office.

"Hey, Mikey-Wikey, whatcha got?" the president asked.

"More enemy combatant IDs, sir," the Chief answered. His smile was obsequious, but it was still apparent that he hated the nickname.

"So, like I told you," the president continued, "The Red Sox ain't goin' nowhere this year. The Curse is still on. I don't give a hoot what ESPN says. And if they do get to the playoffs, the Rangers will be waiting, ready to kick butt big-time."

"Yessir," Karl said. "But what about the Cubs?"

"The Cubs?" The president guffawed. "Don't kid me. Be a cold day in hell when they get to the Series. Twenty years easy."

"Um, meantime, sir, " Karl said, "your brother tells me there could be some problems with the Florida felon's list for '04. That stupid civil rights lawsuit could be closing in on it."

"No problemo, Karlito," barked the president. "Our guys can stall it for at least a couple more years." He glanced up at the ceiling. "After all, the judge is a friend of mine. His son and me were in the Alabama Air National Guard together." A smirk. "Man, those were some serious parties."

"Sir" the Intelligence Chief put in tentatively.

"Oh. Sure." The president grabbed a pen, and initialed the sheets the Chief held out to him.

"Thank you, sir," said the Chief, and turned toward the door.

"Anytime," the president called after him. "You go get them Evildoers, hear?" The president and Karl were still giggling when the door clicked shut behind him.

III

The Director of Quaker House was late for another peace workshop. Closing the new issue of *Baseball Weekly*, he scooped up the last of the handouts from the copier, dropped them into a wrinkled Wal-Mart bag and headed for the door.

Two men were coming up the steps as he locked the door. One was tall, he noticed, almost big enough for the NBA; the other was no more than five feet 4. About the height of Paul Wellstone, and once again he felt that old twinge. He started to smile at them, but their blank expressions brought him up short.

The tall one said, "Your name Chuck? The Director nodded.

The short one stepped quickly behind him, and grabbed his hands.

498

"Hey, what–?" the Director protested, as the Wal-Mart bag dropped to the sidewalk and the plastic handcuffs tightened on his wrists.

The tall one expertly slipped the Director's wallet out of his back pocket, and eyed the drivers license. Then he was saying something.

"The president has determined that you are an enemy combatant, and ordered that you be taken into custody until further notice."

"A what?" the Director shouted. "I'm no such–"

"Shut up!" the short one snapped, and gave a yank on the handcuffs. The pain took the Director's breath away.

"Look at this," the short one said, holding up a sheet from the Wal-Mart bag. "The Lamb's War.'"

The tall one nodded. His face was grim. "Let's go, Mr. Chuck," he said. "You're lucky we don't pop your grape right here."

They hustled the Director toward a gray van idling at the curb.

Part Two

IV

The Treasurer turned to the Clerk of the Quaker House board. "Nope," he said, shaking his head. "The bank accounts are in order. So whatever happened, Chuck hasn't run off with the money. Not," he added, "that it would get him very far in any case. And the house is fine, no signs of break-in or struggle." He frowned. "Just deserted. Only thing, his house plants are wilting from lack of water."

"You're sure he didn't elope or something?" asked the Clerk.

A rueful chuckle from the rest. "I doubt it," murmured Bob, the Board's senior member. "His girlfriend called me last week, looking for him too. She's getting frantic."

"But he's often gone for days at a time doing workshops and such," the Clerk reminded them, "and you know we don't keep close track."

"Sure," Bob agreed, "but not for two weeks. Besides, I had an email from Rocky River Friends Meeting yesterday. They said Chuck was set to do a retreat there last weekend, on the Peace Testimony and The Lamb's War. Never showed up, and no call, no nothing. I'm worried."

"Did you call the police?" Anxiety tightened the Clerk's voice.

"And the FBI," said the Treasurer. "The cops knew nothing. The FBI said nothing."

"This gives me the creeps," Bob declared. "There was a piece on NPR the other day, about the government making some more arrests of so-called 'enemy combatants,' the ones they can hold forever with no charges, no lawyer, nothing."

He leaned forward abruptly. "You don't suppose – ?"

"Now hold on a minute," – the Treasurer cautioned. "Let's not get paranoid. He'll turn up before long."

But he didn't. After eighteen months of uncertainty, the Board hired a replacement. And the new Director stayed for fifteen years.

V

The old man lay on the bunk, eyes closed, his mind almost as blank as the walls of the cell.

Footsteps came down the hall. The rhythm told him it was Hank, the new young guard. Hank was a friendly, this-is-just-business-nothing-personal type. That was often a relief, but it could also rub in the bitterness of the empty years even deeper, and his unfeigned good nature only made it worse.

Hank stopped at his cell. "Hey, Chuck," he boomed, "do I have two amazing pieces of news for you, or what?"

The man stirred and sat up, his mind still sluggish. "What?" He noted that Hank was wearing a newly-pressed uniform, dark blue khaki. A walkie-talkie hung from the wide black belt. A tiny green light flashed on the walkie-talkie. It was the brightest color Chuck had seen in awhile, wasn't sure how long.

"Get this," Hank said. "First, I know you're a baseball fan, or you were anyway. And the playoffs just finished."

"It's October?" the old man asked. How many Octobers had he been in here, he wondered.

"Yeah, it's October," said Hank. "I been meaning to tell you, but they just keep me hoppin'. Well, nobody can believe it, but the Cubs beat the Giants four straight, and last night the Orioles snuck past the Yankees in seven. So we're going to have a World Series with the Birds and the Cubs. If the Cubs win, it'll be the first time in over a century. Bigger than the Red Sox."

The old man's eyes narrowed. "I think I remember," he murmured. "What is it they used to talk about in Boston for so long, some kind of curse'?"

"Yeah," Hank was enthusiastic. "The Curse of the Bambino, 'cause the Red Sox traded away Babe Ruth back in World War One. That's great you remember."

The old man rubbed his eyes and stared at Hank, unable to think of anything more to say. Baseball, like just about all of life, was a million miles away now, often too far away even for memories.

500

His stare seemed to jog Hank's memory as well.

"Oh!" the young man said. "That's the other thing I wanted to mention, was on the news just this morning. The CIA says they caught Muhammad Bin Laden."

The old man blinked uncomprehendingly. "Who?"

Hank was apologetic."Oh yeah, sorry," he said. "He's Osama's son. Took over Al Queda when the old man bought it. But they finally caught him, in Yemen or somewhere. Put up a fight, and he was wounded, but they got him."

The old man nodded, without interest.

"I was deployed in the 'Stan," Hank was rambling on, "with the 82nd Airborne. Man, talk about weather! Cold as hell in the winter, hot as hell in the summer. And no sign of Osama either. Big waste of time know what I mean?"

The old man did not answer. He had returned to his cot, and was staring up at the blank ceiling.

"Anyway," Hank said, "Just thought I ought to tell you. The Pentagon said this knocked a big hole in the whole network. They think in a few more years it'll all be over with."

He laughed with an echo of youthful delight. "Hey, man, won't that be cool? Then maybe they'll let you out of here!"

The old man turned his head toward Hank, just as the walkie-talkie at his belt began to beep and squawk.

"Damn," Hank said, "That's the desk. Gotta get back. Hang in there, Chuck. I'll tell you how the Series goes."

"Thanks," the old man murmured, eyes closed again. He listened to Hank's steps fading down the hallway. "Whatever."

www.ingramcontent.com/pod-product-compliance
Lightning Source LLC
Chambersburg PA
CBHW031228090426
42742CB00007B/113